THE SHIFTS IN
HIZBULLAH'S IDEOLOGY

RELIGIOUS IDEOLOGY,
POLITICAL IDEOLOGY, AND
POLITICAL PROGRAM

Joseph Elie Alagha

ISIM DISSERTATIONS

ISIM / LEIDEN

AMSTERDAM UNIVERSITY PRESS

Cover illustration: The painted picture, across the side of a huge building in Tehran, depicts Iman Khumayni's 20-million-soldier army for the liberation of Jerusalem. The same picture, with the same Qur'anic substantiation, is employed by Hizbullah in Lebanon. Picture taken by Serge Veldhuisen in 2002.

Cover design and lay-out: De Kreeft, Amsterdam

ISBN-13   978 90 5356 910 8
ISBN-10   90 5356 910 3
NUR   741 / 717

© Joseph Elie Alagha / ISIM / Amsterdam University Press, 2006

VRIJE UNIVERSITEIT

The Shifts in Hizbullah's Ideology:

Religious Ideology, Political Ideology, and Political Program

ACADEMISCH PROEFSCHRIFT

ter verkrijging van de graad Doctor aan
de Vrije Universiteit Amsterdam,
op gezag van de rector magnificus
prof. dr. T. Sminia,
in het openbaar te verdedigen
ten overstaan van de promotiecommissie
van de faculteit der Godgeleerdheid
op vrijdag 10 februari 2006 om 10.45 uur
in de aula van de universiteit,
De Boelelaan 1105

door
Joseph Elie Alagha

geboren
te Beirut,
Libanon

Promotor: prof. dr. A. Wessels

To my wife and child

Contents

A Note on Transliteration

The transliteration of Arabic words into English in the dissertation is in conformity with the transliteration system of the *International Journal of Middle East Studies*, with a few modifications.

Acknowledgements

I would like to extend my deepest gratitude and appreciation to the Chairs, the Academic Director, Prof. Dr. Asef Bayat, the Executive Director, Prof. Dr. Dick Douwes, staff, and colleagues of the International Institute for the Study of Islam in the Modern World (ISIM), without whom none of this research would have been possible. I am very grateful to ISIM's generous financial and academic support throughout my M. Phil. and Ph.D. years. I started my research with Prof. Dr. Martin van Bruinessen of Utrecht University on "The Effects of the Liberalization Process in Iran on Hizbullah's Gradual Integration in the Lebanese Public Sphere". After two and a half years, I changed the topic of my research to studying "The Shifts in Hizbullah's Ideology", concentrating specifically on the Lebanese dynamic. I would like to profusely thank my promotor Prof. Dr. Antonie Wessels of the Free University and co-promotor Drs. Paul Aarts of the University of Amsterdam who generously and patiently guided me in my endeavours to write a coherent dissertation and transform it into a book in less than two and a half years. Their rightful guidance, unwavering support, and systematic dedication coupled with their much-appreciated help and guidance resulted in this book. Nevertheless, I take full responsibility of any shortcoming in the final product.

I would like to wholeheartedly thank my colleagues and friends who took the time to read and comment on earlier drafts of this manuscript, especially Dr. Frank Peter and Dr. Vahid Behmardi who conveyed their non-abating assistance in spite of the heavy load of their work. I am indebted to all my colleagues – especially Egbert Harmsen, Nadia Sonneveld, Mujiburrahman, Sindre Bangstad, Caco Verhees, and Robbert Woltering – who have sacrificed their precious time in order to render themselves of service to me and my research, and all those whom I failed to remember. Also, special thanks to Dennis Janssen for his logistical, computer, and technical assistance. I am very grateful to my friend Serge Veldhuizen, who has supplied the photo for the book cover, and who has helped me in collecting sources. Last but not least, I would like to convey my gratitude to the people whom I have interviewed, to the Hizbullah people who helped me piece things up and who gave me access to their archive material and activities.

Prologue

Personal account: My interest in the subject

Lebanon is a myriad of 18 recognized minorities that coexisted in relative peace[1] till April 13, 1975, the date of the outbreak of the 16-year old civil war. From being the "Switzerland of the Middle East", Lebanon plunged into the law of the jungle where various militias undermined the Lebanese state's sovereignty and curved out their own cantons, most of the times based on sectarian affiliation. I am writing from personal experience as a member of what came to be called the "war generation", meaning someone who has witnessed and survived the entire civil war – in all its atrocities and futilities – from 1975 till 1990. Through out the course of the war I lived as a "neutral" civilian, who neither belonged to any political party nor had any knowledge of using any kind of weapon, as such I never participated in the civil war in any capacity whatsoever. As a child, these events left in me a sense of helplessness, helplessness at the internal situation (the civil war), and the external factor (the Israeli invasion). Later on as I matured I endeavoured to understand why so many people gave their lives in the 16-year appalling civil war? Was it in vein? Was it for a cause? Was it for the sovereignty and territorial integrity of Lebanon? The Israeli army was portrayed as the "invincible army". Was it then a matter of beating a dead horse to fight it back?

I was only 14 when Israel occupied Beirut on September 14, 1982 after 83 days of besieging it. The 1982 Israeli invasion left a great mark on my personality because of the physical injury that I have incurred and the psychological scars that I have suffered from. While filling water from the well of the Near East School of Theology (NEST), I was injured in my shoulder and knee, injuries that never healed completely until this present day. On September 24 of that year, my friends and I went to Hamra Cinema Theatre to watch a movie by Bud Spencer and Terence Hill. In the midst of the movie, the Israeli army stormed the theatre, kicked us out, and beat us up ordering us to go home. I was wondering what have we done to be treated this way? The answer was simple: a Lebanese member of the resistance targeted Israeli soldiers at the nearby Wimpy Restaurant, killed three of them with his pistol, and escaped unharmed. This incident among others heralded the withdrawal of the Israeli army 13 days after occupying Beirut. The Lebanese Resistance gained momentum and in 1985, the Israelis withdrew to their 1978 (first Israeli invasion) declared "security zone". After 1985, Hizbullah spearheaded the Lebanese resistance, and the Islamic Resistance, its mil-

11

itary wing, inflicted heavy casualties through a war of attrition on Israeli soldiers occupying Lebanese soil. Hizbullah employed hit and run tactics as well as guerrilla attacks that eventually drove Israel to withdraw out of Lebanon in May 2000.

The civil war taught me to live day by day; thus, my only achievement during that time was survival. After the civil war ended and the barriers between different Lebanese regions were removed, especially the notoriously renowned demarcation line between West Beirut (The Muslim sector where I live) and East Beirut (The Christian sector), I toured Lebanon in order to get to know "the other". At the beginning I was frightened from and critical of Hizbullah's notion of the Islamic state, especially since it was clearly stated on their flag, back then, "The Islamic Revolution in Lebanon". The watershed occurred in 1996 as a direct result of the Israeli "Grapes of Wrath" military campaign, which resulted in an unprecedented national solidarity with Hizbullah, most notably from the Christians who adhered to a diametrically opposed ideology. Fear of the other as well as the bulwark or veil of misconceptions were replaced by sociability and compassion. This encouraged me in 1997 to start attending Hizbullah's activities that were open to the public. This close encounter aroused my interested in the party; my interest was in its "resistance identity" and its achievements on the battlefield. What added to my interest is that, unlike other militias and political parties, Hizbullah did not take part in the civil war[2], concentrating all its energy on driving the Israeli army out of Lebanon. This led me to seek contact with Hizbullah's "Central Information Office", which opened the door for me to a closer look on Hizbullah's social and political activities. Eventually, this prompted me to write my dissertation on Hizbullah in order to construe how can Hizbullah be faithful to its Islamic identity, on the one hand, and at the same time function as a mainstream political party working in a confessional-sectarian system, on the other? This interest led me to start serious research about the party. This dissertation is a result of this research.

Preface

1. Hizbullah's identity and brief history

The basic aim of this dissertation is to study the Lebanese Shiʻite resistance movement Hizbullah as an identity-based movement from its rudimentary foundations in 1978, passing through its official inauguration in 1985, and ending in 2005, thus surveying a period that covers more than a quarter of a century. I question how the movement has tried since its transition to a political party in the 1990s to maintain and integrate its identity through the interplay between religion and politics. My research analyses how Hizbullah's identity construction is taking place by focusing on three key components: religious ideology, political ideology, and political program. Thus, this dissertation studies how Hizbullah's identity as an "Islamic *jihadi* (struggle) movement" changed in the following three stages: (1) from propagating an exclusivist religious ideology; (2) to a more encompassing political ideology; and (3) to what can be considered a pragmatic political program.

Hizbullah defines its identity as an Islamic *jihadi* movement, "whose emergence is based on an ideological, social, political and economical mixture in a special Lebanese, Arab and Islamic context".[3] I study the constituents or contents of this identity throughout Hizbullah's historical development. The body of the dissertation consists of the three parts below, which are explained in the following sequence.

1.1 The development of Hizbullah's ideology:
saliency of religious ideology: (1978-1984/5)

Since Hizbullah absolves itself from abiding by a specific date for its birth, I argue that Hizbullah was founded in 1978 as an Islamic movement of social and political protest by various sectors of Lebanese Shiʻite clergy and cadres, with Iranian ideological backing. The constituents of Hizbullah's religious ideology are the following: (1) belief in Shiʻa Islam; (2) *wilayat al-faqih* (guardianship of the jurisprudent or jurisconsult); (3) and *jihad* (struggle) in the way of God.[4] Ever since its emergence, Hizbullah has been a party in which the *ʻulama* (Muslim religious scholars) played, and still play, an important role. In this chapter, I try to find out what is so specific and different about Hizbullah's interpretation of the Shiʻite religious ideology? In particular, I gauge the role of the *ʻulama* in the formation and development of Hizbullah's Islamist ideology under the presumed Iranian influence.

1.2 The development of Hizbullah's ideology: prominence to political ideology (1984/5-1990)

In 1985 Hizbullah forged its "Open Letter" in which it declared its political manifesto to the public, thus engaging directly in Lebanese political life after operating clandestinely for some years. Over the period 1985 to 1990 Hizbullah became a full-pledged social movement "in the sense of having a broad overall organization, structure, and ideology aiming at social change"[5] and social justice. The components of Hizbullah's political ideology are the following: oppressors and oppressed; Islamic order; relations with the Lebanese Christians; perspective on Israel; unity of the Muslims; stance vis-à-vis the West; and *jihad* and martyrdom. The questions I raise intend to shed light on the reasons and methods through which Hizbullah shifted its emphasis from a religious ideology to a political ideology.

How did Hizbullah employ the transnational link of Iranian political ideology in its dealings with domestic Lebanese politics as well as regional and international relations? Does this explain why Hizbullah followed domestically a radical-violent approach towards the Christian militias and an uncompromising attitude anathematising the Lebanese political system in its entirety, regarding the Lebanese government as an infidel? Does this also account for Hizbullah's regional and international militancy towards Israel, France, and the US?

1.3 The development of Hizbullah's ideology: paramount to political program (1991 to 2005)

Since the early 1990s Hizbullah evolved, more and more, into a mainstream political party, with an extensive network of social services that benefits both Muslims and Christians. Hizbullah participated in elections, assuming not only parliamentary and municipal responsibility, but also governmental responsibility by joining the cabinet in 2005. Hizbullah's political program is based upon the following constituents: oppressors and oppressed; perspectives on the Islamic state; dialogue with the Lebanese Christians; jurisprudential stipulations of parliamentary, municipal, and governmental work; socio-economic program: Non-Governmental Organizations (NGOs) and civil institutions; Lebanonisation and *infitah* ("opening up"); relations with Syria and Iran; perspective on Israel; and *jihad* and martyrdom. I bring up the following questions in order to underscore the rationale and way in which Hizbullah altered its accent from a political ideology to a political program.

Lebanonisation or *infitah* refers to Hizbullah's integration policy in the Lebanese public sphere or Hizbullah's enrolment in Lebanese domestic political life starting the early 1990s.[6] What is the place of Islam in Hizbullah's idea of integration, *infitah*, or Lebanonisation? Can Hizbullah, as a social movement and a full pledged political party, vitally affect society and become a powerful force for social change while functioning within the confessional-sectarian system it anathematised for more than a decade? How could Hizbullah modify its identity from an Islamic *jihadi* movement towards a political party having a "prominent" political role in the Lebanese milieu by propagating a detailed political program? Did the liberalisation process in Iran influence the Lebanese national standard that Hizbullah is trying to portray, or was it Lebanese authenticity all along? How could Hizbullah sell to its followers its commitment to Islamic identity while it abides by a pragmatic political program? Did Hizbullah manage to maintain an Islamic reputation through its parliamentary, municipal, and governmental work, or did it sacrifice its Islamic identity and ideological principles in its bargaining and compromise with other political parties and groups?

In what way did Hizbullah want to appeal to strata and sectors of the population, mainly Christians and Sunnis, it did not reach out to before? What are the implications of including them in Hizbullah's election lists? Are there conditions for representing Hizbullah and speaking in its name? Is it simply *Realpolitik* or pragmatism? Are there usual stable alliances and cooperation with other political parties? How does this resonate inside the party? What has transformed Hizbullah to a mainstream political party that managed to receive the highest number of votes in the 2000 and 2005 parliamentary elections? Is Hizbullah mobilizing all its resources and capabilities to integrate in the Lebanese public sphere?

These questions point out to a process that is reshaping Hizbullah's identity and suggest that the party is going through a remarkable transformation. Each of the three components of Hizbullah's identity – religious ideology, political ideology, and political program – is essential in one of the three stages, prompting a better explanation of the shifts from one stage to the other.

2. **Analytical framework**

I offer the working definition of ideology that this dissertation employs and I endeavour to explain how resource mobilization is important to the survival of a social movement.

2.1 Working definition of ideology

Ideology is any kind of a coherent and systematic whole of ideas on politics and society. This systematised whole functions as a rationale for political and social action. As such, it connotes a worldview held by any social group to justify their actions. Such a worldview can be subject to re-description and reformulation, and it does not have to be accepted in its entirety; it could be amended and reinterpreted. However, an ideological view does not undergo the stringent criterion of empirical tests in the way scientific theories and hypotheses are subjected to. Intellectual ideology is defined as a formal system of belief and a coherent system of thought, which includes political programmes/manifestos, philosophical orientations and religious codification.[7] I employ the latter usage in this dissertation.

2.2 The survival of a social movement and the role of resource mobilization

A social movement is defined as "purposive collective actions whose outcome, in victory as in defeat, transforms the values and institutions of society".[8] In studying the shifts in the ideology of a social movement, I mainly employ the concept of resource mobilization. Resource mobilization refers to the way a social movement mobilizes its capabilities or resources – such as money, political influence, access to the media, and personnel – in order to confront and survive strategic difficulties and challenges facing it. A principal advantage of the theory of resource mobilization is that it attaches a high degree of importance to the survival of a social movement i.e. how it copes with strategic difficulties and challenges while standing its grounds. Thus, a social movement might shift its ideology to facilitate adjustment to a world that is in incessant flux, or else it would risk demise or might not remain a viable-throbbing social movement.[9]

Gramsci argued that all the fundamental sociological questions boil down to political science questions.[10] Thus, paraphrasing Gramsci, social movements are nothing but political movements.[11]. Not all Islamists aim at only mobilizing civil society through a bottom-up process, rather their objective is to take power and govern through a top-down process. As such, Islamism could be conceived as the most salient unitary mobilizational power behind political change and transformation in the Arab and Muslim world.[12] Islamists seem to be effective in pointing at grievances and in expressing them, but this is not enough. In order to eradicate these grievances Islamists must actualise their potential role by constructively addressing societal needs through effective allocation of their resources. Islamism is holistic in its approach since it is "a *religious-cultural-political framework* for engagement on issues that most concern politically engaged Muslims".[13]

And so, social movements thrive on propagating their social, economic, and political legitimacy through efficient resource mobilization. This seems to make up their main modus operandi of mobilization in order to acquire a substantial following and backing in society. Indeed, the way and extent to which social movements acquire resources from their constituencies shape their activities. Thus, resource mobilization dwells on the notion of social movement in a very broad sense. It covers all activities, or even beliefs (ideologies) and preferences (identities), to change society by collective mobilization.

3. **Sources**

The part and parcel of my research is based upon Hizbullah's primary sources. I have analysed Hizbullah's religious ideology, political ideology, and political program, mainly relying on primary sources in Arabic; some secondary sources in Arabic, English, and French; and conducted interviews of representative samples of Hizbullah's rank and file. Primary sources are available in abundance in Lebanon at Hizbullah's Central Information Office (CIO); Hizbullah's think tank, Consultative Centre for Studies and Documentation (CCSD); the Khumayni's Cultural Centre in Beirut; the Cultural Centre of the Islamic Revolution of Iran in Lebanon[14], and other Iranian and Hizbullah affiliated institutions and publishing houses. In addition to many Arabic books, articles, archive material, communiqués, documents, speeches, political declarations, and other Hizbullah publications, the primary sources that I have studied and which provided me with information on Hizbullah's ideology and program are the following: (1) the Open Letter or political manifesto; (2) the parliamentary and municipal election programs of 1992, 1996, 1998, 2000, 2004, and 2005; (3) "Views and Concepts"; (4) "Statement of Purpose"; (5) and "Identity and Goals", Hizbullah's latest self-description.[15] Also, I made use of Hizbullah's Internet sites pertaining to the topics researched. Nevertheless, my reliance on *publicly available* primary sources has its own inevitable limitations in exposing Hizbullah's clandestine nature, given the largely secretive nature of the party and its operations.

4.   **Organisation of the Chapters**

The chapters shed light on the different levels in which Hizbullah's ideology is shifting. The first chapter surveys Hizbullah's historical development from 1978 until 2005. Chapters two, three, and four study the development of Hizbullah's ideology from a phase of religious intensity (1978-1984/5), to a phase of political orientation (1984/5-1990), and to the phase of *infitah* or integration in the Lebanese public sphere (1991 to 2005). Chapter five sheds light on the general shifts in the constituents of Hizbullah's ideology in the three stages. Chapter six offers a conclusion on the main findings of the dissertation in relation to the shifts in Hizbullah's ideology.

1 A Survey of Hizbullah's History
Its Development from Its Rudimentary Foundations in 1978 until 2005

Introduction

This chapter is divided into four parts. The first endeavours to give a brief historical background on the political development of the Lebanese Shi'ites. The second part intends to survey Hizbullah's history between 1978-1984/5. The third part deals with Hizbullah's history over the years 1984/5 to 1990. The fourth and last part adumbrates Hizbullah's History from 1991 till 2005. Thus, I am interested in highlighting some basic facts of the development of the Shi'ite community in general, and Hizbullah, in particular, by examining the important phases, figures, and dates in the lifespan of that social movement.[1]

I A brief historical background on the political development of the Lebanese Shi'ites

1. The Shi'ites of Lebanon

The Lebanese Shi'as are partly authentically from Lebanon proper, and some originated from Iran. The Shi'ite existence in Lebanon is traced back to their presence in the ninth century in the area between the *Awwali* River to the north and the Galilee to the South, a region known as *Jabal 'Amil*[2]. Others resided in the northern part of the *Biqa'* Valley. The history of relations between the Lebanese Shi'ites and their Iranian counterparts dates back to the twelfth century.[3] In the fourteenth century, the Shi'ites were an oppressed minority who were expelled by the Mamluks and were contained in the peripheral areas away from central Mamluk rule (1282-1516).[4] In the sixteenth century, the Safavids assumed power in Iran and adopted Shi'ism as an official state religion for the fist time in Iran's history. Since then, the Iranians had a unique tie with the Lebanese Shi'as. Thus, strong historic ties between the Shi'ite community in Lebanon and the Iranians were consolidated during the Safavid period, when the *ulama* (religious scholars) from *Jabal 'Amil* – which is the den of Shi'ism in Lebanon, and an important Shi'ite centre of higher learning – were instrumental in converting the majority of the Iranians from Sunnism to Shi'ism.[5] Lebanese Shi'ite *ulama* from *Jabal 'Amil* were rewarded by holding high-ranking positions in the Safavid state. Among these was Baha'eddine al-'Amili, who occupied the post of Shaykh al-Islam in Esfahan, and other personalities from *'Amil* such as Al-Muhaqqiq Al-Karaki[6], who in 1510 emigrated from Lebanon to Iran with a considerable number of *ulama*, among whom was Al-Hurr Al-'Amili, the author of the Shi'ite concordance of hadith[7].

After the fall of the Mamluks in 1516 to the Ottoman Turks and the formation of the Ottoman Empire, like other Shi'ites in the Empire, the Lebanese Shi'ites were again reduced to the status of defending themselves against the Sunnis. This period fed the preponderance of the *zu'ama* (feudal leaders) and maintained their grip over the serfs (peasants) who trusted their leaders to maintain good relations with the Ottoman Empire. Among the Shi'ites, the Hamadé family in the *Hirmel* near the *Biqa'* and the As'ad family in *Jabal 'Amil* rose to prominence as *zu'ama*, and they were able to maintain their leadership for a long time.[8] Such Shi'ite families ruled from within a consociational arrangement that formalized their *za'ama* (leadership). Again, it was a time when an oppressed Shi'ite dissidence had to overcome Ottoman repressive measures under any legitimate means, even under the protection of the *zu'ama*. [9]

With the increase of animosities between the Safavids and the Ottomans and the spread of acrimonies to *Jabal 'Amil*, *Biqa'*, and *Hirmel*, the *ulama* in *Jabal 'Amil* found in Iran a safe haven from conscription and Ottoman persecution and bullying. Like in Lebanon, Iraq, and other Shi'ite religious centres, also in Iran, the *'Amili ulama* concentrated on writing and publishing an enormous number of books, which are still taught in the *Hawzas* (religious seminaries or schools)[10] and religious universities. That is how the relationships between the Lebanese and Iranian people started taking an ideological twist enforcing cultural-religious brotherly exchanges. This resulted in intermarriage and a mutual wave of migrations.[11]

After the defeat and disintegration of the Ottoman Empire in 1918, the provisional Arab governments, headed by the *zu'ama*, replaced Ottoman rule. This development was short-lived and the Arab nationalist dream of the Shi'ite *zu'ama* came to a premature end as a result of the May 1916 Sykes-Picot Agreement, which had already divided the Middle East among the British and French. Thus, France created "Le Grand Liban" or the Greater Lebanon on September 1, 1920. From the stance of being their protégé during Ottoman rule, France had vested interest in the Maronites of Lebanon. That is why it extended the borders of Lebanon, at the expense of Syria, to include *Jabal 'Amil*, the *Biqa'*, and the Sunni costal cities and declared its independence from Syria at the great disappointment of the Shi'ites' wish of unification with Syria.[12] Nevertheless, the Greater Lebanon of 1920 opened up a new opportunity for the Shi'ites since the Lebanese state was to be based on the guaranteed proportional representation of the different religious minorities. It is from that day on that the numerical distribution of the religious groups among the Lebanese became a serious volatile issue and a source of inequality and injustice.[13] Still, for that time, under no other circumstance would the Shi'ite *zu'ama* aspire to play a prominent political role. Only in a separate Lebanon could the Shi'ite elite expect to have a substantial role in government.[14] As a result, the Shi'ite *zu'ama* proved their allegiance to the Lebanese state when they refused the Arabic call for the unity between Syria and Lebanon. Their regions (constituencies) were calm and indicated a consensus on the Shi'ite support for the idea of the Greater Lebanon.[15]

The Greater Lebanon had the effect of doubling the territory but also the side effect of complicating its future. It was assured that no community would be pre-eminent, which resulted in the dual imperatives of creating internal alliances and bringing about external support. However alliances like these were destined to fail since no community was homogenous, and even intra alliances were hard to strike or maintain. The Shi'ites' experiences of that period with alliances were, more or less, imposed. For instance, the gap that existed between the two main Shi'ite areas of Lebanon would have hardly made any successful intra community alliance. Indeed, the path that was followed in *Jabal 'Amil* was different from the one in the *Biqa'* Valley and *Hirmel*. The former was an agricultural feudal community where the *zu'ama* reigned along with some *'ulama*. The northern *Biqa'* was characterized by clans' code and honour, which regulated the lives of the semi-nomadic Shi'ites of that region. Joined together, these two regions would constitute 17% of the 1920 Greater Lebanon's population in a country where the size of a community is a prerequisite for its representation. However, the alliance between these two Shi'ite communities was a bit artificial. While it enhanced the power of the *zu'ama*, it alienated the people.[16]

On May 23, 1926 the Lebanese Republic, having a written constitution and internationally recognized boundaries, saw the light.[17] The Lebanese constitution was drafted by Lebanese parliamentarians and dignitaries[18] along French lines, and Charles Debbas, a Greek Orthodox, was elected as the first president of the Lebanese Republic. The 1926 constitution recognized the Shi'ites "as an official community separate from the Sunnis".[19]

2. The deprivation of the Shi'a in the Lebanese socio-economic and political system, and the effects of the Palestinian-Israeli conflict on the mobilization and radicalisation of the Shi'ites

The outcome of this united Shi'ite community was increased backwardness and a low standard of living that lacked any good social organization or viable economy. This resulted in the Shi'ite populace being deprived and marginalized through out the Lebanese system. One of the outcomes behind this is the 1932 census, which was done by the French government and was biased towards the Christians. Shi'ites who lived in predominantly Christian areas were counted as Christians. For example, this was the case in the South, Mount Lebanon (*Jubayl* and *Kisirwan*), and the North (*Akkar* and *al-Kura* district). In other areas, many Shi'ites were either counted as either Sunni or Christians. The practice of *taqiyya* (expedient dissimulation) contributed in decreasing the percentage of Shi'ites. The results of the census were that the Christians (the Maronites) were the majority or the largest community; Sunni Muslims the second largest; and Shi'ites as the third largest, comprising 19.6% of the population in 1932. Because the Shi'ites were the third largest confessional group, they possessed some power, but still disproportionate to their number.[20]

Taking the results of the 1932 census into consideration, with the independence of Lebanon from the French, the National Pact of 1943, which is an oral agreement not written in the 1926 constitution, made the president of the republic a Maronite, the prime minister a Sunni, and the speaker of the parliament, a Shi'ite.[21] The National Pact between the strong Sunni and Maronite minorities, on the one hand, and the French government, on the other was to become the basis for Lebanon's independence. Although the Shi'ites had the symbolic post of the Speaker, the National Pact became one of the many sources of resentment for the Shi'ites who felt excluded from political power or any tangible chance of accretion to it. Thus, they felt as third-class citizens. Moreover, the ratio of appointments in political posts as well as representation in the parliament of six Christians to five Muslims, which was based on the 1932 census, made the Muslims, as a whole, feel second-class citizens.[22] However, article 95[23] of Section 6 of the Lebanese Constitution gave some hope for the Shi'ites of a fairer representation in the future: "Temporarily and from the stance of justice and national reconciliation, the sects are represented in a just manner in public employment and in the formation of the cabinet, without [this representation] harming the [Lebanese] state's interest".[24] Lebanon declared its independence on November 22, 1943. Since then, November 22 has been celebrated as Lebanon's Independence Day. However, real independence did not take place till December 1945, and the French army left Lebanon a year later on December 31, 1946.[25]

During that time, it is estimated that about 80% of the Shi'ites originated from the South. Although a small portion still dwelled in the South, many moved to Beirut and its impoverished suburbs such as *Nab'a*, *Burj al-Barajné*, and *'Ain al-Rimmané*. The remaining 20% lived in the northern part of the *Biqa'*, *Hirmel*, and *B'albak*.[26] Through the process of modernization, the Shi'ite community started loosening its ties with the *zu'ama*. Real power was slipping out of the *zu'ama*'s hands as early as the beginning of the 1960s, largely as a result of the growth of the state bureaucracy that provided as many services of political goods as the *zu'ama* did. Consequently, a relatively free-floating population of politically disoriented individuals were liable to the influence of any discontented member of the elite. Thus, between 1946 and 1962, the Shi'ites were increasingly feeling under-represented and forbidden appropriate access to power,[27] as such they despised being part of the Lebanese state. Most notably those of the South were the most susceptible "to the ideologies of change" demanding a complete overhaul of the political system.[28] Over the years, the Shi'ites became Lebanon's fastest growing community, with the highest birth rate and lowest emigration rate compared to other communities. One can question if their religious identity, which emanates from their doctrines and traditions, heralded that increase.[29] Thus, the Lebanese Shi'ites, the largest demographic group who were at the bottom of the socio-economic ladder, started demanding a place in the distribution of power and spoils.[30] During that time the unjust economic distribution was clearly evident: famine, illiteracy, and deprivation characterized the rural peripheral regions inhabited mostly by the Shi'ites, while Beirut was shining with an impressive apparent prosperity. Thus, Beirut blossomed and become a showplace of wealth and consumption, while the Shi'ite slums became more crowded and expanded.[31]

In 1959 General Fouad Shehab, the Lebanese president at that time, asked the French government to help him lay down a socio-economic and administrative reform program. So the French government dispatched the "Institut International de Recherche et de Formation Education Développement" (IRFED)[32] delegation that conducted intensive research on Lebanese soil and revealed its findings in a report published after three years. According to this study, Louis Joseph Lebret, IRFED's head and founder, revealed that two percent of the Lebanese population owned eighty percent of the means of production and distribution, while the South, the Biqa' Valley, and the North were very primitive. These peripheral areas had no running water or electricity, no infrastructure, and no hospitalisation, etc. In fact, almost all infrastructure, superstructure, modernization, and developmental projects were concentrated in Beirut and Mount Lebanon. Thus, Lebret urged for balanced development.[33] According to Lebret, at that time, the Shi'ites were completely disenfranchised; not only they were underrepresented politically, but also economically deprived. Most of the Lebanese grassroots, who lived from hand to mouth in slum areas, were Shi'ites par excellence. Lebret warned that the discrepancy between the backward peripheral areas and the flourishing centre makes the Lebanese socio-economic structure incapable of sustaining any crisis, thus rendering it not viable, unless this discrepancy is urgently and constructively addressed. Thus, he predicted a bloody civil war in Lebanon in the domain of near-range or middle-range theories (10-15 years).[34]

In conjunction with the socio-economic factor the effects of the Palestinian factor on the Lebanese Shi'ite's population were also at play, especially in southern Lebanon. Starting from 1948, the year of the Nakba (great misfortune), when Israel was created as a state on the remnants of Palestine, hundreds of thousands of Palestinians were uprooted by Israeli forces and sent across the border to many Arab countries, the majority of whom resided in Lebanon. According to Sayyid Ibrahim al-Musawi between 1948 till the creation of the Palestinian Liberation Organization (PLO) in 1964 there was not a single attack carried out against Israel from the Lebanese borders, yet Israel killed more than 100 civilians and wounded many others.[35] The conflict was yet to worsen after the Naksa (small misfortune) of the June 4, 1967 war where Israel annexed by military force Gaza, the West bank, Sinai, and the Syrian Golan Heights.[36] Since then, Lebanon has been the target of arbitrary Israeli aggressions, in the sense that they were not necessarily pro-voked by or retaliatory measures against PLO or Lebanese resistance attacks. With the loss of their launching ground in Gaza and the West Bank, the Pal-estinian fighters used south Lebanon as a replacement. Al-Musawi adds, in 1968, Israeli commandos blew up 13 Middle East Airlines (MEA) planes at the Beirut International Airport as a reprisal for an attack in Athens, to "Leba-nese-trained Palestinian" freedom fighters.[37]

As a result, "The migration of Shi'i families to the suburbs of Beirut became a flood from the late 1950s onwards"[38], especially after the growing PLO military presence in the South and the violent confrontations with the Israelis. The Lebanese state paid a heavy price for siding with the Palestin-ians since Shi'ite grassroots, especially those living in the South, lost their homes and loved ones and encountered great economic losses on behalf of Palestinian freedom fighting.[39] The originated sense of bitterness towards the PLO accumulated and reached a confrontational dimension. "Since the late 1960s, hundreds of thousands of Lebanese have been repeatedly dis-placed from their homes in the South, more often than not as a result of Israeli military action".[40] "[B]y 1971, nearly half of the Lebanese Shi'a popula-tion was found concentrated in the Greater Beirut area".[41] As such, the Pal-estinian-Israeli conflict in southern Lebanon had its toll on the mobilization and radicalisation of the Shi'ites.

Although most political and social scientists dismissed Lebret's pre-diction as a far-fetched possibility, his omen materialized on April 13, 1975, the date of the eruption of the 16-year old civil war.[42] The civil war resulted in drastic demographic changes. Between 1975-76 the Christian Militias embarked on a fierce campaign of "ethnic cleansing"[43] that was success-ful in uprooting the Shi'ites from East Beirut, thus concentrating them in the *Dahiya* (Beirut's southern suburb). "By the early 1980s fully one-third of Lebanon's whole Shi'i population was found there. The large-scale Shi'i migration to Beirut accelerated the process of social change within the sect", especially since the Shi'ites from *Jabal 'Amil* and the *Biqa'* had the chance to fuse together, which gradually helped forge "a single national Shi'i con-stituency".[44] Thus, "events in south Lebanon have resulted in large numbers of refugees moving into the Beirut area with the result that Shi'is are now probably the largest religious community in Beirut".[45]

After the end of the Lebanese civil war in 1990, statistics revealed that four percent of the population owned eighty percent of the means of production and distribution.[46] This made Rashid al-Solh, an ex-prime minis-ter, remark in the wake of May 6, 1992 social unrest, that Lebanon is a country ruled by one thousand families who control everything in the Lebanese milieu.[47]

Contrary to what Norton and Shatz claim, "Even at the most generous estimates, only 40 percent of all the Lebanese are Shiis"[48] and "Shiites, who account for 40 percent of Lebanon's population"[49], currently, as recent estimates from the Ministry of Interior indicate, the Shi'ites in Lebanon comprise about 55 percent of the population – Beirut's *Dahiya* alone houses around 850,000 Shi'ites.[50]

II   The Mobilization of the Shi'a, the role of Imam Musa Al-Sadr, and Hizbullah's Emergence

1.   Imam Musa al-Sadr

Imam Musa Al-Sadr was born on March 15, 1928, in *Qum* (Iran), and was educated in *Najaf* (Iraq), which are considered the most important religious educational centres of Shi'ite Islam. His father, Sayyid Sadreddine al-Sadr, was an Iranian citizen, and his mother, Sayyida Safiyya, was originally Lebanese[51]. After Musa Al-Sadr obtained a degree in law from Tehran University, he began teaching *fiqh* (jurisprudence) and logic in *Qum*. In 1954, he left to *Najaf* and studied *fiqh* and *usul* (principal elements of religion) under the guidance of leading Ayatullahs such as Sayyid Muhsin al-Hakim and Sayyid Abu al-Qasim al-Khu'i.[52]

Musa al-Sadr arrived from Iran in 1958 and gradually acquired following and became the leader of the Lebanese Shi'ite community.[53] The Iranian born Imam Musa al-Sadr later on married a Lebanese woman.[54] In 1963 al-Sadr's Iranian citizenship was revoked due to his criticisms levelled against the Shah's repression of the Iranian people's uprising. Thus, in 1963 al-Sadr became a Lebanese citizen.[55]

In the 1960s and 70s, the advent of Imam Musa al-Sadr opened a new leaf of relationships between the Lebanese and Iranian people, especially after many Iranians fled from the Shah's regime and sought refuge for many years in Lebanon. The basis for that is that Lebanon was regarded as a safe haven for liberal and Muslim movements who were mobilizing against the

Shah. And so, the Iranians used Lebanon as a launching pad to organize their groups against the Shah regime. They were also interested in supporting the Palestinian freedom fighters who used southern Lebanon to launch attacks against Israeli's northern settlements. It is worth mentioning that during Imam Khumayni's stay in *Najaf*, he issued a *fatwa* (religious edict) sanctioning the use of *khums*[56] (one-fifth religious tax) to support the Palestinian freedom fighters in their struggle against Israel.[57]

Imam al-Sadr mobilized the Lebanese Shi'ites effectively in their endeavours to attain a more just political, social, and economic system. He championed the rights of the Shi'ites in an uncontested way, as he was fighting on two fronts at the same time: (1) He started to lobby and exerted pressure on the Lebanese state to adopt a more just approach to the demands of the Shi'ites calling for more representation for them in the Lebanese political structure; (2) At the same time he challenged the large land-holding Shi'ite *zu'ama*, in a bid to contest and undermine the power of his Shi'ite political opponents, most notably Kamel al-As'ad, the speaker of the parliament, back then. This resulted in an internal Shi'ite clash.[58]

His first demand, in founding strong and effective civil society organizations independent of the state, materialized with the formation of the Islamic Shi'ite Higher Council, which aimed at representing Shi'ite demands before the state on an equal footing with other Lebanese sects. This council was officially established in 1969, and al-Sadr became its leader on May 22, 1969. In his inauguration ceremony on May 23, 1969 he presented his political program, which was outlined along the following seven points: (1) To organize the affairs of the Shi'ite community and to improve its socioeconomic conditions. (2) To implement a holistic vision of Islam with regard to thought, practice, and *jihad*. (3) To strive for total unity among Muslims without any discrimination. (4) *Infitah* ("opening up"): To cooperate with all Lebanese sects and communities[59], and safeguard national unity. (5) To fulfil patriotic and national duties, and to protect Lebanon's independence, sovereignty, and territorial integrity. (6) To combat ignorance, poverty, backwardness, social injustice, and moral degeneration. (7) To support the Palestinian resistance and to effectively take part in the liberation of Palestinian "raped" land along with brotherly Arab countries.[60] It is worth mentioning that Shi'ite *zu'ama* such as Sabri Hamadé and political leaders such as MPs Sayyid Ja'far Sarafeddine, Fadlallah Danas, and ex-minister Sulayman al-Din worked hand in hand with Imam al-Sadr, not only in establishing the Council, but also in giving it a leading political and social role.[61]

In the summer of 1969, Imam Musa al-Sadr – along with Shaykh Subhi al-Tufayli, Shaykh Husayn Kawtharani, and Shaykh Hasan Malik[62] – met with his cousin Sayyid Muhammad Baqir al-Sadr[63], in the latter's house in *Najaf*, in order to put him in the picture of the Islamic mobilization in Lebanon and consult with him on organizing the Islamic movement. The five agreed on boosting *da'wa* (Islamic propagation or call) in Lebanon through organizing political, intellectual, and religious circles composed of the Shi'ite youth who regularly attend Imam Musa al-Sadr's lectures and speeches. The aim was to mobilize, organize, discipline, and disseminate the knowledge inculcated in Baqir al-Sadr's two recently published books entitled *Our Philosophy* and *Our Economy*[64]. However, discord ravaged the ranks of the nascent Islamic movement, and its longing for unity through revolutionary mobilization, as Baqir al-Sadr intended, did not materialize. Imam Musa al-Sadr, while working on serving the political, social, and economic interests of the Shi'a community, insisted on safeguarding the Lebanese Republic and working hand in hand with the Christian community based on the Qur'anic verse (2:135): "Say: 'We believe in Allah, in what has been revealed to us, what was revealed to Abraham, Isma'il, Ishaq, Jacob and the Tribes, and in what was revealed to Moses, Jesus and other prophets from their Lord, making no distinction between any of them, and to Him we submit' ".[65]

In the late sixties and early seventies, Iranian cadres and clergy came to Lebanon and served in the mobilization and organization of the Shi'ite community. Among the Iranians who were trained in Lebanon[66] were Ayatullah Khumayni's two sons, Ahmad and Mustafa, as well as Janti, Hamid Sadiqi, al-Gharawi, Muhammad Husayn Muntazari, Mustafa Shamran, the late Minister of Defence[67] in the Islamic Republic, whose wife, Ghada Jaber, is Lebanese.[68] This manifested to a great deal the interlinkage that was prevalent then among the three causes: The Iranian Revolution, the Palestinian struggle, and the process of Shi'ite mobilization in Lebanon.

The Cairo Agreement of November 3, 1969, which was signed between the PLO and the Lebanese Army, gave the *fida'iyyin* (Palestinian freedom fighters) a freer hand in launching their attacks against Israel across the Lebanese border. It sanctioned Palestinian armed struggle from certain parts of south Lebanon, which came to be known as "The *Fateh* Land".[69] The situation turned from bad to worse, when, in 1970, Lebanon witnessed the influx of thousands of *fida'iyyin* following the bloody conflict in Jordan,[70] or what came to be known as "The Black September Massacre". The mounting tension resulting from increased Palestinian military activity in Lebanon resulted in 1973 in a bloody confrontation between the *fida'iyyin* and the

Lebanese Army – that was protecting the interests of the Lebanese state – which considered that the Palestinians manipulated the Cairo Agreement in order to build a state within a state.[71] In turn, Israel did not stand idle while its northern settlements were being continuously targeted. Thus, Israel retaliated aiming at stopping the Palestinians who were using the Lebanese land in order to carry out a war of liberation through their raids against Israeli forces and civilians. As mentioned earlier, the Lebanese Shi'ites living in southern Lebanon paid the heaviest price since Israeli's retaliation primarily targeted them.

Imam al-Sadr was not idle; he mobilized his followers and organized mass rallies that drew tens of thousands. In 1974, Imam Musa al-Sadr, together with Grégoire Haddad, a Greek Catholic archbishop, formed *Harakat Al-Mahrumin* (the Movement of the Deprived) in a bid to alleviate the suffering of the deprived people regardless of their sectarian or ethnic affiliation, as such it was open for all downtrodden people from all sects and not restricted to the Shi'ites.[72] However, this inter-community openness did not last long enough, as the ruling elites (*zu'ama*) were afraid this would undermine the community's patronage system.[73] As time passed, *Harakat Al-Mahrumin* soon developed into a Shi'ite based movement under the leadership of al-Sadr.

Al-Sadr used religious symbolism on political mobilization, thus establishing a sectarian alternative specifically with Shi'ite needs. His movement became a viable alternative to the leftist forces and the Shi'ite *zu'ama*.[74] His leadership could not easily be challenged because his civilian leadership of the community rested on the moral claim he held as the supreme religious leader. As such his religious authority was not contested.[75] In the beginning of his activities, demonstrations and protests were verbal and symbolic in nature, but after a while, demands and forms of actions became more radical and violent. Thus, al-Sadr not only succeeded in reducing the *zu'ama's* influence, he also brought the Shi'ite masses into politics.

Al-Sadr's hopes of changing the political conditions with peaceful means faded away, and in 1975 he founded a militia group. The group was called *Afwaj Al-Muqawama Al-Lubnaniyya* ("The Brigades of the Lebanese Resistance"), known by its acronym *AMAL*. *AMAL* was an activist movement that aimed at social and political reform, but its primary agenda was to liberate southern Lebanon from the Israeli troops. Unlike, *Harakat Al-Mahrumin*, *AMAL* had a military wing.[76] Al-Sadr acknowledged that he established *AMAL* in order to struggle against oppression, and state corruption aiming at a more just representation for the Shi'ites as well as establishing safety and security in the South. Al-Sadr said in a speech in front of a massive rally of his supporters: "Military training is a duty like prayer, and bearing arms is a duty as having a Qur'an".[77] On July 6, 1975, it was the first time that al-Sadr announced the death ("martyrdom") of some of AMAL fighters during military training exercises.[78] In other words, the advent of al-Sadr's charismatic leadership over the Shi'ite community transformed it into one of rebellion and social protest.[79] Some scholars pointed that the motive behind establishing AMAL was to give the Shi'ites an instrument for advancing their claims within a political arena dominated by sectarian militancy. They even contended that by establishing AMAL, al-Sadr made it clear that armed struggle was a necessary means to reach political goals. Aside from the aforementioned, it seems the main reason behind al-Sadr's establishment of AMAL was his perception of threat caused by Israel[80], which made Lebanon, and especially the South, a daily target for its aggressions.[81]

Al-Sadr wanted to defend the southerners, as he believed that the Lebanese state is not capable of doing so because of the great gap in capabilities between Lebanon and Israel; he also wanted to help the Palestinians against the Israeli hostilities. Thus, al-Sadr established a Shi'ite militia in an attempt to integrate "all the militias into a government institution, ... an auxiliary to the regular Lebanese army that would be capable of repulsing Israeli attacks".[82] In one of Sadr's famous speeches he declared, "If Israel invaded the South, I will take off my turban and attire and become a fidda'i (freedom fighter)".

Musa al-Sadr worked within the multi-confessional system, under the legitimacy of the Lebanese state. However, al-Sadr did not hide his intention of reforming the Lebanese system in order to achieve equality and social justice.[83] Al-Sadr's attitude brought him a wide popularity that extended far beyond the direct boundaries of his sect. He stressed in most of his speeches the indispensability of peaceful, fruitful, and interactive coexistence of the different ethnic and communal groups in Lebanon. He was so keen to defend his fellow Lebanese Christians as much as he was for the Shi'ites. After the eruption of the Lebanese civil war in 1975, AMAL took an active part in it as well as continued fighting Israel. During the Lebanese civil war, especially in 1975-76, al-Sadr successfully exerted pressures to defend the Christians in the Biqa' region when some militias tried to attack them as retaliatory actions to the aggressions carried against some Muslim neighbourhoods in East Beirut.

On March 14, 1978, Israel launched its first massive ground invasion, "Operation Litani", in order to prevent PLO rockets from reaching its northern settlements, and established a security zone in south Lebanon. AMAL was supporting the PLO, and during the 1978 invasion an influx of hundreds of thousands of Shi'ite civilians sought refuge in the impoverished southern suburbs of Beirut. Those affected were even more radicalised than they already were. As a result, a gap has been developing between the Shi'ites and the PLO.

Al-Sadr was active domestically and regionally in his endeavours aiming at putting an end to the Lebanese Civil war. Regionally, he embarked on touring some Arab states, which were either considered key players in the fighting in Lebanon or wielded power on the fighting factions. From this perspective, al-Sadr visited Libya, but disappeared in mysterious circumstances on August 31, 1978. His whereabouts are still unknown till now. Although al-Sadr never declared himself as a *marja'* (religious authority) and he was never emulated; yet he held a firm grip on the Lebanese Shi'ite community.

1.1   *AMAL* after al-Sadr

In 1978 the Shi'ites witnessed a great gap in their leadership, and Husayn al-Husayni and Nabih Berri[84] could not match al-Sadr's charisma, charm, and leadership. Thus, the Shi'ites needed a new leader to turn to, and the relief was to come now from another exceptional source, Imam Khumayni. Indeed, the only Arab country that welcomed the victory of the Islamic Revolution in 1979 through massive supporting demonstrations was Lebanon. Many Lebanese Shi'ites were inspired by Imam Khumayni's revolutionary ideology, which eventually led them to actively mobilize and struggle for a more active role in the Lebanese political system.

The Iranian Revolution did not hide its aim to establish contacts with the Shi'a communities in the Arab world. It had already developed close links with many cadres in the *AMAL* movement, and was supporting the Iraqi members of the *Da'wa* ("The Islamic Call") Party present in Shi'a regions in Lebanon.[85] In 1978 the relations between *AMAL* and Iranian opposition groups continued to develop. At the same time, many individual Lebanese and Iranian Shi'ite *'ulama*, who were students at the *Najaf* religious seminary, were closely associated and connected with Iraqi colleagues who were members of the Iraqi revolutionary movement, *Hizb Al-Da'wa Al-Islamiyya*.[86] When the Iraqi regime decided to crack down on them, most of *al-Da'wa* members sought refuge in Beirut, where they found in their co-religionist *AMAL* movement a natural ally.[87]

Iran had encouraged former *al-Da'wa* members to join and infiltrate *AMAL* in order to disseminate a more radical and revolutionary message to a wider audience and to challenge the secular and moderate orientations of

AMAL. A notable individual within *al-Da'wa*, adopting this route was Sayyid Hasan Nasrallah[88], who became an *AMAL* official after serving as a group official in *al-Da'wa* party.[89]

By early 1982, relations between *AMAL* and the PLO had passed the breaking point. After serious clashes, it was a foregone conclusion that Shi'ite interests could no longer be reconciled with the *fida'iyyin*'s presence[90]: "Ironically, the Lebanese sector that suffered most from Palestinian military activity in South Lebanon against Israel until 1982 was the Shi'ite population; the misery generated by the Palestinian presence in South Lebanon was so great that when the IDF [Israeli Defence Force][91] invaded in June 1982 the troops were showered with handfuls of rice".[92] Thus, Palestinian growing military presence and Israeli retaliations constituted another major factor behind the mobilization and radicalisation of the Lebanese Shi'ites. Indeed, the Israel invasion of 1982 was successful in uprooting the PLO from Lebanon, thus heavy military Palestinian presence ceased to be. However, the remaining civilian Palestinian population continued living as refugees in various camps in Lebanon, but they were allowed to only keep their light weapons.[93]

1.2   The schism in *AMAL* and the defection of its cadres to Hizbullah

The major event which led to a division within *AMAL*'s hierarchy between moderates and those adopting a radical Islamic approach, occurred when Nabih Berri, *AMAL*'s leader, decided to co-opt with the Lebanese government, thus joining the National Salvation Committee, which was formed by the Lebanese president Elias Sarkis in mid-June 1982 to deal with the Israeli occupation of Lebanon and its besiegement of Beirut. For many radical *AMAL* members, who were inspired by Ayatullah Khumayni's revolutionary doctrines, Berri's participation was contrary to the line he should have adopted. Thus, his attitude was also judged as un-Islamic.[94]

In protest, some of *AMAL*'s main cadres moved to their opponent, the radical religious party of Hizbullah (The Party of God).[95] For instance, Nasrallah, the current Secretary General of Hizbullah, was *AMAL*'s district leader of the *Biqa'* before he shifted his allegiance.[96] Thus, the divided Shi'ite elite[97] led to a schism in *AMAL*, which eventually resulted in the creation of Hizbullah. Nabih Berri, the current leader of *AMAL* and the Speaker of the Lebanese parliament, has repeatedly stated that *AMAL* was the womb of Hizbullah.[98] He also added, "the brothers in Hizbullah are organically tied to *AMAL*".[99] Thus, most of the cadres who established Hizbullah, including Nasrallah, originated from *AMAL*, but they were against *AMAL*'s compromising attitude; they opted for mobilization and revolution.

Therefore, these radicals abandoned *AMAL* and joined ranks with already existing Islamic Shi'ite groups – including members of the *Da'wa* party, *Itihad al-Lubnani lil Talaba al-Muslimin* ("The Lebanese Union of Muslim Students")[100], as well as independent active Islamic figures and clerics – and established Hizbullah as an Islamic *jihadi* movement against the Israeli occupation, with the material support of Iran and backing from Syria.[101]

2. Iranian ideological and material backing to Hizbullah: ascendancy and emergence of Hizbullah

Since Hizbullah absolves itself from abiding by a specific date for its birth, it seems that Hizbullah's religious ideology could be traced back to 1978, the date of the arrival from *Najaf* of one its primary founders and the teacher of Sayyid Hasan Nasrallah, the late Sayyid 'Abbas al-Musawi who established *Hawzat al-Imam al-Mutazar* and started his *da'wa* in B'albak, in the *Biqa'*. This also coincided with the arrival of dissident Iranian clergy and military personnel who established religious and military training centres with substantial material and spiritual backing from Imam Khumayni who was himself banished to *Najaf* for a period of 13 years.[102] At that time, Ali Akbar Muhtashami, the assumed mastermind of Hizbullah, was the Iranian ambassador to Damascus.[103] Muhtashami, who spend a considerable time in Lebanon, exploited the power vacuum left by the Lebanese state and held regular meetings with leading Islamist cadres such as Imad Maghni-yyé, Husayn al-Musawi, Abbas al-Musawi, and Subhi al-Tufayli, who later on formed Hizbullah's nucleus.[104] At a later stage Muhtashami became the Iranian Interior Minister. He praised Hizbullah's leading Lebanese experience and called on other Islamist movements to follow its lead.[105]

In turn Mustafa Shamran was among the first Iran immigrants who came to Lebanon. He resided in Tyre and was very close to Imam Musa al-Sadr, becoming in charge of his social institutions. Later on Shamran established his own military organization and trained *al-Da'wa* and *AMAL* cadres, mainly in Palestinian camps until he established independent *AMAL* training camps.[106] Shamran became the first central organisational cadre of *AMAL* (*awwal mas'ul tanzimi markazi*).[107] In addition to helping Musa al-Sadr with the founding of *AMAL*, Shamran also had an active hand in the founding of Hizbullah.[108] Thus, the Islamic ideology unified various sectors of the Shi'a community or the *al-hala al-Islamiyya* ("Islamic Milieu"). This led to an increase in Lebanese youth who went to the religious seminaries in *Qum* and *Najaf*, among these, prominent would-be, Hizbullah cadres. All of these factors were conducive to the emergence of Hizbullah's rudimentary foundations that crystallized in the birth of its religious ideology.

Members of the *al-hala al-Islamiyya* converged and established, "the Committee Supportive of the Islamic Revolution, a cultural organization founded in 1979 in the run-up to the revolution in Iran. Since the committee is considered by Hizbu'llah as its 'prospective nucleus', party members emphasize the fact that its birth preceded the [victory of the] Islamic Revolution".[109] In order to coalesce the newly emerging social movement, after the victory of the Islamic Revolution, Sayyid Abbas Al-Musawi along with his students and other leading *'ulama* officially founded "The Hizbullah of Lebanon".[110] Thus, Sayyid Abbas personally coined the name Hizbullah based on the Qur'anic verse (5:56): "Whoever takes Allah, His Apostle and those who believe as friends [must know] that Allah's party [Hizbullah] is indeed the triumphant". However, Hizbullah's "leadership nucleus had been formed before the Islamic Revolution unfolded. Hizbu'allah was therefore the organizational manifestation of a religious current [religious ideology] that can be traced back to the 1960s".[111]

According to Sayyid Husayn Al-Musawi, even when Imam Khumayni was banished in Iraq, he was deeply concerned with Jerusalem and the occupation of Palestine. From this perspective, when Israel invaded Lebanon in 1978, he was in direct contact with *al-hala al-Islamiyya*, but was not able to sent military support, rather material support from his stance as a leading *marja'* responsible for *khums* and *muqadasat* (holy sites).[112] Al-Musawi adds, with the success of the Islamic Revolution and the second Israeli invasion in June 1982, Imam Khumayni could send his *Pasdaran* (Republican Guards) in order to train *al-hala al-Islamiyya*.[113] At that time, the Islamic Revolution was four years old, and already engaged in a fierce war with Iraq. In spite of that, when the Israeli army invaded Lebanon, the Iranians did not hesitate to declare their intention to defend Lebanon against the Israelis. The speaker of the Iranian parliament at that time, Hashemi Rafsanjani, said that the road to Jerusalem passes through *Karbala'* and Lebanon.[114] Syria allowed the dispatching of around 1500 *Pasdaran* to the Lebanese *Biqa'* Valley in June 1982. The *Pasdaran* were at the right place and time to provide Hizbullah with the necessary military and financial support.

And so, Iran played an important part in the emergence of Hizbullah, and it supported Hizbullah's development and profile. Internal Iranian affairs continued to influence Hizbullah during the 1980s, but the influence changed in character and strength. It seems Hizbullah did not make it on its own; part and parcel of its military and social institutions are financed directly by Iran. In fact, to spread the Islamic revolution and help Shi'ite communities outside Iran, Iran provided the Hizbullah of Lebanon with religious (*marja'iyya*), financial, organizational, and military aid.[115] Thus, without Iranian ideological and material backing there could not have been an efficient Lebanese Hizbullah.[116]

2.1   Hizbullah as an Islamic *jihadi* movement

In 1982, Hizbullah's founding members, as represented by the "Committee of the Nine", wrote an internal treatise entitled, "The Treatise of the Nine", which indicated the dimensions of Hizbullah's work and operation stressing its resistance identity as an Islamic *jihadi* movement whose "emergence is based on an ideological, social, political and economical mixture in a special Lebanese, Arab and Islamic context".[117] Nasrallah seconds that, attributing the direct causes of this emergence to the "Zionist invasion" of Lebanon that led to Israel's military occupation of the country from the southern border till Beirut, the collapse of all resistance in the face of the Israeli forces, the expulsion of the PLO from Lebanon, and the formation of a pro-Israeli puppet government led by Amin Jumayyel, etc.[118]

On November 11, 1982, Ahmad Qasir, Hizbullah's first suicide bomber ("martyr"), detonated himself in the Israeli headquarters in Tyre, in southern Lebanon, killing around 76 military officers and wounding 20 others.[119] Begin, the Israeli Prime Minister at the time, declared a three-day mourning in Israel purporting that this is Israeli's worst calamity since its creation in 1948.[120] In Qasir's honour, Hizbullah annually celebrates "Martyrdom Day" on the eleventh of November. On April 13, 1983, Hizbullah conducted its second "martyrdom operation" when 'Ali Safiyyeddine detonated his car into an Israeli convey in *Dayr Qanun al-Nahr* killing six soldiers and wounding four others. On October 14, 1983, Hizbullah conducted its third "martyrdom operation" when Ja'far Al-Tayyar blew himself in an UNRWA building in Tyre housing Israeli soldiers, killing 29 soldiers by the concessions of the Israelis themselves. It is worth mentioning that in the same year (1983), Hizbullah put a lid on an aborted double suicidal operation when the car of the two suicide bombers got blown prematurely on its way to Tyre.

And so, since its founding Hizbullah remained operating underground and anonymously till 1984. Hizbullah's *Shura* (Consultative) Council, or main decision body, passed through different stages from nine members to five and was finalized to seven as of 1984. Hizbullah released several political declarations bearing its name and established its politburo. On June 18, 1984 Hizbullah's mouthpiece and weekly newspaper *al-'Ahd* came to light.[121] And so under Iranian material backing (financial-military-logistical support) and ideological support (adherence to *wilayat al-faqih*), Hizbullah's institutions started to emerge.

Ayatullah Fadlallah's role

Although many social scientists[122] consider the Lebanese Ayatullah Muhammad Husayn Fadlallah, the godfather of *al-hala al-Islamiyya* in Lebanon, as Hizbullah's *murshid ruhi* (spiritual leader), Fadlallah has repeatedly stated that he did not have and does not have "any organizational role, link, or ties with Hizbullah".[123] He added, "I do not concede to this alleged organizational role... I'm the one who reared this generation [of Islamists]... they exercise their own *'ijtihad'* [independent reasoning] or 'hypocrisy' and attribute to me this characterisation of *murshid ruhi*, an accusation that is totally unfounded. I never was and would never be the *murshid ruhi* of any Islamic movement... I'm totally independent and would never confine my role to that".[124] However, this does not rule out informal ties. Fadlallah unequivocally stated that in Islam there is no *murshid ruhi*.[125] Even though Fadlallah is not listed as one of Hizbullah's leaders or ideologues on its official website[126], he is the leading Lebanese Ayatullah who is respected by Hizbullah.[127]

III Hizbullah anathematising the Lebanese political system (1984/5-1990)

1. Hizbullah's Open Letter (*al-risal al-maftuha*)

In the 1980s, Hizbullah followed a radical-violent approach and a rigid political discourse that conveyed an uncompromising attitude anathematising the Lebanese political system in its entirety, regarding the Lebanese government as an infidel. Al-Tufayli, Hizbullah's first Secretary General, said: "We [Hizbullah] consider the regime of Amin Jumayyel [the Lebanese president at the time] as one created by the Western imperialism to destroy the personality of Muslims in this country and to Westernise it. And we will not allow that".[128] Al-Tufayli added: "We should first defend the Islamic Revolution and Iran before considering the formation of a second Islamic state in Lebanon".[129] In that milieu, on February 16, 1985, Hizbullah declared its first detailed official document that outlined its political ideology. The Open Letter, considered to be Hizbullah's political constitution or political manifesto, was published on February 22, 1985, as *Al-Nass Al-Harfi Al-Kamil li-Risalat Hizbullah (Al-Maftuha) ila Al-Mustad'afinin* [The Original Text in Full of Hizbullah's Open Letter Addressed to the Oppressed] in Hizbullah's weekly mouthpiece *al-'Ahd*.[130] It officially revealed what already had been in existence, namely, the establishment of Hizbullah, its military wing, the Islamic Resistance, as well as Hizbullah's identity and objectives. The timing of the propagation of the Open Letter is telling: exactly one year after the assassination of Saykh Raghib Harb, one of its leading cadres in the Islamic Resistance who was mobilizing the masses to fight against the Israeli forces occupying southern Lebanon. It also coincided with the Israeli retreat from Sidon and its preparations to retreat to its self-declared "security zone", which was accomplished by June of the same year.

2.   **Hizbullah's reaction to the aftermath of the Israeli invasion**

In March 1985 Israel blew the *Husayniyya* (centre for male Shi'ites in which religious ceremonies are held and study groups are conducted) of *Ma'raké* and assassinated two leading Hizbullah cadres. In April Israel withdrew from *Nabatiyyé* and *Tyre*. The *Jalil* Operation on May 20 between the General Command of the Popular Front for the Liberation of Palestine (PFLP) and the Israeli government resulted in the release of 1,150 Lebanese and Palestinian detainees from the *Atlit* detention camp in Israel, in exchange for three Israeli soldiers. In June the Israeli Army announced that it has finalised its withdrawal and established an 1100-squared kilometre "Security Zone", which included 168 cities and villages. The "Security Zone" compromised around 15% of Lebanese territory along Lebanon's southern border with Israel, which is reminiscent of the 1978 invasion that aimed at creating a similar security arrangement in order to protect the northern Israeli settlements from missile attacks across the Lebanese border. The Israeli withdrawal resulted in a confrontation between the Christian militias (The Lebanese Forces, the military wing of the Phalangists) and the Muslim and secular militias. The Christian militias were defeated and withdrew leaving behind the Christian population that suffered from atrocities committed by the victors.

On February 16, 1986 the Islamic Resistance captured two Israeli soldiers in an operation in the *Kunin* area of *Bint Jubayl*. Israel launched a limited incursion in 17 villages for six consecutive days in order to retrieve the two soldiers, but with no avail. The Islamic Resistance waged a relentless war against the local collaborators with the Israeli Army, the South Lebanon Army (SLA) posts aiming at occupying them and destroying them, killing and detaining all members, then blowing the entire post. In October an Israeli jet fighter was downed, and Ron Arad, the assistant pilot, was captured. Hizbullah standardised the practice of videotaping military operations against Israeli forces in order to convey the exact number of the Israeli dead and wounded to the Israeli public, thus belying Israeli claims of low casualties.

In 1987, Nasrallah assumed the newly established "chief executive officer" post, in addition to being a member of the Consultative Council, which is Hizbullah's highest leading panel.[131] On the Islamic Resistance's front, the year of 1987 witnessed the reinvigoration of the war of attrition against SLA posts in an unprecedented manner. December marked the beginning of the first Palestinian *Intifada* (popular uprising).

In 1988 the first major military encounter and direct confrontation took place between the Islamic Resistance and the Israeli Army, in an Israeli attack on *Maydun*, in the Western *Biqa'*. On March 11 Hizbullah conducted its fifth "martyrdom operation" when 'Amer Kalakish blew himself in an Israeli convoy near the *Mtulé* settlement at the Lebanese border killing 12 Israeli soldiers and wounding 14 others. The *AMAL*-Hizbullah control war started on April 5 in the South and spread to the *Dahiya* on May 6, which led to the ousting of *AMAL* fighters from the *Dahiya*. This control war ended more than two years later in November 1990. In that war secular Shi'ites (*AMAL*) fought against Islamist Shi'ites (Hizbullah).

On another note, also in 1988 the Consultative Centre for Studies and Documentation (CCSD), Hizbullah's think tank, was created. In May 1988 Hizbullah's *al-Nour* radio station started broadcasting.

On August 19, 1988 Hizbullah conducted its sixth "martyrdom operation" when Haytham Dbuq blew himself in an Israeli convoy on the *Marji'yun* road killing one Israeli soldier and wounding three others according to Israeli military sources. The seventh operation occurred on October 19 when Abdallah 'Atwi blew himself near the Fatima Gate, on the border between Lebanon and Israel, killing eight soldiers and wounding another eight by the concession of the Israelis.

In 1988 Hizbullah still voiced its opposition to the Lebanese political system as Sayyid Ibrahim Amin al-Sayyid declared on the ninth anniversary of the victory of the Islamic Revolution that the Muslim populace in Lebanon does not accept to become part of the (political) project of others

(Lebanese state) heeding to the "president of the Maronite regime"; rather others should find a place for themselves in the project of Islam.[132] Thus, Amin al-Sayyid was inviting others to become part of the Islamic project in Lebanon, refusing to be under the governance of or to co-opt with a non-Muslim regime (Lebanese state), which was an offshoot of Hizbullah's grand program of Islamisation of society in the 1980s.

In these bleak circumstances the tenure of the then Lebanese President Amin Jumayyel[133] ended without electing a successor by the Lebanese parliament. So, on September 23, 1988, Jumayyel appointed General Michel 'Aun, the Lebanese Army Commander, to head a military government composed of three Christians and two Muslims. Deeming the appointment unconstitutional, Muslim clergy met and issued a *fatwa* banning any Muslim from participating in the military government. So General 'Aun virtually ruled the Christian areas in East Beirut and Mount Lebanon, while the rest of the country was under the mandate of prime minister Salim Al-Hoss, who formed a second government in West Beirut. Thus, at that time, Lebanon had two governments, a situation that lasted for almost two years.

On June 3, 1989 Imam Khumayni died and Khamina'i was named as his successor. Hizbullah pledged allegiance to Khamina'i's religious authority.[134] Also in 1989 Hizbullah held its first conclave and revealed the identity of its leaders and cadres. The conclave resulted in the creation of the post of the secretary general and the election of Shaykh Subhi al-Tufayli as Hizbullah's first secretary general. On July 28 the Israeli army abducted Shaykh AdbulKarim 'Ubayd, a leading Hizbullah cadre, from his hometown, *Jibshit*. On August 9 Hizbullah conducted its eighth "martyrdom operation" when Shaykh As'ad Birru blew himself in an Israeli convoy across the *Marji'un* road killing five soldiers and wounding five others according to Israeli military sources.

In an attempt to drive the Syrian Army out of Lebanon, on March 14, 1989, General Michel 'Aun, waged a "Liberation War" against the Syrian forces present in Lebanon since 1976. The "Document of National Accord," known as the Ta'if Agreement, was negotiated by 58 members of the Lebanese parliament in Ta'if, Saudi Arabia, between the 30th of September and the 22nd of October 1989. On Saturday, October 22, 1989 at 10:45 pm, it was officially announced, from the Palace of Conventions at Ta'if, that the civil war ended. However, the nominal declaration of ending the war was not abided by on the ground and the civil war dragged on. 'Aun issued a decree dissolving the parliament, but it fell on deaf ears.

The Ta'if Agreement served as a "bill of rights" or a blueprint for national reconciliation and reform aimed towards a more equitable political system for all sectarian-confessional groups in Lebanon. The bulk and parcel of the agreement dealt with textual changes to the constitution; the rest handled procedural matters such as ending the state of war, dissolving the militias and integrating their members in the Lebanese Army, Lebanese-Syrian relation, etc. The proposed changes in the Ta'if Agreement were officially adopted and written into the Lebanon's new constitution in August and September 1990. The final document is known as "The Constitution of Lebanon after the Amendments of August 21, 1990". The new constitution stipulated the need to share political office on a fifty-fifty basis between Christians and Muslims, as opposed to the earlier 6/5 ratio. Also, the number of seats in the parliament was increased from 99 to 108.[135] The new constitution officially marked the end of the civil war since it stipulated the disbanding of all militias and surrendering their weapons to the Lebanese state. It also called for the integration of the militia members in Lebanese civil society and Lebanese state institutions, most prominently, the Lebanese Army. Nevertheless, the Ta'if Agreement allowed the militias to transform themselves into political parties.

On August 1, 1990 Saddam Husayn invaded and annexed Kuwait. The regional situation dictated on the US to give a green line to the Syrian army to oust General Michel 'Aun, who was considered an ally of Saddam. October 13, 1990 witnessed the actual ending of the 16-year civil war by the ousting of General Michel 'Aun and banishing him to France.[136] Also, the regional situation had its toll on the two and a half-year *AMAL*-Hizbullah war that ended by a final accord on November 9, 1990 brokered between the warring factions through intensive Syrian and Iranian pressure.

3. Hizbullah's views on the Ta'if

Did Hizbullah accept the Ta'if? It seems that Hizbullah's initial reaction was to reject its political component and to accept its security component. On August 13, 1989 Hizbullah issued a political declaration that regarded the Ta'if Agreement "as timid reform that does not touch upon the essence of sectarian privileges, rather it refashions a political system similar to a Maronite Israel in the region" [i.e. a racial state].[137] Hizbullah added, "The Ta'if Agreement constitutes a deadly repetition to the historical sin that was committed in 1943 [National Accord], and which was the main factor behind the disintegration and destruction of the Lebanese state" [a reference to the civil war].[138] That was not all; Hizbullah practiced its own discourse analysis when it issued an official document, which conveyed its stance on Ta'if.[139] Hizbullah criticised the superficial level of the proposed political reforms, but agreed on implementing its security stipulation, pending a clear distinction between militia and resistance. As such, Hizbullah's military wing, the Islamic Resistance was deemed as a legitimate-national resistance by the Lebanese state[140], thus it was allowed to keep its weapons and to conduct its resistance against Israeli forces occupying south Lebanon and the *Biqa'*. However, Hizbullah abided by the security clause of the Ta'if Agreement that prohibits bearing arms and walking in military clothes in the non occupied areas of Lebanon.[141] This arrangement outraged the leaders of the Christian militias since; after all, Hizbullah was allowed to keep its arms and military structure. Also, this move angered secular and leftist militias since it virtually granted Hizbullah a total monopoly in resisting the Israeli forces. Thus, one could say that Hizbullah accepted the Ta'if Agreement out of necessity, rather than conviction.

IV   Hizbullah's infitah ("opening-up") policy (1991 to 2005)

Unlike its uncompromising pre-1990 stance that anathematised the Lebanese state and called it an infidel, Hizbullah conveyed a lenient stance towards the Lebanese state. On January 3, 1991, Hizbullah issued a political declaration, which called on the Lebanese government to safeguard political, intellectual, ideological, and media freedoms. Also, Hizbullah urged the government to differentiate between the role of the different militias in Lebanon and the role of Hizbullah's Islamic Resistance.[142] In March 1991 the Lebanese government officially declared the dissolution of the militias. The end of April was set as a deadline for the militias to hand in their heavy weapons and to close their military and training centres. Hizbullah was exempted as the notable exception to such a decision since the Islamic Resistance, its military wing, was classified as a resistance movement, and not as a militia; as such it was allowed to keep up its arms and continue its resistance against Israel.

Starting May 22, 1991 Hizbullah held its second conclave and elected Sayyid 'Abbas Al-Musawi as its second Secretary General, and Shaykh Na'im

Qasim, as his deputy. Unlike the first conclave in which the seven-member *Shura* Council were nominated, in the second conclave they were elected. The conclave set written moral precepts upon which dialogue would be conducted with the Christians.[143] Thus, the most salient decision of the conclave was Hizbullah's *infitah*. This development was reflected in Hizbullah's 1991 political program, authored by Sayyid Abbas al-Musawi.

In line with its *infitah* policy, Hizbullah changed its discourse and made it pluralistic and inclusive in orientation. Thus, on June 3 Hizbullah's *Al-Manar* TV station was launched. A few months after making its voice heard through its written and audio-visual media, the first swap operation between Hizbullah and Israel, which was brokered by UN[144], took place, on three instalments, between September 11 and December 1. Israel released 91 Lebanese detainees (one from Israeli prisons and 90, including ten women from the *Khyam* detention camp), and the remains of nine fighters in exchange for information about the two Israeli soldiers who were detained by Hizbullah on February 16, 1986.

February 16, 1992 witnessed the assassination of Sayyid Abbas al-Musawi, his wife, and his son, by an Israeli helicopter. Two days later, Sayyid Hasan Nasrallah, Hizbullah's third Secretary General, was elected as well as Shaykh Na'im Qasim as Deputy Secretary General. Both Nasrallah and Qasim retain their posts till the present day. Israel attacked the two villages of *Kafra* and *Yatir*, an act that was met with forceful resistance from Hizbullah fighters. This inaugurated Hizbullah's employment of the Katyusha weapon as a deterrent strategy to protect Lebanese civilians from Israeli aggressions.

The Lebanese electoral system:
The parliamentary elections of 1992

In order to ensure a fairer representation of the sectarian-confessional balance, in 1992 the Lebanese state increased the number of seats in the Lebanese parliament from 108, as stipulated by the Ta'if, to 128. Thus, the Lebanese government embarked on organizing the first parliamentary elections that were not held for the past twenty years[145] due to the civil war. The post-Ta'if Lebanese electoral system has been based on a system of absolute majority of votes received by a candidate who belongs to a certain sect and represents a certain electoral district. The list system reigns where each voter has to choose candidates across the confessional divide according to a rigid sectarian quota system that allocates a certain number of seats to each sect depending on the size of the population in the election district and its confessional make up. The Ta'if Agreement stipulated the division of Lebanon into five *muhafazat* (large administrative districts): Beirut, Mount Lebanon, North Lebanon, *Biqa'*, and South Lebanon. This was precisely done in order to ensure the multi-confessional composition of all lists in an endeavour to safeguard Muslim-Christian co-existence and national unity, and fend off tribalism and sectarianism.

Hizbullah found difficulty in deciding whether to participate in the 1992 elections or not; this resulted in an internal row or discord[146]. Since *al-waliyy al-faqih* (jurisconsult) is the one who determines "legitimacy"[147] (even in practical political matters), Khamina'i had to intercede and grant legitimacy for participation. This caused a considerable schism in Hizbullah because Tufayli contested the decision and pursued a confrontational stance with both the party and the Lebanese state.

After the issue was settled, on July 3, 1992 Hizbullah publicly announced its decision to participate in the elections and launched its political program, which was based on the elaboration of the following pillars: (1) The liberation of Lebanon from the "Zionist" occupation; (2) the abolishment of political sectarianism[148]; (3) amending the electoral law so that it will be more representative of the populace; (4) ensuring political and media freedoms; (5) enacting a modern naturalization law based on meritocracy; (6) the complete return of all the displaced; (7) administrative, developmental, educational and cultural, and social reforms.[149] Based on its 1992 election program, Hizbullah's won all of the twelve seats on its election list: eight were reserved for party members, and four for affiliated sympathizers: two for Sunnis and two for Christians (a Greek Catholic and a Maronite). In commenting on the 1992 election program and Hizbullah's performance, Hajj Muhammad Ra'd, the current head of Hizbullah's 12-member parliamentary Bloc, explained that Hizbullah's MPs tried to show the other side of the party, i.e. Hizbullah as a political party. Hizbullah's deputies defended the Islamic Resistance, addressing and engaging the domestic, regional, and international public opinion as much as the parliamentary public space allowed.[150]

On September 21, 1992, Ibrahim Dahir conducted Hizbullah's ninth "martyrdom operation" when he targeted an Israeli convoy on the *Jarmaq* road, killing and wounding 25, according to Hizbullah.

Hizbullah's dialogue with the Lebanese Christians

On December 1, 1992, Hizbullah set a precedent in its relations with the Christians when its late MP Shaykh Khudr Tlays and Sayyid Nawwaf Al-Musawi, Hizbullah's Politburo member, paid a watershed visit to the

Maronite Patriarch. After the meeting, Tlays stressed the need for Christian-Muslim dialogue and *infitah* adding that Hizbullah regards cultural, political, and religious freedoms in Lebanon as sanctified and, as such, should not be encroached upon, come what may.[151] From this perspective, Hizbullah's leadership embarked on developing a political program of dialogue as a statement of intention aimed at opening up the channels of dialogue with all parties, except those who had blatant connections with Israel such as the Phalangists and Lebanese Forces. The aim behind this political program of dialogue has been to survey common grounds that would set the pace for a fruitful cooperation on common issues as well as solve existing discords without any recourse to confrontation. Hizbullah stressed that this is possible if each party's beliefs, particularities, specificities, and overall visions are respected, while at the same time, leaving room for altering, out of conviction, certain standpoints. According to Hizbullah, dialogue and political relations ought to be based upon a complete respect for citizens' rights, social justice, and peaceful coexistence, all stemming from the conviction that Lebanon is for all its citizens.[152]

In response to Hizbullah's 1992 visit, on January 22, 1993, the Maronite Patriarch sent a delegation headed by his deputy to meet with Hizbullah's Secretary General. In the wake of this meeting a common committee was set to follow up on Christian-Muslim dialogue on a regular basis. Although the Maronite Patriarch indicated divergence with Hizbullah on certain issues, he conveyed his respect for Hizbullah because of its integrity in honouring its words with deeds. In turn, Hizbullah stressed that dialogue should concentrate on and be confined to issues of mutual benefit and things that do not encroach upon sensitivities or lead to repulsion. Rather, dialogue should deal with primary issues that have a high potential of leading to convergence or modification of ideas and opinions among the parties. The various parties adjust themselves to and reconcile themselves with consenting to dialogue regardless if it leads to an acceptable result or roots discord instead, without allowing that negatively to affect the persistence and continuity of dialogue and cooperation.[153]

In the early summer of 1993 Hizbullah held its third conclave, in which it re-elected Sayyid Hasan Nasrallah as its Secretary General, and Shaykh Na'im Qasim as Deputy Secretary General. It is important to note that the Islamic Resistance was rewarded by electing Hizbullah's "Central Military Commander", Hajj Muhsin Al-Shakar, as one of the seven-member *Shura* Council.

From the 23rd till the 31st of July 1993 "The seven days war" or the Israeli "Operation Accountability" erupted as a direct result of the Islamic Resistance's killing of seven Israeli soldiers. "The seven days war" led to the death of 130 people, mostly Lebanese civilians, and it displaced around 300,000. "Operation Accountability" resulted in an unwritten (oral) agreement between Hizbullah and Israel to sideline the civilians on both sides of the border. In spite of PM Rafiq Hariri's government ban on demonstrations, in the wake of the signing of the Oslo Agreement, Hizbullah protested in the *Dahiya* by a peaceful demonstration, which turned out bloody when the Internal Security Forces (ISF) or the Police and Lebanese Army fired at the demonstrations killing thirteen, including two women, and wounding around forty.

In October 1994 the Islamic Resistance stormed the Israeli post of *Dabshé*. Hizbullah exploited the camera as a primary weapon in its psychological warfare against Israel by airing, through its *al-Manar* TV, details of the operation and the Israeli casualties. On May 31, an Israeli commandos unit abducted Hajj Mustafa al-Dirani, an Islamic *AMAL* leading cadre, from his hometown, *Qsarnaba*, in the *Biqaʻ*.

Acknowledging the difficulty of implementing the stipulations of the Open Letter in the Lebanese public sphere and its clash with the political system, in October 1994 Nasrallah hinted to a possible rewording of the Open Letter: "The Open Letter conveyed general precepts and general guidelines of our identity... for some time ago, we have reviewed the Open Letter and I do not consider that there are major alterations that have occurred to our overall doctrines and orientations although we should account for the changes and eventualities that took place in the previous years".[154]

On May 17, 1995, Khaminaʼi appointed Sayyid Hasan Nasrallah, Hizbullah's Secretary general, and Shaykh Muhammad Yazbik, Hizbullah's *Shura* Council member, as *wakilayn sharʻiyyan* (his religious deputies)[155] in Lebanon "in the *hisbi* (things that God does not allow that we forsake) domain and *sharʻi* (religious) precepts, taking over from him the religious duties and disposing them to the benefit of the Muslims; warding off oppression and injustice; conducting *sharʻi* conciliations for the *khums* adherents; and appointing their own deputies".[156]

On April 25, 1995 Salah Ghandur conducted Hizbullah's tenth "martyrdom operation" when he blew himself in an SLA post in *Bint Jubayl* wounding eleven according to Israeli military sources. Hizbullah's fourth conclave was held in July 1995. The Secretary General and his deputy were re-elected. Some of the basic organizational changes that Hizbullah made were the following: (1) The Politburo was renamed the "Political Council" and its jurisdiction was enlarged; (2) The creation of the "*Jihadi* Council", headed by Sayyid Hashim Safiyyeddine, the only new member of the *Shura* Council; (3) The "Executive Council" replaced the "Executive *Shura*" with, more or less, the same jurisdictions; (4) In order to evaluate Hizbullah's experience in the parliament, the party formed a new body called the "Parliamentary Bloc Council".

On March 20, 1996 'Ali Ashmar conducted Hizbullah's eleventh "martyrdom operation" in the Town of *Rub Thalathin* in *al-'Daysé* killing two according to Israel military sources. In an attempt to curtail Hizbullah, from April 11 till April 18, 1996, Israel launched a massive attack against southern Lebanon killing more than 150 civilians – including 102 civilians seeking shelter in the UN headquarters in the Lebanese village of *Qana* – and displacing around half a million others. Also, Israel bombed heavily the Lebanese infrastructure.[157] The "Grapes of Wrath" resulted in an unprecedented national solidarity with Hizbullah. Along with other denominations, Christians, most notably, donated gold and money so that Hizbullah can buy Katyusha rockets to be fired at Israel as a deterrent strategy in an endeavour to halt the attack. Thus, after the Grapes of Wrath there seems to be a consensus among most Lebanese parties on Hizbullah's resistance legitimacy. The Israeli aggression produced what became known as the "April 1996 Understanding/Agreement" that protected both Israeli and Lebanese civilians from military operations. The UN, France, Syria, and the US brokered the April 26 *written* Agreement between Israel and Hizbullah, which established the "Monitoring Group for the Understandings of Operation Grapes of Wrath". Thus, the international community along with Israel seem to have recognised Hizbullah's right to resist the occupation.

The parliamentary elections of 1996
In the shadow of the foregoing pressuring military confrontations, in the summer of 1996 Hizbullah launched its parliamentary election program, which could be outlined as follows: (1) Resisting the Israeli occupation; (2) achieving equality and establishing the just state; (3) pressuring the state to adopt favourable economic policies towards the oppressed, aiming at balanced development; (4) educational and syndicate reforms; (5) social and health reforms; (6) safeguarding public freedoms; (7) and enhancing the foreign policy of the Lebanese state.[158] Muhammad Ra'd stated that in 1996 Hizbullah evaluated its participation in these parliamentary elections, especially after the Lebanese public opinion rallied around Hizbullah[159]. Hizbullah managed to keep nine seats: seven were occupied by party members,

and two others by a Sunni and a Maronite Christian, non-party members. This resulted in changing some deputies with incumbents who are characterised by practical dimensions, rather than theoretical ones (more specialization and division of tasks). This led to more representation of the different geographical areas that form Hizbullah's constituencies: Beirut, the South, and the *Biqa'*. Further, a member of Hizbullah's Bloc was elected as the head of the parliamentary committee of economy.[160] It is worth mentioning that only the head of Hizbullah's parliamentary Bloc was a clergyman, Sayyid Ibrahim Amin al-Sayyid.

Under German sponsorship, on July 21, 1996 Hizbullah exchanged the bodies of 2 Israeli soldiers (kidnapped on February 16, 1986) and 17 SLA collaborators, for 45 Lebanese detainees and 123 remains. In the 1996 parliamentary elections, Hizbullah managed to keep 11 seats. On April 7, 1997 a swap operation between Hizbullah and Israel resulted in the exchange of three Lebanese detainees for the body of a dead SLA sergeant.

On May 4, 1997 conflict erupted between Hizbullah and the Lebanese state when Shaykh Subhi al-Tufayli declared the "Revolution of the Hungry", and on July 4 he called for civil disobedience against the Lebanese government. This culminated in blocking roads on October 26. On September 5 the Israeli operation of *al-Ansariyyé* resulted in the death of 12 high-ranking officials of an elite Israeli military commandos while not a single member of the Resistance was injured. On September 12, Sayyid Hadi Nasrallah, Sayyid Hasan Nasrallah's son, died in a confrontation with the Israel soldiers in southern Lebanon.

The formation of the Multi-confessional Lebanese Brigades

On November 3, 1997 Hizbullah formed *Al-Saraya*[161] *Al-Lubnaniyya Li-Muqawamat Al-Ihtilal Al-Israeli* or the Multi-confessional Lebanese Brigades to Fighting the Israeli Occupation (LMCB), which marks the "Lebanonisation"[162] of the resistance. Although the LMCB was formed by Hizbullah, not a single member of the Islamic Resistance participated in its operations. The former was an attempt to revive something like the secular *al-Muqawama al-Wataniyya al-Lubnaniyya* ("Lebanese National Resistance") that became defunct as of early 1991 as a result of the disbanding of militias in accordance with the Ta'if Agreement. LMCB was based on the nationalist and secular dimension of the resistance to occupation, while the Islamic Resistance is based on the Islamist ideology.[163]

Shaykh Subhi al-Tufayli was officially expelled from Hizbullah by a political declaration issued on January 24, 1998. On January 30 a violent military confrontation erupted between the Lebanese army and al-Tufayli's supporters, who occupied by military force Hizbullah's religious seminary in *'Ayn Burday*, near *B'albak*. The bloody face off – which resulted in some casualties, the most important were the death of a Christian army lieutenant and ex-Hizbullah MP Khudr Tluys, Tufayli's son in law, and wounded many others – ended with the destruction of Tufayli's headquarters and the Lebanese state's issuing of an arrest warrant against Tufayli. However, till this day, he is still at large. After solving the problem of internal discord, Hizbullah held its fifth conclave between June 20 and the end of July. Nasrallah was elected for a third term. For this move to be made, Hizbullah had to amend its internal bylaws by deleting the stipulation that the secretary general cannot serve for more than two consecutive terms.

The municipal elections of 1998

From May 24 till June 14, 1998 Lebanese municipal elections – that reflect true populace representation[164] and which had not been carried out since 1963 – were carried out only after pressure and lobbying from Hizbullah. The Lebanese government used the pretext of lack of financial and technical resources and manpower, but Hizbullah insisted on the reactivation of the elections. In its bid to control the municipal councils in its main constituencies, Hizbullah fielded its party members along with Christian candidates. Hizbullah contested the municipal elections according to the following municipal election program: (1): "Encourage the citizen to play a more active role in the selection process of development projects; (2): increase the functions and powers of municipalities in the provision of education, health care and socio-economic affairs; (3): involve qualified people in developmental projects; (4): finance development projects from both municipal revenues and donations; (5): exercise control over public woks and prevent embezzlement; (6): renovate the physical and administrative structures of municipalities and provide them with computer facilities".[165] Around seventy municipalities could not take part in the elections, either because of the Israeli occupation in the South or due to the displacement of various Lebanese citizens during the course of the civil war. *AMAL* and Hizbullah failed to agree on a common electoral list, which resulted in fielding competing candidates. In Mount Lebanon, *AMAL* and the Lebanese government's candidates lost a lot of ground to Hizbullah and the Christian opposition. Eventually, Hizbullah won a landslide victory in Beirut and a considerable number of municipal councils in its main constituencies in the South and the *Biqa'* (with the exception of the *B'albak* district where it won 4 out of 21 seats), including electoral districts that were supported by the Lebanese government and its candidates. However, the dissident Tufayli was able to take control of his village, *Brital*, and the adjacent village, *Tarayya*. On the whole, Hizbullah won a landslide victory in most Shi'ite electoral districts, monopolizing most of the local municipal councils. The results of the elections revealed Hizbullah as "a major political force" that has to be reckoned with.[166]

On June 26, 1998, by the mediation of the Lebanese government, the remains of an Israeli soldier, who died during the *Ansariyyé* battle of September 1997, were exchanged for 60 detainees (10 of whom were detained in Israel) and the remains of 40 Lebanese resistance fighters, including Hadi Nasrallah. On September 13 Israel released Suha Bshara (who 10 years ago attempted to take the life of the SLA leader, Antoine Lahd) after 10 years of imprisonment and torture at the notorious *Khyam* prison.

In September 1998 Hizbullah overtly acknowledged that it does not consider the Open Letter anymore as a primary authoritative frame of reference (*la ya'tamiduha masdaran asasiyyan min adabiyatihi*)[167], which conveys more and more Hizbullah's Lebanonisation and *infitah* policy.

On February 28, 1999 the Islamic Resistance blew the convoy of the Israeli Brigadier-General in Lebanon, Erez Gerstein, which resulted in his immediate death. Gerstein was the highest-ranking Israeli soldier to be killed in 17 years. In early June Israeli forces and SLA withdrew from *Jezzin* (a predominantly Christian enclave) that comprised around 6% of the "Security Zone", thus reducing the total size of the "Security Zone" to 9% of the Lebanese territory. Through German mediation, Israel released, on two instalments, 13 Lebanese freedom fighters, five of whom were released on December 26 from the Israeli *Ayalut* detention camp, in exchange for a promise from Hizbullah to help track the missing Israeli pilot, Ron Arad, whose plane was downed over south Lebanon in 1986. On December 30, 1999 'Ammar Husayn Hammud conducted Hizbullah's twelfths "martyrdom operation" on the road to *al-Qlay'a* killing 7 Israeli soldiers and wounding seven others according to Hizbullah, while according to Israeli military sources the operation resulted in no Israeli casualties since the suicide bomber detonated himself prematurely.[168]

The confrontation between Hizbullah and Israel continued. From 1992 till 2000, "14 Israeli civilians have died as a direct or indirect result of

Hizbullah's attacks, while over 500 Lebanese and Palestinian civilians have died".[169] Furthermore, "In April 1996 alone, hundreds of thousands of civilians were driven north by IDF bombing... Israeli strikes on Lebanese power plants darkened much of Lebanon in 1996, 1999, and twice in 2000, causing damages estimated at $300 million".[170] In February 2000 the Islamic Resistance blew the farm of the SLA's second man in rank, 'Aqil Hashim, who died in the blast. On April 19 Israel released 13 Lebanese detainees from the Israeli *Ayalut* detention camp. On May 24 Israel withdrew from southern Lebanon after 22 years of occupation; however, Israel failed to relinquish the Lebanese *Shib'a* Farms[171], which are a bone of contention between Israel and Lebanon.

Unlike the atrocities that were committed against the Christians after the Israeli withdrawal in June 1985, nothing happened after the Israeli withdrawal of May 2000. Rather, only civil peace prevailed and stability reigned since Hizbullah acted under the Lebanese state laws and left to it to deal with ex-collaborators and ex-SLA members.[172] Hizbullah won 12 seats in the parliamentary elections held in the summer. On October 7 Hizbullah captured 3 Israeli soldiers from the Lebanese *Shib'a* Farms. On 15 October Hizbullah lured and apprehended, at Beirut, a retired Israeli Mossad colonel.

The Lebanese Shib'a Farms

The Lebanese *Shib'a* Farms border Lebanon and Syria from the side of the Golan Heights from the east and Israel from the southeast; they have an area of around 22 square kilometres, which comprises around 2% of the total area of Lebanon that is 10, 425 square kilometres. They were captured by Israel in the 1967 war.[173] After Israel invaded Lebanon on March 14, 1978, the UN issued Resolution 425 demanding the complete and unconditional withdrawal of Israeli troops from Lebanon.[174] By May 25, 2000[175] and after 22 years, Israel complied and withdrew from southern Lebanon and the western *Biqa'*, but not from the *Shib'a* Farms because it was considered to be part of the Syrian Golan Heights that were occupied in 1967. After the Israeli withdrawal in May 2000, Syria filed a letter to the UN conceding unequivocally, in writing, that the *Shib'a* Farms are Lebanese. From May 25, 2000 till June 6, 2000, the UN and Lebanon were engaged in a painstaking operation of verifying the Israeli withdrawal. As a result, Lebanon regained 17,756,600 square meters of its southern land along the Israeli border, and what has been labelled as the "Blue Line" was drawn between the two countries.

On May 20, 2001, Nasrallah, Hizbullah's Secretary General, affirmed that it is not his concern if *Shib'a* falls under UN Resolution 242 or 425; rather, this is the concern of governments. What he is concerned about is that it is Lebanese land, which is under occupation and Hizbullah will liberate it come what may. He added that it was the Islamic Resistance that forced Israel to accept the implementation of 425, and not the international community.[176] Lebanon still maintains its reservations against the "Blue Line", as President Emile Lahud reiterated in his official visit to France on May 29, 2001, arguing that the "Blue Line" is a demarcation line that does not conform to the official truce border between Lebanon and Israel. He added that, without Hizbullah, the Lebanese resistance, and the Lebanese Army, Israel would not have withdrawn. He also refused to send the Lebanese Army to the south "in order to protect Israel".[177] On June 27, 2001, during his official visit to France, Bashshar al-Asad, the Syrian president, reiterated that *Shib'a* is Lebanese. John Kelly, the ex-US ambassador to Lebanon, corroborates this by stressing, "Both Syria and Lebanon has affirmed that *Shib'a* Farms are Lebanese and send a written memo in this regard to the UN. That is why *Shib'a* Farms are Lebanese".[178] In turn, Asher Kaufman, an Israeli academic, demonstrated that the *Shib'a* Farms are Lebanese.[179]

The 2000 electoral system

The Christian right, who accused Syria of controlling the electoral process, characterized the 2000 election law as neither free nor fair, plagued with gerrymandering, manipulation of electoral lists, and exploitation in the eligibility of voters.[180] It contended that, this resulted in a culture of intimidation, extortion, and bribery of voters as well as vote rigging. Contrary to the Ta'if, the 2000 election law divided the five *muhafazat* into 14 electoral districts: Beirut was divided into three districts; Mount Lebanon into four; North Lebanon into two; the *Biqa'* into three; and the South into two. According to the Christian right, the election law had the inevitable result of electing pro-Syrian candidates, while at the same time barring those who were against Syrian influence from making it to parliament. It is alleged that the late Syrian Colonel Ghazi Kan'an[181] was the orchestrator and godfather of the 2000 parliamentary election law, on which he was handsomely rewarded by a $10 million check from the late PM Rafiq Hariri.[182]

Hizbullah's 2000 parliamentary elections program

Hizbullah's August 2000 electoral program was divided along seven categories which are the following: (1) Resistance and liberation (E.g. the *Shib'a* Farms); (2) Enhancement of Lebanese foreign policy; (3) Reforms on the economic level in order to solve the serious socio-economic crisis; (4) Building of institutions and the state of law as well as the promotion of political participation; (5) Educational and cultural issues; (6) Social and health issues; (7) Environmental issues.[183] Based on this political program, Hizbullah won twelve seats in the 2000 parliamentary elections. Hizbullah's nine candidates, along with two Sunnis, and one Maronite Christian, received the *highest number of votes in the country*.[184] In the 2000 parliamentary elections all Hizbullah's representatives in the parliament were civilian (no *'ulama*). In conformity with Hizbullah's rotation policy, Ra'd and Amin al-Sayyid swapped positions, thus the former became the head of Hizbullah's Parliamentary Bloc, while the latter was appointed as the head of Hizbullah's Political Council. A member of Hizbullah's Bloc was elected as the head of the parliamentary committee of agriculture, and the rest of the Bloc members participated in other parliamentary committees such as finance, defence, security, public administration, and foreign affairs.[185]

In Hizbullah's sixth conclave that ended on July 30, 2001, Nasrallah was re-elected for life, and Sayyid Ibrahim Amin Al-Sayyid and Hajj Jawad Nureddine replaced Hajj Muhammad Ra'd and Hajj Muhsin Shakar in the *Shura* Council. Hizbullah placed its media institutions under the direct command of Nasrallah, aided by the head of the Political Council and that of the Executive Council. This was done in order to upgrade the role of Hizbullah's media, and pursue its ideological hegemony. Also, Hizbullah abolished its "Central Planning Council", and strengthened internal audit and accountability mechanisms. From this perspective, the roles and duties of the municipal councils were expended (horizontally) and upgraded (vertically).

On March 27-28, 2002 the Arab Summit was held in Beirut and the "Saudi Initiative", which aimed at ending the Israeli-Palestinian conflict, was adopted. In late March, early April, the Israeli army conducted a deadly incursion into the West Bank. Hizbullah responded by 12-day military operations in the *Shib'a* Farms in order to buttress the *Intifada*. On June 10, in light of the revival of the prisoner-swap negotiations and as a good will gesture towards Hizbullah, Israel released Muhammad al-Birzawi, a Hizbullah fighter, who has been detained since 1987.

Hizbullah's evaluation of the Open Letter

On June 10, 2002, Na'im Qasim confirmed that the party was intending to release a modified version of its 1985 Open Letter. According to him, the new version will specify the goals and record Hizbullah's vision on new developments during the previous years. Nevertheless, Qasim stressed that Hizbullah's position towards doctrinal issues would remain the same: "We

[Hizbullah] consider that our stance concerning our attitudes is overt and transparent. That is why, the new Open Letter would not shatter these doctrinal positions; rather it will consolidate them. It will be considered as coalescing with earlier stances taken by the party in different contexts".[186]

In October 2002 rumour surfaced that Hizbullah was in the final phases of launching a new updated version of its Open Letter in conformity with an earlier decision taken in Hizbullah's sixth conclave that was held in July 2001. The rumour was substantiated by Qasim's October 28, 2002 published interview in the Daily Star. Qasim argued, "Much has happened and much has changed between 1985 and now... Our basic principles remain the same because they are the heart of our movement, but many other positions have changed due to evolving circumstances developing around us". Locally, Qasim stressed that Hizbullah's position towards the Phalagists has obviously changed, stressing that they are partners in dialogue. Regionally, concerning Hizbullah's stance towards Israel, Qasim affirmed Hizbullah outright animosity towards the "Zionist entity" and the "Small Satan" from an immutable, doctrinal perspective: "Since many positions have changed, we need to be flexible and change ours too... But the resistance against Israel has been the core of our belief and that has never changed" since "the struggle against Israel remains the central rationale of Hizbullah's existence". Internationally, Qasim argued that Hizbullah's relationship with the West has witnessed many changes in line with its *infitah* policy and the West's changing perception towards the party, especially France: "The French were considered our enemy because they attacked our bases in the Bekaa... France's position has changed towards us, so we have to change ours". However, he added that Hizbullah's perception towards the US[187] is still the same, since the party still regards it as the "Great Satan".[188]

On August 21, 2003 Israel returned the remains of two Hizbullah fighters in return for a meeting between the detained Mossad colonel and the German mediator. In response to a suicide operation in Israel a day earlier, in which 19 Israeli civilians died, on December 5 Israeli jets violated Lebanese airspace and bombed an alleged Palestinian training camp near Damascus. This was the first Israeli air strike on Syria in 30 years, since the end of the October 1973 war. Syria exercised restraint after receiving assurances from the UN.

On January 19, 2004 Hizbullah destroyed an Israeli military bulldozer after it crossed the "Blue Line". Hizbullah targeted it by firing an anti-tank rocket when it was 26 meters inside Lebanese territory by the concession of the UNIFIL. One Israeli soldier was killed, and another was seriously wounded. This confrontation came at a time when the prisoner exchange negations between Israel and Hizbullah were at their peak. This exemplifies Hizbullah's two-track policy: military confrontation and negotiations, side by side.

The prisoners' return

On January 29-30, 2004 Hizbullah and Israel conducted the first phase of a watershed prisoner exchange deal after four years of negotiations brokered by Germany. Hizbullah released the Israeli colonel and the bodies of three Israeli soldiers captured in October 2000 in return for 400 Palestinians and 23 Lebanese and Arabs (including two Hizbullah senior cadres: Shaykh AbdulKarim 'Ubayd and Hajj Mustafa Al-Dirani) released from Israeli prisons, and the remains of 59 Lebanese guerrilla fighters, 11 of whom belonged to Hizbullah. It was a groundbreaking operation since it was the first time that Israel acquiesced to Hizbullah's demands and released Palestinians, setting a precedent and bestowing Hizbullah with an unprecedented role in the *Intifada*, thus regionalizing the conflict. By this move, Israel granted Hizbullah a de facto recognition as a legitimate resistance movement, which has managed to release all it cadres from Israeli prisons, as Nasrallah has repeatedly promised.[189]

On May 7, 2004 an Israeli incursion reminiscent of *Ansariyyé* occurred after the elite Israeli Egoz commandos unit crossed the "Blue Line". Hizbullah fighters ambushed it, killed one soldier and wounded 5 others, by the concession of the Israelis themselves. Unlike the precedent set by *Ansariyyé* and in spite of Hizbullah's intensive firing power, the Israelis were able to evacuate their dead and wounded.

Hizbullah's 2004 political program

Almost two years before the 2004 municipal elections took place, Hizbullah held a special conference and produced its election program, setting a precedent to other political parties, which either had sketchy election programs or hardly any election program. I outline the election programs, and then I highlight the results. Hizbullah's 2004 municipal elections program[190] was based on the following two slogans: (1): Hizbullah's principles dictate that the populace constitute the main pillars behind its movement. From this perspective, Hizbullah is under a responsibility to fend off all oppression and injustice in order to serve them and protect their dignity. (2): One of Hizbullah's aims is to adopt the plight of the oppressed and the disenfranchised populace by protecting them and actively working for putting an end to oppression and discrimination towards the deprived areas in order to raise its standards of living in all respects. The election program can be summarised as follows[191]: (1) Administration and organization; (2) The efficiency of the municipal council and boosting the confidence of the citizens in it; (3) Expand the financial revenues of the municipalities; (4) Developmental projects, which are divided into guiding plans and specific projects; (5) Giving importance to environmental conditions within the municipal jurisdiction; (6) Social care: (A) Consolidating a resistance society; (B): Caring for the youth; (C): Children, motherhood, old age, and handicap (disability) care; (D): Pedagogical care; (7): Specifying the domestic, regional, and international resources that the municipalities benefit from.

From the second to the thirtieth of May the second municipal elections were held after a lapse of six years. The usual correlation between Hizbullah's programs and its success[192] materialised once more since it has consolidated its earlier gains and advanced more at the expense of other political parties, most notably *AMAL*. Hizbullah achieved a landslide victory in the *Biqa'* winning 28 out of the 30 municipalities that it was behind their formation; 3 municipalities in which Hizbullah contributed few members to its municipal councils; 16 municipalities were left to their own devices; and 8 municipalities won without competition or by acclamation (*bi-al-tazkiya*), where Hizbullah was behind fielding its candidates. In *Brital*, Subhi al-Tufayli's supporters won a landslide victory. Unlike 1998, Hizbullah secured all the 21 seats in *B'albak*, a constituency composed of roughly 15,000 Shi'a, 10,000 Sunnis and 5,000 Christians. The Ministry of Interior estimated the participation was 70%.[193] As in 1998, Hizbullah achieved a sweeping victory in Beirut securing all municipalities in the *Dahiya*. In the South, where the highest rate of voting was detected, the party won 61% of the municipalities securing 87 out of 142 and penetrating 20 others. Hizbullah won in 5 out of 7 main municipalities. In the South, which has always been considered as *AMAL*'s turf, *AMAL* shared only scattered victories, splitting the 39% with other political parties and independents.[194] Thus, the coordination and cooperation pact or the "understanding" between *AMAL* and Hizbullah did not pay off and resulted in no consensus since each insisted on forming different election lists and not a common slate list. Contrary to 1998 when Hariri won in Beirut and Sidon, his hometown, this time he was able to secure only Beirut, and only one candidate on his list was able to make it in Sidon. Moreover, none of Hariri's candidates made it in Tripoli. Thus, it seems that there emerged two main winners and two main losers in the elections, these being respectively Hizbullah and President Lahud, on the one hand, and the PM and the Speaker, on the other hand.[195]

On May 21, 2004 Hizbullah held a huge demonstration to protest the desecration of the holy sites in Iraq. Around half a million Hizbullah supporters wearing white burial shrouds chanted "death to Israel" and "death to America". This show of force came two days before the municipal elections in the South, which was considered an *AMAL* den and strong constituency. By this, Hizbullah proved itself to be the largest political force in the country.

Unlike the September 13, 1993 unlicensed demonstrations, on May 27, 2004 licensed demonstrations spread over the country in protest for the pressing socio-economic situation triggered by a severe hike in fuel prices. In *Hayy al-Sulum*, in the *Dahiya*, the Lebanese Army fired at the demonstrators who where throwing rocks at it, killing five and wounding several others. As a result, riots spread in the *Dahiya*, and the demonstrators burned the first floor of the Ministry of Labour. On May 29, 2004 Nasrallah held a news conference in which he accused the US Embassy in Beirut of infiltrating the demonstrators and perpetrating the violence, thus giving weight to the hidden hand explanation or the conspiracy theory. He called on the cabinet and parliament to hold emergency sessions to discuss the issue, and he called on the government to launch an investigation about what has happened. On May 31, 2004, conceding to Nasrallah's demands, the Lebanese cabinet held an urgent meeting in which it vehemently condemned the May 27 shootings and offered, as blood money, around $33,000 to the family of each victim. The cabinet asked the Minister of Justice and the Minister of Defence to conduct an investigation into the unrest and report directly to it.

Hizbullah's seventh conclave

From June to August 16, 2004, Hizbullah held its seventh conclave. Unlike, the previous conclaves where information was leaked to the media, hardly any information was disseminated. It seems that Hizbullah's extra clandestine tactic might have to do with the dismantling of a network of underground operatives allegedly linked to Israel, as well as the assassination attempts the party's rank and file suffered from in the last two years.[196]

It is worth mentioning that the followers of Subhi al-Tufayli released a political declaration chastising the conclave and asking for reinstating him and his followers to their "natural, normal position of leadership" in the party after being ousted due to conspiracies that occurred a few years ago. The political declaration added that the convening of this conclave offers a historical chance to conduct honest elections in Hizbullah's rank and file in order to choose leaders who will retain Hizbullah's earlier glory as a religious, Shi'ite social movement. The declaration accused Nasrallah of planting discord in the Shi'ite house (milieu) by his "total hegemony and tyrannical control" over the party and its capabilities and directing them in a way that is not conducive to the Shi'ites, for instance, as exemplified by the criticisms directed towards Sayyid Fadlallah[197] in favour of some (Iranian) personalities and *maraja's*.[198]

Hizbullah released a political document in the form of two political declarations. The first political declaration conveyed that no changes took place within Hizbullah's 7-member *Shura* Council, which includes the following members: Sayyid Hasan Nasrallah, Hizbullah's Secretary General and the head of the *Jihadi* Council; Shaykh Na'im Qasim Deputy Secretary General; Sayyid Hashim Safiyyeddine head of Executive Council; Sayyid Ibrahim Amin Al-Sayyid the head of the Political Council; Hajj Hasan Khalil, Nasrallah's political aide or advisor; Shaykh Muhammad Yazbik head of Religio-Judicial Council, or the "responsible for the dossier of the *shar'i* matters and Islamic scholars' affairs"; and Sayyid Jawad Nureddine. In its second political document, Hizbullah listed four priorities and eight basic modifications or amendments. The most salient amendment was Hizbullah's division of the South into two administrative geographical areas: the first south of the Litani river, and the second to its north. Both function under the auspices of one central organisational leader in order to secure organisational structures that are capable of improving local administration and activate polarisation. In addition, Shaykh Karim 'Ubayd was appointed as the head of Hizbullah's social institutions. Besides that, Shaykh Hasan Izzeddine, Hizbullah's spokesman at the Central Press Office, was appointed as Hizbullah's political representative in the South, and he was replaced by Nasrallah's media aide or advisor, the engineer Hajj Muhammad Afif.[199]

The UN Resolution 1559

On September 2, 2004, the UN Security Council issued Resolution 1559[200] censuring Syrian intervention in Lebanese affairs and criticising both Syria and Lebanon for the intended constitutional amendment that will extend president Lahud's tenure for three more years, till November 2007. Among other things, 1559 called for the disbanding and disarmament of all the Lebanese and non-Lebanese militias which is a direct reference to Hizbullah since it is the only Lebanese political party that still bears up arms. It also called upon all remaining foreign troops to withdraw from Lebanon, which is an indirect reference to the presence of 14,000 Syrian troops in

Lebanon. In spite of the international pressure, on September 3, 2004, the Lebanese parliament amended the constitution, thus allowing president Lahud to remain in office for a second three-year term.

On November 30, 2004 around 250,000 Lebanese people[201], one-third of whom were Hizbullahis, demonstrated against resolution 1559. Clergymen and secular notables representing various leftist and rightist political parties (including the Phalagists, Armenians, Kurds, etc.) as well as civil society organizations participated in the demonstration. In addition to a number of ex-Ministers and ex-MPs, 4 Ministers, and 29 MPs took part in the demonstration. What is noteworthy to mention is that all the participants carried out Lebanese flags including Hizbullahis. It was the fist time that Hizbullah participates in a demonstration without portraying flags, banners, and special slogans. The only two features that pointed out at Hizbullah were the following: (1) the chanting of "death to Israel" and "death to America"; and (2) the Hizbullahi veiled women, who outnumbered Hizbullahi men by a great margin. Contrary to the precedents of spearheading such demonstrations, Hizbullah only marched at the rear of the demonstration. Some of the banners raised by the Hizbullahis were the following: "Unity, unity in Lebanon so that we can defend our country"; "We do not want democracy American style". Hizbullah's presence was symbolic[202], rather than a *taklif shar'i* (legal-religious duty) since Hizbullah wanted to convey its *infitah* and Lebanonisation aspect.

Due to anti-Semitism charges, on December 13, 2004 France banned Hizbullah's satellite TV, *al-Manar*, from broadcasting to France and other EU countries. Hizbullah abided by the ruling and al-Manar voluntarily stopped transmission. However, *al-Manar* continued to broadcast from six other satellites covering most of the globe, including three in Europe, which do not fall under France's jurisdiction. On December 17, 2004 the US followed suit and banned *al-Manar* classifying it as a "terrorist organization".

First woman appointed to a prominent political role

In the beginning of December 2004 and in light of the decisions taken in Hizbullah's seventh conclave, Hizbullah, for the first time in its history, has appointed the head of its Women's Organization, Rima Fakhry, as a member of its 18-member Political Council (Politburo). Also, Hizbullah appointed Wafa' Hutayt, the person responsible for political programs in *al-Nour* radio, as deputy of Hizbullah's Central Information Office.[203] These two moves came as a result of internal debates among Hizbullah cadres and amending some of the party's bylaws.[204]

Rafiq Hariri's assassination and its aftermath

In 2005 dramatic and dynamic events swept Lebanon. The ex-PM Rafiq Hariri was assassinated on February 14, 2005 by a massive suicidal truck bomb attack in the predominantly Muslim West Beirut.[205] Hizbullah offered an outright condemnation of the assassination. For the first time, people took to the streets in the Muslim part of the capital demanding the withdrawal of the Syrian troops and blaming Syria for the Hariri assassination, a charge that it vehemently denied. On March 8, Hizbullah organised a pro-Syrian rally in Downtown Beirut, the heart of the capital. Around half a million Hizbullahis along with their supporters and sympathizers filled the streets of the capital carrying only Lebanese flags. Like the November 30, 2004 demonstration Hizbullah did not convey any party banners or slogans; it just showed banners stating, "Thanks to Syria" and "No to Syria out". Nasrallah addressed the rally calling for national unity, constructive dialogue, and coexistence among all the Lebanese in order to confront the crisis that is rupturing the country.[206]

Although the aim behind Harir's assassination might have been to militarise Lebanon and bring it back to the brink of civil war, the assassination resulted in an unprecedented dynamic mobilisation process. The "Cedar Revolution" of March 14, 2005 organized by the opposition – where around one million Lebanese, mostly Sunnis, Christians, and Druz, took the streets in Martyr's Square of Downtown Beirut demanding the withdrawal of the Syrian forces and unveiling the truth about Rafiq Hariri's murder – accomplished most of its goals: the pro-Syrian Karami cabinet resigned; Syrian forces withdrew; a UN investigation headed by Detlev Mehlis ensued into Hariri's assassination; the heads of the Lebanese security forces resigned; parliamentary elections were held; and a new government was formed.

The Run up to the formation of a technocrat Cabinet: Hizbullah's Dialogue with the US

On April 19, 2005 Omar Karami's government resigned and Nagib Miqati's 14-member Cabinet, which in accordance with the Lebanese constitution was evenly divided between Christians and Muslims, was sworn in. The government promised to fulfil the opposition's demands, especially the holding of free and fair parliamentary elections, where none of the members of the cabinet were entitled to run. In an unprecedented move, Hizbullah not only gave a parliamentary vote of confidence to the Miqati's cabinet, which received 109 votes out of 128, but also fielded Trad Hamadé, a Hizbullah affiliated sympathizer (non-official member)[207], for the first time in its history. Hamadé was accorded the service Ministry of Labour and Agriculture, an appointment that is supposed to serve as a litmus test to Hizbullah's future ministerial work in the cabinet. Keeping in mind that the US Administration brands Hizbullah as a "terrorist organization", it neither voiced its opposition to such an appointment nor threatened boycotting him. On the contrary, in June Hamadé met, with Hizbullah's blessings, senior members of the US Administration, including Elizabeth Dibble, the Deputy Assistant Secretary of State for Near Eastern Affairs, in his capacity as a minister representing Hizbullah in the cabinet. In that meeting Hamadé advised the US Administration to consider 1559 as null and void for the time being and to place it on the shelf for at least two years.[208] This was not the only contact between Hizbullah and the US Administration over the past few years. In an attempt to discuss the problematic that was impeding Muslim-European-US dialogue, a lot of unofficial meetings took place between the two parties in Beirut, Amsterdam, Rabat, Geneva, and Oman. Graham Fuller, a former intelligence officer at the CIA, has conducted dialogue sessions with Hizbullah officials, most notably in March 2005 with Nawwaf al-Musawi.[209]

The May/June 2005 parliamentary elections: The first after the Syrian withdrawal

Hizbullah's political program

Hizbullah called for reforming the election law trying to lobby the government to replace the old law by a new one based on proportional representation, which the party believed would give the 18-ethno-confessional communities a more equitable chance for a proper representation. As soon as the Lebanese state announced that it would conduct the elections based on the 2000 election law, Na'im Qasim outlined the party's 2005 election program: (1) Safeguard the Resistance. (2) Facilitate the mission of the UN investigating team into Hariri's assassination. (3) Maintain a special relationship between Lebanon and Syria. (4) Reject foreign interference in Lebanese affairs. (5) Work hard towards attracting the largest popular support. (6) Affirm the value of national dialogue. (7) Stress the need for a comprehensive socio-economic program.[210] Hizbullah emphasized that its election alliances would not be at the expense of its political alliances. It also clarified that the most salient article in its election program is protecting the Resistance, which comes as no surprise since this has been the first article in all its previous parliamentary elections programs: 1992, 1996, and 2000.

2005 election results

Based on this election program, Hizbullah made a strong showing in the parliamentary elections through a political-strategic alliance with *AMAL* and other players. In the first round of the elections, which took place on May 29 in Beirut, Sa'd Hariri's entire 19-member list was elected, including Hizbullah's candidate. The voter turn out was estimated to be 28%. The second round of the elections took place on June 5 in the South, one of Hizbullah's strong holds and a major constituency. Hizbullah's alliance with *AMAL* won a landslide victory appropriating all the 23 seats. In spite of the calls for boycotting the elections, the turn out was an unprecedented 45%, 1% higher than five years ago. What is telling is that there were more than 100,000 votes difference between the last winner and the first loser.[211] In spite of the Christian boycott that dramatically lowered the overall turn out average, Hizbullah picked up more than 88% of 45% turn out, where all of Hizbullah's 6 candidates made a sweeping victory receiving the highest number of votes in the country. The biggest and most intense round of elections, where 58 seats were out for grabs, took place on June 12 in Mount Lebanon and the *Biqa'*, which is Hizbullah's major constituency and strong hold, "the reservoir of the Resistance", as Hizbullah's cadres term it. In *B'albak-Hirmel* voter turn out was more than 52%. All of Hizbullah's 6 candidates were elected. Also, in Mount Lebanon Hizbullah's candidate was elected. On June 19 the fourth and last round of the elections took place in the North. The Hariri coalition needed 21 seats in order to obtain the majority in the parliament; however, he and his allies captured all of the 28 seats.[212] Unlike the elections in Beirut, the South, and the *Biqa'*, Hizbullah did not have a say at all in the elections in the North, since, according to Qasim, the number of voters it could influence is very small.[213]

Although the 2005 parliamentary elections were conducted according to the 2000 election law, the direct opposite of 2000 happened, maybe because the Syrians were not physically present anymore. The opposition to Syrian influence led by the Sa'd Hariri camp won 72 seats out of the 128.[214] The new parliament was composed of 61 new MPs and 67 former ones. However, many leading pro-Syrian cadres failed to be re-elected and out of the 84 pro-Syrian MPs in the previous parliament, only 4 remained.[215] Sa'd Hariri clarified that he is not anti-Syrian and aspires for good and balanced relations between Syria and Lebanon; rather he is against Syrian tutelage.

In accordance with its rotation policy and in order to ensure better representation, accountability, and transparency, Hizbullah succeeded in fielding 10 new candidates, including a Maronite Christian and two Sunnis, as well as four previous candidates in the 2005 parliamentary elections.[216] Thus, Hizbullah's parliamentary bloc entitled, "Loyalty to the Resistance," added two more seats to its earlier 12-seat representation in 1992 and 2000. A member of Hizbullah's Bloc was elected as the head of the parliamentary committee of media and communication, and the reset of the Bloc members participated in the following parliamentary committees: finance; public administration and justice; education and culture; public health; defence and municipalities; public works and energy; agriculture and tourism; environment; economy, commerce, and industry; youth and athletics; and human rights.

The employment of al-taklif al-shar'i in the elections

The leader of the parliamentary opposition – Michel 'Aun who repeatedly stated that the safety of the Resistance is conducive to the safety of Lebanon – criticized exploiting "God" in the elections blasting Hizbullah's call for its supporters to vote in the elections from the stance of *al-taklif al-shar'i*. Hizbullah responded through the head of its Political Council, Sayyid Ibrahim Amin al-Sayyid, who argued that the party's *al-taklif al-shar'i* is in conformity with its strict obedience and discipline, which constitute the fulcrum of its organizational structure.[217]

Not surprisingly, Sayyid Muhammad Husayn Fadlallah blasted Hizbullah's employment of *taklif shar'i* in the elections, accusing the party of exploiting *taklif* as a commodity in the political bazaar in order to polish its reputation and boost its credentials. He cautioned that, on the long run, people would get used to these "perverted practices" that do not adhere to religious safeguards and injunctions, an eventuality that would ultimately lead to stripping Islamic concepts and norms of their purity, authenticity, and reach out to the populace.[218] Sayyid Fadlallah clarified that Khamina'i considers that Hizbullah's leadership shoulders the responsibility of executing his injunctions through *taklif*, and abides by God's injunctions in both the religious and political spheres. In this way, *taklif* originates from personal choices that people are responsible for in front of God. Thus, Fadlallah added, by choosing a candidate, people are giving that incumbent a blank check. To the contrary, Fadlallah considers the people free to elect their representatives on the objective criteria of merit, probity, and integrity: "I do not consider that *al-taklif al-shar'i* amounts to electing the corrupt, the criminals, the murderers, the wayward, etc." Fadlallah concluded that Hizbullah employs *al-taklif al-shar'i* from the stance of a political-pragmatic *maslaha* (interest) in order to legitimise itself.[219]

Repercussions of the elections

Contrary to the US Administration's stance on Hizbullah, Saʿd Hariri stressed that, like his father, the Lebanese state, and most Lebanese citizens, he considers Hizbullah as a national liberation resistance movement and not a militia.[220] He added that Hizbullah would not be disarmed in the near future, unless a comprehensive peace settlement is reached in the Middle East. In that case, the Lebanese would sit together and discuss Hizbullah's military role.[221] Saʿd Hariri was echoing his father's earlier position as communicated by Nasrallah who revealed that he held regular weekly meetings with Hariri in order to discuss the future of the Resistance. In these meetings, Nasrallah purported that Hariri promised that he would neither fight the Resistance nor allow Lebanon to become another Algeria, rather he would resign and leave the country.[222] Nasrallah stated: "If anybody entertained the idea of disarming Hizbullah, then we will fight him as the martyrs did in *Karbala*".[223]

On the whole, Hizbullah's interpreted its performance in the parliamentary elections as national-political referendum, which constitutes a "slap in the face" of the international pressure to disarm it led by US and France, and presented a great disappointment to Israel.[224] The results of the elections imply that Hizbullah is going to hold on to its arms, being granted legitimacy from the people. Nasrallah stressed that the current parliament is the most important and most dangerous parliament since 1992 because it is obliged to decide the basic political and strategic choices for Lebanon in the decades to come.[225]

To date, Hizballah's record in this "most important" parliament is mixed. The party helped to prevent the proposed pardon of the SLA who fled to Israel in the wake of the "Liberation" or the Israeli withdrawal in May 2000.[226] Nasrallah considered the proposal "a big insult" to the Lebanese people and "an unequivocal threat to national security".[227] But the legislators did pardon Samir Geagea – the leader of the right wing Christian Lebanese Forces (LF) who has served an 11-year jail sentence – and the Sunni Islamists who served a 5-year jail sentence. Hizbullah's bloc opposed this measure by walking out of the parliament before the vote began; however, it endorsed the pardoning of the ex-Minister of Energy, Barsumian, and lifting the ban on the anti-Syrian MTV.[228] Parliament is scheduled to enact a new and more representative electoral law, and is holding weekly hearings to check the performance of the cabinet, a first in Lebanese politics. It is also discussing the disarmament of Palestinians inside and outside refugee camps in accordance with UNSC 1559, which many consider the prelude to discussions of Hizballah's disarmament. To Hizballah's dismay, the parliament debated whether it should avail itself of FBI assistance in training Lebanese security forces to better investigate killings and assassination attempts targeting politicians and journalists.

Four days after Shaykh 'Afif al-Nabulsi, the head of the Shi'ite religious scholars of Jabal 'Amil, granted Hizbullah religious approval and legitimacy to its participation in the Lebanese cabinet[229], on June 10, 2005, Nasrallah delivered a fiery speech in which he announced Hizbullah's intention to play a leading political and developmental role by fully integrating in the Lebanese public sphere through a complete enrolment in Lebanese political and economic life as well as participation in all the Lebanese government's institutions including the cabinet.[230] The party deemed it necessary to seek a seat at the cabinet table so as to be able at least to speak strongly and directly to power against steps it opposes.[231]

The Formation of the first cabinet after the Syrian withdrawal and its aftermath

After Berri's election as Speaker for a fourth consecutive term on June 30, 2005, al-Sanyura, the ex-Minister of Finance and a veteran of the Hariri bloc, was appointed by the Lebanese president, in light of the mandatory parliamentary consultations, which resulted in the historical precedent[232] of 126 out of 128 votes nominating al-Sanyura, to form the new cabinet. The newly elected LF MP Edmond N'im – the Lebanese Maronite judicial, constitutional, and international law expert, who earlier condoned Palestinian suicide bombers[233] – argued from the stance of public international law that Hizbullah should not give up its arms before Israel withdraws from the occupied 1967 Palestinian territories, since Hizbullah or any other group or state are entitled to come to the rescue of the weaker party, as he purported.[234] By this N'im gave Hizbullah's disarmament a regional dimension. On his part, the Syrian PM, Muhammad Naji al-'Utari, stated that Hizbullah's disarmament posses a threat to Syria's national security since Lebanon would become a "playground for Israeli intelligence", as he put it.[235]

The tensed political situation, the spate of bombings and assassinations[236] that rocked civil peace, the Syrian economic transit embargo effective early July, and regional tensions negatively effected the Lebanese tourism season and curtailed a badly needed substantial income in foreign currency. In addition to the explicitly stated reason for Syria's de facto economic punishment of Lebanon, namely fear of smuggling guns and explosives to Syria on board of transit trucks, the Syrian authorities asked for compensation for its alleged killed and abused workers, a claim rejected as unfounded by Lebanese officials.

After 19 days of political bickering over key ministries, and after five meetings between Sanyura and Lahud, and four previous draft line-ups, the first "national unity" 24-seat cabinet after the Syrian withdrawal saw the light on July 19. In addition to Trad Hamadé, who retained his post as Minister of Labour, for the first time, a veteran leading cadre, Muhammad Fnaysh, who was accorded the Energy Ministry, directly represented Hizbullah. Thus, Hizbullah was granted two service ministries and its rival *AMAL* also obtained the ministries of Health and Agriculture. During the negotiations that preceded the formation of the cabinet, Hizbullah endeavoured to break the taboo that bars Islamic movements from obtaining the two sensitive ministries of Defence and Foreign Affairs. Hizbullah lobbied hard for the Foreign Ministry, but International pressure, especially from the US and France, as well as domestic Lebanese reservations barred Hizbullah from realizing its dream. In order to avoid the deadlock, Hizbullah proposed a moderate Shi'ite independent, Fawzi Sallukh, an ex-ambassador and a veteran diplomat who is also acceptable to *AMAL*, and it got what it wanted. However, it is worth mentioning that Hizbullah is represented in the parliamentary committee for foreign affairs by two MPs who were elected for that post.[237]

In response to Fnaysh's appointment, the US Department of State said it would not have any dealings with "terrorists", clarifying that it would only boycott the Hizbullah minister, but would have regular dealings with the cabinet. Fnaysh responded that the US should stop interfering in Lebanese domestic affairs and leave the Lebanese to their own devices. Condoleezza Rice's unexpected visit to Lebanon on July 22 aimed at buttressing "Lebanon's progressive path towards democracy". She affirmed the international community's stance of standing by Lebanon and communicated the US Administration's will of the full implementation of the 1559, stressing Hizbullah's disarmament. Hizbullah's MP Husayn Hajj Hasan stated that the party refuses to have any dealings with the "oppressive US Administration that is aggressing against freedom and democracy" by not recognizing the public will of the Lebanese people that accorded Hizbullah representation in the parliament and cabinet.[238]

On July 30, the parliament granted its vote of confidence to the cabinet, thus approving its policy statement, by a majority of 92 votes.[239] The policy statement upheld Hizbullah's right to bear arms and defend the "sovereignty and territorial integrity of Lebanon", while at the same time stressed its respect to all the UN Resolutions, without specifically mentioning 1559, rather 194 that deals with the Palestinian refugees' right of return. The next day, Sanyura visited Syria in an endeavour to smoothen the relations. His talks bore fruit and on the following day, August 1, Syria partially lifted its economic embargo and opened its border to Lebanese transit trucks.

On a parallel track, between July 31 and August 6, Nasrallah along with members of Hizbullah's *Shura* Council visited Tehran in order to attend the inauguration of the newly elected president Mahmud Ahmadi Nejad as well as conduct meetings with him, Imam 'Ali Khamina'i, and other Iranian officials. The Iranian leadership assured Hizbullah that disarming it is a "mirage". Attempting to capitalise on Hizbullah's gains and boost his regional stance, the Syrian president embarked on a two-day visit to Tehran immediately after Hizbullah's return. Nejad said that Syria constitutes the Islamic *umma*'s first line of defence.

On August 17, Israel relinquished the Gaza strip after 38 years of occupation. Nasrallah termed this eventuality as a historical victory for the Palestinian resistance and the *Intifada* as well as the second triumph for Hizbullah's model of resistance in five years: "The choice of resistance liberates Gaza". He added that this constitutes further proof for the utility of holding on to the weapons of the Hizbullah's Islamic Resistance. Qasim termed the Israeli withdrawal as defeat expropriated by the Palestinians through military force.[240]

On October 21 the Lebanese government received an official copy of the Detlev Mehlis Report, which Mehlis presented 36 hours earlier to Koffi Annan, the UN Secretary General. The Report was almost immediately leaked to the press. Although the Report was "legally inconclusive", but "politically powerful"[241], it implicated high-ranking Syrian and Lebanese officials in the assassination. Unlike other political parties and politicians who commented in an impromptu way on the Report, Hizbullah declined to comment until it thoroughly studied it. On October 24, *AMAL* and Hizbullah released a three-point joint declaration: (1) criticising the report for failing to disseminate the long awaited truth. (2) The statement suggested that cracking the truth requires a more thorough and serious judicial investigation based upon tangible-conclusive evidences as opposed to attempts aiming at politicising the report. In spite of that, the statement endorsed the Lebanese government's decision to extend the mandate of Mehlis' team till December 15, 2005. (3) In order to confront the US-Israeli led campaign against Syria, both *AMAL* and Hizbullah anticipated any UN Security Council resolution that might censure Syria, by refusing any imposition of sanctions on the Syrian regime.[242] It is worth mentioning that this stance mirrors, more or less, the Syrian position that blasted the report as being politicised, inconclusive, and dogmatic – aiming at serving the US-Israeli interests in the Middle East.

2 The Saliency of Hizbullah's Religious Ideology (1978-1984/5)

Introduction

This chapter presents the constituents of the Shi'ite religious ideology that form the background of Hizbullah's religious ideology. The constituents of Hizbullah's religious ideology are the following: (1) belief in Shi'a[1] Islam; (2) *wilayat al-faqih* (guardianship of the jurisprudent or jurisconsult); (3) and *jihad* (struggle) *fi sabili Allah* (in the way of God).[2] "Section I" describes the classical Shi'ite doctrines or the fundamentals of the Shi'ite faith and its basic historical development in order to determine which lines and outlook Hizbullah follows; "Section II" discusses Imam Khumayni's elaboration of the Shi'ite religious ideology; "Section III" outlines Ayatullah Fadlallah's possible contribution to Hizbullah's ideology and thinking; and "Section IV" highlights Hizbullah's acceptance, choice, and application of this heritage indicating on what does Hizbullah put emphasis on. This will be followed by a summary of the basic constituents of Hizbullah's religious ideology.

I The Basic Shi'ite Foundational Religious Ideology

1. Belief in Shi'a Islam

Traditionally, Twelver Shi'ite communities – in addition to their belief in the (1) *Imama* (doctrine of the Imamate) as a fundamental requirement of faith – believed also in the necessity of practicing (2) *taqiyya* (expedient dissimulation) as a quietist practice for protecting the self, and (3) *ta'bi'a* (mobilization), at a later stage, as an activist practice for defending the self. These three principles offer an insight into the basic Shi'ite religious ideology.

1.1 *Imama*

The *arkan* (five pillars) of Islam are the following: *al-shahadatayn*[3] (Muslim confession/declaration of faith), *salat* (the five daily ritual prayers), *sawm* (fasting), *hajj* (pilgrimage to Mecca), and *zakat* (alms giving). To these, Twelver Shi'ism adds *khums*[4] (one-fifth religious tax), *jihad*, and *al-amr bi al-ma'rub wa al-nahi 'an al-munkar* (enjoining the good and prohibiting the evil). Parallel to the *arkan*, Twelver Shi'ism believes in *usul al-din* (the foundations of faith), which consist of: *tawhid* (divine unity), *nubuwwa* (Prophethood), *Imama*, *'adl* (justice), and *al-ma'ad* (resurrection).[5] *Imama*, the most distinctive mark of Shi'ite Islam, stipulates that the essential, primary, and sufficient attributes of the Imam boil down to three principles, which form the essence of the Shi'ite theocratic dogma: (1) apostolic succession; (2) *al-'isma* (immunity from sin and error); and (3) perenniality or perpetuity of the Imamate.

1.1.1 *Apostolic Succession*

The Shi'ites believe that God instructed the Prophet to select 'Ali as his successor and designate him and his two sons, Hasan and Husayn, as Imams down to the Twelfth Imam; as such, the Prophet would have named the eleven Imams that would succeed 'Ali in the Imamate.[6] Thus, from that time onwards, the Imams always designated their successors. However 'Ali, the first Imam, accepted Mu'awiya's *tahkim* (arbitration) in order to salvage Islam from internal or civil strife. After 'Ali was killed in January 661, Mu'awiya became Caliph.[7]

According to Shi'ite doctrine, the succession of the Imamate is determined only by *nass* (divinely inspired designation). *Nass* refers to the specific designation of an Imam by the preceding Imam. According to Shi'ite traditions, the *nass* is stipulated in the Qur'an (4:58): "God has ordered you to make over the trust to those who are entitled to them".[8] Thus, apostolic succession means that the Imams succeed each other exclusively in the Household of the Prophet. This first principle is labelled as *Imamat al-nass* (divine designation or textual *Imamat*) or "the conferment of the Imamate by designation or covenant". *Imamat al-nass* was first practiced when God conferred the title upon the Prophet. In a similar vein, the Imamate after the Prophet should be established solely by designation in order to determine his successors.[9] According to Imam Ja'far al-Sadiq, the sixth Imam, every Imam has foreknowledge of the Imam who is going to succeed him. That is why he designates him by *nass*.[10] Thus, *nass* is blended with *'ilm* (religious knowledge), a subsidiary characteristic or attribute of the Imam. *'Ilm* stipulates that the Imam is the most learned in all branches of religious knowledge (al-'ilm al-muhit or al-ihatah fi al-'ilm), and he transmits his special religious knowledge to his successor.[11]

Since God, the Prophet, and the members of the House are the only ones knowledgeable about the Truth of Islam,[12] the Imam, in his capacity as being designated by God through his Prophet as being the most learned in all branches of religious knowledge, is the only one entitled and capable of providing ta'wil (hermeneutics or an esoteric interpretation of the Qur'an), which is of fundamental importance and is the principal source of shari'a (divine law, Islamic law). Like the Mu'tazala and most mystics, the Twelver Shi'ites consider the Qur'an as created in time, the created Word of God, thus open to allegorical interpretation.[13] And so, for the Shi'ites, religion, and especially the Qur'an, has besides the exoteric meaning an esoteric meaning that can only be known through spiritual contact with Imam al-Mahdi.[14] On these grounds, the Shi'ites believe that the twelve Imams are endowed with both esoteric and exoteric knowledge of the Qur'an and hadith (Prophetic Traditions). The divergence with the Sunnis is that the latter consider solely the Qur'an and Traditions as the primary sources of shari'a, while the Shi'is consider that religion cannot be perfected except through the pursuit of both the exoteric (Qur'an and Traditions) and the esoteric (the Imam). The departure from the Sunnis in this respect is in the belief that Islam is not revealed to man once and for all in the Qur'anic text; rather, it is a continuous process awaiting the successive rise of the Imams. Thus, the Imam being the legatee and guardian of the shari'a, the source of trust in the interpretation and the understanding of both the esoteric and exoteric meanings of the Qur'an and hadith, is definitely the most erudite in religious matters. The Imam is the hujja (apodictic proof) of God to mankind, thus engendering a mandatory obedience on each and every Shi'ite.

Indeed, the Shi'ites consider the Imamate a divine appointment by designation (al-istikhlaf bi al-nass wa al-ta'yyin) or appointment of the successor or vicar by a divine designation, unlike the Sunnis who consider the Caliphate a product of consensus, thus a political process (al-istikhlaf bi al-shura wa al-bayy'a) or appointment of the successor or vicar by consultation and mutual homage. The Shi'a abide by the following hadiths: "The Imams will not confer upon an error"; "Islam is still a fortress of the Twelve Imams", while the Sunnis adhere to the following hadith: "The umma will not confer upon an error".[15]

1.1.2 *Al-'isma (immunity from sin and error)*

The second principle is *al-'isma* or infallibility and impeccability of the prophets and the Imams, which only God has foreknowledge of. The source of this infallibility from errors and immunity from sins is the Divine Light, which in turn will lead to *hikma* (divine wisdom).[16] The Shi'ite Imams, the guardians of the *shari'a*, who are deemed perfect and do not suffer from any defect, are infallible and pure from any defilement; they do not commit sins whether major or minor. According to Shi'ite traditions this is substantiated by the Qur'an (33:33): "People of the House, God only desires to put away from you abomination and to cleanse you" ['make you really pure' according to other renderings].[17] This has been interpreted to signify the sinlessness of the Prophet, Fatima and the twelve Imams, which has also been demonstrated by tradition, the most eminent being: "I [Prophet Muhammad], 'Ali, Hasan, Husayn and nine of the descendants of Husayn are pure and sinless".[18] Moreover, 'isma entails impeccability, sinlessness, and infallibility of the Imams. As Imam Ja'far al-Sadiq maintains: "The one who is sinless (*ma'sum*) is the one who is prevented by God from doing anything that God has forbidden. For God has said: 'He who cleaves to God is guided to the Straight Path' [*al-Sirat al-Mustaqim*]".[19]

1.1.3 *Perenniality or perpetuity of the Imamate*

The third principle is perenniality or perpetuity of the Imamate, namely, the necessity for the permanent existence of an Imam. Thus, the earth is not left without a living Imam who is the *hadi* (guide) and *hujja* of God. The theory of the Imamate stipulated the necessity of the perpetual existence of a living Imam to guide mankind. The occultation of the Imam made him aloof from politics without encroaching on the principle of his perenniality. Ja'far al-Sadiq placed the Imam above the ruler, who must abide by what the Imam's religious edicts since he is the supreme religious authority.[20]

A corollary of this category is the necessity of recognizing the living Imam. Shaykh Saduq or Ibn Babawayh[21] (306/918-381/991) asserted that remuneration is for belief in the Imam and recognizing him. Imam Ja'far al-Sadiq stressed that God prepares the ground for the death of a prophet only after He has ordered him to appoint a successor from his lineage... The Shi'ites should always recognize their Imam and obey him as a religious duty. And so, the existence of the Imam is a necessary grace. Indeed, it is the religious obligation of every Shi'ite to recognize and obey the Imam of his time. He who perishes without recognizing the Imam of his age – even though he has recognized past Imams – is doomed to eternal damnation, condemnation, and *jahiliyya* (pre-Islamic pagan) death. Thus, a Shi'ite cannot ascend to heaven without acknowledging the living Imam.[22]

Recognizing the Imam has been a complicated process for the Shi'ite community after the disappearance of the Twelveth Imam, al-Mahdi, at the age of seven, thus starting the Lesser Occultation in 874 AD. With this eventuality, the line of the twelve Imams came to an end. For the next 67 years Imam al-Mahdi maintained communication with the Shi'ite community through four directly appointed intermediaries or private deputies. In 941 AD, a few days before the death of the fourth deputy, Imam al-Mahdi is believed to have declared the end of the Lesser Occultation, thus he severed communication with the Shi'ite community and declared the beginning of the Greater Occultation.[23] In the Greater Occultation no deputies were appointed as intermediaries between Imam al-Mahdi and the Shi'ite community, rather the mode of representation of Imam al-Mahdi changed to a *na'ib 'am* (general deputy) by high-ranking *mujtahids* (Shi'ite jurists) whose integrity is unquestionable and who possess insight into temporal and religious matters. And so, the Shi'ite community has been waiting for the Mahdi's return, who will found justice and peace on earth by establishing an Ideal Islamic order (*nizam Islami*).[24]

Around the end of the eighteenth century[25], the leading *mujtahid* became synonymous with the *faqih* (jurisprudent) or *marja' al-taqlid*, who is considered the supreme Islamic legal authority to be emulated, or accepted for emulation, by the majority of the Shi'a in matters of religious practice and law since he is regarded as the most knowledgeable.[26]

1.1.3.1 The Development of *marja'iyya* (religious authority)

Shi'ite history has been replete with or characterised by a plurality, polarity, and multiplicity of *marja*'s (religious authorities) who monopolised religious knowledge. *Marja'iyya* came about as a result of a struggle between the *Akhbari* and *Usuli* schools of jurisprudence, a struggle that slumbered for centuries and was only finally adjudicated a few centuries ago in favour of the *Usuli*s, who stressed, among other things, the right of the *'ulama* to ijtihad (independent reasoning) and the *taqlid* (emulation) of living *mujtahids*, practices which were totally opposed by the *Akhbari*s. *Marja'iyya* in Shi'ism got its prominence as a real power in society since the *Safavid* period. In fact, religious knowledge has been for centuries the sole prerogative of the institution of *marja'iyya* that appropriated, constructed, and disseminated that religious knowledge to the faithful Shi'ite populace, and through this process it accumulated and transformed this religious knowledge into religious legitimacy. Since the *marja's'* authority is measured by the following they muster, the relationship between them and the populace has been one of interdependence whereby the populace, through their payment of *al-huquq al-shar'iyya* (legal rights) of *zakat* and *khums* financially sustain the institution of *marja'iyya*, and in return the populace is granted a religious authority to emulate. Since the hierarchy of the *marja's* is measured by the size of their following and wealth, and is not solely determined by their reli-gious-academic qualifications – adhering to a certain *marja'iyya* not only wielded religious legitimacy, but also conferred a certain religious ideology to the populace. In principle, the Shi'ites follow the *marja'* whom they feel *itmi'nan*[27] (peace of mind) with.[28]

1.1.3.2 Stages of *ijtihad* leading to *marja'iyya*

The person who intends to become a *marja'*, also called *muqallad* (emulated or followed), should fulfil certain scholarly requirements to attain the degree of *marja'iyya*. Basically, he has to cover the following three levels: *al-muqaddimat* (the prolegomena), *sutuh* (corpus of knowledge), and *bahth al-kharij* (extracurricular research). In *al-muqaddimat* the student spends an average of three to five years learning grammar, rhetoric, and logic.[29] In the *sutuh* the student studies jurisprudence and positive law (man-made law).[30] The student spends three to six years in this stage, where he could freely choose his mentor/s who would recommend certain textbooks to be studied, in preparation to exercise independent reasoning. The *bahth al-kharij* is the third and final stage of religious study in which the graduate student heavily participates, in a seminar setting, in the ongoing debates taking place in the religious seminary. It is worth mentioning that this stage is referred to as the extracurricular research since there is no specific textbook; rather the men-tor would lecture from his own notes, which are based on his knowledge. After fulfilling these criteria, the student acquires the title of *mujtahid*. It is note worthy to mention that only after the *mujtahid* publishes his judicial decisions or *fatwas* (religious edits), he becomes a *marja'*.[31]

The essential function of the *marja'* is to guide the community of those who "imitate" his teachings and follow his precepts, in particular concerning the following two issues: (1) the application of the rules of the *shari'a* as *furu' al-din* (subsidiary principles of religion) and (2) *ahkam* (judicial solutions or legal qualifications) in regard to the problems of contemporary life. Theo-retically, the imitation or following of the *marja'* has no connection with *usul al-din*, which are derived from *iman* (faith) and from *yaqin* (inner conviction). The *mujtahid* established as *marja'* must pronounce judicial decisions and write one or more books as a *risala 'amaliyya* (practical treatise) in order to guide his followers. Only after publishing his *risala 'amaliyya* he becomes recognised as a Grand *marja'* or Grand Ayatullah.[32]

1.1.3.3 Choosing the *marja'*

This is one of the hotly debated issues in Shi'ite history that has not been resolved yet, simply because there is no clear cut established method for choosing the *marja'*. The process of choosing a *marja'*, i.e. deciding on who is the most knowledgeable among the *mujtahids*, is influenced by many factors such as political, social, and even geographical considerations. Another problematic has to do with ethnicity; for instance, being an Arab or a Farsi (Persian). Being a graduate of the Iraqi *Najaf* religious seminary or the Iranian *Qum* religious seminary is also at stake since the two religious seminaries have been in fierce competition over the leadership of the Shi'ite community. Usually the person who intends to become a *marja'*, who is a *mujtahid*, is "marketed" by a narrow clique that constitutes his entourage, who usually are either his disciples or his relatives. He is often promoted to attract more followers who emulate his religious authority, and thus pay the *khums* to him. Although the religious seminary has not provided a crystal clear method of choosing a *marja'*, nonetheless two very important elements has been accounted for in this regard. First, is the number of followers and their proximity. Second, is the number of *mujtahids* attending his lectures. A third less salient factor to be taken into consideration is his practical treatise and publications. Upon the fulfilment of the aforementioned premises the *marja'* enjoys *shaya'* (wide reputation), which enables him to join the club of grand *marja'*s who could have a say in establishing him as such.[33]

1.2   *Taqiyya* (expedient dissimulation) as a quietist practice

Taqiyya is rendered into English as precautionary, expedient, or religious dissimulation or concealment of one's true convictions or belief. It was practiced when the Shi'ites were facing great perils, which they could not shun or had no prospect of triumphant struggle and victory against.[34] This precept of practice was employed when Shi'ism was still an underground movement in embryonic form struggling to face the Sunnite majority who had the upper hand in political matters. As such, *taqiyya* became part and parcel of Shi'ite tenets[35], to the extent that it was regarded as their primary trait par excellence.[36]

1.2.1 *The legitimisation and justification of taqiyya*

1.2.1.1 Qur'an

The legitimisation of *taqiyya* is based on the Qur'an and *hadith*. The Qur'anic injunction of "enjoining the good, and forbidding the evil" (22:41) is regarded as one form of *taqiyya*.[37] *Taqiyya* is warranted in the Qur'an in verses such as (3:28), (16:106), and (40:28).

Verse (3:28): "Let not the believers take disbelievers for their friends in preference to believers. Whoso doeth that hath no connection with Allah unless (it be) that ye but guard yourselves against them [*tattaqu minhum*, from the same root as *taqiyya*] taking (as it were) security [*tuqatan*, again from the same root as *taqiyya*]. Allah biddeth you beware (only) of Himself. Unto Allah is the journeying". Thus, God adamantly prohibits any kind of intimate relationship with unbelievers or infidels. Therefore, the believer should use his discretion to scout out danger and avoid a relationship that might unnecessarily endanger his life.[38]

Verse (16:106): "Whoever disbelieves in God after believing – *except for those who are compelled while their hearts are firm in faith* – and then finds ease in his disbelief, upon him will be the wrath of God' (The section of this verse in italics is held to refer to *taqiyya*)".[39] This verse illustrates Prophet Muhammad's divine forgiveness, redemption, and purification from sin of 'Ammar ibn Yasir, an 'Alid companion of the Prophet, who was coerced under the threat of swords into denouncing his faith in Islam and accepting to worship the gods of *Quraysh*. 'Ammar did that nominally, outwardly; however, he remained a pious Muslim wholeheartedly which explains why Prophet Muhammad redeemed him.

Verse (40:28): "Then a believing man of Pharaoh's folk, who kept hidden his belief, said: Will you kill a man for saying: 'My Lord is Allah', and he has brought you the clear proofs from your Lord? If he is a liar, his lying will recoil upon him, but if he is truthful, you will be smitten with some of what he is promising you. Allah will not guide one who is an extravagant impostor". This verse exemplifies the story of a pious man, who, while concealing his faith, questioned the benefit of killing a man for the sake of his religion.[40]

1.2.1.2 *Hadith*

There is a whole body of *hadiths* attributed to Imam 'Ali and other Imams such as Imam Hasan, Imam al-Baqir, and especially Imam Ja'far al-Sadiq sanctioning *taqiyya* and emphasizing its vital role as an integral part of religion and true piety.[41] Imam 'Ali stated: "It is the mark of belief to prefer justice if it injures you, and injustice if it is of use to you"; "He among you who is most honoured before God is the most fearful (of God)", i.e. he who employs *taqiyya* the most; and "*Taqiyya* is our *jihad*".[42] Imam Ja'far al-Sadiq asserted that *taqiyya* was practiced by Joseph and Abraham.[43] Ja'far al-Sadiq stressed *taqiyya* as the distinguishing trait of Shi'ite faith: "He who has no *taqiyya*, has no religion".[44] Al-Sadiq affirmed that the person who disclos-es the concealment and *taqiyya* of the Shi'ite faith is the one who rejects them.[45]

In addition to the legitimisation and justification of the *taqiyya* prac-tice by the Qur'an and *hadith*, throughout the course of history almost every volume on Shi'ite jurisprudence contains a justification of *taqiyya* or out-lines its principles. Ibn Babawayh stressed that whoever leaves the practice of *taqiyya* before the appearance of the Mahdi will be considered as aposta-tising and disobeying God, His Prophet, and His Imam. And so, *taqiyya* is a religious obligation imposed on every Twelver Shi'ite.[46]

In practicing *taqiyya*, the Shi'ites are guided by the precepts of prac-tice and way of life as exemplified by their Imams, in particular, Ja'far al-Sadiq. The Shi'ites considered the occultation of the Twelfth Imam as the exemplary *taqiyya*.[47] Following their Imams' model of political quietism, the Shi'ites practiced *taqiyya* in order to prevent their persecution and oppres-sion, trying to adjust their roles to the various political regimes of the time. In practicing *taqiyya* the Shi'ites, especially the *'ulama*, did not take active part in politics, rather they favoured the practice and observance of reli-gion. In summary the persecution of the Shi'a as a religious minority led them to resort to *taqiyya*, as an esoteric quietist practice, in life-threatening situations. *Taqiyya* does not only include the concealment of one's convic-tions, but also the concealment of one's right to politics. Indeed, the *taqi-yya* imprisoned the Shi'ites in political quietism, and provided the doctrinal bases for the depolitisation of the sect.[48]

1.3 *Ta'bi'a* (mobilization) as an activist practice and Imam Husayn's martyrdom

Ta'bi'a is a militant practice in Shi'ism, as in other Muslim sects, although its implementation varies among different sects in accordance with their ideological background. In the specific Shi'ite case, *ta'bi'a* is defined as an act of mobilization whereby the Shi'as – emulating Imam Husayn's revo-lution – rebel, mobilize, and endeavour to seize power and take control of government in order to establish the rule of God or Islamic *shari'a*, in other words, an Islamic order.[49] The *ta'bi'a* approach has a major historical precedent. Imam Husayn – *Sayyid al-Shuhada* (the leading martyr) according to Shi'ite doctrine – mobilized his followers and revolted against the Umayyads, who according to him, deviated from Islam, in order to restore the right of the Holy House of the Prophet to government. Imam Husyn marshalled his followers and faced the Umayyads at the eminent battle of *Karbala'* in the tenth of *Muharram*[50] 61 AH (October 9, 680 AD) where he and around 70 of his family, close relatives, companions, and faithful followers were killed and overrun by the Umayyads who outnumbered them and were by far better equipped. It is believed by devout Shi'ites that Imam Husayn was "martyred" in defence of reform in the *umma*, wholeheartedly knowing that his stance will lead to his martyrdom: "I [Husayn] fought for the reform in my grandfather's [Prophet Muhammad's] *umma*, and in order to uproot the tyrannical, oppressor ruler… God willed to see me killed and slaughtered aggressively and oppressively"[51], as attributed to him.

Because this eventuality occurred on the tenth of *Muharram*, it was dubbed *'Ashura*. Since then, the Shi'ites, all over the world, classified *Karbala'* as one of the greatest incidents in history and commemorated *'Ashura*, mourning the martyrdom of imam Husayn by walking barefooted while beating their chests, slashing their scalps with swords, and whipping themselves with chains.[52] Over the period 750 to 950 AD, the Shi'ites split into Zaydis, Twelvers, and Isma'ili factions. In general, the Zaydis favoured political action, the Twelvers were political quietists, and the Isma'ilis adhered to *batin* (esoteric) and *'irfan* (gnostic) ideas.[53]

Although some authors[54] seem to refer to the martyrdom of Imam Husayn as being "unnecessary and useless" i.e. futile, it is most likely that the classical denotative meaning of *jihad*[55] has been radically transformed through his martyrdom. An important significance of Imam Husayn's martyrdom is its mobilizational effect on the Shi'ites through a bitter feeling of injustice, enjoining them to alter that injustice by practicing *ta'bi'a* and activism against unjust governments.[56]

1.4 Conclusion on *taqiyya* and *ta'bi'a*: Shi'ism as a religious ideology: quietism and activisim

Historically, Twelver Shi'ism has been characterised by quietism and activisim[57], which find their respective application in *taqiyya* and what is defined as *ta'bi'a* in Arabic and *bassidj* in Persian:

> As a religious ideology Shi'ism functions within a specific sociopolitical order which constantly calls upon its adherents whether to defend and preserve or

to overthrow and transform... Shi'ite religious ideology is both a critical assessment of human society and a program of action, whether leaning toward a quietist authoritarianism or an activist radicalism, as the situation may require, to realize God's will on earth to the fullest extent possible.[58]

It is worth mentioning that in both practices, namely *taqiyya* and *ta'bi'a*, the Shi'ites are guided by the precepts of practice or ways of life of their Imams. For instance, Imam Ja'far al-Sadiq practiced *taqiyya*, while Imam Husayn practiced *ta'bi'a*. And so, the Shi'ites have been split into two factions: those calling for *taqiyya* and adapting themselves to the various regimes; those calling for *ta'bi'a* with the aim of assuming power under the guardianship and authority of the *'ulama*. During the historical period in which *taqiyya* was practiced, *'Ashura* celebrations were carried underground due to fear of persecution by the successive ruling Sunni regimes. Thus, with the practice of *ta'bi'a*, quietism was replaced by activism. However, this mobilization and activism remained underground – form roughly 680 AD until the period of the Great Occultation in 941 AD – due to the successive Sunni regimes repression on the Shi'ite population. Establishing an Islamic order had not been realized because the Shi'ites, up till the mid-twentieth century, interpreted the martyrdom of Imam Husayn in mystical, lyrical, and emotional terms, which were devoid of any political-activist application:

> [F]ollowing numerous unsuccessful attempts by the Shi'ite leaders at different times in their history to overthrow the ruling power (even when the power was Shi'ite), Shi'ites adopted the quietist attitude rather than the activist one. There is *sufficient historical precedent* to argue that the quietist attitude was at times adopted as a strategy for survival rather than as principle in itself. In the face of unfavorable circumstances it became imperative to protect Shi'ite life from destruction. Moreover, such quietist passivity was justified as a religiously sanctioned strategy *(taqiyya)* to allow for time to regroup and reorganize for future activism. These realities render difficult the task of charting precisely the ebb and flow of Shi'ite activism, for given the proper sociopolitical conditions, the activist mentality may be seen as merely dormant or latent within Shi'ite quietism... recent Shi'ite activism has, as in the past, emerged after a period of relative quietism in large part because of the central role played by Shi'ite religious leaders and their radical teachings in response to specific sociopolitical conditions.[59]

Although it seems that the theory of *ta'bi'a* and activism dates back and can be traced to Imam Husayn's martyrdom, however, the successful implementation of that theory by Twelver Shi'ites in modern times dates back to the third quarter of the twentieth century. *Ta'bi'a* started with Imam Husayn, then it withered away for many centuries (at least exoteric mobilization), and then it was revived again by Imam Khumayni starting the early 1960s. By emulating Imam Husayn, *ta'bi'a* materialised in the victory of the Islamic Revolution in 1979.[60] It should be noted here, however, that following the death of Imam Husayn, the Shi'ite leadership went through a state of quietest resistance that was manifested mainly in the literary and poetic enterprises by Shi'ite scholars. This continued till the sixteenth century when the founder of Safavid Persia, Shah Isma'il, launched his war to unite the country under his rule by employing the slogan of retaining the lost rights of the Prophet's Household (through *ta'bi'a*). Thus, for the first time after a lapse of centuries, Shi'ite militant activism was revived and a Shi'ite state was established in Iran.[61] In brief, this change that took place by the advent of the Safavids continued to show its impact on the Shi'ites till today. The Constitutional Revolution in Iran in 1905, and before that the Tobacco Crisis a decade earlier, and finally the Islamic Revolution in 1979, were all variant manifestations of what Shah Isma'il has started and changed in the nature of Shi'i *ta'bi'a*.[62]

2.   *Wilayat al-Faqih* (Governance of the Jurisprudent or Jurisconsult)

2.1   Definition of *wilaya* (governance, spiritual guidance)

Wilaya can have two connotations: (1) temporal government or the authority to govern with the right to demand obedience; and (2) spiritual guidance and sanctity.

According to Imam Ja'far al-Sadiq,

> The Imam is seen as the spiritual friend or supporter [*wali*] who guides and initiates mankind into the mystical or inner [esoteric] truth of religion. It is through him that God's grace reaches the Earth... the Imam [guides] mankind onto the path of spiritual enlightenment and progress [he is] master and friend in the journey of spirit.[63]

Thus, *wilaya* is "the primary expression of the Islamic belief system. [It] is not the conventional fundamental pillars of Islamic faith, but rather the comprehensive relationship of the Muslim community to the legitimately constituted authority in Islamic public order. This is the meaning of the cardinal doctrine of wilayah, and it is the sole criterion for judging true faith in Shiism".[64]

2.1.2 *Historical survey of the wilayat al-faqih doctrine*

Wilayat al-faqih refers to the rule of the religious jurist. Throughout the course of history many Shi'ite *'ulama* have contributed to the *wilayat al-faqih* doctrine with varying degrees, from a rudimentary perspective to an evolutionary one.[65] The precursor who paved the way and laid the foundation of this doctrine is al-Karaki[66] (1465-1533) who pioneered the suggestion that the *'ulama* were the *na'ib al-'am* of Imam al-Mahdi. Al-Karaki's disciple, Shahid al-Thani (1506-1558) is considered as the founding father of the doctrine. His contribution to the *wilayat al-faqih* doctrine consists in that he "took the concept of *Na'ib al-'Amm* to its logical conclusion in the *religious* sphere and applied it to all the religious functions and prerogatives of the Hidden Imam. Thus, the judicial authority of the *'ulama* now became a direct reflection of the authority of the Imam himself...".[67]

Bihbahani (1706-1792) had the conviction in the *mujtahid's* ability to establish *hujja*. Prior to that the title of *hujjat al-Islam* was only confined to Imam al-Mahdi. Moreover, in addition to his endorsement of the *Usuli* school on the right of the *'ulama* in *ijtihad*, Bihbahani settled the way for recognizing the legitimacy of the transfer of the Hidden Imam's religious authority, but *not* his political authority. A *mujtahid* was no more considered a general deputy of the Hidden Imam; rather, *mujtahid* and *faqih* became one and the same. Thus, Bihbahani considered the *mujtahids* as vicegerents of the Prophet in *religious matters only*. Therefore, his contribution lies in fusing the religious and social dimensions, but not the political.[68]

Mulla Ahmad Naraqi (1771-1829), Bihbahani's disciple, supported the legitimacy of the legal speculation on the part of the *faqih* in the absence of the Hidden Imam. His emphasis on Prophet Muhammad's succession as being the prerogative of religious authority is of special importance since it brought the political dimension into the *wilayat al-faqih* doctrine. As such, al-Naraqi was the first to recognise the *faqih's* right in *political authority*. Moreover, when he compared a *faqih* and a king, he placed the former above – not even juxtaposed to – the latter, thus, making him the supreme political figure of the community. And so, al-Naraqi was the first to stipulate that the

political, religious, and social authority of the Hidden Imam can be trans-
ferred to and vested in the *faqih*. To recapitulate, his major contribution lies
in adding the political dimension to the religious and social ones.[69]

Shaykh Muhammad Husayn Na'ini (1860-1936) became the lead-
ing *marja'* in Iran in 1920. Na'ini[70] stressed that in the Greater Occultation
period, the best way to prevent an authority from becoming wayward is
to abide by an Islamic constitution that guarantees the rights and duties
of the citizens as well as those of the state. He recommended establishing a council comprised of leading *mujtahids*, intellectuals, and wise men
who act in the interest of the people by supervising the implementation
of the constitution and the affairs of the state. Na'ini stressed *wilayat al-
umma 'ala nafsiha* (the governance of the *umma* by itself) as a legitimate
right in the period of the Greater Occultation because this issue falls under
the *hisbi* domain (things that God does not allow that we forsake)[71], rather
than general *takalif* (delegated responsibilities, plural of *taklif*[72]) i.e. the
governance of the *umma* by itself is a *political* and not a *shar'i* (religious-
legal) issue. Since it is a practical impossibility for a Shi'ite to have the delegated responsibility to establish God's Governance, then he has delegated
responsibility to institute the political-*hisbi* domain in conformity with the
interest of the *umma*. This implies that his enrolment in politics is for the
sole purpose of transforming a tyrannical power to a democratic authority
that represents the *umma*.[73]

3. ***Jihad* in the way of God from a Shi'ite perspective**[74]
The etymology of the word *"jihad"* is derived from the verb *"jahada"*,
which means to exert a person's energy or to do ones best to overcome
trouble, difficulty, or hardship. *Jihad* is total devotion in performing one's
religious duty, be it in action or in intention.[75]

3.1   The general Shi'ite understanding of *jihad* and its justification
in the Qur'an and *hadith*
The following Qur'anic verse demonstrates the high stature of *jihad*
and the *mujahidin* (those who carry out *jihad*) in Islam (9:88-89): "But the
Apostle and those who believe with him struggle [*jahadu*] with their wealth
and their lives. To those are the good things reserved, and those are the
prosperous. Allah has prepared for them gardens beneath which rivers flow,
abiding therein forever. That is the great triumph!" The saliency of *jihad* is
also noticed in a *hadith* attributed to the Prophet: "Heaven has a door called

the 'door of the *mujahidin'*. When it opens, they go toward it, wearing their swords while the Angels are greeting them".[76]

Imam 'Ali enjoined *jihad*: "*Jihad* is one of the doors of Heaven, God opened it for his special saints. *Jihad* is the garment of the pious; it is God's shield and his assured Heaven". Another saying attributed to Iman 'Ali that conveys the paramount role of *jihad* is the following: "Belief has four pillars: patience, strong conviction, justice, and *jihad*". Imam Ja'far al-Sadiq exhorted believers to conduct *jihad*: "*Jihad* is the best thing after religious duties".[77]

A different *hadith* stresses that engaging in *jihad* leads to dignity, while not engaging in it leads to humiliation, loss, degeneration, and disintegration of the individual as well as the *umma*: "God clothes a person who leaves *jihad* with humiliation, poverty, and the destruction of his/her religion. God has dignified my [the Prophet's] *umma* with the hoofs of the horses[78] and the centres of the spears". The person who puts *jihad* aside will live humiliated on the personal level because he is crushed and totally impotent in front of his enemies, surrendering to their demands. He lives in paucity because his enemies manipulate his life and the resources of his country. He gradually loses his religion because he was not committed to *jihad*, which strengthens religion and fortifies the believers.[79]

Another *hadith* states that if the believer is incapable of performing *jihad*, or if the objective circumstances preclude him from engaging in it, then, at least, he should live interacting with *jihad* and have the desire or intension to conduct it (as persuasive *jihad*), even if he communicated this desire to perform *jihad* within himself[80]: "If a person died and he did not participate in *jihad*, and did not even talk within himself about it, then he died the death of a hypocrite". This constitutes a different evaluation to life, preferring life with *jihad* in order to stand up for the right and dignity of the *umma*, as opposed to death in humiliation and capitulation, as Imam 'Ali had said: "Death is living your life crushed with humiliation, and eternal life is granted to you if you die while performing *jihad*".[81]

3.1.1 *Exoteric and esoteric jihad: smaller and greater jihad*

The Qur'an portrays both exoteric and esoteric *jihad*. The former is warranted in (9:36): "... fight [*qatalu*] the polytheists all together just as they fight you all together; and know that Allah is on the side of the righteous". The latter is merited in (29:79): "And those who strive [*jahadu*] in Our cause We shall guide in our ways, and Allah is with the beneficent". The Prophet is reported to have said when he returned from some battles (*ghazawat*, singular of *ghazwa*): "We returned from the smaller *jihad* (*al-jihad al-asghar*) and we still have [to conduct] the greater *jihad* (*al-jihad al-akbar*)". When the Prophet was asked, what is the greater *jihad*? He replied: "the struggle with the self (*jihad al-nafs*)".[82] God has sanctioned the smaller *jihad* in order to consolidate His religion, uphold His word, disseminate His mercy to whomever he wishes from his faithful servants, and to "... cause the Truth to triumph and nullify falsehood, even though the wicked sinners dislike it "(Qur'an 8:8). God has enjoined the greater *jihad* in order to save and lift up the souls of righteous people to heaven, and rid them from living according to the flesh and its material desires in women and wealth: "Attractive to mankind is made the love of the pleasures of women, children, heaps upon heaps of gold and silver, thoroughbred horses, cattle and cultivable land. Such is the pleasure of this worldly life, but unto Allah is the fairest return". "Say; 'Shall I tell you about something better than that?' For those who are God-fearing, from their Lord are gardens beneath which rivers flow, and in which they abide forever [along with] purified spouses and Allah's good pleasure. Allah sees His servants well!" (Qur'an 3:14-15).[83]

3.1.2 *Smaller jihad: initiative (ibtida'i) offensive jihad and defensive (difa'i) jihad*

The classical distinction of smaller *jihad*, as offensive and defensive *jihad*, is well known in Shi'a literature and interpretations. It is adequately discussed in the Shi'ite "manual" of *jihad* and martyrdom.[84] The jurisprudents divide military *jihad* (smaller *jihad*) into the following two categories: (1) initiative offensive *jihad*, and (2) defensive *jihad*. Prophet Muhammad conducted offensive *jihad* in order to get rid of the infidels and build the foundations of the requisite social milieu for propagating Islam and disseminating its teachings. The following Qur'anic verses testify (justify) to that (9: 12-13): "But if they break their oaths after their pledge [is made] and abuse your religion, then fight the leaders of unbelief; for they have no regard for oaths, and that perchance they may desist"; "Will you not fight a people who broke their oaths and intended to drive the Apostle out, seeing that they attacked first? Do you fear them? Surely, you ought to fear Allah more, if you are real believers". "And fight them, so that sedition might end and the only religion will be that of Allah. Then if they desist, Allah is fully aware of what they do". (8:39).[85]

3.1.2.1 Defensive *jihad*: military *jihad* and persuasive non-military *jihad*

Defensive *jihad* branches into military *jihad* and persuasive non-military *jihad*. Military *jihad* is carried by the Muslims in defence of Islam and the Islamic *umma*. According to the Shi'ite "manual" of *jihad* and martyrdom, defensive military *jihad* is a religious duty in the following nine contexts or circumstances[86]:

1. If the enemies of Islam attack the Muslim countries in order to terminate Islam, or contrived to do so, then: "And fight for the cause of Allah those who fight you, but do not be aggressive. Surely Allah does not like the aggressors" (2:190).

2. If the enemies of Islam attacked any of the Muslim countries in order to control it and colonise it, then: "Permission is given to those who fight because they are wronged. Surely Allah is capable of giving them victory". "Those who were driven out their homes unjustly, merely for their saying: 'Our Lord is Allah'... ". (22: 39-40).

3. If a Muslim country is attacked by another Muslim country, then other Muslim countries should take the initiative to reconcile the two warring countries. If the aggressor refuses to yield to justice, then other Muslim countries should come to the aid of the aggressed upon Muslim country: "If two parties of the believers should fight one another, bring them peacefully together; but if one of them seeks to oppress the other, then fight the oppressor until it reverts to Allah's command. If it reverts, then bring them together in justice and be equitable; for Allah loves the equitable" (49:9).

4. If there is an onslaught on the public wealth of Muslims and the national riches of the Muslim countries.

5. If there is an offensive against the selves, possessions, and dignities of the Muslims.

6. If there is an onslaught on worshiping God, and the mosques and places of prayer are attacked by the enemies in order to obliterate Islam: "... Had Allah not repelled some people by others, surely monasteries, churches, synagogues and mosques, wherein the name of Allah is mentioned frequently, would have been demolished. Indeed, Allah will support whoever supports Him. Allah is surely Strong and Mighty" (22:40).

7. Conduct *jihad* in order to defend Islamic culture and ethical norms, and preclude anti-Islamic cultural and moral campaigns from targeting the Islamic *umma*.

8. Conduct *jihad* in order to defend the oppressed *(mustad'afin)* who did not have the capacity to defend themselves against the aggression and injustice of the oppressors *(mustakbirin)*: "And why don't you fight for the cause of God *[fi sabili Allah]* and for the down-trodden *[mustad'afin]*, men, women and children, who say: 'Lord, bring us out

of this city whose inhabitants are unjust and grant us, from You, a protector, and grant us, from You, a supporter" (4:75).

9. Conduct *jihad* in order to prevent the propagation of materialism and atheism: "So let those who sell the present life for the life to come fight in the way of Allah. Whoever fights in the way of Allah and is killed or conquers, We shall accord him a great reward" (4:74).

In these nine contexts or similar contexts and circumstances, the Shi'ites have the inalienable natural right in defending their honour, pride, dignity, and wealth. For Islam has made this responsibility incumbent upon their shoulders; if they portray any negligence in conducting this delicate responsibility of *jihad*, then the enemies of Islam will exercise despotism on the Muslims by controlling the political, social, economic, cultural, scientific, and military aspects. In addition, those Muslims who shun *jihad* will be punished and severely tortured at the day of judgement because they have deserted and abandoned their faith:

(9:24): "Say: 'If your (1) fathers, your (2) sons, your (3) brothers, your (4) spouses, your (5) relatives, the (6) wealth you have gained, a (7) trade you fear might slacken, and (8) dwellings you love are dearer to you than Allah and His Apostle or than fighting [*jihad*] in his way, then wait until Allah fulfils His decree. Allah does not guide the sinful people' ".[87]

(9:39): "If you do not march forth, He will inflict a very painful punishment on you and replace you by another people, and you will not harm Him in the least; for Allah has power over everything".[88]

3.1.2.2 Persuasive non-military *jihad*

Persuasive non-military *jihad* is *jihad* by the tongue and heart, while military *jihad* is *jihad* by the hand. The following *hadiths*, attributed to Imam Ali, support this interpretation: "Practice *jihad* in the way of God with your hands, if you could not, then practice *jihad* by your tongue, if you could not either, then practice *jihad* by your hearts"; "God enjoined you to practice *jihad* with your possessions, selves, and tongues in His way"; "The first type of *jihad* you practice is *jihad* by the hand, then *jihad* by the tongue, then by the heart. He who neither enjoined a good by his heart nor dissuaded an evil, he would be turned upside down"; "If a person engages in *jihad* in way of God, with his hand, tongue, and heart, then God would shower him with victory and dignity". In addition, Imam Ali specifies four categories of persuasive *jihad*: "Enjoin the good, forbid the evil, honesty in appropriate situations, hatred of the sinful. If a person enjoins the good, God will support him; if he forbid the evil, then he humiliates the hypocrites; if he is honest in appropriate situations, then he performed his due; if he despised the sinful and was angered for the way of God, then God's anger would be on his side". The "manual" of *jihad* stresses that Imam Ali's *hadith*s resonate the Prophet's *hadith*s: "The believer practices *jihad* with his sword and tongue"; "If a person among you sees evil, then let him change it with his hand; if he could not, then by his tongue; and if he could not, then by his heart, and this is the weakest of faith".[89]

3.2 The connection/link between *jihad* and martyrdom

According to Shi'ite sources, *jihad* is related to martyrdom. *Jihad* has two glorious fruits (*husnayayn*). The word *husnayayn* in (9:52) is taken to refer to martyrdom and victory[90]: "Say: 'Do you expect for us anything other than one of the two fairest outcomes (martyrdom and victory); while we await for you that Allah will smite you with a punishment, either from Him, or at our hands?' So wait and watch, we are waiting and watching you".[91]

3.3 Summary of the general Shi'ite understanding of *jihad*

The major distinction is between the smaller *jihad* (exoteric, external *jihad*) and greater *jihad* (esoteric, inner *jihad*). In addition, the following types of smaller *jihad* have been discussed: (1) Initiative *jihad* or offensive *jihad*, which cannot be practiced anymore after the death of the Prophet and the Eleven Imams and the occultation of Imam al-Mahdi. Therefore, only Imam al-Mahdi can exercise offensive *jihad* upon his return. (2) Defensive *jihad*, which in turn branches into military *jihad* (fighting the enemy in the battlefield including martyrdom) and non-military *jihad* (persuasive *jihad*, such as by the tongue and heart, for instance). The distinction between greater *jihad* and smaller non-military *jihad* is meticulous. Greater *jihad* is transcendental-metaphysical, spiritual, and inner *jihad*; while non-military smaller *jihad* has to do with this world, with the here and now. Although non-military smaller *jihad* is mainly concerned with material things, however, it could also have a spiritual dimension, but not to the extent of the transcendental-spiritual dimensions of greater *jihad*.

II   Imam Khumayni's elaboration on the Shi'ite religious ideology

2.   Imam Khumayni's stance on *taqiyya* and *ta'bi'a*: quietism and activisim

Imam Khumayni blatantly rejected the *taqiyya* practice, which he considered to be one of the major sources of the quietism of the Shi'ites. According to Khumayni, *taqiyya* sanctions a person – in order to safeguard his life, money, honour or those of others – to utter an injunction contrary to factual evidence (reality) or to commit an action against the *shari'a*. He added that *taqiyya* is a non-binding practical necessity, which is an exception to the norm, rather than being a basic *shar'i* principle. His alternative was opting for mobilization and political activism; thus, he rejected the quietism of some *'ulama* who argued that sins should proliferate for the Mahdi to appear in order to redress injustice. By contending that if sins did not proliferate then the Twelveth Imam would not appear, they retreated from their guidance role. And so, Khumayni considered that the practice of *taqiyya* is legitimate only if it is intended to safeguard the self and others from the dangers resulting from the application of religious laws and rituals; however, he stressed that under the Islamic state the necessity and *maslaha* (interest) of resorting to *taqiyya* ceases to be. Khumayni affirmed that if Islam is in danger, then there is no room for *taqiyya* or quietism; he also enjoins the *'ulama* not to practice *taqiyya* and not to work for an unrighteous government. Moreover, according to Imam Khumayni another factor that contributed to the quietism of the Shi'ites was their belief that every government in the absence of the Hidden Imam is perverted and unjust even if it were headed by a Shi'ite.[92] As a result, the Shi'ite *'ulama* used to recommend to their followers not to indulge with government and to refuse governmental positions due to the fact that these governments were deemed unjust and *kuffar* (infidel), apostate governments anathematising the political order. According to Khumayni, this attitude seems to explain why the Shi'ites until recent decades were not fairly represented in governmental positions; their negative attitude towards established government made them quietists and hampered their active participation in public and political life.[93]

Imam Khumayni depicted *Muharram* as the month of the victory of blood over the sword, which he regarded as a characterization of the Islamic Revolution as such.[94] Khumayni argued that everything that the Islamic

Revolution has achieved is the result of 'Ashura; he enjoined the Shi'ites to generate an 'Ashura in their struggle for establishing an Islamic order. He added, if Imam Husayn did not inspire[95] the Islamic Revolution, then it would not have been victorious. Khumayni asserted that Imam Husayn's mourning ceremonies (majalis al-'aza') should not be given up because they give life to the Shi'ites and vitalise them.[96] According to Khumayni, 'Ashura means the radical change and establishing the community and the state by Islam. That is why any Islamic revolution regards Imam Husayn as its ideal, in the present and the future, by trying to emulate his revolution that rejected partial solutions and was adamant on Islam being the governing (or guiding principle) of all men's activities in this life.[97] Khumayni added, if it were not for the leading martyr (sayyid al-shuhada), Imam Husayn, then Yazid, his father (Mu'awiya), and his successors would have made the people forget Islam (by their hereditary succession)... Husayn's revolution protected Islam and led the way to the people to mobilize, revolt, and confront anything that would endanger the Message (Islam) through deflection and forgery... 'Ashura is the real perpetual revolution till God inherits the earth and everything on it.[98]

2.1 Imam Khumayni's contribution to *wilayat al-faqih*

Imam Khumayni highlighted the crucial role of *al-waliyy faqih* or *faqih*[99] as a leader of the state and people through his theory of *wilayat al-faqih*. According to Imam Khumayni, *wilayat al-faqih* denotes the guardianship of the jurisprudent or jurisconsult who is the most just and learned in all branches of religious knowledge.[100] Khumayni's contribution to *wilayat al-faqih* doctrine is his bringing the theory of *na'ib al-'am* to its logical end in the *political* sphere by stipulating and sanctioning the right of the *faqih*, not only to religious and social issues, as his predecessors have argued, but also to *political leadership*.[101] In line with the doctrine of the Imamate – which stipulates the Imam as the most learned in all theological sciences as well as the legitimate authority in all religious, social, and primarily political spheres – the *wilayat al-faqih* sanctions the same legitimate authorities to the *faqih*.

In other words, Khumayni's contribution to *wilayat al-faqih* lies in his joining of *Imama* (Imamate) and *Wilaya* in one person for the first time after the Greater Occultation of the Twelfth Imam, which made possible, in the absence of the Hidden Imam, the establishment of an Islamic order. As such, *wilayat al-faqih* is bestowed upon and practiced by one person who is the universal authority in all religious, social, and *political* matters during the period of the Greater Occultation on behalf of the Hidden Imam. From this perspective stems its perennial importance to the Shi'ites in the whole Muslim world since they believed that the legal and just government could not be re-established until Imamate and *Wilaya* were united in one person. Moreover, since for them there was no explicit recognition of the separation of temporal and religious authority, the Imams were considered the supreme political and religious leaders of the community. And so, the *faqih*, in line with the Imam, is deemed the *hujja* of God to mankind, thus engendering a mandatory obedience (*wajib*) on each and every Shi'ite.[102] Imam Khumayni became the first supreme *faqih* who established the principal and tradition that future supreme *faqihs* should be selected by their predecessors, in line with the Imams who were designated by their predecessors.[103]

Indeed, the bestowing of political authority, in addition to religious and social ones, upon a just *faqih* provided the legitimate and religious framework for the establishment of an Islamic order which was previously considered as a practical impossibility due to the monopoly of political authority by the Imams, and later on due to the Greater Occultation. Imam Khumayni stressed the necessity of establishing an Islamic order: "It is taken for granted or self-evident that the necessity of abiding by the imperatives/injunctions that stipulated the establishment of Prophet Muhammad's government are not confined or limited to his time; rather they are a continuous process after his death". Basing himself on a host of Qur'anic verses[104], Imam Khumayni added that the imperatives/injunctions of Islam are not transient being confined to a specific place and time; rather they are perpetual (religious) duties that should be implemented till eternity.[105] On these grounds, Khumayni stipulated and strongly advocated that Muslims, in general, and Shi'ites, in particular, have an obligation (*wajib*) to establish Islamic order that would enlighten the Muslim populace through the following process: making it conscious of its rights; by halting injustice and oppression: every non-Islamic system is polytheism (*shirk*) and its ruler is regarded as a tyrannical and illegitimate (*taghut*); by stopping the corruption in the land[106]: eliminating polytheism and illegitimate rule; by guiding people to the right path; and by protecting the Muslims from the tutelage of the enemies and their interference in the affairs of the Muslims.[107]

And so, the *faqih*, who like the Imam is infallible[108], is the only one who has the final say in all executive, legislative, and judicial matters. As God's representative on earth, the *faqih* supervises the government and has the absolute power to declare its acts null and void. Khumayni affirmed, opposition to *wilayat al-faqih* "is denying the imams and Islam... *I must point out, the government which is a branch of the absolute governance of the Prophet of God is among the primary ordinances of Islam, and has precedence over all secondary ordinances such as prayer, fasting, and pilgrimage".*[109] Therefore, Khumayni stipulated that the *maslaha* of the Islamic order or its agencies gains priority over any other principle in the social and political affairs. As such, Khumayni developed the theory of *al-wilaya al-mutlaqa* (absolute *wilaya*) in a way that could perfectly serve his political ends through giving the *waliyy al-faqih* absolute political and religious power.

In conclusion, although the doctrine of *wilayat al-faqih* cannot be only ascribed to Imam Khumayni since it is deeply rooted in classical Shi'ite thought; however, Khumayni was the first to implement the doctrine by combining the social, religious, and *political* dimensions, thus moving Shi'ism from *Imama* (Imamate) to *wilaya* (governance and spiritual guidance). The *faqih*, in the absence of the Hidden Imam is *the political and a religious leader* of the *umma*.[110] Khumayni forcefully asserted that the *faqih* should depose or oust the ruler and rule in his place, thus establishing an Islamic order. And so, Imam Khumayni was the first *faqih* after the Great Occultation and in contemporary history to assume the title of the deputy of Imam al-Mahdi and to establish an Islamic order through political revolution.

Khumayni practically proved, by the application of his *wilayat al-faqih* theory, that an Islamic order could be established during the period of the Great Occultation, before the return of Imam al-Mahdi. In other words, Khumayni's *wilayat al-faqih* made possible the establishment of a just government in the absence of the Hidden Imam. Such possibility turned out to be the springboard of mobilization and political activism since it conferred upon the Shi'ites the religious duty to establish such a government. Khumayni's theory of government delegates a minimal role to the people (populace) because he passionately believed in the role of the *'ulama* as leaders in both public affairs of the state and as spiritual advisors to the faithful. And so, the *'ulama* were not quietist anymore; on the contrary, they resorted to political activism being regarded as successors of the Hidden Imam, thus, engendering complete allegiance from the masses. Thus, *wilayat al-faqih* embeds and is flavoured by a revolutionary character because it calls for the active involvement (mobilization) of the *'ulama* in politics and government.

Khumayni's innovation was to unequivocally and cogently metamorphose *Wilayat al-Faqih* into a system of political administration. Khumayni in his capacity as *al-waliyy al-faqih* and *marja' al-taqlid* (authority of emulation), blended *Imama* with *wilaya* with *marja'iyya*, which is a precedent in Shi'ite religious ideology. This is of vital importance since in Shi'ite jurisprudence "the ruler's ordinance abrogates the *mujtahid's* fatwa" (*hukum al-hakim yanqud fatwa al-mujtahid*), if the *maslaha* of the Islamic order requires such a course of action. Thus, Khumayni believed in and practiced absolute *wilaya*.

2.2   *Tadhiyat al-Nafs* (self-sacrifice) in connection to *jihad* and martyrdom

2.2.1   *Smaller military jihad and martyrdom*

Imam Khumayni asserted that it is a must to obey *al-waliyy al-faqih* in general matters among it the defence of Islam and the Muslims against the infidels, the tyrants, and the aggressors.[111] Khumayni employed sacrifice in the context of smaller *jihad* and martyrdom. He argued that there is nothing to be achieved without sacrifice and martyrdom; martyrdom is eternal bliss and dignity. In line with the classical Shi'ite understanding on the relationship between *jihad* and martyrdom (9:52), Khumayni stressed that pious Muslims who long for martyrdom are inevitably victorious; they have won eternal life, therefore, they are living martyrs. In according the martyrs a special status, Khumayni emphasized that they have sacrificed what God has granted them, so they have received God's blessings and eternal felicity; however he acknowledged that the rest of people, including himself, are different from them.[112] Khumayni added that this conviction in martyrdom is a source of tranquillity and the secret of the triumph of the Islamic Revolution.[113]

Khumayni declared that it is a legitimate and religious duty to sacrifice the self and possessions in defending the land and harbours of the Muslims that are besieged by a foe who threatens the Muslim community and territory or pale of Islam.[114] According to him the raison d'être or legitimisation for the sacrifice of the self and possessions is found in a host of Qur'anic verses.[115] Khumayni was the first *faqih* to sanction martyrdom operations, for both men and women, arguing that they constitute the highest level of self-sacrifice for the sake of religion:[116] "[A]s Shi'ites we welcome any opportunity for sacrificing our blood. Our nation looks forward to an opportunity for self-sacrifice and martyrdom"[117]; as such, "Red death is much better than black life".[118] During the Iran-Iraq war (1980-1988) Imam Khumayni legitimised and enjoined martyrdom by ordering members of the *Bassidji*[119] (1.5 million 12-year-old martyrs), who were wearing the "key to heaven", to walk through Iraqi landmines. He idealized kids who blew themselves in front of enemy tanks as leading martyrs.

2.2.2 *Greater jihad (esoteric jihad)*

According to Khumayni, greater *jihad* is the dynamic process that aims at altering reality by freeing the human being from the chains and bonds of material desires that weaken his soul and threatens his self with disintegration. He exhorts man to transcend worldly pleasures and the love of the world, with all its vices and corruption, and become engaged with spirituality (*ruhaniyyat*), having no aim save the love of God and His service in order to be able to practice greater *jihad*. Khumayni explains that man reaches this Truth when he moves to the hereafter where all the veils are ruptured (3:182) and (18:49). Then man realises the significance of his deeds in the world of the here and now and how they are weighed and reflected in the hereafter (99:7-8). All man's deeds would be exposed (41:21). Khumayni adds that people who believe in these things should restrain their selves in the transitory-transient world they live in and uphold their deeds, safeguard their tongues, watch out where they trod, and invest in reforming, purifying, and rectifying their selves.[120]

Khumayni describes how this process of change takes place, which ultimately leads to self-refinement and self-purification as well as reformation of character. He stresses that God dispatched his prophets in order to deliver people from vices, corruption, and moral turpitude, and to inculcate them with virtue, good manners, and noble ethical virtues (*makarim al-akhlaq*).[121] He explains that the veils of darkness cover man when God is not the fundamental and basic goal as well as when man seeks engagement in vices and corruption (7:176). According to Khumayni, the Truth is hidden from man by a canopy of successive veils, which correspond to man's mortal sins and carnal desires. He explains that man cannot perform smaller *jihad* when his carnal desires have blinded his intellect and blurred his vision of the Truth. He should first transcend the here and now in order to tear down the veils of darkness and live according to the spirit and the love of God. This could only be done when man purifies his intentions, rectifies his deeds, and expels the love of glory, fame, and the self from his heart, directing all his attention to worshiping and prostrating to God, thanking him for His mercy and benevolence. Only then, man reaches a high stature that allows him to penetrate the veils of light and reach the source of Greatness and Truth by being completely detached from everything except God. Thus, the Muslim believer must engage in perpetual, non-abating *jihad* by striving to remove these veils so that God's light may enlighten his heart and mind and purify his soul or self; man has to remove these veils to become closer to God. Khumayni terms the struggle to remove the veils as greater *jihad*. He cautions that the believer cannot engage in smaller *jihad* unless all of these veils have been removed, thus purifying his self.[122]

According to Imam Khumayni, the practitioners of greater *jihad* should be well mannered and well versed in the tenets of Islam so that they could be the party of God (Hizbullah). He added that they ought to hold back themselves from the outer crust and the pleasures of life and be generous in sacrificing their selves in order to please God, uphold His word, advance Islamic ideas, and be of service to the *umma*.[123] Khumayni stressed that after the believers build up, reform, purify, and refine their selves, then they could be of service to the *umma*: "Those who believe and do what is right, the Compassionate will favour with love [His love and that of their fellow creatures]" (19:95). On these grounds, Imam Khumayni enjoined the believers to practice *jihad* in the way of God, to exert and sacrifice their selves, and surely they would be handsomely rewarded and remunerated (*ajr*) by God, if not in this life, then in the life to come, which is much better for them since the heavenly remuneration is boundless and infinite. According to Khumayni, exercising greater *jihad* eventually leads these wise individuals (prospective martyrs) to conduct smaller military *jihad* by spilling their immaculate blood in the battlefield of martyrdom on the front lines.[124]

In conclusion, building on the general Shi'ite understanding that differentiates between smaller military *jihad* (fighting the enemies of Islam in the battlefield), and greater *jihad* (the struggle with the self), Imam Khumayni broadened the mandate of greater *jihad* by arguing that any Muslim who does not engage in greater *jihad* is not a true believer and upholder of the faith. Instead of struggle with the self (*jihad al-nafs*), Khumayni preferred to use self-exertion (*mujahadat al-nafs*)[125] in the sense of a perpetual struggle that aims at annihilating the egocentric self. Khumayni reversed the classical order of practicing smaller *jihad* before greater *jihad*; for him smaller *jihad* is only a very minute dimension in the process of destroying the bonds and obliterating the bulwarks and veils of darkness and light that stand in the way of man's coalescence (*takamul*) with the greater good that bonds the Muslim community and allows him to reach the Truth. He stressed that the Muslim believer should first practice greater *jihad* before engaging in smaller *jihad*, greater *jihad* being the spearhead of change and the human being the fulcrum of this change. Khumayni emphasized that greater *jihad* is Islamic reform, reforming the person, the self, before reforming society. He radically redefined greater *jihad* giving it a mystical (*sufi*) and gnostic ('*irfani*) dimension.

This warrants some explanation. In brief, according to Khumayni gnosticism is delving into the essence of things in order to discover them i.e. convey things and portray them to the realm of vision and foresight. The esoteric and the exoteric can respectively be expressed through the transcendental-supernatural and the reality, which are complementary dimensions according to Khumayni. He based his distinction between exoteric and esoteric on the Qur'anic verse (30:7) "They Know the outward aspect of the present life [exoteric], but they are heedless of the Hereafter [esoteric]". This verse implies that the esoteric in this life leads to the hereafter, or, in other words, reaching the esoteric amounts to reaching the hereafter i.e. engaging in greater *jihad* amounts to a meta-level of spiritualism and transcendentalism that elevates man from the here and now to asymptotically reaching the hereafter. Thus, confining oneself to the exoteric dimension of living on the outer crust of the world leads to neglecting the hereafter, which also amounts to disregarding the Truth and reality in this world.[126]

III   Fadlallah's possible contribution to Hizbullah's ideology and thinking

Although Ayatullah Muhammad Husayn Fadlallah rejects and is adamantly against Khumayni's *wilayat al-faqih*[127] and is continuously contesting Iranian religious authority, and even though Fadlallah is not Hizbullah's spiritual leader, this does not mean that his writings and thought did not influence Hizbullah's ideology[128] and thinking, especially Fadlallah's two most prominent books *Al-Islam wa Mantiq Al-Quwwa* (1976) and *Al-Haraka Al-Islamiyya* (1984), which *al-hala al-Islamiyya* (the "Islamic Milieu") in Lebanon based its aspirations and goals upon.

In *Al-Islam wa Mantiq Al-Quwwa* Fadlallah addresses the logic of power in intellectual, political, social, economical, and military struggles. According to him, the revolutionary ideology of the logic of power is very important, especially when pressures mount on the *umma*, thus endangering or even jeopardizing Muslim religious beliefs, doctrinal causes, and the destiny of the *umma*. Hizbullah might have built on Fadlallah's logic of power in order to alter the notions of disinherited, downtrodden, and oppressed into empowerment.[129]

In *Al-Haraka Al-Islamiyya* Fadlallah lays down the descriptions and prescriptions for Hizbullah's *umma* advocating the governance of the *umma* by itself as opposed to absolute *wilaya*, which, according to him, is idealistic and not deeply rooted in the Islamic state and society at large.[130] However the book as a whole constitutes a thorough research in the *shar'i* and jurisprudential foundations of Islamic politics and polity. Based on this theory and detailed vision, Fadlallah draws the milestones for any Islamic movement that bases itself on the Qur'an and the Sunna, taking into consideration the future of the Islamic movement in the wake of the chaos of conceptions rupturing the Islamic world at the time. After ten years of its publication, the book became a frame of reference to the Islamic movement since it, most likely, based its ideological conceptions on it. As such, Hizbullah identified with this collective Islamic identity as a guiding framework and precept of practice.[131]

Thus, it appears that Hizbullah's organizational-*jihadi* order concurs with Fadlallah's encyclopaedic religious and cultural authority, both from the perspective of temporary political order and in relation to the broader Islamic project[132]: "Hizbullah's deeds amplified Fadlallah's words, carrying his voice far beyond his own pulpit to a wider world. Fadlallah's words interpreted and justified Hizbullah's deeds, transforming resentment into resistance".[133] However, the differences between Hizbullah and Fadlallah visibly come to the fore if one delves into the particularities and specificities of each party. For instance, during the 1980s, Fadlallah has openly called for the rationalisation and routinisation of Hizbullah's charisma arguing against Hizbullah's enthusiastic-unbalanced discourse.[134] And so, the Hizbullah-Fadlallah relationship can be characterised from the following perspective: "Render unto Hizbullah what is to Hizbullah, and render unto Fadlallah what is to Fadlallah".[135]

IV Hizbullah's application of the Basic Shi'ite Foundational Religious Ideology

4.1 Belief in Shi'a Islam

4.1.1 Doctrine of the Imamate

As Twelve Shi'ites, Hizbullah's followers recognise the twelve Imams and pay homage to their established religious authority. However, since in Shi'ism emulating a dead *marja'* is considered an anomaly rather than the norm, Hizbullah stresses the absolute necessity of recognising the living Imam[136] who is infallible and has absolute knowledge about the Qur'an, Traditions, and *shari'a*. Hizbullah specifically places heavy emphasis on this point since God, the Prophet, and the members of the House are the only ones knowledgeable about the Truth of Islam. Hizbullah acknowledges that in Shi'ite history there has always been disagreement on the issue of *marja'iyya*. As such, Hizbullah has repeatedly stated, "It is not the first time that disagreements surface over the religious authority. This is a normal issue in Shi'ite history".[137] Hizbullah regarded highly Imam Khumayni, the official *marja' al-taqlid* of the Islamic Republic and paid homage to his religious authority as the first *faqih* after the Great Occultation and in contemporary history to assume the title of the deputy of Imam al-Mahdi.[138]

4.1.2 Taqiyya

Sayyid Hasan Nasrallah, Hizbullah's Secretary General, argues that the *taqiyya* was a necessity imposed due to the political crackdown that was practiced against the Shi'ites during particular historical epochs. As such, persecuted Shi'ites resorted to *taqiyya* to prevent confrontation with unjust rulers. Nasrallah stated that this is precisely why Hizbullah's leaders and cadres exercised political *taqiyya* as a survival strategy and operated underground till 1984. According to him, the second reason of following *taqiyya* is to avoid *fitna* (dissention) and schism among the ranks of Muslims. From this perspective, Nasrallah declared that *fitna* should be warded off at all costs since its consequences would be catastrophic on the *umma*. As a practice of political *taqiyya*, Hizbullah has always called for unity, both in the Islamic and domestic fronts, in order to avoid *fitna*.[139]

4.1.3   Ta'bi'a or mobilization

Hizbullah makes use of the *Karbala'* incident in order to marshal support and following through *ta'bi'a* or mobilization. Indeed in line with Imam Khumayni, Hizbullah followed the exoteric activist line of mobilization against century's backdrop of political quietism that was practiced by the majority of the Shi'ites. In line with the classical Shi'ite definition and Imam Khumayni's view of *ta'bi'a*, Hizbullah regards *ta'bi'a* as an act of mobilization whereby the community of the faithful, led by the *'ulama*, try to seize power and take control of government in order to establish the rule of God or Islamic *shari'a*, in other words, an Islamic order. This had been Hizbullah's motto and objective since the beginning, as conveyed by its first political declarations that were released in 1984-1985 and were signed as: "Hizbullah – The Islamic Revolution in Lebanon".[140]

Hizbullah outlines the framework of its method of Islamic mobilization by claiming that it is the most authentic and efficient way among the Islamists since it safeguards Muslim cultural authenticity from the materialism, consumerism, moral decadence, and cultural invasion of the East and West. As an Islamic *jihadi* movement, Hizbullah calls for mobilizing all resources in fighting the enemy as a doctrinal and practical necessity, while at the same time exercising balance in this confrontation.[141] Hizbullah stresses that mobilization forms the backbone of its recruitment strategy, which serves as a baptism ritual training. Mobilization and strict discipline are Hizbullah's salient features that set it apart from other movements, groups, and political parties.[142]

4.2   Wilayat al-faqih

4.2.1   Hizbullah's adoption of wilayat al-faqih

Hizbullah adopted Khumayni's *wilayat al-faqih* as a major pillar of its religious ideology. Since its early beginnings, Hizbullah abided by the legitimate leadership of Imam Khumayni as the successor to the Prophet and the twelve Imams. Khumayni, who, being the most knowledgeable, had the epistemic competence and the leadership qualities, was the one who draws the general guidelines for work within the *umma*; that is why his orders and prohibitions should be enforced. Hizbullah considered Imam Khumayni as *waliyy amr al-Muslimin* (jurisconsult of the Muslims) or *al-waliyy al-faqih*, thus commanding to him absolute allegiance and loyalty in accordance with *al-mas'uliyya al-shar'iyya* (the legitimate and religious responsibility) to the *faqih*, who is the official Iranian *marja' al-taqlid*. The *faqih* specifies the *taklif* and he is the only one who determines legitimacy.[143]

4.2.2 *Hizbullah's application of wilayat al-faqih*

Hizbullah's connection to *wilayat al-faqih* falls within the domain of *taklif* and commitment, which are binding upon all the *mukalafin* (followers). The *mukalafin* might refer back to another *marja'*[144]; however, when it comes to *taqlid*, the final ordinance, in the general Islamic procession is for the *faqih*.[145] Qasim is making the distinction between "referring" to (consulting with) the *marja'* and emulating him. Qasim means that in terms of the private domain of *ibadat* (ritual practices) and *mu'amalat* (daily dealings) Hizbullahis can refer to or consult with another *marja'*; however, when it comes to the public domain of political matters, the only court of appeal and the only *marja'* to emulate is Khumayni who determines the political legal obligation.[146] Qasim adds that the limitations imposed by the *faqih* take into consideration the following two main points in the chain: (1) implementing the *shar'i* edits, and not engaging in acts contrary to them; (2) respecting the specificities or particularities, which affect the circle of delegated responsibility of every community or country. Qasim affirms that Hizbullah's commitment to the *faqih* constitutes a circle in this chain: it is work in the domain of the Islamic circle and the implementation of its edits; it is behaviour in conformity with the directives and the rules dictated by the *faqih*.[147]

I learned from my interviews that in the early 1980s Imam Khumayni ordered and entrusted Khamina'i, who was at the time Deputy Minister of Defence, to be fully responsible of the Lebanese Hizbullah. Since then, Khamina'i became Hizbullah's godfather. That is why, since the beginning, Hizbullah from a religious and an ideological stance fully abides by the ideas and opinions of Imam Khumayni as communicated by Khamina'i.[148] During that period, the religious-ideological nexus between the Islamic Republic of Iran and Lebanon could be examined from the following declarations by Hizbullah and Iranian officials: "Iran and Lebanon are one people in one country... We do not say that we are part of Iran, we are Iran in Lebanon and Lebanon in Iran"; "We are going to support Lebanon politically and militarily as we buttress one of our own Iranian districts"; "We declare to the whole world that the Islamic Republic of Iran is our mother, religion, *ka'ba*, and our veins".[149]

4.2.3 Views on the Islamic order (nizam Islami) in relation to wilayat al-faqih

Sayyid Sadiq al-Musawi is a Hizbullah religious scholar ('alim) of Ira-nian origin, who has complied in a 1300 pages, a two-volume work on the declarations and opinions that are supportive of immediately erecting an Islamic republic in Lebanon without any postponement. In line with *wilayat al-faqih* that enjoins the establishment of an Islamic order under the guardi-anship of the jurisconsult, Imam al-Mahdi's deputy, Sadiq al-Musawi argued that the Qur'an is the eternal divine constitution of the Muslims; they ought to abide by it and act according to its injunctions because it is the revealed word of God. He added that the Muslims should obey God and his Prophet, execute their *wajib shar'i*, and destroy every unjust ruler in order to estab-lish *al-hukuma al-Islamiyya* (Islamic government) that will instate justice and equality and ward off the waywardness of evil and discords among the Muslims. According to him, *hakimiyya* (governance) and sovereignty only belongs to God: (12:40). God's divine law prescribes the precepts of human behaviour and the ordinances of government on a global scale. He stressed that Islam executes the injunctions through a just government in the person of the Prophet, the Imams, and the *'ulama*, the heirs of the prophets: (4:58). In line with Imam Khumayni, Sadiq al-Musawi affirmed that God commanded the Muslims to anathematise and to regard as infidel every authority or gov-ernment that does not rule by what God has revealed. God has prohibited governance by tyrants deeming that as hypocrisy and vice, in this world and the world to come: (4:60-61) and (4:51). Also under the influence of Imam Khumayni, Sadiq al-Musawi argued that abiding by *al-qawanin al-wad'iyya* (positive or man-made laws and legislations) instead of Islamic *shari'a*, is totally un-Islamic.[150]

Sayyid Husayn Al-Musawi[151] stressed that Hizbullah's religious ide-ology dictated upon the party to establish an Islamic order based upon Khumayni's *wilayat al-faqih*. He rationalised Hizbullah's choice of the reli-gious-ideological slogan of *al-Jumhuriyya al-Islamiyya* (the Islamic repub-lic) as it is used in Iran and the feasibility of its application in Lebanon. Al-Musawi argued that, in general terms, Islamic government is based upon divine principles mentioned in the Qur'an, Traditions, and the jurispruden-tial deductions or stipulations derived from them, which deal with man's social, economic, and political concerns. He contended that the contem-porary concept of the "Islamic Republic" is an extension to the efforts of prophets and imams, and is a live personification of the long experience of the divine massages. Al-Musawi argued that the system of governance that was in existence during the Prophet's time did not bear a specific name. However, with the complexities of modern life, the Muslims used different words such as Caliphate, Emirate, or state to denote the Islamic order. He took this to imply that the door is open for the Muslims to choose the label they deem fit in expressing Islamic order and governance depending on the context. According to al-Musawi, this explains why the Muslims do not feel any discomfort in choosing the name of the system that makes it incumbent upon itself to implement Islamic *shari'a*, even if it is different than the names used by the early Muslims. Since "republic" implies a political system based on the will of the populace, and since "Islamic" means that the opinions of the people lose their credibility if they are not in conformity with the Islamic *thawabit* (immutable set of values or principles), then Hizbullah uses the slogan of "The Islamic Republic in Lebanon" to denote a system that enforces Islamic laws in Lebanon based upon God's injunctions in the Qur'an as laid down by *wilayat al-faqih*: "Whoever does not judge according to what Allah has revealed – those are the unbelievers [*kafirun*]", evildoers (*zalimun*), and transgressors (*fasiqun*) (5:44-46).[152]

4.3   *Jihad* and martyrdom

Jihad

4.3.1   *Hizbullah's stance concerning jihad and its justification*

Hizbullah's religious ideology depicts *jihad* as the fulcrum of belief in Islam.[153] Hizbullah's religious ideology abides by the classical Shi'ite under-standing on smaller military *jihad* as well as that of Imam Khumayni, as expressed by (22:78): "And strive [*jahidu*] for Allah as you ought to strive. He elected you, and did not impose on you any hardship in religion – the faith of your father Abraham. He called you Muslims before and in this [the Qur'an], that the Apostle may bear witness [*shahidan*] against you and you may be witness against mankind. So, perform the prayer, give the alms and hold fast to Allah. He is your Master; and what a blessed Master and a blessed supporter!" Hizbullah stresses that what is meant by *jihad* in the aforementioned verse is the general meaning i.e. *jihad* solely in the way of God. Like Khumayni, Hizbullah emphasises that by practicing *jihad* believers enter paradise, while infidels go to hell.[154]

Like the classical interpretation, Hizbullah's religious ideology places *jihad* above the following eight mundane (worldly/material) relations mentioned in verse (9:24): "Say: 'If your (1) fathers, your (2) sons, your (3) brothers, your (4) spouses, your (5) relatives, the (6) wealth you have gained, a (7) trade you fear might slacken, and (8) dwellings you love are dearer to you than Allah and His Apostle or than fighting [*jihad*] in his way, then wait until Allah fulfils His decree. Allah does not guide the sinful people' ". Thus, the priority is to love God and Prophet Muhammad and practice *jihad* in their way, rather than loving the eight mundane relations and material desires mentioned in (9:24). Hizbullah stresses that this priority becomes noticeable when there is a conflict between (1) giving money for *jihad* and keeping it because of fear of losing it, and (2) when a parent prevents his offspring from sacrificing themselves. Both cases are regarded as a deflection from obedience to God. However, in the case of sacrifice in the way of God and *jihad* in His way and the Prophet's way, there is no conflict between the eight mundane relations listed above and *jihad*. In that case, the eight mundane relations are considered as helping factors towards performing the *taklif* to the *faqih*.[155]

Hizbullah's religious ideology broadens the classical understanding of the verb *jahada* by interpreting it, as doing one's utmost in defending oneself against the enemy.[156] Hizbullah portrays *jihad* as a contractual dimension (tacit consent) with God based on *mubaya'a* (homage or a pledge of allegiance) to Him, in order to enter heaven in return for this sacrifice (9:111): "Allah has bought from the believers their lives and their wealth in return for Paradise; they fight in the way of Allah, kill and get killed [*yuqtalu*]. That is a true promise from Him in the Torah, the Gospel and the Qur'an; and who fulfils his promise better than Allah? Rejoice then at the bargain you have made with Him; for that is the great triumph".[157]

4.3.2   *The safeguards of jihad: abiding by the injunctions of the faqih*

In line with Imam Khumayni, Hizbullah's religious ideology emphasises that *jihad* is based upon sacrificing the self and possessions. The fruits of *jihad* can only be realised by the sacrifices and offerings of the fighters, their families, and the wounded because the aggressions of the enemy are founded on inflicting pain, suffering, and hopelessness in order to impose capitulation. *Jihad* is a means of defence to preclude the enemy from accomplishing its goals even though this might lead Hizbullah to pay a heavy price and a lot of sacrifices and pains, which are warranted by a competent and responsible *faqih* and based upon a clear *shar'i* objective.[158]

Hizbullah upholds Khumayni's assertion of obeying the *faqih* in general matters including the defence of Islam and the Muslims against the infidels, the tyrants, and the aggressors, which is in concert with the views of the jurists. The *faqih* estimates and judges objectively and contextually whether *jihad* has to be conducted only to attain victory or set special limitations on the level of sacrifice. Since the *faqih*'s decision is absolute and irrevocable, Hizbullah cannot contest it using its own logic and analyses.[159]

Indeed, the stated policy of Hizbullah is that the decision to wage *jihad* is incumbent upon *al-faqih* who diagnoses if the situation falls within the narrow confines of defensive *jihad*. He also determines the rules of engagement and its safeguards. This is of vital importance because there is a grave responsibility for spilling blood since the fighters should not engage in any battle, neither without establishing the duty of *jihad* in it nor without a solid foundation in establishing its goals. Since it is the jurisdiction of the *faqih*, then the final say and decision is his, and it is binding upon all the Muslims who follow him.[160]

One Hizbullah member, who would like to remain autonomous, told me that as practice of indoctrination and as a baptism/initiation ceremony, new Hizbullah recruits had to repeatedly state: "*idha qala laka al-waliyy al-faqih ‘an auqtul nafsak, fa ‘alayka dhalik* (If Imam Khumayni told you to kill yourself, then you have to do it)". This not only illustrates indoctrination, but also the total obedience to the *faqih*.

4.3.3 *Engaging in greater jihad before smaller jihad*

Hizbullah's religious ideology argues that the Islamic connotation of the word *jihad* conveys something more than militarily combating the enemy. The mandate of *jihad* could be extended to greater *jihad*, which is fighting the internal enemy of the human being. Hizbullah's religious ideology adjusts Khumayni's interpretation of greater *jihad* by distinguishing between: (1) insinuations calling on the individual to perform all kinds of vices and (2) the Devil who enjoins committing delinquent, corrupt, and evil acts.[161] Nevertheless, in line with Imam Khumayni, it stresses that a person needs to prepare himself before engaging in smaller military *jihad* by showing willingness to sacrifice the most precious things a person has: his self and his possessions, rather than a part of them. This could only be accomplished after a lot of effort and *jihad* with the self (greater *jihad*). [162]

In line with Imam Khumayni, before engaging in smaller military *jihad*, a Hizbullahi has to undergo systematic and stringent indoctrination aimed at inculcating the spirit of greater *jihad* in his heart and mind. Thus, in order to achieve successful and efficient mobilization, for many years, Hizbullah has embarked on giving extensive lessons on the importance of self-sacrifice, and made these the centre of its educational or indoctrination movement. Hizbullah's religious ideology mobilized its followers and indoctrinated them on ideological and religious grounds through a gradual process based on a spiritual transformation, which ultimately led to fostering the inner strength required for self-sacrifice that would empower the weak over the strong, the oppressed over the oppressors.[163] Thus, sophisticated and intensive military training (smaller military *jihad*) is not enough for the transformation of the individual who is willing to sacrifice himself. Rather, this should be accompanied by psychological mobilization and spiritual transformation as a basic indoctrination technique of greater *jihad* in order to instil the spirit of self-sacrifice in their hearts and actualise their potential strength.[164]

Hizbullah's religious ideology mentioned the excessive and encumbering *ta'tir* (process of screening) that Hizbullah's prospective members undergo so that they know how to go beyond enjoining the good and forbidding the evil, to go beyond engaging in persuasive *jihad* (smaller non-military *jihad*).[165] He referred to the special spiritual guidance that new recruits pass through in order to inculcate the spirit of greater *jihad* in their soul and cause a metamorphosis of the self through a perpetual process of spiritual building. Only then they can engage in smaller military *jihad* and self-sacrifice. According to Hizbullah there is an urgent need to revive the culture of *jihad*, *jihad* in the way of God, and indoctrinate its principles and injunctions to the children and the populace of the *umma*.[166] He stressed the need to go beyond both intellectual *jihad* (persuasive *jihad*: smaller non-military *jihad*) and smaller military *jihad* since the distinguishing feature of Hizbullah's culture *par excellence* is inculcating the culture of spiritual *jihad*, greater *jihad*, the *jihad* of polishing the self to go beyond the here and now to practice *ta'bi'a* and *ta'a* (strict discipline and obedience) to the *faqih*. Hizbullah stresses that mobilization and obedience convey a religious-ideological commitment.[167]

The salient feature of Hizbullah's culture of greater *jihad* is piety, spiritual renaissance, sufism, and gnosticism along the lines of Imam Khumayni's *halal shar'i* (religiously sanctioned) practices. Hizbullah's religious ideology adjusts Imam Khumayni's interpretation of greater *jihad* by emphasizing that there is a need not only to build spiritualism but also to continuously reinvigorate and strengthen it by fighting in the way of God since fighting the enemies helps to deeply and speedily inculcate this spiritualism in the soul or self. That is why God ordained religious devotion by way of hurling to the battlefield: (9:122) "Why doesn't a company from each people go forth to instruct themselves in religion" because God is fully conversant that the *umma*'s battle with its enemies is open-ended, pending the Islamisation of the whole world. Hizbullah adds that God wants the battles of the *umma* to take a global dimension where both close and remote people would hasten to join. The justification for this behaviour is that God knows that the circumstances of facing the enemy and sacrificing the self make the self of the Muslim individual understand the truth of Islam and religious devotion without the veils of darkness and light.[168]

4.3.4 The connection between jihad and martyrdom

Hizbullah's religious ideology affirms that the passion to martyrdom does not in any way compromise the desire to victory. Thus, in the line with the classical Shi'ite view and Imam Khumayni's perspective, Hizbullah's religious ideology stresses that *jihad* has two glorious rewards or outcomes (*husnayayyn*): martyrdom (of the self/person) and victory (of the *umma*) (9:52).[169]

Building on Khumayni's logic and argument, Hizbullah's religious ideology defends its martyrdom operations from a religious perspective as an expression of obedience to God to perform smaller military *jihad* as well as fulfilling the religious duty of martyrdom, which is incumbent on the believers in order to defend their rights and their occupied land.[170] Hizbullah explains that upbringing on the notion of *jihad* buttresses the spirit of martyrdom and readiness to die in the way of God. The logic of martyrdom is based upon the religious understanding and belief in another life in heaven, where the human being lives in felicity and where all his/her dreams are realized, in addition to the fruits that the *umma* reaps from his/her martyrdom. Martyrdom transcends the materialistic dimension of liberating occupied land; it is a religious duty and a testimony to abidance by Gods injunctions as that is why it is martyrdom in the way of God.[171]

Martyrdom

4.3.5 Hizbullah's justification of martyrdom operations

Hizbullah's religious ideology exhorts parents to raise their children on the notion of martyrdom in the way of God.[172] The logic behind martyrdom is based on a religious understanding and belief in the hereafter where people live happy and realise all their dreams in addition to the fruits that behold the *umma* as a result of martyrdom. Hizbullah affirms that martyrdom as the duty of defending and liberating occupied land transcends the material dimension. Martyrdom is an embodiment of the concept of obedience to God and it is a religious-legal obligation that leads to eternal life. Hizbullah stresses that the strong desire to martyrdom based on strong religious convictions. Hizbullah learned that upbringing on the concept of martyrdom leads to effectiveness and adoption of the curriculum of martyrdom, where remuneration is tied to the delegated responsibility of conducting martyrdom operations (smaller military *jihad*). In line with Imam Khumayni, Hizbullah's religious ideology stresses that conducting martyrdom is a serious choice requiring belief and interaction with the prospective martyr. In order to accomplish the feat of martyrdom, a lot of indoctrination based on religious and spiritual upbringing is required; martyrdom is a religious duty incumbent upon the believer who is rewarded by going to heaven.[173] In this regard, it is reportedly stated that Hizbullah's Secretary General would meet with every martyr before he conducted his operation against the Israeli forces occupying southern Lebanon and the *Biqaʿ*. "To raise their morale, he would stress that they are going to heaven, because religious war (*jihad*) was an obligation in Islam, and tell them: 'Give my regards to the Prophet Mohammed'".[174] That is way there are so many Hizbullahis who are willing to fulfil their *taklif* by being "honoured" by martyrdom in order to receive God's blessings and acquire his obedience. Thus, there should be no astonishment in the believer's hurling towards martyrdom, for this part of the commitment and religious mobilisation.[175]

Building on its religious ideology Hizbullah justifies martyrdom operations by arguing that they are part of a rationale and vision, an overall vision that is based on the necessity to use all possible force in facing the Israeli enemy. That is why martyrdom operations were launched against the Israeli army occupying south Lebanon as a policy and curriculum/program, which Hizbullah considers as a practical way in order to achieve consecutive hits against that enemy, thus depleting its morale and straining its resources. The motivation behind these martyrdom operations was targeting the Israeli occupying army with violent hits that would shake its military capabilities, so that it would feel impotent and eventually it would withdraw. By this, Hizbullah would have achieved its goal of liberation of occupied land. Hizbullah stresses that martyrdom operations were part of a scrutinized plan, which came into being as the *only* possible way capable of altering the formula in facing the superior Israeli enemy.[176]

Ayatullah Fadlallah stressed that Hizbullah's martyrdom operations rendered Hizbullahis with a sense of empowerment over the seemingly invincible Israeli army. He argued, "There is no alternative to a bitter and difficult *jihad*, borne from within the power of effort, patience and sacrifice – and the spirit of martyrdom".[177] Ayatullah Fadlallah and Hizbullah's religious scholars could never permit the positive outcome of martyrdom operations to serve as their legitimisation.[178]

4.3.6 *Hizbullah's application of Imam Husayn's model and emulation of Khumayni's theory on martyrdom as a ticket to heaven*

Shaykh Ali Yasin, a Hizbullah religious scholar, emphasized that Hizbullah's religious ideology considers those who conducted martyrdom operations against the enemies of Islam as living martyrs in heaven.[179] Basing itself on Imam Husayn's precedent[180] and Imam Khumayni's religious-ideological stance, which regards martyrdom as a religious duty and a ticket to heaven, Hizbullah picked up and applied Imam Khumayni's slogan of "Everyday is *'Ashura*, and every land is *Karbala'* ".[181] According to Qasim, when society is brought up on the model of Imam Husayn and his companions, it acquires *madad* (support and reinforcement) from their leading behaviour and sacrifices.[182] Hizbullah learned from the martyrdom of Imam Husayn in *Karbala'* the love of martyrdom through the love of God, and the passion for *jihad* in the way of Islam. Also Hizbullah is fully conversant with the great feats/accomplishments that were actualised through Imam Husayn's martyrdom after the "renaissance" in *Karbala'* since his major concern was with the future of Islam and the Muslims.[183]

Hizbullah's religious ideology, in addition to relying on Imam Khumayni's views on martyrdom, most likely has been influenced by Ayatullah's Fadlallah's views[184]. Building on the Shi'a religious scholars' endorsement and sanctioning of martyrdom operations[185], Hizbullah equated its martyrdom operations conducted against the Israeli army occupying south Lebanon with the martyrdom of Imam Husayn in Karbala': "Do you want to suffer with Husayn? Then the setting is ready: the Karbala of the South [Lebanon]. You can be wounded and inflict wounds, kill and be killed, and feel the spiritual joy that Husayn lived when he accepted the blood of his son, and the spiritual joy of Husayn when he accepted his own blood and wounds. The believing resisters in the border zone [the self-declared Israeli security zone in southern Lebanon] are the true self-flagellants, not the self-flagellants of Nabatiyya[186]. Those who flog themselves with swords, they are our fighting youth. Those who are detained in [the Israeli camp in] al-Khiyam, arrested by Israel in the region of Bint Jubayl, they are the ones who feel the suffering of Husayn and Zaynab. Those who suffer beatings on their chests and heads in a way that liberates, these are the ones who mark 'Ashura, in their prison cells".[187] Thus, Hizbullah explicitly identified its martyrs as being inspired by and following the lead of Imam Husayn.

4.3.7 Hizbullah's religious ideology distinguishes among the four senses of martyrdom

Hizbullah unequivocally acknowledges that the four senses of martyrdom are *thawabit* that constitute an important pillar of its religious ideology since its early beginnings.[188]

(Martyrdom 1): *al-istishhadi al-mujahid* (the martyred fighter): The word *al-mujahid* is implied, but not directly stated. The martyred fighter corresponds to a Muslim person who – in performing smaller *jihad* – intentionally and willingly blows himself in the battlefield or keeps on fighting till he dies in order to inflict the highest amount of damage and fatalities on the enemy. In line with the classical Shi'ite perspective and Ayatullah Fadlallah, Hizbullah affirms that Prophet Muhammad stipulated that this person is neither washed nor wrapped in a burial shroud (*la yughsl wa la yukaffan*)[189], although it is generally stipulated as a religious obligation to do so.[190] As it is acknowledged in the *hadith*, the "angels wash him". In line with the classical Shi'ite understanding and Imam Khumayni, Hizbullah stresses that this special treatment is done in recognition of his special status, or performed as a token of gratitude and a sign of *takrim* (special commemoration) for his great deeds. This corresponds, for instance, to the twelve Hizbullah fighters who blew themselves targeting Israeli military and intelligence personnel during the occupation of Lebanon. According to Hizbullah the martyred fighter is a hard-core altruist who performed a supererogatory act i.e. he sacrificed himself for the *maslaha* (benefit and interest) of his community and the *umma*, and his sacrifice is regarded as an act beyond the call of duty. It is supererogatory since martyrdom is not incumbent upon every individual.

(Martyrdom 2): *al-shahid al-mujahid* (the martyr fighter): corresponds to a Muslim person who, in performing smaller *jihad*, falls in the battlefield while facing the enemy. For instance, this is the case of Hadi Nasrallah and other Hizbullah fighters who confronted Israel in conventional warfare without blowing themselves. Like category one, the martyred fighter, the martyr fighter is neither washed nor wrapped in a burial shroud. The angels wash him. This corresponds, for instance, to the Hizbullah fighters who had died in confronting the Israeli occupation.[191] Using the same reasoning as employed in (martyrdom 1), Hizbullah argues the martyr fighter performed an altruistic, supererogatory act.

(Martyrdom 3): *al-shahid* (the martyr): corresponds to an innocent civilian Muslim person who died without taking part in the fighting. He/she is washed and wrapped in a burial shroud because he/she died outside the battlefield. However, the final evaluation is for God (*al-taqyyim 'inda Allah*). Hizbullah abides by Ayatullah Khamina'i who argues that martyrdom is a special prerogative for every person. If God responded to his/her call (*du'a'*) and considered his death as martyrdom, then God has bestowed upon him/her the highest dignity and prerogative in return for his/her essence that has gone to heaven.[192] Sayyid Husayn al-Musawi seconds that arguing whosoever demands martyrdom from God in uprightness obtains the place of a martyr, even if he should die in his bed.[193] Qasim argues that the martyr is a victim who did not perform a supererogatory act.

(Martyrdom 4): *shahid al-watan* (the martyr of the nation-state) or *shahid al-qadiyya* (the martyr of a cause): corresponds to a non-Muslim who died in the battlefield fighting for his country or the cause he believes in. God is the only One who evaluates if he/she could take the *ajr* (remuneration) of a Muslim martyr and be elevated to the level of (martyrdom 2) in the full Islamic jurisprudential sense of the word. This corresponds, for instance, to the non-Muslim Lebanese Army soldiers who died in the confrontation with Israel, the same day Hadi Nasrallah and his two companions died. Also, non-Muslim fighters of the September 1997 Hizbullah formed "Lebanese Multi-Confessional Brigades" (LMCB) fall in this category. These are buried according to the specific rites of their respective religions. According to Hizbullah, this category of martyrdom in an altruistic-supererogatory act since it is not every citizen's duty to fight the enemy in the battlefield.

4.3.8 *Martyrdom and ithar ("preference")*[194]

Hizbullah's religious ideology explains the significance of the concept of "preference" in relation to martyrdom. It stresses that martyrdom is a voluntarily-willed act that is based on the intellectual and theoretical foundations of a religious, psychological, and cultural upbringing embedded in the Qur'anic concept of "preference", preference of life in the hereafter, rather than the here and now, and preference of the *umma* over the individual: "And they give food, despite their love of it, to the destitute, the orphan and the captive. [They say]: 'We only feed you for the sake of Allah; We do not want from you any reward or gratitude'" (76:8-9). Thus, Hizbullah's religious ideology broadens the mandate of preference – from fasting for three days and preferring to feed others, rather than the self –to include the giving of blood for the sake of the *umma*.[195]

4.3.9 *The distinction between martyrdom and suicide*

Shi'ite religious scholars have unanimously vilified suicide as foolish behaviour leading to perdition. They extolled and sanctioned martyrdom operations carried out in the way of God against aggressive armies for the sake of liberating occupied land in wars of national resistance. Building on the consensus among medieval Muslim jurists who sanctioned a soldier or a few soldiers to attack a large hostile army, Shi'ite religious scholars affirmed if the Muslims in the early centuries of Islam had been in possession of modern explosives, they would have used them in the same manner as today's martyrs who blew up themselves in the enemy, intending to inflict the highest amount of possible casualties in its ranks.[196] Hizbullah's religious ideology emphasizes that the carrying out of martyrdom operations is a religiously sanctioned act of self-sacrifice that is diametrically opposed to suicide, which is completely prohibited in Islam, the punishment being eternal damnation in hell. In other words, Hizbullah's religious ideology regards self-sacrifice conducted on the basis of greater *jihad* as legitimate martyrdom operations, rather than suicide. However, Hizbullah clarifies that if a person blows up himself without securing a prior authorisation from the *'ulama*, then his act amounts to suicide.[197]

Hizbullah's religious ideology stresses that martyrdom is a voluntary-willed act conducted by a person who loves life, holds on to it, and has all the reasons to live.[198] Hizbullah argues that the West has been perplexed by the degree and level of volitional martyrdom operations, which it terms suicide. The West thought that for the youth to become martyrs, then they definitely have been drugged, confronted with difficult living circumstances, faced with complicated psychological problems, or showered with enormous financial or material rewards. Hizbullah adds that the West has been "indoctrinated" according to its intellectual background to sanctify material life and get hold of it come what may. That is why the West is incapable of construing the meaning of the existence of martyrs except by materialistically and secularly explaining the martyrs' religious beliefs. Hizbullah stresses that the West has the right not to understand the effects of religious indoctrination on the curriculum of Islam because understanding a phenomenon (martyrdom) is not only based upon or confined to rational explanations and justifications; rather it needs real and a close encounter with, and a follow up to, the different stages that the lives of the would-be fighters and martyrs pass through. It also requires knowledge of the Islamic Milieu that gives rise to such a devotion to martyrdom based upon the spirit of greater *jihad*. Hizbullah concludes that the Westerners who have witnessed the reality of martyrdom cannot deny it, even if they were perplexed in interpreting it because they were not able to construe the real motivation behind martyrdom.[199]

Ayatullah Fadlallah delineated the distinction between suicide and martyrdom (self-sacrifice) sanctioning martyrdom by arguing that if the objective of a person who scarifies himself in a martyrdom operation "is to have a political impact on an enemy whom it is impossible to fight by conventional means, then his *sacrifice* can be part of [smaller military] *jihad*". In line with Hizbullah's first sense of martyrdom, 'the martyred fighter', Fadlallah affirmed, "Such an undertaking differs little from that of a soldier who fights and knows that in the end he will be killed. The two situations lead to death; except that one fits in with the conventional procedures of war, and the other does not[200]… the Muslims believe that you struggle by transforming yourself into a living bomb like you struggle with a gun in your hand. There is no difference between dying with a gun in your hand or exploding yourself".[201] Fadlallah added, "What is the difference between setting out for battle knowing you will die *after* killing ten [of the enemy], and setting out to the field to kill ten and knowing you will die *while* killing them?"[202]

4.3.10 *The aims and prohibitions of martyrdom operations*

Since the beginning, Hizbullah placed practical safeguards on martyrdom operations; the most important was that that the number of Israeli soldiers killed should be at least thirty, in order for the operation to be religiously sanctioned.[203] According to Hizbullah's religious ideology, martyrdom is the epitome of self-sacrifice, which is conducted on the basis of specific religious safeguards in confronting a stronger occupying enemy. If inflicting heavy casualties on the enemy or achieving victory over it depends upon the martyrdom of a few resistance fighters, then their endeavour is crowned with legitimacy.[204]

Likewise, Fadlallah argues martyrdom operations "should only be carried out if they can bring a political or military change in proportion to the passions that incite a person to make of his body an explosive bomb".[205] Fadlallah stressed that there are certain prohibitions tied to the act of martyrdom. According to him, a "martyrdom operation is not permitted unless it can convulse the enemy. The believer cannot blow himself up unless the results will equal or exceed the sacrifice of the believer's self. Self-martyring operations are not fatal accidents but legal obligations [*taklif shar'*] governed by rules, and the believers cannot transgress the rules of God".[206]

V   Chapter Conclusion

The backbone of Hizbullah's religious ideology centres upon the following constituents or specifics: belief in Shi'a Islam {doctrine of the Imamate; *taqiyya*; and *ta'bi'a*}; (2) the adoption and application of the *wilayat al-faqih* doctrine; and (3) *jihad* in the way of God.

Hizbullah views *wilayat al-faqih* as its true Islamic cultural authenticity. Basing itself on the classical Shi'ite interpretation of the doctrine of the Imamate, Hizbullah recognized Imam Khumayni as the official *marja' al-taqlid* of the Islamic Republic and as the first faqih after the Great Occultation, and in contemporary history, to assume the title of the deputy of Imam al-Mahdi. Believing that Khumayni blended Imama with *wilaya* with *marja'iyya*, Hizbullah followed the religious authority of Iran and paid homage and allegiance to Khumayni as the political and a religious leader of the *umma* and abided by his *wilayat al-faqih* as a major pillar in its religious ideology.

Hizbullah practiced *taqiyya* as a socio-political necessity (*darura*) as well as a survival strategy, but not on doctrinal grounds since it kept its name, identity, and goals secretive so as not to risk annihilation from its enemies while it was still evolving in a rudimentary form. This behaviour is in line with Imam Khumayni who, after the victory of the Islamic Revolution in 1979, banned the practice of *taqiyya* since there was no need to have recourse to it after the establishment of an Islamic order. The only exception being the preservation of life and religion in conformity with the purposes of Islamic *shari'a*. Hizbullah's religious ideology broadened the mandate of *taqiyya* and abided by it only in the specific case of avoiding dissention. This behaviour is warranted since Hizbullah is operating in Lebanon in a multiconfessional sectarian state, and not within an Islamic order.

Hizbullah's mobilized a substantial portion of its resources to fight the Israeli occupying forces, making mobilization and self-discipline the distinguishing traits of its Islamic method as well as its recruitment strategy that aimed to uphold Islamic cultural authenticity. It employed *ta'bi'a* as an act of mobilization whereby the 'sons of Hizbullah's *umma*' endeavoured to get hold of political power through a top-down process in order to establish an Islamic order governed by *shari'a* and *hakimiyya* in accordance with Imam Khumayni's *wilayat al-faqih*.

Hizbullah endorsed and applied Imam Khumayn's stipulation of the necessity of engaging in greater *jihad* before practicing smaller military *jihad*. However, Hizbullah slightly adjusted Khumayni's theory by sanctioning prospective fighters to hasten to the battlefield in order to inculcate religious devotion in their souls. In line with Khumayni, Hizbullah's religious ideology affirmed that greater *jihad* metamorphoses the individual into a coalescent, spiritually refined human being. Hizbullah regarded spiritual mobilization and strict obedience and discipline to God and the *faqih* as the religious-ideological components of greater *jihad*. Mobilization and self-disciple became the two most salient components of Hizbullah's greater *jihad*. Thus, giving up the pleasures of the body through giving primacy to the spiritual dimension for the promise of heaven and God's blessings, gives the Hizbullahi a strong volition to stay firm in his belief and to defend his convictions. Hizbullah members follow specific religious safeguards when it comes to giving blood and following the way of God, irrespective of the sacrifices encountered, if the order is given from the legitimate leadership that is represented by the *faqih*.

Hizbullah stressed that the base and foundation of Islamic belief is smaller military *jihad* that is practiced against the Israeli occupation army in southern Lebanon. Thus, in line with Imam Khumayni's view of the sacrificing of the self and possessions, which he regarded as a social liberating force in this world and as a ticket to heaven, Hizbullahis engaged in smaller *jihad* and sacrificed themselves in battle against the enemy. Hizbullah claimed that it conducted *jihad* in a realistic, practical, and efficient matter because it follows the Islamic teachings and abides by the *faqih*'s safeguards, guidance, and supervision.

In conformity with its *taklif*, Hizbullah conveys Islamic upbringing based on the spirit of martyrdom. Hizbullah regarded martyrdom operations launched by freely willed individual self-sacrificial martyrs against the Israeli occupation forces in the early 1980s as legitimate and religiously sanctioned operations conducted against a superior military "aggressive" army, where conventional means of smaller military *jihad* proved futile. However, Hizbullah stressed that there should always be a *fatwa* – religious justification or legitimisation – behind every martyrdom operation or else it would be regarded as suicide. Thus, Hizbullah's religious ideology does not consider blowing oneself in enemy troops or engaging them in the battlefield till death as suicide, rather as "glorified" martyrdom based upon the Qur'anic concept of preference, preference to uphold the honour and dignity of the *umma* over living in disgrace under the occupation; preference to live eternally in heaven, rather than continuously being humiliated in this world.

Building on Imam Khumayni's and Ayatullah Fadlallah's religious-ideological justifications of martyrdom, Hizbullah explicitly identified the martyrs as being inspired by and emulating Imam Husayn's martyrdom in *Karbala'*. Hizbullah's argument that there is no distinction between dying while fighting in the battlefield and blowing up oneself, seems to have shattered the commonly held theological view that regards giving one's life for the faith to die as a martyr as not the same thing as blowing up oneself. However, the religious-ideological justifications of self-sacrifice and martyrdom do not rule out the political practicality of forcing the enemy to withdraw from occupied land and achieve victory, since this practicality is based on and sanctioned on religious-ideological grounds which regard *jihad* as having two glorious fruits (*husnayayyn*), which are martyrdom of the self and victory in battle, as mentioned in the Qur'an (9:52). This is a mark of the collective identity of self-sacrifice and martyrdom whereby the community, the *umma* benefits and reaps the rewards of martyrdom.

One could argue that Hizbullah's religious ideology was to a greater extent successful in dominating the Lebanese state's identity, at least in Hizbullah's major constituencies as well in *al-hala al-Islamiyya* where it wields power. Thus, Hizbullah was triumphant in increasing Islamic influence and identity in its Islamic Milieu at the expense of the Lebanese state.[207]

3 The Prominence of Hizbullah's Political Ideology (1984/5-1990)

1. Introduction

This chapter presents Hizbullah's political ideology as formulated over the period 1984/5 to 1990. It is compiled from and described on the basis of the available sources: the Open Letter of February 1985[1], a series of political declarations issued from 1984 onwards, and the speeches and statements issued by Hizbullah's leaders and cadres between 1984/5 and 1990.[2] The speeches and statements that are quoted in this chapter were delivered, most prominently, by Hizbullah's leaders and cadres: Shaykh Subhi al-Tufayli[3], Sayyid Abbas Al-Musawi[4], Sayyid Husayn Al-Musawi[5], Sayyid Ibrahim Amin Al-Sayyid[6], Sayyid Muhammad Husayn Fadlallah[7], Sayyid Hasan Nasrallah[8], and Shaykh Na'im Qasim.[9] Also, heavy reliance has been placed on Muhammad Z'aytir's book entitled *An Outlook at the Proposal of the Islamic Republic in Lebanon*[10], and brief mention of 'Ali Al-Kurani's book entitled *Hizbullah's Method of Islamic Mobilization*[11].

Below I will offer a seven-point thematic exposition of the constituents of Hizbullah's ideology: (2.1) Hizbullah's standpoint towards the oppressors and oppressed; (2.2) its perspectives on the Islamic state (*al-dawla al-Islamiyya*) or Islamic government (*al-hukuma al-Islamiyya*) or Islamic republic (*al-jumhuriyya al-Islamiyya*)[12]; (2.3) its position on relations with the Lebanese Christians; (2.4) its perspective on Israel; (2.5) its viewpoint towards the unity of the Muslims; (2.6) its stance vis-à-vis the West; and finally (2.7) its views on *jihad* and martyrdom. This will be followed by a summary of the basic constituents of Hizbullah's political ideology.

2. The Constituent Points of Hizbullah's Political Ideology

2.1 Views on the Oppressors (*mustakbirin*) and Oppressed (*mustad'afin*)

"Whoever takes Allah, His Apostle and those who believe as friends [must know] that Allah's party [Hizbullah] is indeed the triumphant" (5:56).

The Open Letter presents Hizbullah as the party of the oppressed serving the interests of the entire world oppressed and their perpetual revolution for achieving social, economic, and political justice. Hizbullah considered Third World Countries, which included all Muslim countries, as the world oppressed. According to Sayyid Ibrahim Amin Al-Sayyid, *mustad'afin* applies to all the oppressed and downtrodden of the earth. He added that Hizbullah's friends are all those Muslims and Christians who face off the oppressors.[13] Hizbullah clearly stated in its Open Letter that it extends its invitation to all the downtrodden or oppressed non-Muslims.[14] Hizbullah mentioned that although its oppressed friends convey ideas that do not originate from Islam (such as Jesus is the son of God and belief in Trinity, for instance), this does not preclude Hizbullah from cooperating with them in order to achieve the goals (of getting rid of arrogance and oppression and achieving a just society), especially since Hizbullah feels that the motives (of fighting the aggressors), which exhort the oppressed to struggle, are Muslim motives in the first place (such as the protection of the self, family and descent, religion, and property[15]), originating from the oppression and tyranny that has been practiced and imposed upon the oppressed, even if these motives were formed by un-Islamic ideas (such as liberation theology[16]). Although Hizbullah's cadres argued that Liberation theology is un-Islamic since it is based on Biblical and Marxian notions, they conceded that the following Qur'anic verses could be interpreted as referring to liberation theology concepts: (2:220); (7:56); (7: 7:85); (7:170); (11:88); (11:117); (26:152); (38:28).[17] Hizbullah added that its friends are all the world's oppressed peoples as well as all those who fight its enemies and ward off their evil. In addition, Hizbullah exhorted the entire world oppressed to bond together in order to face the conceit of the world oppressors by forming an international consortium of liberation movements. Thus, Hizbullah's struggle is aimed at achieving these objectives across the Muslim *umma* and beyond by confronting the oppressors who exploit the world's oppressed.[18]

Ayatullah Fadlallah argued that the Qur'an differentiates between two oppressed groups. The first group are the oppressed who have the capabilities but they do not exercise their volition to alter their plight by sacrificing their security and status out of fear and indolence. The second group are those who suffer from an innate, inborn condition of oppression, but take action in order to rid themselves of this situation. The first group are chastised because they do not abide by the Qur'anic injunction of migrating: "Those whom the angels cause to die while they are unjust to themselves will be asked [by the angles]: 'What were you doing?' They will say: 'We were oppressed in the land'. They [the angels] will add saying: 'Was not Allah's land spacious enough for you to emigrate to some other part?' Those people –their refuge is Hell, and what a wretched destiny! Except the oppressed men, women and children who have no recourse and cannot find a way out. Those, Allah may pardon them; Allah is All-Pardoning, All-Forgiving" (4:97-99). Thus, according to Fadlallah, the Qur'an stipulates several means[19] of facing off oppression such as emigration, for those who are capable, to a new and prosperous land where they can exercise their religion freely.[20]

Internationally and regionally, Hizbullah depicted the imperial-capitalist First World Countries as the oppressors, led by the "Great Satan" (US), France, and the "Little Satan", the "Zionist Entity" (Israel). Domestically, Hizbullah stressed that the oppressors were the political Maronites[21] and their right-wing militias (Phalangists, Lebanese Front, Lebanese Forces).[22] Z'aytir purported that the oppressor, arrogant, and hypocrite political Maronites spread the reigns of terror among the oppressed Muslims, being inspired by the oppressors, the "crusader Pope in Rome" as well as their masters: the French, the Americans, and the Zionists.[23] He stressed that the Maronite oppressors should be punished according to the level of their oppression, injustice, tyranny, exploitation, betrayal, treason, and crimes. Justice is what the oppressed demand as retribution from the oppressors.[24] In a similar vein, Ayatullah Fadlallah argued that in order to alleviate the plight of the oppressed, the causes of oppression should be uprooted, most prominently the power elite represented by the political Maronites.[25] Z'aytir contended that the confrontation between the oppressors and oppressed should constitute an impetus for the Muslims to rebel against their tyrannical-arrogant governments that have enslaved them, squandered their natural resources, and plundered their wealth.[26]

Hizbullah bases its political-ideological legitimisation of the notion of oppressors and oppressed on a host of Qur'anic verses[27], which depict the *mustad'afin* as the downtrodden and oppressed, or those who were deemed weak; and the *mustakbirin* as the arrogant and oppressors (34: 31-33): "The unbelievers say: 'We will never believe in this Qur'an, nor in what came before it'. If you could only see when the wrongdoers are arrayed before their Lord, each one reproaching the other, the downtrodden saying to the arrogant: 'But for you, we would have been believers'. The arrogant will say to the downtrodden: 'Did we really bar you from the guidance after it came to you? No, you were rather ungodly'. Then the downtrodden will say to the arrogant: 'It was rather your cunning night and day, when you commanded us to disbelieve in Allah and assign equals to Him'. They will be secretly remorseful, when they see the punishment. We will put shackles round the necks of the unbelievers; will they be rewarded but for what they used to do?" Other Qur'anic verses, stress that God would always favour the oppressed and grant them victory over the oppressors: "We wish to favour the downtrodden [oppressed] in the land and make them leaders [Imams] and make them the inheritors; And establish them firmly in the land..." (28:5-6)[28]; "And remember when you were few and were deemed oppressed in the land, fearing that the people will snatch you away; but He gave you a shelter, strengthened you with His support and provided you with the good things, that perchance you may give thanks" (8:26)[29]; "And those who, if they are oppressed, will overcome" (42:39).

Sayyid Ibrahim Amin Al-Sayyid said that these Qur'anic verses appeared in many of Hizbullah's publications in the 1980s[30] and crowned the speeches and statements of its leaders and cadres who reiterated Imam Musa al-Sadr's deprivation discourse. Most importantly, he added that Imam Khumayni has already given the significance of the aforementioned verses arguing that Hizbullah decries the Marxist dialectical historical materialism and does not view history from the perspective of class struggle as the socialists do, rather as a struggle between the Qur'anic concepts of oppressors and the oppressed. In line with what Khumayni sanctioned and enjoined, al-Sayyid stressed, as an Islamic duty (taklif), helping and supporting all the deprived and oppressed – irrespective of their social class, race, or religion – from the grip of the oppressors. Al-Sayyid added that Khumayni emphasized that the Muslim religious scholars have a religious duty to fight the oppressors and colonizers by precluding them from exploiting and alienating the oppressed. The Muslim religious scholars should not allow the oppressors to plunder the natural resources of the umma and disseminate hunger and deprivation among its populace. Imam Khumayni called on the oppressed to mobilize and rebel, as such being the catalysts of the Islamic Revolution that would eventually rapture the chains of despotic-unjust rulers and establish an Islamic government that protects the umma.[31]

The political-ideological content of the understanding of oppressors and oppressed was also articulated by Ayatullah Fadlallah. Fadlallah offered an Islamic theory of oppression by depicting world history as a dialectical-perpetual struggle between the powerful arrogant oppressors, and the weak downtrodden oppressed, between injustice and justice. Fadlallah condemned economic and political imperialism; he regarded oppression, colonialism, imperialism, and Zionism as mafasid (evils and vices), and he legitimatised and justified the use of power by the oppressed against these *mafasid*. He argued that oppression leads to dehumanising, humiliating, and robbing the oppressed of their inalienable liberty that is granted to them by the Qur'an.[32] Fadlallah added that *mustad'afin* is a Qur'anic concept where the oppressed suffer from social, economic, and political exploitation and alienation, which makes them feel an acute sense of helplessness and deprivation. According to him, the Qur'an urges the oppressed to revolt against their oppression.[33]

Although the roots of the notion of oppressors and oppressed were underscored by Imam Musa al-Sadr in his theory of the downtrodden Lebanese Shi'ites who were deprived and dispossessed[34], Hizbullah stresses in its Open Letter[35] and political declarations that it was also influenced by Imam Khumayni's revolutionary Qur'anic notion of oppressors and oppressed.[36] Hizbullah also emphasized that it supports the struggle of all the oppressed against the oppressors in order to achieve their rights on a global level.[37]

2.2 Views on the Islamic State and the Lebanese Political System (Political Maronism)

Hizbullah conveyed its obligation to the rule of Islam (Islamic State) calling upon the populace to opt for the Islamic system (*al-nizam al-Islami*), which is the only one capable of warranting justice, liberty, and security. Hizbullah portrayed its discourse in political-ideological terms by affirming that only the Islamic system is capable of halting any new colonialist-imperialist intervention in Lebanon.[38] In line with Imam Khumayni, Hizbullah argued that abiding by *al-qawanin al-wad'iyya* (positive or man-made laws and legislations) instead of Islamic *shari'a*, is the second out of four ways colonialism seeks to distort Islam.[39]

In line with Ayatullah Fadlallah's views[40], according to the Open Letter[41] and its political declarations, one of Hizbullah's objectives is to grant the Lebanese populace (both Christians and Muslims) the right of self-determination by freely choosing the form or system of government they deem fit based on mutual agreement:[42] "There is no compulsion in religion; true guidance has become distinct from error. Thus he who disbelieves in the Devil and believes in Allah grasps the firmest handle [bond] that will never break. Allah is All-Hearing, All-Knowing. Allah is the Supporter of the believers. He brings them out of darkness into light. As for those who disbelieve, their supporters are the devils who bring them out of light into darkness. Those are the people of the Fire in which they shall abide forever" (2:256-7). However, Hizbullah anticipated the result by contending, "they would definitely choose Islam". That is why it calls for the implementation of the Islamic system. Indeed, Hizbullah emphasized in the Open Letter and its political declarations that it does not want Islam to reign in Lebanon by force as the "oppressive system" of political Maronism was governing.[43]

Na'im Qasim commented on the aforementioned by arguing that the Open Letter is clear in its call to establish the Islamic state (*al-dawla al-Islamiyya*) in Lebanon based on the free will and free choice of the populace. He added that Hizbullah is totally in harmony with its convictions and with the practical-objective circumstances in which it operates (i.e. the Lebanese milieu). Thus, according to Qasim, as long as these circumstances preclude Hizbullah from establishing an Islamic state because the choice of the people is otherwise, then the populace should bear the responsibility of the political system that they have chosen: "Had your Lord willed, everybody on earth would have believed. Will you then compel people to become believers?" (10:99).[44]

In *al-'Ahd*, Hizbullah stressed that the Muslims have no right whatsoever to even entertain the idea of a Muslim canton (a mini-Islamic state)[45] or a Shi'ite canton, or a Sunni canton... Talking about cantons annihilates the Muslims, destroys their potential power, and leads them from one internal war to another. Only the Islamic state (*al-dawla al-Islamiyya*) upholds their unity.[46]

In the Open Letter Hizbullah stressed that Islam[47] or the Islamic order is characterised by ideology, doctrine, political order, and mode of governance[48], without specifying the components or contents of these terms, while Z'aytir did. He argued that based on strict religious criteria, the Islamic government takes its decisions, conveys its projects, wages wars, ratifies or rejects treaties, and deals with the international situation from the stance of changing it and Islamising it. He added that the Islamic government constitutes a practical embodiment of the Islamic laws and injunctions. It is stipulated that the governor should be well conversant with Islamic laws and injunctions, and he must be just in applying them because the ignorant governor would lead the people astray, and the unjust would steal money, downgrade the rights, and destroy the *umma*: "My covenant does not apply to the evil-doers" (2:124). Z'aytir stressed that Hizbullah seeks the realization of two important objectives in establishing an Islamic Republic in Lebanon: (1) To prevent any governor from becoming a tyrant abusing the people in their security and freedom; and (2) to consolidate the Islamic content of the system. He stressed that the concept of Islamic state means that Hizbullah ought to build its Islamic republic, establish its Qur'anic government, and erect an Islamic community based on the foundation of an Islamic knowledge of the universe and human life, which, according to him, is the best system for humanity.[49]

Z'aytir concretely outlined the constituents of the Islamic order. He argued that authority in Islam is a means to care for people's rights, and for the improvement of their daily dealings and lives. He affirmed that the system of Islamic governance, in addition to applying penal law (hudud), orders social, political, economic, and monetary relations; coordinates and balances between rights and duties. It is based upon the following: social solidarity and social justice; righteousness, fear of God, confidence in Him, and obedience to the Qur'an and Sunna; rendering people their rights and giving them security; justice, fairness, equity, compassion, liaison with the people, and mutual trust. In short, according to Z'aytir, the system of Islamic governance prepares the adequate ground for raising free and noble human beings through holistic social programs, execution of the shari'a, encouraging education and progress, and treating everyone equally in front of the law based upon the hadith and Qur'an respectively: "There is no preference between an Arab and a non-Arab except on the grounds of piety; you are all from Adam, and Adam is from dust"; "O mankind, We have created you male and female and made you nations and tribes, so that you might come to know one another. Surely the noblest of you in Allah's sight is the most pious. Allah is indeed All-Knowing, All-Informed"(49:13).[50]

2.2.1 *The place of the Christians in the Islamic state*

In conformity to the Open Letter, in one of its political declarations Hizbullah stated that it sees in the presence of the peace-loving Christians, who reside in the areas under its control, the credibility of its "opening-up" (infitah) and the tolerance of Islam. Hizbullah stressed that the dhimmis or ahl al-dhimma[51] share with the Muslims the social values of overt and purposeful tolerance such as love, fraternity, and solidarity. However, Hizbullah clarified in its political declaration that political Maronism is exempted from such tolerance being regarded as hypocrites: "When the hypocrites came to you, they say: 'We bear witness that you are indeed Allah's Apostle'. Allah knows that you are indeed his Apostle and Allah bears witness that the hypocrites are liars" (63:1).[52]

Sayyid Fadlallah explained that the first constitution of Islam, the constitution of al-Medina (al-Sahifa) stressed the security as well as the protection of the person and property of ahl al-dhimma as long as they were not treacherous. Fadlallah clarified that in the Islamic state the relations between the Muslims, on the one hand, and the Jews and Christians, on the other, were governed by the "*dhimmi* contract", which regulated these relations and enforced them with specific contractual obligations based on mutual consent, by which the Jews and Christians had the same rights and duties as any Muslim citizen. Fadlallah added since justice[53] has always been closely related to freedom, freedom that grants benefits and precludes harms[54], the *dhimmi* contract granted *ahl al-dhimma* freedom, especially the freedom of religion and the protection of their religious practices.[55] In turn, 'Ali Kurani stated that the freedom accorded to *ahl al-dhimma* in the Islamic state is within the confines of the safeguards of Islamic *shari'a*.[56] He clarified that the Christian minorities who live under Muslim governance are accorded all their civil and religious rights, but not their political rights since they are governed and are not ruling anymore, as was the case with political Maronism.[57]

According to Z'aytir, The Islamic republic that the Muslims are striving to instate in Lebanon does not impose upon the Christians, in general, and the political Maronites, in particular, to convert to Islam because Islam does not need them to be in its ranks, rather they need Islam. He warned that governance and administration of the *umma* should only be the prerogative of the Muslims, and the Muslims must not allow others to interfere in their affairs: "O believers, do not take as close friends other than your own people [co-religionists]; they will spare no effort to corrupt you and wish to see you suffer. Hatred has already been manifested in what they utter, but what their hearts conceal is greater still. We have made clear Our signs to you if only you understand" (3:118). Based on this verse, Z'aytir posed the rhetorical question: since it is a religious imperative not to allow the Christians to participate in government, then how could the Muslims accept to be ruled by them?[58]

In this respect, Sayyid Abbas al-Musawi said that compulsion in religion is not allowed or else Prophet Muhammad would not have revealed the constitution of al-Medina. Sayyid Abbas considered the Prophet as the inter-religious arbitrator among the Muslims, *ahl al-dhimma*, and others. Sayyid Abbas emphasized that the constitution of Medina pointed out that although the city was made up of many religious communities, Medina was a monolithic political community headed by Prophet Muhammad. Thus, non-Muslims conferred legitimacy to the Prophet as the political leader and final arbitrator. Sayyid Abbas stressed that since the Prophet's religious authority over non-Muslims was restricted, *al-Sahifa* granted each religious community full rights to follow its own religion and to practice its own internal affairs as it deems fit. Sayyid Abbas conveyed that this is how Hizbullah treats the People of the Book in accordance with the Constitution of Medina that distinguished between religious authority and political authority or leadership.[59]

2.2.2 Hizbullah's stance towards political Maronism

According to Z'aytir, the principal points of the Maronite political ideology are the following: (1) The exclusive Maronite identity of Lebanon has been established for thousands of years. (2) Xenophobic nationalism: "We are the Christian Lebanese nation, and the others do not belong". Since Lebanon is the nation-state of the Maronites, the Muslims are considered foreigners and should be deported.[60] (3) Maronite Christian supremacy: The Lebanese populace is Maronite and the word "Maronite" means Lebanese. Thus, the Lebanese are Maronites, and Lebanon and the Maronites is one and the same thing. (4) The Maronite history does not mention Islam as such, rather it refers to the "Arab conquest" stressing the need to liberate Lebanon from Muslim presence and transform it into a Maronite nation-state. Since the Arabic language is the language of the Muslim conquerors, the Maronites have called for its abolishment and its replacement with Latin script. (5) The coalescence among the Maronites, "crusaders", and "Zionists" as a means of empowerment by reliance on the West and its tutelage.[61]

Since the Islamic state contradicts and is the direct opposite of the Lebanese sectarian political system, Hizbullah's Open Letter chastised political Maronism and anathematised the infidel Lebanese government, which should be uprooted so that an Islamic system could be established in its place. Hizbullah stressed that the Lebanese regime is so arrogant and inequitable to the extent that no reform or amendment can overhaul it. According to Hizbullah, that is why it should be fundamentally altered[62] since it is an unjust regime.[63]

In its Open Letter, Hizbullah mentioned that the Phalangists are one of their basic enemies in the Middle East, and one of its major goals is to submit them "to a just power and bring them all to justice for the crimes they have perpetrated against Muslims and Christians".[64] Z'aytir stressed that the Muslims would annihilate the crusader political Maronites who killed and massacred Muslims. He added that Islam prohibited, and regarded as haram (religiously prohibited), killing innocent people as a hadith of the Prophet says: "The shaking up of Heaven and earth is easier to God than killing a Muslim person". He argued that the Maronites heeded the orders of the "despicable Crusaders"[65] by crushing and terrorising the "Islamists" (al-Islamiyyun).[66] According to Z'aytir, political Maronism is subservient to Zionist's and Cru-

sader's legitimacy that is transient, tribal, *jahili*[67] (pre-Islamic period of ignorance), and illegitimate because it is based on killing and terrorism, and does
not place any regard to human rights.[68] In turn 'Ali Kurani blasted the blatant
and wayward secularism of political Maronism, which ignores or brushes
aside Islamic political ideology and the ideological bond in favour of liberal-
izing political, humanistic, social, and economic contexts and dimensions
that are totally governed by the materialism of the West and East.[69]

Z'aytir emphasized that from a religious duty, it is always incumbent
upon Islamist political movements to find a way to acquire political power
through a top-down process aiming at replacing the current regime. On a
practical level, he argued that Hizbullah thought that Lebanon was qualified
to rupture the chains of political Maronism and establish an Islamic republic,
as long there was an Islamic revival and Islamist movements that wielded
power on the Lebanese scene. From this perspective, Z'aytir stressed the
urgent need to topple the existing regime and establish an Islamic government in its place. Z'aytir criticised the measured pace or cautious approach
of *al-hala al-Islamiyya* (the Islamic Milieu) towards the establishment of an
Islamic state in Lebanon.[70] He clearly stated Hizbullah's grand design of
Islamization through a top-down process aiming at annihilating and uprooting the infidel Lebanese political system.[71]

Z'aytir clarified that Hizbullah's disagreement with political Maronism
is not on the number of seats in the parliament or cabinet, neither on administrative positions in the state apparatus, nor on superficial amendments to
the constitution; rather, the issue is upholding the cause as well as the survival of the *umma* that did not exist except to rule others: "And thus we have
made the Muslim nation a just nation, so that you may bear witness unto the
rest of mankind, and that the Apostle may bear witness unto you" (2:143).[72]
He threatened that the road is clear to destroy the alleged Maronite superiority and to crush the political Maronite Lebanese system that made it its
duty to exterminate Muslims.[73]

In place of political Maronism, Z'aytir calls for instating an Islamic
republic. Z'aytir warned that Hizbullah and the Islamists would in the end
cut the hands of the traitors and liberate Lebanon from the political Maronite
infidels and tyrants. He stressed that Islam is unequivocal in rejecting any
authority of the infidels (Maronites) over the believers (Muslims). That is why
the political Maronites are afraid of Islam and are attempting to terrorise the
Muslims and prevent them from changing the system and establishing an
Islamic state, contending that it stands in sharp contrast to the Lebanese
constitution and traditions.[74] Z'aytir stressed that there is no legitimacy to

the Maronite minority because any 'legitimacy', which is opposed to Islamic *shari'a*, is rejected. Only the authority given by Islam is legitimate (12:40). According to him, Islam rejects the governance of infidels, and bars Muslims from accepting their authority without any regard to their higher status. That is why the Maronite system can never be legitimate. Legitimacy is only for Islam and anything besides that is *jahiliyya* governance: (5:50). Z'aytir added that even if the Maronites transformed Lebanon into a piece of heaven, then still their rule would remain rejected and illegitimate from an Islamic perspective. He clarified that every government and every authority, which does not govern by what God has prescribed and stipulated, is an infidel-illegitimate government and dealings with it are prohibited.

He added that political Maronism, which is facing a precarious situation, is living the fear of Islam and is doing its utmost to uphold the Lebanese political system using the argument that the Muslims want to create an Islamic republic. Z'aytir abhorred equating Islam with political Maronism, arguing that political Maronism is an emergency intruding system on the country of the Muslims. He concluded that the Maronites are afraid of the resurgence of Islam in the *umma*, a resurgence that would destroy the infidel Maronite system, as it has destroyed the infidel Shah of Iran, and establish an Islamic republic that would return the rights to its rightful owners.[75]

Z'aytir stressed that even if the Muslims took over the state and established a patriotic, democratic, or nationalist system of government, then still their rule would be illegitimate and apostate because it is rejected from God and his Prophet being regarded among the *jahiliyya* systems that are devoid of the bare necessities of legitimacy: (5:44-46); (5:50).[76] Z'aytir affirmed that every government that does not abide by the obedience of God and the traditions of the Prophet is rejected by Islam no matter how progressive and civilized it might be. Islam enjoins the rejection of infidel governments, calling for fighting them till the very end. For the legitimate government is the Islamic government, and the *shar'i* governance is the binding Muslim rule. He concluded as long as the president or the government or both of them do not abide by Islam, then all their decisions and injunctions are considered unjust and illegitimate.[77]

Sayyid Ibrahim Amin al-Sayyid stated that the Muslim populace in Lebanon does not accept to become part of the political project of the Lebanese state or political Maronism; rather the Lebanese state should find a place in the project of Islam.[78] More emphatically, Z'aytir argued that in history all entities have a transient existence, and the Lebanese Republic, which was the volition of the colonialists and the crusaders, ceased to be.

He stressed that Hizbullah should earn the dignity of inculcating the rule of God on earth by establishing an Islamic republic: (6:106).[79]

2.3   Hizbullah's relations with the Lebanese Christians [80]

By addressing the Lebanese Christians in general and the Maronites in particular, the Open Letter set apart the Maronites from the rest of the Christians.[81] The Open Letter also differentiated among the Maronites themselves on the following grounds: (1) the leading Maronite notables and their retinue who constitute the symbols of the political system i.e. political Maronism, or those with blatant connections with Israel; and (2) the rest of the Maronite notables and the ordinary citizens. Hizbullah considered that its primary problem was with the symbols of the political system i.e. political Maronism and the collaborators with Israel. Hizbullah called upon the chiefs of political Maronism to stop using their Christian militias in order to exercise oppressive policies against the Muslims because such policies would backfire on the Christians and would endanger their peace and security, especially since such exploitation was based on narrow-minded particularism, sectarian privileges, and collaboration with colonialism and Israel. Also, the Open Letter enjoined the Christians to liberate their thoughts, minds, and hearts of the despicable sectarianism, fanaticism and parochialism.[82] In addition, Hizbullah clarified in the Open Letter, that its views against political Maronism do not imply that Hizbullah is seeking revenge against all the Christians, stressing that it does not wish any inconvenience or harm neither to the Christians who live peacefully in the areas that are under its control nor to those who are "patriotic" and live elsewhere.[83]

However, in the Open Letter, Hizbullah practiced its Islamic propagation by exhorting all the Christians to convert to Islam in order to have felicity in this world and the world to come: "Open your hearts to our Call (da'wa)[84], which we address to you. Open yourselves up to Islam where you will find salvation and happiness upon earth and in the hereafter". Hizbullah called on the Christians to rid themselves of narrow denominational allegiance and of monopolising privileges to the disadvantage of other communities. Hizbullah stressed that the Christians should answer the appeal from heaven and have recourse to reason instead of arms; to persuasion instead of sectarianism. Hizbullah encouraged the Christians to review their calculations and know that their interest lies in what they decide, by their own free will, not by what is imposed upon them: "Say: 'O People of the Book, come to an equitable world [kalimat siwa'] between you and us, that we worship none but Allah, do not associate anything with Him and do not set up each other as lords besides Allah' " (3:64). In an attempt to convey Hizbullah's tolerance towards non-Muslims, Z'aytir argued that Prophet Muhammad always placed the Qur'anic verse (3:64) as a header on all the letters he addressed to them. Z'aytir stressed that this conveys the "absolute freedom granted to non-Muslims, freedom that ruptures the chains of slavery, freedom that is based upon human coalescence, intuitive trends, and the spiritual dimension of human existence"[85], i.e. religious and social freedom, but not political freedom, as was explained in the previous section. The Open Letter added, however, if the Christians refuse to adhere to Islam, Hizbullah would not force them to do otherwise, rather it just expects them to respect and honour their covenants with the Muslims and not to aggress against them.[86] Most importantly, Hizbullah stressed in the Open Letter that there is "no compulsion in religion" (2:256).[87]

Z'aytir clarified that Islam rejects dialogue between an oppressed Muslim and an oppressor crusader (political Maronism), especially since these crusaders have been conspiring for centuries against the Muslims with the Zionists. He stressed that it is a well-known fact that anyone who allies himself with the enemies of Islam becomes an enemy of Islam even though he was not classified as such from the beginning. Thus, according to Z'aytir, the friend of my enemy is my enemy: "O believers, do not take the Jews and Christians as friends; some of them are friends of each other. Whoever of you takes them as friends is surely one of them. Allah indeed does not guide the wrongdoers [al-zalimin]" (5:51). He added that in reality the political Maronites do not aspire for dialogue; rather they need allies. As such, dialogue was only a means to reach the contrived end of controlling the Muslims: "Neither the Jews nor the Christians will be pleased with you until you follow their religion. Say: 'Allah's guidance is the [only] guidance'. And were you to follow their desires after the Knowledge that came down to you, you will have no guardian or helper [to save you] from Allah" (2:120). Z'aytir affirmed that the political Maronites do not mind to hold a meeting with all the militia leaders and come up with decisions that call for a political settlement, which would stress upholding, what they call, 'legitimacy' and 'constitutionality'. By this the political Maronites deceive the populace, absorb the rising discontent against them, and deceive God: "The devils shall insinuate to their followers to dispute with you; but if you obey them, then you will surely be polytheists" (6:121). He concluded by posing a rhetorical question, namely that since the political Maronites are responsible for the destruction of Lebanon, then why should anybody negotiate with them, and on what?[88]

Hizbullah echoed the Open Letter's views towards the Christians through its political declarations. In 1986 Hizbullah issued a political declaration stating that it does not find itself obliged to conduct dialogue with political Maronism that is collaborating with is enemies; rather Hizbullah opens its heart and extends its hands to dialogue and understanding with the Christians and other religious confessions based on the unshakable conviction of enmity to the USA and Israel.[89]

2.4   Hizbullah's stance towards Israel

In one of its earliest political declarations, Hizbullah affirmed its stance of the continuity of the struggle of the Islamic Resistance until the obliteration of Israel, a notion upon which Hizbullah based and erected its entire military, political, intellectual, and ideological resistance to the Israeli occupation. The declaration stressed that the Zionist entity's presence is illegal; it has no right to exist, no right in the land of Palestine, and no Arab or Muslim has the right to grant Israel any recognition or legitimacy.[90] Hizbullah declared that its enmity to Israel is a banner raised against Zionism for the Liberation of Jerusalem[91] and all the holy sites.[92] Sayyid Ibrahim Amin al-Sayyid indicated a high degree of concordance between Musa al-Sadr's discourse and rhetoric and that of Khumayni. Amin al-Sayyid argued that there is no difference between Khumayni's saying that "Israel should be wiped out existence" and al-Sadr's statements that "Israel is the absolute evil"; "Fight the Israeli's with your teeth and nails"; and "The honour and dignity of Jerusalem would only be liberated by the [Muslim] believers".[93]

Hizbullah's Open letter affirmed its ideological position of enmity towards Israel springs from "a political-ideological and historical awareness that the Zionist entity is aggressive from its inception, and built on lands wrested from their owners, at the expense of the rights of the Muslim people".[94] Other political declarations reiterated that Israel's very existence is rooted in "racist, colonialist Western expansionist ideology that aims at raping Muslim land". Hizbullah emphasized that the Zionist entity is a colonial settler state that was enabled and supported by Western colonial powers that artificially created it by raping Palestinian land, annihilating, and uprooting the Palestinian state and people in order to safeguard Western interests in the Middle East. Hizbullah stressed that the Western colonial powers were instrumental in the establishment of Israel and continuously supported it in order to become their Western outpost. Hizbullah added that the Zionist entity is an artificial expansionist entity that aims at devouring the whole region from the Nile to the Euphrates, not only militarily, but also politically and economically. As such, Israeli hegemony through Western penetration poses a great threat to the Muslim presence in the Middle East. Hizbullah grounded its firm ideology on the destruction of Israel and the total liberation of historic Palestine. Finally, the three political declarations clarified Hizbullah's ideology of rejecting any negotiations with Israel that might lead to a settlement of the 'so-called' Arab-Israeli conflict.[95]

In line with its political declarations and statements that conveyed Hizbullah's ideology of resistance against Israel's occupation and oppression, in the Open Letter, Hizbullah called for the death of Israel, referred to it as "occupied Palestine", and called for the restoration/reinstatement of the 1948 Palestine. The Open Letter added, Hizbullah enjoins the international community to adopt a resolution to fire Israel from the UN because it is an "illegitimate-rapist entity, which is opposed to humanity at large".[96] In this regard, Z'aytir claimed that the demise of non-Muslim regimes is necessarily followed by the annihilation of Israel. According to him, that would ensue the downfall of all the powers and the international organizations that support Israel as well as the satellite regimes that collaborate with it (such as political Maronism).[97]

Although Hizbullah concentrated its attack on the Zionists, in the Open Letter Hizbullah hardly mentions the Jews, "You shall find the most hostile people to the believers to be the Jews and the polytheists" (5:82).[98] Hizbullah's political declaration on the occasion of its first martyrdom operation referred to both the Jews and the Zionists: "the operation of *Khaybar*, the operation that spread terror in the heart of the Zionist enemy [Israel], convulsed its foundations and military balance, and signified a great historical conquest against the Jews..."[99] According to Sayyid Abbas, the choice of the name is telling because it is based on the historical precedent of enmity to the Jews. Sayyid Abbas explained that the Constitution of Medina granted non-Muslims full partnership in the political structure based on the essential components of freedom, justice, and equity. As such, the Jews were part and parcel of the political structure and subject to it. They were even allowed to fight side by side with the Muslims and take part in peace making. Sayyid Abbas stressed that although the Jews were accorded a high status in the Constitution of Medina, they broke the covenant with the Prophet, so he had to fight them because they had to submit to what God has revealed. He quoted the Qur'an to substantiate his claim: "Those, who each time you make a covenant with them, break it, and do not fear God. So, if you should come up with them in the war, scatter[100] them with those behind them, that perchance they may pay heed. And should you fear treachery from any people, throw back their treaty to them in like manner. Allah does not like the treacherous. Let not the unbelievers think that they can escape [Us]. They will never be able to escape. And make ready for them whatever you can of fighting men and horses, to terrify thereby the enemies of Allah and your enemy, as well as others besides them whom you do know, but Allah knows well" (8:56-60).

Sayyid Abbas explained that Prophet Muhammad's army repeated the following slogan when they were storming the gate of Khaybar: "*Khaybar, Khaybar ya yahud, jaysh Muhammad qadimun* [Khaybar, Khaybar you Jews, the army of Muhammad is coming]". He added that Hizbullah replaced the anti-Judaism, which was prevalent at the time of the Prophet, with Imam Khumayni's political ideology of anti-Zionism: "*Khaybar, Khaybar ya sahyun,* Hizbullah *qadimun* [Khaybar, Khaybar you Zionists, Hizbullah is coming]".[101] Sayyid Abbas stressed that from this perspective Hizbullah refuses to negotiate with Israel because historically the Jews were treacherous and did not honour their covenants, and because the Jews in occupied Palestine are rapists of the land and Zionists who will never be accorded any legitimacy by Hizbullah whatsoever.[102]

However, in *al-'Ahd* Hizbullah clarified that from an Islamic legal perspective it considers the Jews as "people of the Book" who should be accorded their religious, legal, cultural, and political rights as stipulated in Islamic law. Hizbullah rationalized this stance by analogy with the way the Prophet treated the Jews under the Constitution of Medina and the way the Islamic Republic treats its Jewish citizens. Hizbullah resorts to Khumayni, who clarified that unlike the Jews, the Zionists are neither "people of religion" nor *dhimmis*. Khumayni added that the Islamic Republic stands firm against the Zionists who are driven by a political ideology that exploits Judaism and despises all other races. Khumayni stressed that if the Muslims and Palestinians defeat the Zionist Entity, then only the Zionists (all Jewish Israelis) would have the same fate as the Shah, while the rest of the Jews, who live in the Arab and Muslim countries, would not be harmed and would be accorded the same rights as any other populace or race.[103] As such, Hizbullah clarified that its enmity is not towards the Jews as a race or religion, rather towards the Zionists who have raped Palestinian land and established their Zionist Entity.[104]

In line with its political declarations, Hizbullah reiterated in the Open Letter that it rejects the "land for peace" principle, and does not acknowledge any truce, ceasefire, or peace treaty with Israel, the "enemy". Hizbullah's Open Letter refused to acknowledge the 'so called' Arab/Palestinian-Israeli conflict and totally rejected any negotiations[105] or peace talks with Israel since it would grant legitimacy to its "Zionist occupation of Palestine". Hizbullah blasted the Lebanese government for negotiating with Israel considering the negotiators as enemies who are committing "grave treason" towards Hizbullah: "the negotiations with the enemy can only be regarded as a conspiracy aiming at acknowledging the Zionist occupation and according it legitimacy as well as privilege on the crimes it had committed against the oppressed in Lebanon..." The Open Letter added that Hizbullah would not cease its struggle "until the Zionists evacuate the occupied lands, which is seen as a step in the right direction to obliterate them from the face of the earth".[106]

As conveyed in *al-'Ahd*, Hizbullah's standard and official position concerning the Israeli-Palestinian conflict demands the return of all Palestine, namely, 1948 Palestine, from the Jordan river till the Mediterranean Sea, and the repatriation of all the Jews who came after the 1916 Sykes-Picot Agreement, which divided the Middle East among the British and French after the demise of the Ottoman Empire and placed Palestine under British Mandate.[107]

2.5 Views on the Unity of the Muslims

Hizbullah's political ideology discussed the inner and outer causes of discord (*fitna*) among the Muslims. The Open Letter warned against the imperialist discord that is threatening to rapture the whole Muslim world. It blamed the "devilish conspiracy" of the imperialist-colonialist nations for killing and concealing righteous *'ulama* – such as Musa al-Sadr, Ayatullah Murtada Mutahhari[108], and Ayatullah Sayyid Muhammad Baqir al-Sadr[109] – who opposed its "aggressive plans" and were calling for Islamic unity in order to thwart Western conspiracy and ward off its venomous discord that is being disseminated among the Muslims.[110]

Z'aytir admonished that inner strife would lead to destroying the most important battlements and bulwarks that stand up against the plummeting of the Muslim society into discord and conspiracies. He warned that every individual should stay alert and ward off discord that the political Maronites are investing a lot in to materialize, so that its unjust system would remain in power.[111] According to him, the "despicable" political Maronites should be annihilated; only then fighting would stop after getting rid of all the conspirers: (4:91).[112] According to Kurani, the unity of the Muslims would be a grave disaster on the Zionist entity and the Great Satan and their allies. That is why, they are adamant in sowing the seeds of discord by way of provoking internal conflicts among the Muslims so that they constantly battle each other.[113]

Fadlallah emphasized that any local collaboration with Israel and the US creates *fitna*, urging the Muslim populace to be responsible and to mobilize against the perpetrators of *fitna* in order to safeguard Muslim existence and future. He also stressed that *fitna* can also result from partnership with political Maronism, the ruling elite. Therefore, Fadlallah cautioned that the seeds of *fitna* should be uprooted so that the Muslims could forge their unity.[114] Z'aytir clarified that all the conspiracies, even those that seem to be coming from within the Muslims, are the product of the West.[115]

In spite of Hizbullah's avoidance of the issue, the era of the political ideology was replete with examples of Sunni-Shi'a discord. Unlike the mainstream Hizbullah official discourse, Kurani admits that the conspiracies did not only originate from the West, but they were also contrived from within the Muslims. Kurani refers to the "Zionist-political Maronite conspiracy", aided by the Muslim feudal leaders who were part of political Maronism, to annihilate the Palestinian refugees in Lebanon and subdue the Muslims by mobilizing them, in general, and the Shi'ites, in particular, against the Palestinians.[116] Kurani is referring to the 1985-88 War of the Camps between the Sunni Palestinian refugees in Lebanon, on the one hand, and *AMAL* and the Shi'a defecting brigades of the Lebanese Army, on the other. Hizbullah condemned the war as an imperialist conspiracy against the unity of the *umma* and Hizbullah's cadres, at times, intervened on the Palestinian side or provided humanitarian support for the camps.[117] Other examples of *fitna* coming from within was the notorious 1988-1990 *AMAL*-Hizbullah control war[118] as well as Hizbullah's control war with the secular leftist political parties[119] who were fighting side by side with *AMAL* and Hizbullah against political Maronism and the Israeli occupation.

In response to discord, Hizbullah stressed the unity of the Muslims. It depicted itself as an "*umma* tied to the Muslims in every part of the world by a strong ideological-doctrinal, and political bond" of Islam. Hizbullah stressed that it is an indivisible part of the Muslim *umma* sharing its wails and woes under the guidance of the supreme jurisconsultant, the Rahbar, Imam Khumayni. Hizbullah stated that it was inspired by the idea of the unity of the Muslims from Imam Khumayni who declared the week commemorating the birth of the Prophet as the week of Islamic unity[120] and emphasized the defence of the rights of all the Muslims.[121] Hizbullah symbolized this unity to a bulwark that ruptures the conspiracies of the oppressors and arrogant nations.[122]

Hizbullah emphasized that the awareness and vigilance of the Muslims should fend off discord and invest in unity, which is God's injunction: "And hold fast to Allah's bond [His religion], all of you, and do not fall apart. And remember Allah's grace upon you; how you were enemies, then He united your hearts [by becoming Muslims] so that you have become, by His grace, brethren. You were on the brink of the pit of Fire, but He saved you from it" (3:102); and "Those who have made divisions in their religion and become sects, thou art not of them in anything" (6:159).[123] Ayatullah Fadlallah called for the unity of the Muslims stressing that the Qur'an cautions against *fitna*.[124] According to him the Qur'anic usage of fitna connotes a state of chaos among the believers or populace that leads to psychological and mental suffering, hardship, and chastisement.[125] Z'aytir exhorted the Muslims to avoid discord and urged them not to be the fuel that would burn them and burn their countries.[126] He stressed that discord should be contained in its early stages or else it would spread like fire in hay that can hardly be contained.[127] Prophet Muhammad has precisely warned the Muslims not to engage in or help spreading discord since they would be labelled as infidels and would have a *jahiliyya* death.[128]

The Open Letter called on all Muslims to be united against the oppressors, the imperialists, and Zionists by following the stipulations of the righteous *'ulama*, and not corrupt state jurists since they would deflect from the teachings of Islam and follow the interests of the Great Satan and Little Satan. Most importantly, Hizbullah called on the Muslim *'ulama* to be united stressing the dangers of the Sunni-Shi'a discord (*fitna*), which the imperialists and oppressors are trying to fuel in order to divide and conquer the Muslim *umma*: "Be aware of the malignant colonial discord [*fitna*] that aims at rupturing your unity in order to spread sedition among you and enflame Sunni-Shi'a sectarian feelings... Do not allow the policy of 'divide and rule' to be practiced among you".[129] Z'aytir added that the crusaders were contriving to rapture and disintegrate the Muslims by spreading discord and enmity among them. He stressed that the enemies of Islam know very well that the Islamic unity renders the Muslims a superior power that can impose its will on the ruling minority governments, and by extension force the imperialists and colonizers to comply to the Muslim populace, which, by far, comprise a majority.[130]

Hizbullah affirmed that the jurisprudential particularities of the Sunnis and Shi'ites should be respected, but this does not mean that there could not be a unity in the political-ideological stance towards Israel and the US, for instance. Therefore, Hizbullah added, that the political-ideological unity of the Lebanese Sunni and Shi'a should be directed against the Western onslaught, spearheaded by the US and Israel on all Muslims.[131] Kurani stressed that the unity of the Muslims in Lebanon means the unity of both the Sunni and Shi'ite *'ulama* as well as their populace as a first step in broadening this unity to encompass all the Muslims in the *umma*.[132]

Hizbullah's leading cadres such as Hasan Nasrallah, Husayn al-Musawi, and Shaykh Subhi al-Tufayli highlighted the importance of the unity of the Muslims on a global level through an all-encompassing Islamic state.[133] In addition, they stressed the Islamic doctrine of the consciousness of unification in the Muslim *umma*. Thus, for Hizbullah the unity of all Muslims is a legitimate duty incumbent upon them in order to ward off the discord of infidelity (*fitnat al-takfir*).[134] Z'aytir argued that the erection of a global Islamic state would ultimately lead to the unity and dignity of the Muslims after being ruptured by desires, nationalities, and sects. As such the most important function of Islamic government is to unify the *umma*.[135]

2.6   Hizbullah and the West, the US in particular

Hizbullah's political ideology towards the West was influenced by Imam Khumayni, the *Rahbar*, who repeatedly stated that the US, "the mother of all vice", is behind all the calamities that have been rupturing the Muslim world.[136] Hizbullah unequivocally conveyed its enmity towards the US and Israel in many of its political declarations. Hizbullah labelled the US Administration as infidel stressing the centrality of Hizbullah's struggle with the US and Israel, taking pride in "breaking the American-Zionist arm" under the attacks of the oppressed Muslim warriors (Hizbullah's Islamic Resistance). These attacks led to the US's humiliating military defeat and its withdrawal, along with its NATO allies, from Lebanon. The declaration added that Hizbullah reminds the Muslims with an important saying of the great leader of the Muslim *umma*, Imam Khumayni, who said that even if the US and Israel declared "there is no God but Allah", this call would not be accepted, and the Muslims would continue their struggle against them till they crush the US hegemony and uproot the cancerous gland (Israel), which is implanted in the midst of the Muslims.[137]

The Open Letter considered the US, Israel, France and NATO as its basic enemies in the Middle East. It stressed uprooting the US's and Israeli vice from the Middle East, blaming both for the calamities, injustices, aggression and humiliation that have been rupturing the Muslim *umma*. Further, Hizbullah chastised the "reactionary" Arab regimes that are corroborating with the aforementioned countries.[138]

Like Iranian political ideology, the enmity to the US and Israel has been a motto constantly repeated by Hizbullah's leaders and cadres where the US has been depicted as the Great Satan and Israel as the Little Satan: 'death to America' and 'death to Israel'. Sayyid Ibrahim Amin Al-Sayyid contended that the Qur'an enjoins the Muslims to fight the Great Satan (US) and the Little Satan (Israel): "And make ready for them whatever you can of fighting men and horses, to terrify thereby the enemies of Allah and your enemy" (8: 60).[139]

Fadlallah cautioned against the dangers of colonialism and imperialism, branding the West as the first and foremost enemy of the Muslim world. He blamed the West, especially the US and Israel, for the misfortunes that are rupturing the Middle East and Lebanon. He stressed that the face off between the West and Islam is mainly due to the Palestinian question.[140] Fadlallah warned the Muslims from heeding to or compromising with imperialism since their attitude would be regarded as un-Islamic.[141] Therefore, the only salvation to the Muslim populace is the founding of socio-political movements (such as Hizbullah), which exercise the ideology of resistance and revolution, in an attempt to rid the Muslims from imperialist domination. According to Fadlallah, this could be accomplished only when the Muslims bond together raising the banner of Islam and freedom.[142]

Hizbullah stated in its Open Letter that it embraced many principles of Iran's political ideology. Following Iran, Hizbullah viewed itself as a movement, under the guidance of Imam Khumayni, struggling against the injustices of imperialism and colonialism that are hostile to Islam.[143] Hizbullah stressed that it was influenced by Imam Khumayni's revolutionary notion of no East, no West, only Islam i.e. an Islamic Republic (*La sharqiyya wa la gharbiyya, innama jumhuriyya Islamiyya*). Thus, no East, no West, rather only Islam embodies man's renaissance because "It is kindled from a blessed olive tree, neither of the East nor the West. Its oil will almost shine, even if no fire has touched it. Light upon light, Allah guides to His light whomever He pleases..." (24:35).[144] Hizbullah affirmed that its goals were "to save Lebanon from its dependence upon East and West, to put an end to foreign occupation, and to adopt a regime freely wanted by the people of Lebanon".[145]

In *Al-'Ahd*, Hizbullah furnishes its understanding of the political-ideological content of Khumayni's slogan of: "No East no West, only Islam". According to Hizbullah, the main motivation and the essence of the Islamic Revolution is not political and social, rather the holy matrimony between cultural and religious life. Hizbullah adds that this cultural-religious fibre has been one of the principal pillars of the Muslim community since its early foundation. In order to substantiate its claim, Hizbullah quotes Ayatullah Murtada Mutahhari who stressed that not all revolutions erupt because of exploitation, deprivation, poverty, alienation, and subjugation. Mutahhari added that it is also not certain whether appealing to the government or engaging in civil disobedience are the driving shafts of every revolutionary movement. According to Hizbullah these are only means; the end is Islam.[146]

Hizbullah questions the real motivation behind Western and Westernised (Arab) revolutionary political ideologies. Hizbullah clarifies that its criticism against the West is by no means limited to capitalism, imperialism, and colonialism; rather it encompasses all secular ideologies including those of the left-wing leanings such as socialism and communism. Hizbullah criticises Western political ideologies as being grounded in materialism, while the Islamic Revolution's pioneering achievement is that it aimed at firmly establishing the Islamic and cultural identity of the Muslim community. According to Hizbullah, this is where the Islamic Revolution's cultural authenticity lies, and this is what the party is endeavouring to emulate. Hizbullah purports, from this perspective the Islamic Revolution's cutting edge is its original curriculum, strategy, and programs, which do not owe anything to the West, neither from the stance of its liberal democratic ideologies nor from the perspective of the Marxist ideology. Again quoting Mutahhari, Hizbullah argues that the conflation is between the Islamic Revolution, which regards Islam as the end, and revolutionary Islam, which considers revolution and strife (nidal) as the end, while Islam is the means.[147]

According to Hizbullah, Khumayni's slogan of rectifying and reforming oneself before rectifying and reforming others summarises a lot of the political-ideological principles of the Islamic Revolution. For instance, Hizbullah contends that in the West a revolution is usually delineated by a coup d'état, by strife against imperialism, by developing the productive sectors, by a quest for social equality, and maybe cultural independence. Hizbullah stresses that all of these dimensions are present in the Islamic Revolution, but they only comprise its means since struggle against the Shah's arbitrary power as well as strife against tyrannical-oppressive imperialism do not define the Islamic Revolution. Rather, the important dimension is to reconsolidate Islam by the founding of an Islamic government (hukuma Islamiyya), not only from a cultural dimension, but also from a socio-political, and most importantly, the spiritual dimension of Islam since Islam is holistic and all-encompassing in its orientation.[148]

2.7 The Banner of *Jihad* and Martyrdom

2.7.1 *Smaller military jihad and greater jihad: Practicing greater jihad before smaller military jihad*

Sayyid Ibrahim Amin Al-Sayyid stressed the uniqueness of Hizbullah's political ideology that is grounded in the Islamic prescription of smaller military *jihad* as a philosophy of resistance against the occupation and the oppression of the Zionist entity.[149] In addition, Hizbullah preached smaller military *jihad* as an obligatory duty against the oppression of political Maronism, the remnants of the crusaders, who made it incumbent upon themselves to crush Islam and the Muslims.[150]

In the Open Letter, Hizbullah distinguished between smaller and greater *jihad*, but not in considerable detail. Hizbullah argued that it took the lead of the Prophet in austerity, the passion to ascend to heaven, conducted martyrdom in the way of God, and engaged in smaller military *jihad* against the enemies of Islam, most notably the "rapist Zionist entity" and the Great Satan. Hizbullah's reference to Imam Khumayni's repeated emphasis on the need to rectify, reform, and refine the self, before rectifying reforming, and refining others and the world at large[151] is a direct reference to his argument on greater *jihad* in his book that bears the same title.[152]

Hizbullah amplified its distinction between smaller and greater *jihad* in an article in *al-'Ahd*[153], where Imam Khumayn's statement of refining the self before refining others is repeated and born out through an analytical exposition. Hizbullah contended that Khumayni's statement summarises a lot of the political-ideological concepts that the Islamic Revolution rests upon. Hizbullah stressed that the Qur'anic understanding of the word *jihad* does not always denote holy war (smaller military *jihad*), but could also connote the effort exerted to accomplish the duties of the believer (greater *jihad*). Hizbullah added that the freedom fighter (*mujahid*) who is willing to engage in smaller *jihad* has first to build up internally his self[154] through a process of perpetual, non-abating *jihad*, in conformity with what Imam Khumyni has said, namely that the great powers (East and West) fear Islam because it builds up an ethically and morally complete (*mutakamil*) holistic-coalescent-monolithic individual, who is capable of striking a balance between spiritual, intellectual and cognitive aspects on the one hand, and emotional, physical, and psychological aspects, on the other hand, thus controlling his inner self.

In the same article, Hizbullah explains that smaller *jihad* is struggle with the external enemies of Islam. Hizbullah stresses that smaller *jihad* is either fighting in battle or generous self-sacrifice (martyrdom) originating internally from the self i.e. greater *jihad*. Hizbullah clarifies that smaller military *jihad* is based upon the external struggle with the enemies of Islam, while greater *jihad* is struggle with the self in order to nourish the soul. As Ayatullah Mutahhari had stated after the victory of the Islamic Revolution in April 1979 that the danger that surrounds the Islamic Republic lies inside the selves of the Iranian people (greater *jihad*), rather than being an external threat. Hizbullah broadened the horizon of its argument on greater *jihad* emphasizing that the distinguishing traits of society and the development of good morals are things that could be put to practice, through exercising concepts such as honour, piety, virtue, trustworthiness, chastity, probity, diffidence, assertion, integrity in honouring oaths and commitments, rectitude, self-sacrifice, kindness, justice, mercy, sharing one's fate and caring for others, and upholding human rights.[155] According to Hizbullah, these concepts, which are the product of the vigilant conscience of the individual, run against personal benefit and individual egoism. Thus, greater *jihad* could be practiced but it needs a perpetual process of training, building, and refining the self to exercise temperance.[156]

Ayatullah Fadlallah portrayed the importance of greater *jihad* arguing that Islam is the religion of perpetual, non-abating *jihad*, on all levels and at all fronts, whose objective is to build the individual. Islam aims to achieve the principles of dignity and liberty from all sorts of imperialism and slavery. He emphasized that the *shari'a* gave prominence to both spiritual and physical *jihad* (smaller military *jihad*).[157]

In turn, Nasrallah termed greater *jihad* as the "power of spiritual progressive ascent". According to him, the practice of greater *jihad* is based upon the principle of obedience to the *faqih* and God as a vital necessity to the implementation of the concept of strict organizational discipline. Nasrallah argued that smaller military *jihad* should only be practiced after mastering greater *jihad*. According to him, the testimony for that is the long list of martyrs who are being taught revolutionary mobilization and mentality (indoctrination) as well as the observance of strict discipline and obedience (*ta'a*) in order to inculcate a certain way of thought that leads to a *mutakamil* individual who is capable of accomplishing two roles: (1) an unforeseen moral-spiritual role (greater *jihad*), and (2) a foreseen material role (smaller military *jihad*). In other words, Nasrallah argued that the ethically and morally complete individual should be moulded in the culture of spiritual *jihad* in order to become ready to engage in smaller military *jihad*. Then Nasrallah specified four domains of smaller military *jihad*: (1) The *jihadi* role has to defend the ideologues and resources of the movement of change (Hizbullah); (2) It has to strike at the enemy's fulcrum and curtail its movement so that it ceases its humiliation of the *umma*; (3) It has to rupture the bulwarks that political Maronism is placing between the people of change (Hizbullah's rank) and the populace of the *umma* (Hizbullah's file); (4) It has to safeguard the accomplishments of revolutionary work that has been realized by the movement of change.

Nasrallah has affirmed that the *jihadi* culture translates itself into a viable revolutionary alternative that offers conducive solutions to the *umma*. He regarded the *jihadi* operations against the US Marines[158] as such an example. According to Nasrallah, the Islamic *jihadi* culture makes the revolutionary alternative a real eventuality to the extent of making the US impotent in facing it, since the *jihadi* culture crushed its morale and forced it to withdraw from the country due to the heavy blows it suffered at the hands of the Lebanese *mujahidin*. He ends up by stressing that the culture of *jihad* opens new horizons to the populace, to the *Rahbar*, and to the *umma* at large so that "it sees with the eyes of God and functions under His care".[159]

2.7.2 *Martyrdom*

Ayatullah Fadlallah regarded martyrdom operations that are conducted by Muslim believers upon the approval and sanctioning of Muslim religious scholars, as religiously sanctioned self-sacrificial defensive *jihadi* acts of resistance against the occupying Zionist enemy. As such Fadlallah defined martyrdom as a legitimate act of resistance viewed as a practical necessity that is conducive to alleviating the suffering caused by the occupying forces and their superior military arsenal. Fadlallah emphasized that martyrdom inculcates the Muslim populace with a sense of collective action, identity, and empowerment that project to the world the plight of the oppressed. Thus, according to him continuous engagement in martyrdom is the only solution to the Zionist violent occupation.[160]

Hizbullah cadres condoned, explained, and justified martyrdom operations both on religious and political-ideological grounds. Shaykh AbdulKarim 'Ubayd, a Hizbullah leading cadre and religious scholar, stressed the religious foundation of martyrdom by arguing that there can be no martyrdom except in the way of God; this unequivocally implies that every martyr would be lifted to Heaven.[161] Sayyid Husayn al-Musawi separated between the martyrdom operations against the Israelis, French, and Americans, on the one hand, and the kidnappings of foreign nationals on the other. He vehemently condemned the latter, but refused to condemn the former.

He buttressed, praised, and blessed martyrdom operations conducted by the resistance and justified them as legitimate defensive *jihadi* acts waged by the oppressed against foreign occupation led by the world oppressors. Husayn al-Musawi regarded those who conducted martyrdom operations as honest and courageous people who fulfilled their patriotic and religious duty. However, he added that Islam prohibits martyrdom operations in the presence of alternative actions that could achieve the same goals as martyrdom.[162]

As its leading cadres argue, Hizbullah's inspiration on the notion of martyrdom originated from Imam Khumayni and Ayatullah Fadlallah[163]. Shaykh Yusuf Da'mush, a Hizbullah religious scholar, stressed that the Hizbullahis consciously and willingly conducted martyrdom operations, as opposed to suicide, under the tutelage of Hizbullah's leaders. The Hizbullahis martyred themselves in the occupying Israeli enemy in accordance with a *fatwa* issued by Imam Khumayni, the *marja' al-taqlid* and *al-waliyy al-faqih*.[164] Sayyid Ibrahim Amin al-Sayyid stressed more the dependence on Khumayni by arguing that the freedom fighters, who devastated the US marines headquarters in Beirut and the Israeli military intelligence headquarters in Tyre[165] by vehicles laden with explosives, martyred themselves in the way of God because Imam Khumayni sanctioned their martyrdom operations, inculcated the spirit of martyrdom and self-sacrifice in their heart and soul, and led them to the hereafter in honour and dignity for their great feat of triumph over Israeli and the American invaders and occupiers.[166] Sayyid Abbas al-Musawi gave the credit to the school of the *Pasdaran*[167] that indoctrinated Lebanese youth to aspire for martyrdom. Therefore, it does not come as a surprise that after a few weeks of the arrival of the *Pasdaran*, a Shi'ite youngster welcomed death with a smiling face while carrying in his car 1.2 tons of TNT.[168] Thus, in line with Imam Khumayni and Ayatullah Fadlallah, Hizbullah's cadres argued that martyrdom is the highest and most extolled form of *Jihad* where the martyr fulfils his political-ideological duty of defeating the enemy and enjoys the fruits of his sacrifices in heaven.

2.7.3   Suicide and martyrdom

In distinguishing between suicide and martyrdom, Fadlallah argued that martyrdom for a Muslim engaged in resisting the enemy is a constant necessity emanating from his own volition, which is taken on the basis of the doctrinal religious and political ideological convictions of the believer. Fadlallah unequivocally stated that Islam regards suicide as a crime[169] since a person is not free to dispose of his own life as he deems fit. He stressed that every person's life is God's property and it is a great transgression to inflict harm on it as well as on others. According to Fadlallah, if a person takes his life or that of others without the endorsement of Muslim religious scholars, he would be punished in the hereafter by being immortalised in hell. He added that suicide, not martyrdom, might be conducted by morally depraved individuals who are suffering from hopelessness, social stress, depression, and despair; suicide is irrational, immoral, and against the very foundations of religion. From this perspective, Fadlallah stressed that the psychological approach[170] to the study of martyrdom that equates martyrdom with suicide is untenable.[171]

3. **Conclusion**

Hizbullah's Open Letter, political declarations, al-'Ahd, as well as the discourse of its leaders and cadres specified the constituents of its political ideology: oppressors and oppressed; Islamic state; relations with Christians, anti-Zionism, pan-Islamism, anti-imperialism, and jihad and martyrdom. Hizbullah employed Qur'anic legitimisation of its political ideology in the form of Qur'anic verses to justify its stance. One can notice that only the first section of the Open letter explicitly refers to Hizbullah's religious ideology: belief in Shi'a Islam, wilayat al-faqih, and jihad in the way of God.

3.1 Oppressors and oppressed

The concept of oppressors and oppressed is central to a proper understanding of Hizbullah's political ideology. Although, Hizbullah seems to employ an exclusivist discourse[172] in which it labels/classifies people according to the Qur'anic classification/dichotomy of Hizbullah (The Party of God) (5:56) or Hizb al-Shaytan (The Party of the Devil) (58: 19), Hizbullah used the Qur'anic term or Islamic expression of oppressed and produced an all-inclusive concept in order to uphold political and social justice. On the face of it, it appears that Hizbullah is using Marxist terminology, which is translated or interpreted in Islamic terms along the lines of economic, political, and social justice, thus producing some kind of "Islamic socialism", as some scholars have claimed.[173]

However, Hizbullah clearly argues in the Open Letter and its political declarations that its friends are the entire world oppressed irrespective of their colour, race, or religion. Hizbullah interpreted and applied the contemporary concept of mustad'af by stressing that it is a Qur'anic concept that came to prominence with the advent of the Islamic Revolution. Hizbullah emphasized that this usage conveys and is in conformity with its identity as an Islamic *jihadi* movement struggling to address and redress the injustices the oppressed suffer from. However, Hizbullah clarified that its usage of the term *mustad'af* is different from the political concept that is used by the socialists to refer to the poor peasants or the proletariat, the Qur'anic concept being more encompassing and holistic in its orientation because it touches upon the existential level of oppression and offers prescriptions and remedies in dealing with the oppressors and warding them off. Hizbullah emphasized that *mustad'afin* applies to the wronged, unjustly treated, tyrannised, and impoverished who cannot own their daily bread, and who are oppressed in their freedom, dignity, and endeavours without any consideration if they are Christians or Muslims. Therefore, Hizbullah's political ideology stresses the universality of the Qur'anic concept – as opposed to the specificity of the Marxist concept – that cuts across class, cultural, and religious cleavages.

Even though Fadlallah is not among the main establishment of Hizbullah, Hizbullah might also have been influenced by his views on oppression. The point of convergence is that both Fadlallah's and Hizbullah's Islamic theory of oppression differs from liberation theology. Although liberation theology places the oppressed, marginalized, discriminated minorities, women, workers, etc. at the centre of its discourse, siding with the oppressed in their struggle for their rights, it does not call for an overall Christianisation of society or aims at establishing a religiously based society and political system. Rather, liberation theology builds on religious sources reinterpreting them for secular-Marxist aims by supporting the struggle of the oppressed "wretched of the earth" for social justice. In spite of that, there seems to be a considerable difference between the two views since Fadlallah's political-ideological legitimisation conveys specificity in his characterisation of oppression that is at variance with Hizbullah, especially his Qur'anic legitimisation, which distinguishes between two groups of the oppressed. It seems as if Fadlallah is insinuating a distinction between negligent; idle oppressed who let grass grow under their feet and do not even exercise persuasive *jihad*, on the one hand, and committed oppressed who mobilize in order to confront their oppressors (smaller military *jihad*) or alter their condition of oppression by emigrating to the Muslim heart land, if they are capable of doing so, on the other.

3.2   Islamic state

The Open Letter, inter alia, classified Hizbullah as a social movement that called for the establishment of an Islamic state[174] in Lebanon modelled along Iran's Islamic Republic. Hizbullah's political ideology advocated an end to political Maronism and rejected any participation in Lebanon's sectarian-confessional political system. In spite of that, Hizbullah's political ideology stressed that it would not impose an Islamic state in Lebanon by coercion, rather Hizbullah would erect an Islamic state, if and only if, the majority of the Lebanese populace demand it and consent to it, since it is necessary to choose a political system in Lebanon by mutual agreement between the Muslims and the Christians. Thus, Hizbullah was inviting others to become part of an Islamic state in Lebanon, refusing to be under the governance of or to co-opt with the un-Islamic Lebanese regime.

The Open letter did not specify the political-ideological content of the Islamic order; rather it only referred to the Islamic state as an ideological doctrine, political order, and mode of governance. However, Z'aytir did outline the most salient traits of the Islamic or Qur'anic government, Islamic state, or Islamic republic. Hizbullah uses these terms interchangeably because it is concerned with instating an Islamic order (*nizam Islami*), and it does not matter which label it gives to it. According to Z'aytir, the Islamic order is based upon practical application of the *shari'a* and divine injunctions; organisation of social, economic, and political relations in order to inculcate social solidarity and disseminate social justice; mutual agreement and trust among the subjects and rulers; and justice, fairness, equity, compassion as well as an equilibrium between rights and duties.

However, Z'aytir's views on the Islamic state were couched in stronger terms than what the Open Letter and other cadres expressed since he stressed the forceful application of God's governance and sovereignty. Z'atir seemed to be much more radical in his political-ideological views than the Hizbullah establishment. This might suggest that he represented a certain militant trend within the party that advocated the establishment of the Islamic state by force to the effect of annihilating the political Maronites. He seemed to be against the too conciliatory, and too compromising attitude of the party. Z'atir's criticism of the Islamic Milieu might be interpreted as an indirect attack on Ayatullah Fadlallah who, according to Z'atir, was not forceful enough in his Islamisation project. Z'atir did not accept Fadlallah's Qur'anic logic of truce/ceasefire (*muhadana*)[175] and the step by step application of Islamisation through a bottom-up process, rather Z'atir called for a violent and radical overthrow of the regime through a top-down process even if the balance of power does not favour the Islamists. As mentioned in the previous chapter, Hizbullah adopted the idea of Islamic order from Imam Khumayni, being influenced by his views on *wilayat al-faqih*. Hizbullah's anathematising of the Lebanese political system might also be attributed to Imam Khumayni's views.[176] However, in practice, the official Hizbullah establishment did not heed to Z'aytir's views.

In its Islamic order, Hizbullah maintained the *dhimmis* category, and as such, Hizbullah stressed that the common grounds between *ahl al-dhimma* and Muslims are the social values of mutual tolerance, respect, brotherhood, and solidarity. On this basis, Hizbullah accorded the Christians their human freedom i.e. social and religious freedom, but not political freedom. Thus, contrary to the Prophetic tradition that granted non-Muslims partnership in the political structure, Hizbullah's tolerance or inclusiveness clearly excludes Christians from political life. Hizbullah seems to imply that tolerance is the responsibility of the "majority" and integration is the responsibility of the "minority".

Most likely Hizbullah's treatment of the Christians as *dhimmis* is a specific interpretation of the Prophet's political constitution of Medina, which was also inspired by the Islamic Republic's constitution. In addition, possibly Hizbullah might have also been influenced by Sayyid Muhammad Husayn Fadlallah who, grounding his argument on the Qur'an, argued that the Muslim stance towards the Christians is anchored upon the horizon of mutual co-existence, cooperation, and dialogue that should be based on points of convergence and common grounds that all parties agree upon.[177]

3.3   Relations with Christians

Hizbullah's political ideology was selective in its treatment of the Lebanese Christians. Although on face value it appears that Hizbullah's call was addressed to all Christians, in reality Hizbullah shunned any contact with political Maronism, Maronites, and any collaborator with Israel. Though Hizbullah had some low-level contacts with the Christians living in its constituencies, nonetheless no high-level or tangible dialogue materialised between Hizbullah and the Christians. In spite of Hizbullah's exhortation of the Christians to convert to Islam, it did not impose this conversion by force; rather Hizbullah applied its theory of tolerance to those Christians living in the areas it controlled as well as to other Christians as long as they are not treacherous or aggressive.

Some writers claimed that Hizbullah was abiding by a political ideology that was not only intolerant towards the Christians, but also Hizbullah was accused of imposing its will and its Islam on all the Lebanese from different denominations, sects, and religions.[178] I do acknowledge that there appears to be a certain tension between Hizbullah's two propositions: (1) Hizbullah's intention not to impose Islam and its coercing the Christians to adhere to it its call; and (2) Hizbullah's mission of establishing an Islamic order. Maybe the confusion has to do with Z'atir's denial of the need to convert Christians and the Hizbullah establishment's call for conversion through peaceful means. Nevertheless, both Z'atir and the Hizbullah establishment agreed that there should be "no compulsion in religion" (2:256) and an "equitable world" or common grounds (3:64) should guide the relationship between the Muslims and Christians.

3.4 Anti-Zionism

Hizbullah's anti-Zionist political ideology seems to often conflate Jewish identity with Zionist ideology, thus equating Jews with Zionists. Also, there seems to be a contradiction between Hizbullah's views concerning the people of the book and how it treats the Jews in Israel. However, the Open Letter and the political declarations clearly stated that Hizbullah equated all Israelis with Zionists. Further, Hizbullah's al-'Ahd and the discourse of its leaders clarified that it does not discriminate against the Jews as a race or religion and it would accord them their human and civil rights as the constitution of Medina had done, in spite of their discouraging Qur'anic and historical precedents of treachery, hypocrisy, and breaking the covenant with the Prophet and fighting him at Khaybar.

Hizbullah's doctrinal behaviour is also warranted by Khumayni's ideology that distinguished between the Jews living in Muslim lands under Muslim rule and the "Zionists" in Israel. Simply stated, Hizbullah's political ideology considers that there are no Jews in Israel, rather only Zionists. That is why the Zionists can be driven out and their country annihilated. From this stance, Hizbullah unleashed its venom towards the "Zionist Entity" that has occupied Palestine by military force. Hizbullah characterizes Israel as aggressive, racist, expansionist, anti-humanist, cancerous glad instated by Western colonial powers in the Muslim heartland. Hizbullah's political ideology conveyed no recognition of Israel, called for wiping it out of existence, and stipulated a continual commitment to the liberation of Palestine. This political-ideological stance mirrors that of the Islamic Revolution: "Today Iran, and tomorrow Palestine" i.e. the liberation of Iran from the Shah would be followed by the liberation of Palestine from the Zionists. From a principal and doctrinal perspective, Hizbullah's political ideology seeks to restore

Arab-Muslim historical rights in Palestine and is totally against any ceasefire, truce, land for peace, peace negotiations, or normalisation of relations with Israel.

3.5   Pan-Islamism

Hizbullah's political ideology heeded Imam Khumayni's call for pan-Islamism, especially in the wake of what he termed the worldwide conspiracy against the unity of the Muslims. Hizbullah's political ideology has always called for unity, both in the Islamic and domestic fronts, in order to avoid the dangers of discord. In its Open Letter, Hizbullah allotted section 22, entitled "God is With the Unity of the Muslims" advocating pan-Islamism in order to render special attention to the dangers of discord, stressing a revolutionary distinction between upright Muslim religious scholars and the corrupt ones, or state jurists who follow the injunctions of the imperialist colonizers by applying the precept of divide and conquer. Hizbullah based its call for the unity of Muslims and warding off *fitna* on a host of Qur'anic verses: (3:103); (6:159); (2:191); (2:193); (8:28); (8:73).

On the basis of what has been presented in section 2.5, it seems that the conspiracy theory has governed a lot of Hizbullah's visions. That is why Hizbullah considered any political or military dispute between Sunnis and Shi'as as an oppressor's-colonizer's conspiracy aimed at spreading discord and dissention among the Muslims. Thus, Hizbullah blames internal discord on the West. Hizbullah has repeatedly warned against this and called upon the Muslims to uphold common grounds that ultimately lead to enforcing the power of the Muslims in the face of the mounting challenges facing the *umma*.

Hizbullah's discourse is general in the sense that it does not give specific examples on Sunni-Shi'ite disagreements, since this would lead to discord, when Hizbullah's aim is the unity of all the Muslims. However, Hizbullah's efforts to unify the Muslims remained on a theoretical level as a kind of persuasive smaller *jihad* by the tongue and heart, rather than real Sunni-Shi'a unity, mainly due to mutually branding each other with infidelity (*khutab al-takfir*) and the disintegration that the Islamic community was passing through. Nevertheless, in the local Lebanese context "The Union of Muslim 'Ulama"[179] has covered some grounds on the way to unifying Islamic work among the Sunni and Shi'a *'ulama* as well as their respective populace. Hizbullah argued that respecting the jurisprudential differences among the Sunni and Shi'ites does not preclude unity and cooperation among the Sunni and Shi'a Islamists on common political-ideological concepts such as anti-imperialism, anti-Zionismism, "the liberation of Jerusalem", etc. In fact, such political-ideological concepts forged a unity of interests and common goals between Hizbullah and Sunni Islamists such as the Lebanese *Harakat Al-Tawhid Al-Islamiyya* and *Al-Jama'a Al-Islamiyya*,[180] as well as Palestinian Sunni Islamists, which all received material support from Iran.

3.6   Anti-imperialism

Hizbullah stressed that it is exercising its legitimate right of defending the rights and the dignity of the *umma* by confronting its basic enemies: the US, France, and Israel. Imam Khumayni clarified that the sensitivity of the Iranians is not towards the American people, rather the American government.[181] Thus, Hizbullah is against Westoxification[182] and does not practice xenophobia (antipathy to the West and East). Nevertheless, Hizbullah's Westoxification is rooted in its hatred of the US Administration, not the US people.

Hizbullah employed a specific reading of Khumayni since it took one aspect, namely reforming the individual before reforming others, and integrated it in another debate as a critique of Western concepts of revolution. By this Hizbullah intended to convey the superiority to the Islamic order – that is holistic concerned with all aspects of life, especially the spiritual dimension – over the materialist outlook of the East and West, socialism and capitalism. Hizbullah did not address the assumption that Western capitalism is rooted in specific cultural and societal traits.

Thus, Hizbullah's political-ideology claims a sense of moral superiority vis-à-vis the West. By building a holistic-coalescent individual, Hizbullah purports that the project of the Islamic Revolution does not aim at modernizing Islam, rather Islam aspires for Islamising modernity, which poses a binary threat to materialism and rationalism that are found in the West. According to Hizbullah, this is what Islam has to offer in response.

3.7   *Jihad* and martyrdom

Hizbullah distinguished between smaller military *jihad* and greater *jihad*, relegating the role of the former to defensive *jihad* in the battlefield against the enemies of Islam and the latter to the internal struggle against one's self. Hizbullah practiced smaller military *jihad* against the local enemies of Islam, the political Maronites, as well as against the regional and international enemies – Israel, France, and the US. Hizbullah emphasized the ideological-political dimension of greater *jihad* whereby mere membership in the Hizbullah amounts to engaging in greater *jihad* in the generic, overall encompassing metaphorical sense of membership in the community of 'the son's of Hizbullah's *umma*'. By this Hizbullahis would have accomplished their legitimate political responsibility (*taklif*). Therefore, Hizbullah amplified greater *jihad* to encompass all stages of membership in Hizbullah's activity. Employing a high-level theological discourse, Nasrallah distinguished between greater *jihad* and smaller *jihad* arguing along the lines of Khumayni that greater *jihad* should be practiced before engaging in smaller military *jihad*. Based on Khumayni and Fadlallah, it could be inferred that Hizbullah's conception of greater *jihad*, as spiritual-transcendental *jihad*, aims at constructing a distinct Islamic identity of the individual.

Hizbullah consciously extolled martyrdom as a religiously sanctioned legitimate defensive *jihadi* act conducted in order to face a superior invading or occupying army equipped with high-tech arsenal. While Hizbullah viewed the reward of martyrdom as eternal life in heaven, it vilified suicide as a ticket to hell in a moment of despair, hopelessness, and frustration. Hizbullah legitimised its martyrdom operations on the basis of religious edicts and reiterated it prohibition of conducting them if the same objectives would be realised by smaller military *jihad*.

4 **Primacy to Political Program** (1991 to 2005)

Introduction

This chapter presents Hizbullah's political program as formulated over the period 1991 to 2005. It is compiled from and described on the basis of the available sources: Hizbullah's 1992, 1996, 2000, and 2005 parliamentary election programs; its "Views and Concepts" of June 20, 1997; its "Statement of purpose" of March 20, 1998; its 1996 and 2004 municipal elections programs; its August 2004 "Identity and Goals";[1] and Hizbullah's political declarations and the discourse of its rank and file over the period 1991 to 2005. The quoted discourse in this chapter refers mainly to Hizbullah's leaders and cadres: Sayyid Abbas al-Musawi[2], Shaykh Na'im Qasim[3], Sayyid Hasan Nasrallah[4], Nayef Krayyem[5], Bilal N'im[6], Ali Fayyad[7], Hajj Muhammad Ra'd[8], Hajj Husayn Shami[9], Sayyid Nawwaf al-Musawi[10], and Sayyid Hashim Safiyyeddine[11].

I start by giving a prelude to Hizbullah's 1991 political program and the debates for participation in the 1992 parliamentary elections. Then I present a nine-point thematic exposition of the constituents of Hizbullah's political program as conveyed in the abovementioned sources: (2.1) Hizbullah's standpoint towards the oppressors and oppressed; (2.2) its perspectives on the Islamic state (*al-dawla al-Islamiyya*); (2.3) its dialogue with the Lebanese Christians; (2.4) Hizbullah's jurisprudential stipulations of parliamentary, municipal, and governmental work; (2.5) Hizbullah's socio-economic program: its Non-Governmental Organizations (NGOs) and civil institutions; (2.6) Hizbullah as a nationalist Lebanese political party; (2.7) its stance towards Syria and Iran; (2.8) its perspective on Israel; and (2.9) its views on *jihad* and martyrdom. This will be followed by a summary of the basic constituents of Hizbullah's political program.

1. Prelude to Hizbullah's political program

1.1 Background to Hizbullah's 1991 political program

As mentioned in the history chapter, the Ta'if Agreement of October 1989 was the closest thing or a substitute to a peace conference, which materialised in the ratification of Lebanon's new constitution in September

1990. However, the 16-year old civil war in Lebanon ended a year later, in October 1990, and not on October 22, 1989 as it was officially announced from the Palace of Conventions at Ta'if. Thus, "With the ending of the hostilities, political parties, like other political actors, entered the post-war phase of Lebanese politics. Militias had to adopt to this new state of affairs and quickly revert to their political party status".[12] Hizbullah found itself facing a new situation; it could no longer mobilize almost all of its resources to fighting the Israel forces occupying Lebanon. And so, a new reality transpired through the opening up of a domestic public sphere that Hizbullah could not afford to ignore. However, Hizbullah had a serious problem when, in March-April 1991, the Lebanese government acted on the basis of implementing the Ta'if Agreement and officially called for the dissolution of all the militias, ordering them to hand in their weapons to the Lebanese Army and to close their military and training centres. In order to counter that, Hizbullah launched a public relations campaign by issuing political declarations and a political program. Hizbullah was exempted as the notable exception to such a decision since the Lebanese government classified Hizbullah's Islamic Resistance, its military wing, as a resistance movement, and not as a militia; as such it was granted permission to keep up its arms and continue its struggle against Israel. Thus, Hizbullah's public relations campaign paid off, and Hizbullah was adjusting to its new dual role of confronting the Israeli occupation in the South and gradually integrating in the newly created domestic Lebanese public sphere, which came about as a result of the civil peace.

1.2   Hizbullah's 1991 political program and *infitah* policy

On January 3, 1991, Hizbullah issued a political declaration, which called on the Lebanese government to safeguard political, intellectual, ideological, and media freedoms as basic duties of the state towards its citizens. In addition, Hizbullah exhorted the government to differentiate between the role of the different militias in Lebanon and the role of Hizbullah's Islamic Resistance, calling for disbanding the militias, while classifying the Islamic Resistance as a legitimate, legal, and humanitarian right that the state ought to be clearly and unequivocally committed to buttressing.[13] This approach was followed by Sayyid Abbas'[14] 1991 four-point political program[15], which he addressed to all the Lebanese, Muslims and Christians: (1) The continuation and reinvigoration of the Resistance against the Israeli occupation.[16] (2) Ending all the repercussions of internal discords (*fitan*) that were prevalent at that time[17] in various (geographical) Lebanese areas[18], and constructively dealing with their consequences through serious public debate that permits open discussion of political and social issues, not only with allies, but also with former enemies.[19] (3) Embark on a "Lebanonisation"[20] (*Labnana*) process or *infitah* "opening-up", aimed specially towards the Christians, through the launching of a unprecedented and far-reaching public and political relations campaign directed at fostering ties, in spite of the ideological differences, with all the social and political powers that comprise the Lebanese myriad[21], especially the political parties present at that time in the local Lebanese scene. *Infitah* or Lebanonisation aims at inculcating an open dialogue policy in a pluralistic setting through interaction and cooperation with all Lebanese sects and communities in order to rid Lebanon of its political and social problems, foster national unity, and build a stronger-united Lebanon on the common grounds of respecting human values. (4) Allocate greater importance and devote a constructive effort towards alleviating socio-economic and communal issues that touch upon all walks of life, especially the strata inhabiting the deprived areas. Mobilize Hizbullah's institutions to improve their services to the oppressed grassroots and cater to their needs without hampering the continuation of the Resistance.[22]

1.3 Hizbullah's arguments for participation in the 1992 parliamentary elections

Hizbullah's decision to participate in the 1992 parliamentary elections was not easy. It was taken after much heated internal debate and discussions, followed by Iranian arbitration (*tahkim*). Hajj Muhammad Ra'd, the current head of Hizbullah's 12-member parliamentary bloc, downplays the internal Hizbullah row and the Iranian intervention, which favoured participation. Ra'd gives weight to the domestic dimension in Hizbullah's "favourable decision" to participate. He argues that when Hizbullah took the decision to take part in the 1992 elections, a chain of ideological, intellectual, and political debates ensued among the leading cadres of the party. He added that these debates were sometimes heated, at other times constructive. According to Ra'd, the debates evaluated the benefits of participating in a sectarian political system, which remarkably differs from the ideological and intellectual vision of the party. Ra'd continued that these debates ended up with the decision to participate on the basis that there are a lot of common grounds that Hizbullah shares with the Lebanese political myriad. Ra'd stressed that political life dictates practical interaction with other groups without delving into the ideological background of every party.[23]

In turn, Naïm Qasim gave a detailed exposition[24] of Hizbullah's position on the nature of the debates[25] regarding participation in the Lebanese political system, in general, and the parliamentary elections, in particular. According to Qasim, the issue of joining the Lebanese parliament or not led to extensive internal discussion and debate among Hizbullah's leading cadres. Hizbullah's seven-member *Shura* Council along with five leading cadres formed a twelve-member committee to assess the situation. The debates centred upon four main junctures: legitimacy; Islamic vision; interests and vices (*al-masalih wa al-mafasid*) as advantages and disadvantages; and priorities.

According to Qasim, the committee was interested in finding answers to the following four questions: (1) The key question dealt with the *legitimacy* of participating in a parliament that is part and parcel of a political-sectarian system, a system that does not reflect Hizbullah's vision towards the best regime. (2) Supposing the issue of legitimacy is solved, does participation mean an implicit recognition of the reality of the political system, a recognition that might ultimately lead Hizbullah to defend the system and adopt it, forgoing its *Islamic vision*? (3) Are there clear and certain *interests*, which outweigh the *vices*? (4) Does participation lead to an adjustment in Hizbullah's *priorities*, to the extent of giving up the Islamic Resistance for the sake of integration in the domestic Lebanese political game?[26]

1.3.1 *Legitimacy*

Concerning the issue of legitimacy, the committee conceded that it could not take a decision since this is the prerogative of *al-waliyy al-faqih*, Imam Khamina'i. However, some considered that participation in a non-Islamic system is not in accordance with the holistic Islamic vision, since Hizbullah's legitimate responsibility and legal obligation is confined to founding an Islamic state. Anything beside that should remain outside the framework of *al-anzima al-wad'iyya* (positive man-made or situational systems). The committee added that the fear of granting legitimacy to a non-Islamic system could lead to its perpetuation. According to the committee, the "Islamists'" (*al-Islamiyyun*)[27] participation in the regime could stand as a barrier to reforming the system or altering it all together. The committee decided to voice its concerns to Khamina'i and wait for his decision.[28]

1.3.2 *Participation*

The committee argued that *participation* in the parliamentary elections is an expression of taking part in the political structure of the present system, as such lending support to it. However, according to the committee, this does not imply that it is bound to protect its current structure as well as to defend its loopholes and deficiencies. Participation in the parliament carries with it popular representation whereby the deputy could defend his[29] point of view and has the freedom to approve what is in conformity with his vision and reject what is not. Based on his belief system or background knowledge (religious and political ideology), the deputy can engage in discussions pertaining to the constituents of the system, propose changes to it, influence draft legislations and propose suitable ones, all this while being faithful to his constituency. The committee stressed that participation in the parliament does not imply a de facto recognition of the system. Rather, participation and representation gives the deputy a big margin to manoeuvre and to express his opinion and defend it without being hostage to the current political system.[30]

1.3.3 *Interests (advantages) and vices (disadvantages)*

According to the committee, there are many pros to parliamentary participation, the most salient of which are the following: (1) making use of the parliament as a political podium, which accords due care to the Resistance, discussing and debating its support as well as laying the ground for a conducive environment so that others can hear the voice of the resistance from the viewpoint of popular parliamentary representation. (2) Through participation in parliamentary discussions and the debates of the parliamentary committees, Hizbullah could articulate in draft legislations issues pertaining to the improvement of people's livelihood, development, health, and social concerns and worries. Also, Hizbullah would promote alleviating the plight of the oppressed areas by allocating to them the necessary funds from various ministries. (3) Prior cognisance of draft legislations, which makes its plausible to study them in advance in order to propose the required amendments, rather than being confronted with an officially adopted binding law. (4) Building a network of political contacts with the representatives of sects and districts in order to conduct with them direct dialogue on standing, unresolved issues. Since it removes false barriers and wrong impressions, this process of familiarity and interaction opens the horizons for developing dialogue and accepting the differences of others.[31] (5) Granting Hizbullah official recognition from the Lebanese parliament, one of the institutions of

153

the Lebanese government that reflects popular representation. This would confer upon the Islamic Resistance the Lebanese state's legitimacy, which would make it part and parcel of both the popular and Lebanese state fabric. (6) Present an Islamic vision on the different issues put to debate, making it readily available to engage other viewpoints put to the fore.[32]

The committee pointed out that there are also cons to parliamentary representation; the most noticeable are the following: (1) There are difficulties in securing a precise popular representation because of the particularity of the political circumstances that specify a certain number of candidates, which renders presence in the parliament as a political representation, rather than a numerical representation. (2) The enactment of laws that are in contradiction to the *shari'a* although Hizbullah's deputies opposed them. (3) People might hold deputies responsible for delivering the services they promised their constituencies with. However, the parliament legislates the laws and holds the cabinet accountable for its actions, but it does not execute, execution being the prerogative of the government.[33]

1.3.4 *Priorities*

The committee highlighted that the priorities fall under the prerogative of Hizbullah's political decision making apparatus[34], which gave prominence to the Resistance against Israel. After deliberations and thorough readings of the Lebanese constitution, the committee found no prior connection between parliamentary participation and the specificity of the resistance. In spite of that, the committee insisted on contesting the elections with a well-formulated declaration that lucidly emphasize the continuation of the Resistance.[35] After evaluating the pros and cons of the situation, the committee concluded that the fear of the parliamentary elections affecting the Islamic Resistance is unfounded; on the contrary, parliamentary elections constitute an additional supporting asset to the Resistance. The committee stressed the convergence between Hizbullah's enrolment in Lebanese political life and the continuation of the resistance, a convergence that would lead to realizing the following two objectives: (1) practical coalescence between people's interests and the endeavour to realize it and enhance it; and (2) the interest of Lebanon and the *umma* in the liberation of the land from the "Zionist" (Israeli) occupation.[36]

After balancing the debates, Hizbullah's 12-member committee took a favourable decision to participate in the elections by a majority of ten to two, arguing that the interests, by far outweigh, the vices. In view of the committee's favourable outcome, Hizbullah presented its findings to Imam Khamina'i and requested form him a formal legal opinion (*istifta'*) on the legitimacy of participating in the elections. As soon as Khamina'i authorized and supported (*ajaza wa 'ayyada*)[37] participation, Hizbullah embarked on drafting its election program and officially announced its participation in the elections.[38]

2.   The Constituent Points of Hizbullah's Political Program

2.1   Views on the oppressed and oppressors, the US and Israel in particular

Hizbullah inaugurated its 1992 parliamentary elections program with a Qur'anic verse portraying itself standing up against the oppressors in the service of the oppressed by employing the concept of human empowerment (*tamkin*)[39]: "Those who, if we establish them firmly in the land, will perform the prayer, give the alms, command the good and prohibit evil. To Allah belongs the outcome of all affairs" (22:41).[40] Domestically, Hizbullah's program conveyed its commitment to confront the plots that are being contrived against Lebanon and to defend the "loyal Lebanese oppressed" with the purpose of upholding their rights, honour, and dignity.

In a similar vein, Hizbullah's 1998 and 2004 municipal elections programs were based on fending off oppression targeting the oppressed: (1) Since the populace constitute the main pillars behind Hizbullah's movement, Hizbullah is under a responsibility to fend off all oppression and injustice in order to serve them and protect their dignity; (2) One of Hizbullah's aims is to adopt the plight of the oppressed and the disenfranchised populace by protecting them and actively working for putting an end to oppression and discrimination towards the deprived areas in order to raise its standards of living in all respects.[41]

Regionally and internationally, Hizbullah's 1992 parliamentary elections program cautioned that the project of the oppressors, spearheaded by the US, is putting its stake on subordinating Lebanon and the Middle East with the purpose of achieving recognition in the legitimacy of the "Zionist Entity", and normalising relations with it, thus fusing the cultural identity of the people of the region and tying its destiny to the market economy and Western mode of production. Hizbullah's program warned that this leads to plundering riches, the depletion of natural resources, the imposition of tyrannical regimes, and the execution of programs, policies, and plans, which are contrary to the interests of the oppressed.[42] In addition, Hizbullah pledged to liberate Lebanon from the "Zionist occupation" as well as the arrogant oppressors' manipulation and hegemony. Hizbullah reiterated the same stance in its 1996 election program by blasting the policies of US hegemony and "Zionist terrorism".[43] Hizbullah stressed that it would confront the US's interference in Lebanese domestic affairs and conspiracies of the US's arrogance and oppressive policies that are giving a green light to Israeli continuous daily aggressions.[44]

2.2   Views on the Islamic State

All of Hizbullah's 1992, 1996, 1998, 2000, 2004, and 2005 parliamentary and municipal election programs do not state anything about instating an Islamic order in Lebanon.[45] Nevertheless, Hizbullah's views on the Islamic state (*dawla Islamiyya*) in the era of the political program are discussed and addressed by the discourse of its leaders and cadres, most notably Nasrallah and Qasim.

Hizbullah stated in its 2004 "Identity and Goals" – its latest self-description that includes aspects of its political ideology and political program – that one of its strategic ideals aims at the establishment of an Islamic Republic (*jumhuriyya Islamiyya*). Hizbullah argued that verily, there is no Islamic movement that does not advocate the establishment of an Islamic state in its own country.[46] Hizbullah stressed that there is no committed Muslim, who bears the Islamic doctrine and believes in its legitimacy, and does not advocate the project of establishing an Islamic state as one of the natural expressions of his Islamic commitment since it conveys and stands for the (social) justice that man aspires for.[47] However, Hizbullah clarified in its 1998 "Statement of Purpose" that its objective is the presentation of Islam that addresses people's minds and reasoning. Hizbullah added in its "Identity and Goals" that it does not aim at the application of Islam by force or violence; rather through peaceful political action, which offers the opportunity for the majority in any society to adopt or reject it. Hizbullah clarified that if Islam becomes the choice of the majority[48] of both the Lebanese Christians and Muslims, then it would apply it. However, if the majority decline it, then Hizbullah would continue to coexist, discuss, negotiate, and bargain until a consensus is reached. Hizbullah emphasized that its Islam rejects violence as a means to gain power, exhorting non-Islamists not to have recourse to force in order to enforce their agendas.[49] In conformity with the aforementioned, Hizbullah rejected recourse to power in order to establish an Islamic state (*dawla Islamiyya*). It argued that the Islamic state needs massive popular backing, and is not only a theoretical option. Hizbullah clarified that a 51% majority does not satisfy the objective stipulation of establishing an Islamic state; rather the Lebanese state and political system should be based on the volition of the entire populace, both Muslims and Christians. Hizbullah stressed if the populace reject the Islamic state, then it would not impose it in 50 years, not even in 100 years.[50]

2.3   Hizbullah's dialogue with the Lebanese Christians

In 1992 Hizbullah reached out to the Christians and conducted a watershed visit to the Maronite Patriarch, thus opening up the channels of dialogue with the Christians.[51] The Patriarch reciprocated, and a common committee was established in order to supervise a dynamic Christian-Muslim dialogue, which included all Christian and Muslim denominations in addition to political parties as well as civil society groups and organizations. Hizbullah called for open dialogue that deals with all doctrinal and political issues.[52] Hizbullah stressed that it always believed in dialogue with the various Lebanese sects (myriad) in order to tackle differences and disagreements, thus consolidating a smooth national coexistence and national unity.[53] In most cases, dialogue leads to beneficial discussions and constructive criticisms that would ultimately reshape Hizbullah's *infitah* policy towards more openness.[54] On these grounds, Hizbullah included Christians and Sunnis in its parliamentary and municipal representation, allowing Christians to speak in its name[55] as long as their discourse remained faithful to the party's immutable set of values (*thawabit*), such as resisting the occupation. The Maronite Patriarch argued that Hizbullah's Islamic Resistance has the right to liberate Lebanese occupied land. He added, that he has great confidence in the Resistance and its rationalisation in managing the conflict.[56]

These meetings set the pace and become the corner stone of Hizbullah's dialogue with the Christians, mainly based on the "Papal Guidance" that was communicated to the Lebanese during the late Pope's visit to Lebanon on April 10, 1997. In this regard, on August 20, 1997, Hizbullah's "Central Information Unit"[57] issued a two-sided book in English and Arabic entitled "A Reading in Papal Guidance: Hizbullah's Perspective", which included the following three issues: (1) "The Last Call" released by the Synod held by the Catholic Assembly at the Vatican on December 20, 1995; (2) "The letter addressed by Hizbullah to His Holiness the Pope John Paul II, on the occasion of his visit to Lebanon" on April 6, 1997; and (3) "A lecture delivered by the head of the Political Council of Hizbullah, Deputy Muhammad R'ad in the seminar organized by the cultural council of Byblos about the Papal Guidance" on June 13, 1997.

In its political declaration commenting on the "Last Call", Hizbullah praised the need to consolidate national coexistence (al-'aysh al-mushtarak) and the founding of common grounds among the Lebanese through a constructive dialogue that leads to national unity around fundamental issues that comprise a national unifying identity, which is conducive to upholding civil peace. It also applauded and encouraged the convention's call to unprejudiced discussions and calm, objective dialogue.[58]

In its letter to the late Pope John Paul II, Hizbullah emphasized that difference in religious belief does not constitute a pretext to ebb a human right. According to Hizbullah, dialogue is the religious trait of the prophets and messengers. Both Jesus Christ and Prophet Muhammad were very keen on engaging in dialogue with their own people as well as others. From this perspective, Hizbullah considers Christian-Muslim dialogue as a key to a productive, prosperous, and constructive cooperation locally and internationally in global forums, especially the Conference on Population Control held in Cairo.[59] Finally, Hizbullah stressed the necessity of real dialogue that ought to include the Muslims who comprise civil society and the Lebanese public sphere, and not only deal with the political authorities since they do not represent the real socio-political fibre of the Muslim countries.[60]

In his lecture, Hajj Muhammad Ra'd[61] commented on the Papal Guidance. He seconded the Pope's call to the Christian youth to obliterate the walls that stand between them and the other, calling on them not to forget and to preserve their Christian-Arabic identity. The Pope also exhorted them to integrate and peacefully coexist and interact with their Arab milieu in order to enrich it, while at the same time highlighting the dangers of exclusion, isolation, and reactionaryism since they are a minority living among a Muslim majority. Ra'd extolled the Pope's usage of the word "brothers" when he referred to non-Christians, as such emphasizing fraternity among the human beings. The Pope stressed that the Catholic Church declares that the building of society on serious, cooperative, and brotherly dialogue is a common endeavour to all the Lebanese. Ra'd added that the Papal Guidance affirmed that the different communities that constitute Lebanon are the wealth and authenticity of the country. He stressed that on the whole the Papal Guidance called for total infitah among the Lebanese, comprehensive daily dialogue on all levels among them, mutual recognition, and giving up stereotyping and discrimination.

According to Ra'd, the Papal Guidance called on the Lebanese to be one-united populace even though they have different political, intellectual, and religious loyalties. He emphasized that the national unity, which the Papal Guidance calls for, constitutes peaceful coexistence, far removed from the majority-minority concepts and logic. In line with the section of the Papal Guidance entitled, "Secularism and the Modern World", Ra'd emphasized that national cohabitation under the umbrella of the human values, which are affirmed both by Christianity and Islam, is much better for society than the adoption of secularism. Ra'd underscored the Papal Guidance's call for a constructive Christian-Muslim dialogue, national coexistence, solidarity with the Arab world, building of a virtuous society that upholds human values and dignity as well as peace and reconciliation. Ra'd reiterated that Hizbullah's position towards the Papal Guidance is that it set a framework for a realistic reform of the Lebanese system and specified a general consensual policy between the Muslims and the Christians in order to erect together a unified society capable of conveying a distinguished civilizational message based upon fraternity so as to achieve the common good and promote a well-functioning civil society.[62]

Hizbullah's overall political program reflected its *infitah* trend. Hizbullah's "Identity and Goals" called for dialogue, tolerance, and acceptance of the other. Hizbullah added that it also has its own cultural plan to attract and convince through civilized and humanitarian means as stipulated in the International Bill of Human Rights, without any recourse to violence or coercion. From this perspective, Hizbullah opens its heart to friendship with everyone on the basis of mutual self-respect.[63] Hizbullah's Islam is the Islam of virtue and morality; the Islam of dialogue with the other; the Islam of unity and cooperation; and the Islam of guidance that displays what it has on others so that they abide by God's injunctions on the ground of: "Let there be no compulsion in religion" (2: 256).[64]

In its 1992 parliamentary elections program, Hizbullah did not vilify the Lebanese government or the political Maronites; rather Hizbullah called for the abolishment of political sectarianism[65], blaming the Lebanese state, not only for the corruption of the political system, but also for all the cultural, security, social, and developmental calamities that have ruptured Lebanon for decades. Hizbullah also blamed political sectarianism for the malevolent entrance of the arrogant-gluttonous foreign powers to interfere in domestic Lebanese affairs, thus endangering Lebanon's destiny and future.[66] In its 1996 election program and 1997 "Views and Concepts", Hizbullah repeated its call for the abolishment of political sectarianism in order to achieve a just and equitable political system.[67] In its political declaration commenting on the "Last Call", Hizbullah regarded the call to shift from sectarian loyalty to national loyalty as synonymous with the abolishment of political sectarianism. However, Hizbullah condemned the call to a consensual democracy based on political sectarianism in order to avoid the tyranny of the majority. Instead of the proposed system, Hizbullah called for an alternative to the political sectarian system that upholds religious and cultural diversity in the framework of the unity in cultural belonging based upon the abolition of political sectarianism that the Lebanese had already consented to and included in the new constitution (Ta'if Agreement) with a mechanism of implementation.[68] In its 2000 election program, Hizbullah urged the Lebanese government to establish the "National Body for the Abolishment of Political Sectarianism".[69] This culminated in Nasrallah's 2001 call for the abolition of political sectarianism in the mentality, before abolishing it in the texts (*ilgha' al-ta'fiyya al-siyassiyya fi al-nufus, qabla al-nusus*),[70] which bears a striking resemblance to the Maronite bishops' declaration that cautioned that deleting political sectarianism from legal texts before wiping it out from Lebanese people's mentality – through an efficient education of coexistence and mutual respect – is hazardous.[71]

Hizbullah 1992 parliamentary elections program addressed the Lebanese, in general, and the Christians, in particular, by promising them to fortify domestic peace, on the basis of political consensus, and to ward off appalling sectarian strife, narrow zealous partisanship, and fanaticism. Hizbullah called for the removal of the remnants of the obliterating civil war that has ravaged Lebanon, and objectively, constructively, and responsibly address its causes and consequences so that justice and equality would be served. Hizbullah added that attaining justice and equality among the Lebanese is regarded as a fundamental pillar for establishing a stable dignified and prosperous country in which all the Lebanese take an active part in the reconstruction process with impetus and solidarity governed by equality of opportunity as well as equality in political, economical, or social rights and duties.[72]

In its "Views and Concepts" Hizbullah allocated a separate section to its dialogue with the Christians. After Hizbullah conveyed its adherence to Islam that calls for upholding human values and abhorrence of all forms of discrimination, be it racial, sectarian, or denominational, Hizbullah portrayed its readiness and willingness to conduct a comprehensive dialogue with others dealing with all issues such as its convictions, beliefs, curricula, and political positions, without any impediments or taboos. Hizbullah stressed its interest (*maslaha*) in reaching common grounds and a mutual understanding with others, without any force or coercion. Hizbullah believes solely in continuous dialogue as the best means to rectify visions and clarify positions. Finally, Hizbullah emphasized that dialogue is one of the most salient tenets of its political program. In addition, "Views and Concepts" presented Hizbullah's fundamental characteristic of dialogue: it uproots exclusiveness and arrogance in human passions and inculcates modesty; it also enhances pluralism, pluralism construed as unity in diversity. That is why wisdom dictates the reduction of conflict since the lack of proper communication and understanding led to it, as exemplified by the Lebanese civil war. Hizbullah added that dialogue is possible among the eighteen sects who comprise the Lebanese myriad[73] and who have different ideologies, mindsets, understandings, viewpoints, and belief systems. Hizbullah stressed freedom, right, justice, security, and peace as the most important human values. Thus, *infitah* is needed since everybody needs to "open up" and live in the moment with awareness and dynamism.[74]

2.4 Hizbullah's jurisprudential stipulations of parliamentary, municipal, and governmental work

The introduction of Hizbullah's 1992 parliamentary elections program emphasized that its participation in the elections through a comprehensive political program is a religious duty and legal obligation (*taklif shar'i*)[75] in front of God, a patriotic obligation, and an expression of the popular will. Hizbullah added that its participation is based upon a realistic diagnosis of the clear and possible dangers as well as the opportunities available to the "Islamists" to take a leading role in the path of consolidating the Islamic project, in harmony with *jurisprudential stipulations* based upon Islamic law or *shari'a*, which serves as an authoritative guide. Hizbullah's program promised that its work in the parliament would be firm in preserving the country and safeguarding the social, economic, and political interests (*masalih*) and needs of the Lebanese populace.[76] The content of Hizbullah's jurisprudential stipulations was communicated by its 2002 municipal conference, Hajj Muhammad Ra'd, Bilal N'im, and Shaykh 'Afif al-Nabulsi, who stressed the role the *shari'a* plays in connection with non-*shar'i* laws.

In its first municipal conference held in July 2002, Hizbullah embarked on organizing detailed studies dealing with the jurisprudence or religious safeguards (*dawabit shar'iyya*) of municipal work and municipal decisions. On the whole, Hizbullah legitimised its participation in the electoral process by employing the following Qur'anic concepts[77]: *shura*[78] (consultation) and its modern Islamic constructions as a democratic consultative government reflecting the public will of the people; *ijtihad*[79] (independent reasoning) as Islamic interpretation or independent opinion formation; *ikhtilaf*[80] and its modern Islamic expressions as pluralism; and *al-huquq al-shar'iyya*[81] (human or 'legal' rights) and its modern Islamic conceptions as human rights. Hizbullah stressed that although the Qur'an, Sunna, and the *shari'a* are the sources and bases of legislation; however, some issues in life could be referred to other sources such as "situational laws" (*al-qawanin al-wad'iyya*) i.e. positive (man made) laws and legislations.[82]

In commenting on the aforementioned, Hajj Muhammad Ra'd argues that there is no conflict between Hizbullah's Islamic identity and its parliamentary work since there is no big practical difficulty between the two, the reason being that the roots of civil legislation or situational laws (*al-tashri' al-wad'i*) are derived from jurisprudential legislations (*al-tashri' al-dini-al-fiqhi*) although their applications might be different. Ra'd adds that Hizbullah bases itself on the following rule of thumb: what falls within the domain of the legally prohibited (*haram shar'i*), Hizbullah endeavours to prevent from coming into being or Hizbullah stands in its way; what stands in sharp contrast to the legally sanctioned (*halal shar'i*), Hizbullah tries to abort it or append it; what falls within the domain of the 'permitted' (*mubah*), Hizbullah does its best to find the most just implementation in conformity with its religious vision. Ra'd explains that as Hizbullah interacts with other groups that form the Lebanese myriad, in its parliamentary work Hizbullah engages in negotiations and bargaining, making compromises when it is confronted with a draft resolution that might pose a grave damage to its religious and ethical vision. Ra'd adds that according to the stipulations of the democratic game, maybe Hizbullah's MPs are not able to abort the draft legislation except by voting in favour of another that is deemed less damaging though sometimes Hizbullah's MPs are not able to accomplish that. Thus, according to Ra'd, Hizbullah's parliamentary work is based on two basic principles: (1) keeping away the vices (*al-mafasid*) has precedent over advancing interests (*al-masalih*); (2) the confrontation between the most damaging and the least damaging. In conformity with *ijtihad*, Ra'd concludes that the jurisprudential principles, which constitute the bases for civil legislations, sanction a great margin of manoeuvre in influencing legislations and decisions.[83]

In turn, Bilal N'im stresses what distinguishes Islam from other religions is that it is a comprehensive system of legislation that covers all aspects of life.[84] He argues against the contentions that Islamic legislation falls short of guiding modern life, does not have the flexibility to deal with man's progress, and addresses only the generalities, failing to deal with the basic particularities that have to do with man's necessities and needs. N'im emphasizes that Islam is the religion of governorship (*hakimiyya*: God's governance) and governance; it is the religion to administer daily life and lead it; it is a religion that has all the necessary legislations to accomplish that; it is a religion that has enough conformity and immutability to *preserve its identity*; and it is a religion that is endowed with flexibility that makes people's lives easier. He clarifies that Islam in its immutable legislations (*tashri'at thabita*) has addressed the immutable natural disposition of the human being[85]. This branch of legislation is connected with eternal interests and vices (*al-masalih wa al-mafasid*) that are only known to God. That is why it is difficult for human reason to meddle with this legislation. N'im adds that Islam in its dynamic legislation (*tashri'at mutaharika*) has focused upon eternal-temporal interests and vices that are capable of being discovered by human reason (*ijtihad*) i.e. what the mind judges based on its knowledge of good and bad... If the mind has done its role and issued the necessary legislations and abided by them, then it is as if the mind has applied a part of the divine Islamic legislations. According to the laws, the person who does that receives his/her share of this commitment as God has willed, even if that person was a *non-Muslim*. He concludes that the problematic is in *practice* and not in *theory*, for Islam has a comprehensive civilizational project dealing with all aspects of human life, thus it is holistic in its orientation.[86]

Shaykh 'Afif al-Nabulsi, the head of the Shi'ite religious scholars of *Jabal 'Amil*, granted Hizbullah religious approval and legitimacy to its participation in the Lebanese cabinet. He argued that from a political standpoint there is a certain wisdom and interest (*maslaha*) that calls upon Hizbullah to participate on the basis of the maxims of Islamic jurisprudence (*qawa'id al-fiqh*), which state that "necessities permit what is prohibited" and "what can not be accomplished in its whole, can not be left in its entirety". According to al-Nabulsi, the current political situation lifts any prohibition on Hizbullah's participation since one of the tenets of purposes of *shari'a* (*maqasid al-shari'a*) stipulate the safeguarding of the Resistance as a corollary to safeguarding law and order in Lebanese society. He adds that safeguarding law and order is a strict legitimate/legal responsibility (*taklif shar'i*) in order to preclude chaos and discords (*fitan*) from rupturing Lebanese society as well as to prevent Israel from attacking Lebanon.[87] Nabulsi added that the Resistance and its weapons constitute an existential necessity to Lebanon as well as a strategic necessity tied to its national security.[88]

Hizbullah's political program as well as Na'im Qasim's, Muhammad Ra'd's, Bilal N'im's, and 'Afif al-Nabulsi's usage of the vices and interests (*al-masalih wa al-mafasid*) in order to grant participation in electoral and democratic processes warrants some explanation. In brief, Islamic jurisprudence theories developed in three main stages: (1) from the principles of jurisprudence (*usual al-fiqh*); (2) to the maxims of Islamic jurisprudence (*qawa'id al-fiqh*); and (3) finally to the purposes of the *shari'a* (*maqasid al-shari'a*).[89] Hizbullah stresses the second and alludes to the third.

1. The principles of jurisprudence deal with the methodology used to extract the law from the authoritative sources. It has to do with the way a scholar tries to understand the text.

2. The maxims of jurisprudence are pragmatic 'principles' that scholars usually refer to from the stance of authority to justify. They are pragmatic, and as I see it, very pragmatic because they give a framework that can be used to confront different situations in a flexible matter. They are principles in the sense of being employed authoritatively to justify things. In short, the provisions of the maxims of Islamic jurisprudence are based on pragmatism. As such, they form a bridge between politics and religion. The following are some maxims of Islamic jurisprudence that I have heard during my fieldwork or I came by while reading Hizbullah's discourse: (A) difficulties will lead to easiness (*al-mashaqqa tajri bi al-tayysir*); necessities permit what is prohibited (*al-darurrat tubih al-mahdhurat*), which is based on (2:173) "But he who is constrained, without intending to disobey or transgress, will commit no sin. Allah is Forgiving, Merciful". (B) What cannot be accomplished in its whole, can not be left in its whole (*ma la yudraku kuluhu, la yutraku kuluhu*), which implies an opposition of all to nothing. (C) Things are attributed to their final causes (*lil umur maqasiduha*), based on the intention (*niyya*), which should be in line with one's action. (D) The maxim of "mutual competition" (*tazahum*): "If two duties conflict (compete), then it is a must to follow the one deemed more important than the other, or the one more pressing than the other" (*idha tazahama amran wajiban fa yajib taqdim al-aham 'ala al-muhim, wa al-mulih 'ala al-aqal ilhahan*). However, the most salient maxim – that was employed by Na'im Qasim, Muhammad Ra'd, and Bilal N'im – is that "the warding off vices is preferable to obtaining interests" (*dar' al-mafasid muqadam 'ala jalb al-masalih*). This is what they mean when they refer to interests and vices.

3. The purposes of *shari'a* are based on the following natural and inalienable rights as well as their corollaries (derivatives): (a) the protection of reason (*hifz al-'aql*); (b) the protection of the self (*hifz al-nafs*); (c) the protection of family and descent (*hifz al-nasl*); (d) the protection of religion (*hifz al-din*); and (e) the protection of property (*hifz al-mal*). According to the purposes of *shari'a*, the *shari'a* was revealed to the human beings because of interest (*maslaha*) for reinterpretation of the law. It is most likely that when Hizbullah refers to *al-huquq al-shar'iyya* as human rights, Hizbullah is referring to them from the stance of the purposes of *shari'a*, which is a liberal interpretation in its own right. The purposes of *shari'a*, being based on a humanistic interpretation of the *shari'a*, deal more with the interest (*maslaha*) of the human being, thus sanctioning engagement in democratic practices and calling for the upholding of human rights.

2.5 Hizbullah's socio-economic program: its NGOs and civil institutions

Another key plank in Hizbullah's electoral platform is its commitment to a comprehensive socio-economic program[90]. Hizbullah's 1992 socio-economic vision remained vague since its major aim was to protect its Islamic Resistance. It just outlined certain policy measures dealing with administrative reform, and the enhancement of social, and educational services. In 1996 Hizbullah listed a series of socio-economic ideas without developing a clear policy line. The important change occurred in 2000 when Hizbullah's entire election program was mainly concerned with socio-economic issues since the Israeli withdrawal dictated an alteration in priorities and strategies.[91] This trend continued with Nasrallah's 2001 domestic political program[92] and reached its peak in Hizbullah's 2004 municipal elections program and its August 2004 "Working Document"[93] of the Central Workers' and Syndicates' Unit.[94]

Hizbullah emphasized that a constructive solution to the socio-economic problem requires the exertion of exceptional efforts aimed at the formation and execution of a general reformist economic plan. Hizbullah outlined the elements, priorities, and emphases of its socio-economic program stressing, in addition to political reforms, administrative, social, and economic reforms in order to stamp out corruption, inefficiency, waste, red tape, favouritism, nepotism, and replace the spoils system by meritocracy based upon economic function, specialisation, transparency, and accountability. Most importantly, Hizbullah exhorted the Lebanese state to concentrate on enhancing human resources (*bashar*) i.e. the plight of the human being and not only material resources (*hajar*) through laying scientific foundations of a comprehensive socio-economic program aimed at eliminating poverty by boosting the productive sectors, protecting the natural resources and the state's capabilities, pursuing balanced development, achieving social justice, and improving the state's care to its citizens.[95]

Hizbullah's cadres regarded the municipal elections as a socio-economic eventuality par excellence. Qasim stressed that the municipal elections are a developmental, socio-economic entitlement having a political flavour.[96] Sayyid Hashim Safiyyeddine stated that the *umma* upholds its pride, honour, and dignity by participating in the municipal elections that wield (Hizbullah controlled) municipal councils, which industriously work to improve the socio-economic conditions of the Lebanese.[97] Finally Hizbullah's 2005 parliamentary elections program stressed the need for establishing a comprehensive socio-economic program aimed at eradicating poverty by boosting productive sectors such as agriculture, industry, and trade that are conducive to rendering basic services to the Lebanese citizens.

Hizbullah's humanitarian duties, which are legitimised on the basis of the Qur'an, dictated upon it to redress the negative effects of "conspicuous consumption"[98] by targeting the periphery and upholding human rights.

Hizbullah blasted the Lebanese government negligence in fulfilling its humanitarian and socio-economic duties toward its citizens.[99] According to Hajj Husayn Shami, while the Lebanese government pursued conspicuous consumption concentrating on the "centre", Hizbullah embarked on reciprocity and a redistribution system targeting the deprived "peripheries".[100] He added, historically, the Lebanese government engaged in modernization projects and developmental plans focusing on the centre i.e. Beirut and Mount Lebanon, and ignored the periphery that constitutes the southern suburbs of Beirut and deprived areas such as the North, South, and *Biqa'*. Shami stressed that Hizbullah's aim behind its NGOs, social institutions, and welfare programmes is to reverse this trend, lobbying the government, through parliament, to take conducive measures to eradicate unbalanced development.[101]

In line with its political program where Hizbullah prided itself for indiscriminately bestowing its humanitarian services upon the Lebanese in various geographical areas[102], most notably the periphery, Hajj Shami emphasizes that Hizbullah's social and humanitarian services are not confined to Shi'ites or Muslims only; rather a lot of Christians of various denominations benefit from these services.[103] As such, a Lebanese martyr's family is Hizbullah's responsibility regardless of its religious affiliation.[104] In line with Shami, Hajj Imad Faqih stresses that a human being receives his share by virtue of his humanity, the inalienable right of being human without any regard to the person's political or religious beliefs. Faqih purports that Hizbullah's NGOs indiscriminately offer their services to the populace at large belonging to all denominations and political parties without aspiring for any remuneration or pressure to elect its representatives. He claims that Hizbullah has a strong social base and is investing its legitimacy for the establishment of social justice. Faqih adds this is the true vision of the humanistic life that Hizbullah aims at and strives for, so that every person can realise it.[105]

In line with its *infitah*, Hizbullah stresses and deals with almost all social, economical, religious, and political domains, thus, it is holistic in its orientation. In fact, Hizbullah's NGOs and civil institutions conducted many services, some of which has been restoring damaged buildings, farming guidance, providing utilities for a token amount and sometimes for free, according medical care and hospitalisation, offering primary and intermediate schooling, granting scholarships to needy students in order to continue their college education as well as providing them with career and guidance orientation, and securing fresh water to the areas that are deprived of it.[106] In order to broaden its support base among the masses, Hizbullah built a network of infrastructure, civil institutions, NGOs, and social welfare that deals with all aspects of life.[107] Also, efficient twin ship programs exist with Iran, and some of Hizbullah's institutions are a replica of Iranian ones. Particular attention has been accorded to education, hospitalisation, and welfare programs giving prominence to the role of women in the public sphere, thus emulating the Iranian experience.[108]

Hizbullah emphasized that it strives to present Islam as the guardian of human rights (*al-huquq al-shar'iyya*) defining choices, adopting convictions, and articulating them across the lines of a socio-economic program. Hizbullah added that it opts for the formation of political pressure in education, pedagogy, medical care, and other socio-economic benefits asserted in the International Bill of Human Rights.[109] Hajj Shami stresses that Hizbullah's NGOs target the deprived grassroots, in particular, and develop an overall welfare system that blends social democratic experience with the Islamic doctrine of human or 'legal' rights (*al-huquq al-shar'iyya*)[110] of *zakat* and *khums*, which are religious duties incumbent upon every believer. In this regard, Faqih quotes Imam Musa al-Sadr who has claimed that if all the Shi'a performed their religious duty of *khums*, then poverty among the Shi'a community in Lebanon would have been eradicated. According to Faqih, this is social justice proper because it safeguards the dignity and humanity of the poor and the oppressed. He adds, the poor have their own needs, which ought to be appropriated from the rich, and this is what Hizbullah is endeavouring to do within the domain of *al-huquq al-shar'iyya*.[111] Both Shami and Faqih added that Hizbullah does not impose prohibitions on cooperation with voluntary welfare and development associations as such; rather only those who threaten or undercut its Islamic Resistance are excluded.[112] From this perspective, in its 2004 municipal election program, Hizbullah stated that it cooperated and coordinated not only with local NGOs and civil society organizations, but also with competent international associations and regional and international organizations such as the UNICEF and the UNDP.[113]

Hizbullah legitimised its humanitarian duties by a Qur'anic verse that enjoins the need of good deeds and benevolence in this life: "But seek, thanks to what Allah gave you, the Hereafter, and do not forget your portion of the here below [the present world]. Be charitable, as Allah has been charitable to you, and do not seek corruption in the land; for Allah does not like the seekers of corruption" (28:77).[114] Hizbullah's political program considers it a religious duty to serve the populace, safeguard their rights, uphold their interest, and exert effort in order to pursue economic development and recovery, which affords the citizens with the requirements of a dignified and honourable life.[115]

Hizbullah's socio-economic program and NGOs are inspired by the same ideals of social justice. Hizbullah's political program emphasized a consorted effort between its resistance identity, on the one hand, and its socio-economic, intellectual, and cultural work, on the other.[116] Hajj Imad Faqih highlights the importance of social justice stressing that Hizbullah is not only a military party[117]; rather it has a "humanistic" dimension. According to him, Hizbullah was compelled to liberate occupied Lebanese land within an overall humanistic project that carries the banner of Islam.[118] Faqih regards military victory over Israel as a step in the right direction towards the establishment of social justice.[119]

2.6 Hizbullah as a nationalist Lebanese political party (Lebanonisation)

Hizbullah's cadres affirm that the party never took part in the Lebanese civil war.[120] They purport that the party never imposed (by force) its ideas, opinions, or its religio-political ideology and political program on any one; on the contrary, Hizbullah always respected the opinions, beliefs, and ideas of others.[121] Hizbullah has repeatedly stated that it refuses to be a social, political, or security alternative to the Lebanese state and its institutions, thus working with the narrow confines of the Lebanese state, rather than aspiring to form a state within a state.[122]

Hizbullah purports that it is not only an Islamic movement, but also a nationalist-patriotic Lebanese political party. Hizbullah's political program portrayed it as one of the foremost mainstream Lebanese political parties, which is embraced by both the populace and government. It also aimed to present it as a Lebanese nationalistic political party that upholds its patriotic duty while at the same time being faithful to its Islamic identity.[123] Hizbullah stressed that it has been mobilizing its "noble religious" and "national struggle" in order to serve freedom, right, justice, and peace in Lebanon.[124] Basing itself on its nationalistic responsibilities, Hizbullah emphasizes that its resistance identity and struggle will continue until it liberates all occupied Lebanese land because it took on its shoulders the duty of defending the security, sovereignty, honour, dignity, and interests of all the Lebanese.[125] From this perspective, Hizbullah formed the Multi-confessional Lebanese Brigades to fight Israel (LMCB) on November 3, 1997 almost two months after Sayyid Hadi Nasrallah, Sayyid Hasan Nasrallah's son, died in a confrontation with the Israel soldiers in southern Lebanon. Hadi Nasrallah's death galvanized the Lebanese to a sense of national unity around the Resistance. Hizbullah capitalised on this and founded the LMCB, which attracted a strong response from the Lebanese youth across the sectarian spectrum. The multi-confessional-sectarian nature of LMCB testifies to Hizbullah's sincerity in its efforts to Lebanonise itself. This move marks the "Lebanonisation" or *infitah* of the Resistance.[126] Hizbullah exploited the Israeli Army's labelling of its fighters as "freedom fighters" to convey its unwavering Lebanonisation[127]: "If this is the testimony of the enemy in us, then who are those who dare to question our nationalistic background"?[128]

The discourse of Hizbullah's leaders stressed its *infitah* policy and its Lebanonisation process. In its 1991 political program Hizbullah outlined its *infitah* policy in an attempt to open up to other groups that form the Lebanese myriad, most notably the Christians. Since then, different nuances of Hizbullah's *infitah* policy or Lebanonisation were given. Lebanonisation is defined as "a political approach where the Islamic movement examines the prevailing circumstances in Lebanon and formulates its strategy within that framework, making allowances for Lebanon's particular circumstances, its confessional sensitivities, and its perception of its environment".[129] In general, Hizbullah employs the term *infitah* or Lebanonisation to denote its political discourse, deeds, and policies in the era of the political program[130], or to signify its enrolment in Lebanese domestic political life.[131]

Hizbullah's leading cadres explained how *infitah* works. Since working within a certain country is linked to its particularity, specificity, and circumstances, Hizbullah's work balances its "Islamic program" (*Islamiyyat al-manhaj*) and "Lebanese national loyalty/allegiance" (*Lubnaniyyat al-muwatana*). Hizbullah is a Lebanese political party in all its particularities and specificities, and all of its leadership, cadres, and rank and file are Lebanese. Indeed, Hizbullah is concerned with what is happening in the *jihadi*, political, social, and cultural domains, carrying the banner of Islam. There is no contradiction between caring for the causes of the Islamic world and the plight of the oppressed (regional and global dimensions), on the one hand, and being concerned with national-patriotic issues (domestic dimension) that are bound to reject tyranny and occupation, as well as working towards the achievement of social justice and taking care of domestic priorities and interests.[132]

Other cadres stressed that, in its daily dealings with the Lebanese mosaic, Hizbullah tries to keep a balance between its nationalist political commitments and its Islamic background. Hizbullah unequivocally stated that it engages in negotiations and bargaining, making compromises (even by allying itself with formal ideological enemies) in its political work, so that the overall political decisions taken might not harm its Islamic and ethical vision.[133] Hizbullah affirms that its Islamic identity endorses the establishment of a civil society governed by the values of democracy, civil peace, public freedoms, as well as a functional-efficient political system.[134] These are priorities that go hand in hand with the party's political program and Islamic doctrine and are conducive to the service of the Lebanese society at large. Hizbullah claims that the establishment of civil society in Lebanon does not contradict its project; rather it is concomitant with it because one of the tenets of Islam[135] urges the enactment of civil society.[136]

Hizbullah's practical performance has its own objective contexts, foundations, and fundamentals, which sanction the preservation of its Islamic identity while working within the domain of Lebanese state's sovereignty. Hizbullah stresses that this should not be seen as a deflection from God's *shari'a* since the party considers that its political experience in the domestic sphere in Lebanon has proven to be in accordance with the Islamic vision in a multicultural, confessional-sectarian society – in a country that cannot bear the Islamic "thought" or ideology[137] as an administration, orientation, and basic conviction in the system of government.[138] Hizbullah purports that its Lebanonisation is in harmony with its Islamic identity.

Conveying pragmatism, it added that there is no objection from benefiting from its morale, competence, rectitude, and popular following, and invest these in domestic politics in the framework of the integrity and decency of the performance.[139]

Finally, a few examples of identity construction on the symbolic level illustrate the waning of identity determinants, giving more weight to Hizbullah's nationalistic character: (A) After the liberation or the nearly complete Israeli withdrawal from south Lebanon in May 2000, the logo on Hizbullah flag, "The Islamic Revolution in Lebanon" was replaced by "The Islamic Resistance in Lebanon". Hajj Imad Faqih contends that it changed as early as 1998 in an endeavour of rapprochement towards the Christians and other confessional groups.[140] (B) In 2001, Hizbullah's weekly mouthpiece Al-'Ahd not only changed its name to al-Intiqad, but also its orientation, thus conveying a "secular" image by dropping the Qur'anic legitimisation (5:56), on the right side, and removing the portrait of Khumayni and Khamina'i, on the left side. In the beginning, there was only Khumayni's portrait; after his death Khamina'i's portrait was added. Also, in the beginning AH dates were written with their AD equivalent. After the name change, the trend was reversed: AD dates, then their AH equivalent.[141] (C) During the municipal elections of 1998, in the Dahiya (Beirut's southern suburb) Hizbullah removed all religious and ideological symbols – including pictures and banners – from areas surrounding the Christian polling stations in order not to offend or scare the Christians. This was done from the stance of respecting the specificity and particularity of the Christian displaced population that was competing for municipal seats. (D) Even before Hariri's assassination, Hizbullah started to portray its national character in street politics, rather than its ideological-Islamic identity. As a case in point, I take the November 30, 2004 and March 8, 2005 demonstrations where Hizbullah marched carrying Lebanese flags, rather than portraying it flags, banners, and special slogans. Thus, the vanishing of the symbols of Hizbullah's identity marks an important victory for the logic of operating within the bounds of the Lebanese state over the logic of the revolution.

2.7   Hizbullah's stance towards Syria and Iran

From its stance of pan-Arabism and pan-Islamism, in its political program Hizbullah stressed its amicable relations to Syria and Iran. In its 1996 election program Hizbullah stated as a priority the preservation of good, brotherly Lebanese-Syrian relations as a practical application of Lebanon's Arab heritage, identity, belonging, and cultural authenticity.[142] Hizbullah considered these relations as a bulwark standing against any endeavour aimed at isolating Lebanon in the face of regional challenges. According to Hizbullah, the previous years have proven that these relations present an element of stability to Lebanon.[143] In the introduction to its 2000 parliamentary elections program, Hizbullah emphasized that distinctive relations with Syria are an element of strength to Lebanon and Syria in the face of the mounting challenges and international pressures that are being waged against the two countries.[144] The third article in Hizbullah's 2005 parliamentary elections program exhorted the Lebanese government to lay scientific foundations for systematising the special relationship between Lebanon and Syria. Also, Hizbullah's 2000 parliamentary elections program laid emphasis on expanding the Lebanese-Iranian relations, thanking the Islamic Republic of Iran that has always been firm in buttressing Lebanon.[145]

Hizbullah affirms that it is a Lebanese political party that derives legitimacy from its struggle for the liberation of Lebanese occupied land by Israel, and from the support of Lebanese people and government (domestically), and that it is buttressed by two strong regional players, namely, Iran and Syria (regionally). Hizbullah concedes that Iran furnishes it with economic, social, political, military, and financial assistance.[146] Hizbullah admits that it consults on a regular basis with Iran, Syria, and other key players, and that this renders any decision it embarks upon more ripe, wise, and perspicacious.[147] Hizbullah, as a political party, has domestic, regional, and international junctures that are in accordance with its overall vision and interests (*masalih*). This leads to harmony and coordination between Lebanon, on the one hand, and Iran and Syria, on the other, that grant Hizbullah assistance and backing in its legitimate right for resistance and liberation. Hizbullah benefits from the positive convergence of its interests and strategy with Syria and Iran to recover occupied land from Israel, be it Lebanese or Palestinian.[148] However, the details are left to the particularities and specificities to the Lebanese to deal with. Hizbullah takes its decisions independently of Iran and Syria, because Iran and Syria have their own convictions and responsibilities that might not always be in agreement with Hizbullah's domestic Lebanese politics.[149]

The discourse of Hizbullah's leading cadres demonstrated a political-strategic partnership between Hizbullah and Syria. Before the Syrian withdrawal, Hizbullah defended Syria's "legitimate" intervention in Lebanon arguing that the Syrian forces entered Lebanon in 1976 by an official request from the Lebanese authorities and contending that the continuous Syrian presence was sanctioned by the Ta'if Agreement. Hizbullah criticised calls, most notably by the Christians, for the evacuation of the Syrian forces whom they regarded as a threat to civil peace. Hizbullah vehemently refused equating the Syrian presence with "colonialism and occupation", labelling that presence as beneficial in the wake of Israeli occupation and continuous threats.[150] Hizbullah's official stance regarding its relations with Syria was summarised by its Political Council member and foreign relations officer, Sayyid Nawwaf al-Musawi who acknowledged that Lebanon has been advantaged from Syria's standpoint towards the Arab-Israeli conflict and its support for resistance movements against the occupation. Al-Musawi argued that this came about from the concordance of interests (malasih) between Lebanon and Syria in fighting the Israeli occupation of Southern Lebanon. Although al-Musawi conceded that Syria might have benefited from Hizbullah's resistance, he vehemently denied that Syria used Hizbullah as a tool of policy in order to further its strategic interest of recovering the Golan Heights, or to pressure Israel and the US by urging Hizbullah to enflame the northern front with Israel.[151]

After the Syrian withdrawal, Nawwaf al-Musawi argued that the party embarked on the decision to involve itself more in the domestic Lebanese political scene by joining the Lebanese cabinet, in the wake of the Syrian President's decision on March 5, 2005 to withdraw his army from Lebanon. He explained that Hizbullah took this decision in order to fill the vacuum that resulted from the Syrian withdrawal and to stop the Western powers, most notably the US and France[152], from exercising their influence in Lebanese domestic affairs.[153] Qasim revealed that the Syrian withdrawal dictated a change in Hizbullah's tactics. He added that Hizbullah took an irrevocable decision not to join the cabinet as long as the Syrians were present in Lebanon since their presence accorded Hizbullah political protection. Also the general trend in Lebanon and the Syrian-Lebanese coordination were conducive to offering that protection. Qasim added, however, after the Syrian withdrawal Hizbullah felt that the Lebanese cabinet would have to take important political decisions that might have grave consequences on the future of Lebanon, the face off with Israel, and the specificity of the Resistance. From this perspective, Hizbullah deemed it an "executional and implementational" necessary to join the cabinet since this move would shelter the party with bona fide protection.[154] Hajj Muhammad Ra'd stressed the importance of putting the Lebanese-Syrian relations on the right track on the basis of mutual benefit and interest to the two countries, especially in the domain of political-strategic as well as economic coordination and coalescence. In addition, Ra'd called for total coordination and cooperation between the two countries in order to ward off any Israeli aggression and foreign intervention, tutelage, and hegemony over Lebanon, Syria, and the Middle East.[155] Nasrallah stressed that becoming a foe to Syria is counterproductive to Lebanese interests.[156]

The discourse of Hizbullah's leading cadres conveyed an ideological-strategic alliance between Hizbullah and Iran. After the death of Imam Khumayni, Hizbullah ideologically commanded allegiance to his successor, Imam Khamina'i, the official *faqih*. Hizbullah unequivocally stated that it does not regard the regime in the Islamic Republic of Iran as the jurisconsult of *all* the Muslims, and in consequence, not all Islamic movements have to abide by the orders and directives of the *faqih* or the regime.[157] Hizbullah's leadership is represented by the *Shura* Council[158], which gets its legitimacy from the *faqih*. Thus, it has a wide margin of prerogatives and delegated responsibilities that facilitate the performance of its duties in line with an individual and specific margin and in harmony with the *Shura* Council's estimation of the executive performance, which is deemed beneficial for its purpose and its general line of work.[159]

In May 1995 after Khamina'i achieved the level of *marja' al-taqlid*, he nominated Sayyid Hasan Nasrallah, Hizbullah's Secretary general, and Shaykh Muhammad Yazbik, Hizbullah's *Shura* Council member, as his representatives in Lebanon. This move granted Hizbullah special prerogatives and delegated responsibilities that reflect a great independence in practical performance. Even though the *faqih* need not monitor, on a daily basis, or keep his eye on Hizbullah, the party's leadership takes the initiative to question, or ask the permission of the *faqih* if it needs to know the *shar'i* judgment concerning a particular issue, such as participation in the 1992 elections, for instance. Hizbullah also consults with the *faqih* if it needs to know if a certain act could be deemed as legitimate or not; if it confronts a basic juncture or watershed; and if it faces grave issues that might lead to a retrogression or deflection in the performance, or affect a basic principle.[160] Although the watershed decision to participate in the Lebanese cabinet ideologically requires the *shar'i* judgment and legitimacy of the *faqih*, for the first time in its history, Hizbullah secured the legitimacy from Shaykh 'Afif al-Nabulsi, the head of the Shi'ite religious scholars of Jabal 'Amil of south Lebanon, and not Imam Khamina'i, which indicates more independence in decision-making. Indeed, administrative matters; following and keeping update with the nitty-gritty daily political work; cultural and social issues; even *jihad* against the Israeli occupier, in all its details, are the prerogatives and responsibilities of the elected leadership of Hizbullah's cadres in conformity with the internal bylaws of the party.[161] Thus, Hizbullah does not blindly follow and adhere to Iranian policies, because the Lebanese circumstances differ from Iranian ones in many respects. Islam is universal; it is a worldly phenomenon. When this Islam is practised in Iran, it results in dynamism and gives a positive experience. However, Hizbullah does not abide by Islam only on the basis of its presence in Iran.[162]

Since Iran is obliged and committed to abide by the directives of Khamina'i, the *faqih*, then this obligation and commitment resulted in an easy convergence of ideological and strategic interests between Iran and Hizbullah's vision towards the problems of the Middle East, which particularly resulted in boosting Hizbullah's resistance identity. Hizbullah's ideological relations are with the official *marja' al-taqlid*, Imam Khamina'i, and Iranian state institutions that are mostly controlled by the conservatives. Hizbullah does not take part in the internal Iranian debates and dynamics; rather what concerns Hizbullah is its good relations with both the conservatives and reformers as well as with other sectors in Iran, who, according to Hizbullah, all support its right to resist the Israeli occupation and are with the liberation of the land.[163] As such, Hizbullah contends that internal Iranian disputes and problems have no bearing on it since they are domestic Iranian affairs that Hizbullah does not interfere in.[164] Also, there is no connection between the management of the affairs of the Islamic Republic and Hizbullah's administration, for these are two different things having their own particularities and specificities, each in its own right. Hizbullah and Iran have also different administrative visions, even if they share a convergence in abiding by Khamina'i's directives and ordinances.[165] Hizbullah's relations with Iran do not dictate limitations on its domestic, regional, and international agendas and policies. Domestically this commitment does not hinder Hizbullah's *infitah* or the building of various relationships with different institutions of civil society, especially political parties, interest groups, and NGOs. Also, it does not interfere with Hizbullah's regional relations and international cooperation.[166]

2.8   Hizbullah's position regarding Israel

Hizbullah referred to Israel as the "Zionist Entity, which, in its very origin, creation, and makeup is based upon a malicious belligerence and rape of the Palestinian land and its people".[167] According to Hizbullah, "The Zionist Entity is absolutely and completely groundless and baseless (*batil*); it is a rapist, vanquisher, occupier, terrorist, cancerous entity that has absolutely no legitimacy or legal status. This is a solid belief/faith and commitment in the Islamic Resistance and its rifles and bullets (weapons) and the blood of its holy warriors (*mujahidin*): Death to Israel".[168] Hizbullah put the accent on its identity as an Islamic *jihadi* movement against the "Zionist Entity" since, on an existential level, Hizbullah's doctrinal foundations leave no room for granting any legitimacy or recognition to 'Israel'.[169] Hizbullah blasted the "Zionist enemy" and its "brutal" invasion, extortion, threats, and aggressions. Hizbullah emphasized that it will liberate Lebanon from the "rapist Zionists" and their occupation and terrorism.[170]

Hizbullah blasted the Israelis as "racist Zionist Jews".[171] Likewise, Hizbullah vilified Israel as a "racist aggressive entity".[172] Also, Hizbullah exploited the Knesset's (Israeli parliament's) passing of a bill stopping Palestinians from obtaining Israeli citizenship in order to accuse Israel of being "racist and discriminatory".[173] Hizbullah affirms that Israeli society is a military society.[174] Hizbullah stresses that in the state of 'Israel' the distinction between Jews as "People of the Book" and Zionists does not hold anymore because all the citizens are considered Zionists. Hizbullah affirms that in Israel, it does not distinguish between a civilian and a military, a woman, a child, and an elderly. Hizbullah argues, with a strong qualification[175], that in Israel there are no civilians: they are all conquerors, occupiers, rapists of the land; they are all taking part in the crime and the massacre... they are all Zionists and must be killed.[176] Hizbullah adds that killing them is a religious obligation, and the persons who do it are regarded as martyrs.[177] However, Hizbullah stresses that the formula of equating civilians to the military applies *only* to Israel, not outside its borders, or is the particular case of the Zionist entity. Hizbullah stressed that in all other places the Jews have the status of "The People of the Book".[178]

Hizbullah added, "No one has the right to give up one pebble of sand of Palestine's land; no one has the right to relinquish one letter of the name of Palestine".[179] Hizbullah affirmed that it is totally against any negotiations, normalisation of relations, cultural invasion, and peace negotiations[180] or treaties with Israel that would grant legitimacy to its rape of the land and aggression against the Palestinian people and would only give back 22% of the "historic" Palestine – the June 4, 1967 borders.[181] Hizbullah clarified that its stance conforms to the Islamic Republic's solution to the Palestinian crisis, namely, a general referendum that includes the "indigenous Palestinian people" composed of the Muslims, Jews, and Christians – who are spread worldwide and inside the Occupied Territories – in order to determine their future and the type of government they aspire for.[182] In other words, Hizbullah demands the return of all the 1948 "historic" Palestine, from the Jordan river till the Mediterranean Sea, and the repatriation of all the Jews who came after the 1916 Sykes-Picot Agreement that divided the Middle East among the British and French after the demise of the Ottoman Empire, placing Palestine under British Mandate.[183]

2.9   The Banner of *Jihad* and Martyrdom

2.9.1   *Smaller military jihad and greater jihad*

Hizbullah's distinction between halal and haram in smaller military jihad

Hizbullah clarified its stance on the killing of innocent civilians when it offered an outright condemnation of the Madrid March 11, 2004 terrorist bombings[184]. Hizbullah denounced the bombings, which cannot be warranted by any standards or criteria, as a horrible crime and a blatant attack against innocent civilians and people. Hizbullah stressed that every attack that targets innocent civilians, to whichever country or religion or nation they belong to, is a cowardly act that is vehemently censured from an Islamic, Qur'anic, and Muhammadi perspective.[185]

Hizbullah affirmed that not all fighting is *jihad*, stressing that the Islamic-Qur'anic terminology (*mustalah*) or definition of *jihad*, is that *jihad* is the specificity of fighting in the way of God: "Oh believers, if you journey [fight with the sword] in the way of Allah be discerning... And he who kills a believer intentionally will, as punishment, be thrown into Hell, dwelling in it forever; and Allah will be angry with him, curse him and prepare for him a dreadful punishment" (4:94+93). Hizbullah added that this is par excellence the toughest punishment in the Qur'an inflicted upon a person who intentionally kills a believer, for this the worst sin (*kabira*). According to Hizbullah, *jihad* has its own religious injunctions and jurisprudence; there is religiously sanctioned (*halal*) and religiously prohibited (*haram*) in *jihad*. That is why, Hizbullah stressed the need to ask the jurisprudents about the jurisprudential details dealing with the *jihadi* work, or else this work would not be done for God, rather for some other end. And so, Hizbullah stressed that *jihad* in the way of God should be governed by God's *shari'a*, God's legitimacy, and the total subjugation and obedience to God's volition.[186]

However, Hizbullah's smaller military *jihad* against the occupying Israeli forces falls within the domain of *halal jihad*, since it is not only sanctioned by the Qur'an, religious injunctions, and jurisprudence, but also by the International Bill of Human Rights as well as the UN Charter.[187] Based on the aforementioned, Hizbullah emphasized its identity as an Islamic *jihadi* movement against the "Zionist" invasion and occupation of Lebanon. Hizbullah underscored the legitimate right of its Islamic Resistance to practice self-defence as a natural and inalienable right in accordance with international legitimacy.[188] Hizbullah affirmed its resistance identity by mobilizing a large proportion of its resources in building a full-pledged resistance society (*mujtama' al-muqawama*) in order to safeguard the Lebanese populace. Hizbullah depicted itself as the party of "Resistance and Liberation". As such, a *jihadi* is a person who sacrifices his self and possessions in a war of national resistance against occupying forces.[189] Hizbullah praised its model of resistance, which accomplished Lebanon's liberation from Israeli occupation, exhorting the populace in the Middle East, in general, and the oppressed Palestinian people, in particular, to adopt it.[190] As a practical political dimension, Hizbullah founded its "*Jihadi* Council" is 1995 in order to closely monitor and supervise its *jihadi* activities. It is worth mentioning that the *Jihadi* Council gained more importance after the May 2000 nearly complete Israeli withdrawal, since in its last 2004 conclave, the Secretary General himself became its head.

A new dimension to greater jihad

Hizbullah's *Jihadi* Council gave a new practical dimension to greater *jihad*. Hizbullah portrayed its participation in the 1996 parliamentary elections as greater *jihad*. Hizbullah crowned its election program with the following Qur'anic verse: "But those who struggle [*jahadu*] in Our cause, surely We shall guide them in Our ways [paths]; and God is with the good-doers" (29:69). It is worth mentioning that Hizbullah considered the Lebanese government's acquiescence to its demand of the creation of a separate governarate in *B'albak-Hirmel* in July 2003 as a victory in greater *jihad*. Hizbullah celebrated this political victory as it used to celebrate successful *jihadi* operations against the Israeli forces in the battlefield.[191] The discourse of Hizbullah's leaders stressed the importance of greater *jihad*. Nasrallah has remarked, in addressing the municipal councils and the majors of the South, that greater *jihad* is directed against the self, and that the greater struggler (*al-mujahid al-akbar*) is the one who can immune, hold back, and control himself from committing vices and engaging in corruption. Nasrallah stressed that the Hizbullahi's endeavour and contriving, their presence on the ground, meetings in the municipality and elective councils, and daily efforts to serve the public are all *jihad*. Nasrallah emphasised that the greater *jihad* is when man refrains from theft and embezzlement.[192] Nasrallah added that this holding back is the greater *jihad* and is the measure of victory and defeat as well as of success and failure. He called for transparency and accountability as the best means to face corruption.[193] Nasrallah added that fighting corruption is much more difficult than resisting Israel. According to him, the Islamic Resistance could defeat 100 'Israels', but the corruption in Lebanon is stronger than 100 'Israels'. Nasrallah stressed that in fighting the Israeli occupation there was a national consensus; however, in fighting corruption one has to fight with a considerable number of his fellow citizens. Nasrallah concluded, the *jihad* of resisting corruption is more severe and more bitter than resisting the occupation.[194]

Hizbullah's distinction between suicide and martyrdom

Reflecting on the political debates that took place before the 1992 elections, Hizbullah stressed that its decision to contest the elections is based on permanent-principled political convictions, which are enforced by the blood of its martyrs and their families, the suffering and pain of its prisoners of war, detainees, wounded, and the oppressed. Hizbullah emphasized that it has sacrificed for these principles and convictions its best cadres who martyred themselves in resisting and driving out the "Zionist Occupation".[195]

In conformity to its resistance identity as an Islamic *jihadi* movement, Hizbullah sanctioned martyrdom operations (*al-'amaliyyat al-Istishadiyya*) in its political program as a specific resistance strategy against a superior, well-equipped army when conventional smaller military *jihad* tactics prove to be futile. Hizbullah unequivocally states that it employed martyrdom operations as one of its distinguished techniques and a tactic of resistance against the allegedly "invincible" Israeli forces occupying Lebanon. In addition to elevating the spirits across the *umma*, Hizbullah purports that its martyrdom operations inflicted heavy casualties on the Israeli occupying forces and spread the reigns of terror among them.[196] Hizbullah regards martyrdom in the way of God as the epitome of self-offering, giving the self and possessions, self-sacrifice, and the "preference" (*ithar*) of a dignified life in heaven, as to living under the disgrace of occupation; and the preference of the well being of the *umma* over that of the individual.[197] Hizbullah added that the most vital human right that it has been sacrificing the blood of its martyrs to is the right of the Lebanese to their land.[198] Hizbullah stressed that martyrdom in the way of God should be governed by God's *shari'a*, God's legitimacy, and the total subjugation and obedience to God's volition.

From here comes the devotion to martyrdom and the love of meeting God. In all other circumstances martyrdom becomes suicide; however, the final evaluation (*taqyyim*) is for God.[199]

Hizbullah distinguishes between suicide operations and martyrdom operations mainly in response to the West's accusations[200]. Hizbullah contends that suicide, not martyrdom, is an expression of *hopelessness*, frustration, and despair of life that usually occurs in the case of *non-believers* who are facing, for instance, economic, social, or political hardships. Hizbullah is confident that while, a believer surrenders to the will of God and knows that his/her patience will lead to rewards in heaven; however, a person who commits suicide will go to hell because he/she is not free to dispose his/her life as he/she deems fit. That is why understanding martyrdom and agreeing to it is not subordinate to international conventions or the enemies' and the oppressors' policies.[201]

Hizbullah argues that it is quite natural that those who wage an organised campaign against martyrdom in order to distort it and label it with demeaning connotations do so because it has given Hizbullah a special and extraordinary power that made the party's will to attain victory stronger, especially when power shifted in the direction of the enemies.[202] According to Hizbullah, the West resorts to threats and intimidations that are of no avail to the martyrs since they live in this world, but are not part of it. Martyrdom is as dangerous as non-conventional weapons because the target can never prepare a defence mechanism to deal with it, unlike the defences that have been created to deal with almost any weapon. That is why, martyrdom as a weapon is tenable and cannot be controlled or contained by the enemy.[203]

Hizbullah has reiterated, on various occasions that victory is always the result of martyrdom. It referred to the enormous pride and dignity in the hearts of the martyrs. Hizbullah emphasized that the Palestinian people in the (West Bank and Gaza), as well as the Lebanese, possess a substantial power; they are lovers of martyrdom, lovers of meeting God, lovers of departing to the vicinity of God and the eternal gardens (garden of Eden).[204] Hizbullah " 'does not pursue martyrdom as an end in itself', but as a means of achieving victory... without the imperative need for a defensive *jihad*, martyrdom becomes suicide, which is clearly proscribed in Islam and thereby not rewarded with an everlasting life in paradise, as is true martyrdom: 'Maybe some people think we crave martyrdom because we like to die in any way. No, we like to die if our blood is valued and has a great impact [on Israel]' ".[205]

Hizbullah, Ayatullah Fadlallah, and Iran[206] condemned September 11, 2001, and the London July 7, 2005 attacks[207] as suicide-terrorist attacks that cannot be considered martyrdom operations, which are being carried out by national resistance movements that aim at the liberation of land still under occupation.[208]

Ayatullah Fadlallah denounced the September 11 operations as criminal-suicidal acts that constitute an ugly human genocide in all respects. These, according to him, are not martyrdom acts. He added that neither offensive nor defensive *jihad* justifies such acts that are denounced religiously (*shar'an*). These are vicious acts that are not sanctioned by any religion, civilization, and human logic. It is not right to use innocent-peaceful civilians as bargaining chips and means of leverage to change a certain [US] policy. Islamically speaking, it is wrong to get engaged in such acts because there is no *shar'i* justification for such acts. September 11 is a horrendous act that is not authorized by any religion or approved by any "heavenly message", he affirmed. Thus, Fadlallah is adamantly against targeting civilian means of transportation because their safety and security is a worldly, humane concern from a *shari'* perspective.[209]

Hizbullah condemned the September 11, 2001 suicidal attacks against the US, showing sympathy towards the US people, while blasting the US Administration:

> After many Muslim clergy men stated their position toward the bloody attacks which recently occurred in New York and Washington, we call for caution and not falling prey to a state of fear and panic that was intended to be spread throughout the world to give the US administration free rein to practice all types of aggression and terrorism under the pretext of fighting aggressions and terrorism, Now the big question is whether what the American administration is planning really has to do with responding to the perpetrators of the latest attacks, or whether it wants to exploit those tragic events to exercise more hegemony over the world and practice more unjust policies which have led to this level of hate against the US by many peoples and governments in the world. The world, which is now waiting for the U.S response, must not forget that there are massacres carried out against the Palestinian people by the Israeli occupation, which feels proud, that the world is silent towards its crimes. We are sorry for any innocent people who are killed anywhere in the world. The Lebanese, who have suffered repeated Zionist massacres in Qana and elsewhere, massacres that the US administration refused to condemn at the UN Security Council, are familiar with the pain and suffering of those who lost their loved ones in bitter events.[210]

181

Ayatullah Fadlallah's *fatwa* stated that the London July 7, 2005 attacks are criminal-suicidal acts unacceptable to any religion, reason, and abhorred by any *shar'i* or positive (man-made) law. He added it is a kind of savagery that is totally rejected by Islam in spite of some people's endeavours to accord an Islamic flavour to these attacks, or insinuate that Islam accepts these attacks. In turn, Hizbullah's political declaration stressed that targeting the innocent is censured by all human, ethical, and religious standards. Hizbullah extended its consolation to the victims of the attacks, expressing its empathy and compassion with the families of the victims, in particular, and the Britons, in general.[211]

3. Chapter conclusion

Hizbullah's 1991 political declaration and Sayyid Abbas' 1991 political program announced its *infitah*, dialogue, and Lebanonisation process as major pillars of its down to earth political program for the coming decades.

As regards Hizbullah's arguments for participation in the 1992 parliamentary elections, the committee recommended that participation in the elections is a beneficiary must, which is in harmony with Hizbullah's *holistic* vision that favours living up to the expectations of the people by serving their socio-economic, and political concerns. Hizbullah's greater *jihad* and dedication to addressing the plight of the people does not contradict its priority of smaller military *jihad* for the sake of liberation of occupied land. Participating in the elections leads to the achievement of good political results, and is also regarded as a leading step towards interaction with others. By this Hizbullah presents a novel experience in the *infitah* of a young Islamic party. The committee stressed that this participation is in accordance with the Lebanese particularities and specificities as well as the nature of the proposed elections, which allow for a considerable margin of freedom of choice. In short, the committee concluded that the sum total of the pros (*masalih*) outweighs the cons (*mafasid*) by far; that is why participation in the parliament is worthwhile since it is viewed as one of the ways of influencing change and making Hizbullah's voice heard, not only domestically, but also regionally and internationally. Thus, it seems that Hizbullah is forced by the political circumstances, the Ta'if Agreement and the end of the civil war, to change to a new phase in its history by propagating of a matter of fact political program and by co-opting with the Lebanese system.

3.1 Views on the oppressed and oppressors, the US and Israel in particular

Hizbullah offered an Islamic justification to sanction its participation in the parliamentary elections by buttressing the oppressed against the oppressors. The opening Qur'anic verse of Hizbullah's 1992 election program (22:41) serves such a purpose because it stresses the Qur'anic concept of human empowerment that leads to the production of the doctrines of general human sovereignty and the responsibility of the community. It is worth mentioning that "establish them firmly in the land" connotes granting them political power. This is reminiscent of the Prophet who established the Islamic community in Medina. Hizbullah seems to be arguing that acquiring authority or political power through parliamentary representation, would not deflect it from giving due attention to the private sphere of prayer, and the social or public sphere of alms giving as well as commanding the good and prohibiting the evil. I think that Hizbullah's apologetic discourse, which sanctioned the "Islamists" to participate in the electoral process, also reflects the internal heated debates, among Hizbullah's cadres and leadership, which eventually led to the production and propagation of such a program.

Domestically, Hizbullah's political program stressed that its parliamentary and municipal work would wholeheartedly protect the socio-economic and political interests of the Lebanese oppressed. Regionally and internationally, Hizbullah's political program blasted Israel and the US as oppressors: the US for aiming to hegemonise Lebanon and the Middle East, while at the same time buttressing Israel's occupation and "aggression". Hizbullah criticised the imposition of the market economy and the Western mode of production on the people of the Middle East by the US, which has been aiming at robbing the wealth, natural resources, and planting despotic regimes in order to crush, dominate, and mutilate the cultural identity of the oppressed.

3.2 Hizbullah's views on the Islamic State

None of Hizbullah's 1992, 1996, 1998, 2000, 2004, and 2005 parliamentary and municipal election programs mentions, refers to, or advocates the founding of an Islamic state in Lebanon. Hizbullah emphasized that the establishment of an Islamic state could not be the result of the logic or adoption of a certain group or faction of people, who enforce it or enforce their own opinions on other groups or factions in society. Hizbullah neither applies nor accepts coercion in its project of Islamisation; rather the establishment of an Islamic state should be the result of freedom, will, and direct choice of the people. Hizbullah would only move in the direction of implementing an Islamic State in Lebanon on the basis of a democratic, tolerant process sanctioned by the majority of the non-Muslims and Muslims.

Thus, it seems that due to practical reasons of political expediency, Hizbullah has put to rest, once and for all, the issue of the establishment or implementation of an Islamic state in Lebanon. That is why its political program can be regarded as pragmatic. This accounts for Hizbullah's participation in electoral politics, and its decision to take an active part in the Lebanese public sphere. It seems that Hizbullah was in its political programs down-to-earth and practical since it most probably saw that it is counter-productive and politically unwise to mention its earlier commitment to an Islamic order. However, there appears to be a discrepancy between these political programs and the discourse of its leaders who continued to give lip service to the old ideological commitment of establishing an Islamic order. Thus, it is most likely that Hizbullah was guided by political expediency since in its political programs it accepted the fact that the majority of the Lebanese do not opt for an Islamic order, and imposing it by force is not an option.

3.3 Hizbullah's dialogue with the Lebanese Christians

In conformity to Sayyid Abbas's political program, which called for a Lebanonisation process, *infitah*, and dialogue, most notably, with the Christians, Hizbullah took the initiative in 1992 and visited the Maronite Patriarch. The talks centred mostly upon Christian-Muslim dialogue and Hizbullah's gradual integration in the Lebanese public sphere. However, with the passage of time, Hizbullah's dialogue did not remain confined to the Maronites only, rather it was extended to encompass the rest of the Christians that comprise the Lebanese mosaic. Hizbullah conducted dialogue with the Christians and other groups on the basis of transparency in order to reach common grounds. As to the content and subjects of the dialogue, Hizbullah tried to avoid engagement in theological or religious issues, which are the specificity and particularity of every sect in the Lebanese myriad, and concentrated on nurturing dialogue dealing with political, socio-economic, and civil society issues. In its political program, Hizbullah blamed political sectarianism for Lebanon's malaise, calling for its abolishment in line with Lebanon's 1990 new constitution. Hizbullah embarked on an open, peaceful, and constructive dialogue with all sects, political parties, and civil society groups and organizations in order to tackle the source or origin of cultural, political, theoretical, and practical differences.

Hizbullah tried to portray itself as a big Muslim-Christian co-existence promoter stressing the importance of pluralism through multi-confessional representation. It incorporated Christians, including Maronites, in its parliamentary elections lists and granted them the right to speak in its name as long as they do not deflect from the party's established doctrines. Also, it shared municipal council seats with Christians. Thus, Hizbulah made it clear that the only condition for a sympathizer to speak in its name is to abide by its policy guidelines. Hizbullah's dialogue with the Christians, as stipulated in its political program, garnered the party support in its resistance against Israel and *infitah* policies, especially among the Christians. By adopting what many observers would consider "Christian discourse", namely, the abolition of political sectarianism in the mentality, before abolishing it in the texts, Hizbullah is portraying a progressive-liberal, and pragmatic view on the abolishment of political sectarianism, which is in conformity with the stance of the Maronite Church and the Papal Guidance. The Pope's call for fraternity and the inculcation of dialogue and tolerance among the Lebanese had a responsive cord in Hizbullah's circles since most of it was reminiscent of Imam Musa al-Sadr's discourse on Christian-Muslim understanding, mutual coexistence, and open and permanent dialogue. Thus, in an endeavour of rapprochement towards the Lebanese Christians, Hizbullah based its political program of dialogue with them on the Papal Guidance.

3.4 Hizbullah's jurisprudential stipulations of parliamentary, municipal, and governmental work

Hizbullah's jurisprudential stipulations conveyed its understanding and usage of Islamic law in dealing with non-*shar'i* laws through the purposes of *shari'a* and the maxims of Islamic jurisprudence such as "necessities permit what is prohibited", "what can not be accomplished in its whole, can not be left in its entirety", and most notably "the warding off vices is preferable to obtaining interests". Based on this pragmatic-religious legitimisation, Hizbullah was able to strike a balance between its Islamic identity, on the one hand, and its parliamentary, municipal, and governmental work, on the other, thus justifying its participation in the Lebanese system. This reasoning falls in line with, what Hizbullah calls, Islam's comprehensive-holistic project that deals with all aspects of human life through its flexible *shari'a*, which covers man's needs, necessities, and progress.

Although it is typical of Hizbullah's discourse and political program to consider the ultimate principle of legislation to be Islamic law in accordance with the *shari'a*, Hizbullah's political program highlights the possibility of making the *shari'a* flexibility through the employment of a pragmatic approach in its distinction between situation bound laws or legislations (non-*shar'i* laws) that are transient, on the one hand, and religious or juris-prudential legislations, on the other. Also, Hizbullah's characterization of the two principles that it bases its political work upon, namely warding off vices and the face off between the most and least damaging, is pragmatic because it is based on interest and necessity. Hizbullah concluded that juris-prudential stipulations, which form the backbone of civil legislations, per-mit a substantial margin of manoeuvre in influencing non-*shar'i* legislations and decisions. Building on this reasoning, Hizbullah legitimises its partici-pation in the democratic process on the basis of a practical application of the Qur'anic concepts of *shura, ikhtilaf, al-huquq al-shar'iyya*, and *ijtihad*: the Islamisation of democracy by way of consultation (*shura*) through popular empowerment (*tamkin*); tolerance and acceptance through pluralism (*ikhti-laf*); respect, honour, and dignity through human, 'legal' rights (*al-huquq al-shar'iyya*).

After the theoretical dimension dealing with the religious legitimacy of participating in the cabinet was settled, Hizbullah has to objectively and practically weight between the interests and vices that might result from this participation. It seems Hizbullah joined the Lebanese cabinet when its strategic calculations legitimatised by its interpretation of *shari'a* dictated such participation.

3.5   Hizbullah's socio-economic program:
       its NGOs and civil institutions

Hizbullah conveyed in its parliamentary and municipal elections programs[212] that it is a project for national Resistance and liberation, which founded its NGOs and civil institutions for a more effective and compre-hensive socio-economic support. Hizbullah's political program stressed that socio-economic, intellectual, and cultural work is concomitant with resist-ance and should go hand in hand with it. In being faithful to its socio-eco-nomic program, Hizbullah built an efficient network of NGOs and civil insti-tutions dealing with all aspects of life ranging from socio-economic issues to cultural, educational, and health concerns. Since Hizbullah extended its services to all the Lebanese living in its constituencies, Hizbullah's NGOs and civil institutions granted it popular and political support even among non-Muslims. Hizbullah's civil institutions and NGOs are a testimony to its capac-ity to merge in civil society and engage in democratic practices once the services of its Islamic Resistance are not needed anymore.[213]

Hizbullah stressed that its political program dwells upon its civilizational belonging and commitment, which aspires to accord man with felicity and dignity. As religious legitimisation, Hizbullah employed the Qur'anic verse (28:77), which implies that its engagement in the elections is based upon the stance that one should not neglect the here and now, the present life for the sake of the hereafter since any Hizbullahi aspires for felicity in this world and the world to come (*al-sa'da fi al-darayn*). Hizbullah broadened the horizon of the Qur'anic concept of *al-huquq al-shar'iyya* to include, in addition to *zakat* and *khums*, the basic human rights, which the International Bill of Human Rights mentions and which Hizbullah's NGOs and civil institutions grant to the people.

3.6 Hizbullah as a nationalist Lebanese political party (Lebanonisation)

Hizbullah expressed its Islamic legitimisation in democratic form by portraying itself as a mainstream nationalist Lebanese political party while at the same time upholding its Islamic identity. Hizbullah's *infitah* and Lebanonisation endeavoured to convey how it was able strike a balance between its Islamic identity and program, on the one hand, and its Lebanese national loyalty, on the other through "opening-up" to the various constituents of the Lebanese myriad. Although Hizbullah denies it, it seems its success in weighing between nationalist political commitments and its Islamic background was at the price of negotiations, bargaining, and compromises (even on some doctrinal issues), which characterise an open democratic system. Through buttressing civil peace, public freedoms, and a functioning civil society, Hizbullah attempted to preserve its Islamic identity while working within the domain of Lebanese state's sovereignty, within a non-Islamic state and a multi-religious-confessional-sectarian state. Thus, Hizbullah cannot go beyond being a political party operating within the Lebanese public sphere by accommodating its protest through contestation[214], co-optation[215], and empowerment[216]. Hizbullah's Lebanonisation and *infitah* fall under contestation; its participation in electoral politics and governmental work could be regarded as co-optation; and Hizbullah's ascendancy to the political scene becoming a nationalistic political party can be viewed from the stance of empowerment. Thus, it is most likely that the Lebanese public sphere is dictating certain policies on Hizbullah, and the Lebanese political structure seems to be co-opting Hizbullah to take decisions that may not be that popular to the rank, file, and leaders. On the whole, Hizbullah's decisions are based on *realpolitik*, political expediency, benefit, and interest (*maslaha*). This calls into question the extent to which Hizbullah is willing to be co-opted into the Lebanese political system/government and state institutions as well as its possible diffusion in the public sector.

3.7   Hizbullah's stance towards Syria and Iran

Even though there is an ideological-strategic alliance between Hizbullah and Iran, on the one hand, and a political-strategic partnership between Hizbullah and Syria, on the other, the previous presentation has shown that Hizbullah is not a tool of policy in Syrian and Iranian hands. Rather, Hizbullah has pursued an independent course of decision-making and action that suits the particularities and specificities of the Lebanese political equation by putting into practice its political program of Lebanonisation, *infitah*, and integration in the Lebanese public sphere.

3.8   Hizbullah's position regarding Israel

In its political program, Hizbullah considers Israel as the Zionist Entity that should be wiped out from the face of the earth so that the state of Palestinian could be reinstated along the pre-1948 borders. In other words, Hizbullah still adopts the pre-1967 Arab nationalist discourse that grants no legitimacy or recognition to Israel, refuses peace negotiations with it, and stands firmly against any normalisation of relations with it.

Hizbullah considers the Jews as "People of the Book", and *only* regards the Jews living in Israel as Zionists, who should be killed, as Nasrallah puts it. From the stance of regarding discrimination as a form of oppression, Hizbullah has blasted the Israelis as "racist Zionist Jews". Although on occasions Hizbullah has censured Israel for being "racist and discriminatory", Hizbullah neither discriminates against the Jews as a religion nor as a race. Thus, it seems that Hizbullah is not anti-Semitic in its overall orientation.[217] It is worth mentioning that Hizbullah's equating the civilians with the military in the state of Israel, as radical as it seems, is neither new, nor is it confined to it or to Islamic movements.[218]

3.9   The banner of *jihad* and martyrdom

In all its election programs Hizbullah stressed the feats of its Islamic Resistance that engaged in smaller military *jihad* against the occupying Israeli army, thus enforcing Hizbullah's resistance identity. Hizbullah prided itself in erecting a resistance society and in exporting its model of resistance as an exemplar to other resistance movements. In addition to the religious legitimacy of resisting occupation through smaller military *jihad*, Hizbullah added the legitimacy of the international community and international bodies. Hizbullah's struggle against Israel falls within the domain of smaller military *jihad* or the *jihad* against the enemy, while greater *jihad* is the internal *jihad* with the self and holding it from living according to the flesh and being engaged in corruption. Hizbullah gave a new dimension to greater *jihad* since it emphasised that its mission in fighting domestic corruption in the Lebanese political and administrative system is much more difficult than defeating 100 'Israels'. In other words, Hizbullah seems to be arguing that engaging in greater *jihad* is 100 times more difficult than engaging in smaller military *jihad*.

Hizbullah also extended the use of greater *jihad* to its participation in the elections.[219] It used as a legitimisation the Qur'anic verse (29:69), which is usually employed to sanction and justify smaller military *jihad*, and which theologically falls within the domain of the controversy regarding free will and predestination. Hizbullah opted for free will, and broadened the mandate of the verse: 'God will help us if we perform greater *jihad* in the elections'. According to Hizbullah this is another way of the giving of blood.[220] Since 1995, both smaller military *jihad* and greater *jihad* has been supervised by Hizbullah's *Jihadi* Council, which gave a new dynamic and pragmatic dimension to both.

Hizbullah introduced a groundbreaking distinction between religiously sanctioned (*halal*) and religiously prohibited (*haram*) *jihad*. It drew a line between *jihad* in the way of God, on the one hand, and vengeful piety i.e. when the suicide bombers regard themselves as avengers of God, on the other. Hizbullah exalted the former and vilified the latter. Building on the Qur'anic verse (4:93-4), religious injunctions, and Islamic jurisprudence, Hizbullah emphasized that religiously sanctioned *jihad* is only carried out when fighting in the way of God. Hizbullah affirmed that intentionally killing innocent civilians would be rewarded by hell fire. From this perspective Hizbullah condemned the March 11, 2004 Madrid terrorist attacks as well as the September 11, 2001 and the London July 7, 2005 suicide-terrorist attacks. Hizbullah also vehemently condemned all other terrorist attacks targeting innocent civilians worldwide. Since the international community regards all martyrdom operations as suicide actions, Hizbullah could not claim their support in its martyrdom operations, rather it contended itself with religious and strategic legitimisations as a resistance tactic against a superior army. Hizbullah regards martyrdom as a strategic means towards achieving victory, rather than an end in itself. Like the *jihadi*, the martyr in the way of God is willing to sacrifice the self and possessions.

5 A Specific Perspective on the General Shifts
in the Constituents of Hizbullah's Ideology in the Three Stages

1.   Introduction

The Lebanese Shi'ite resistance movement, Hizbullah, is going through a remarkable political and ideological transformation. Hizbullah was founded in 1978 by various sectors of Lebanese Shi'ite clergy and cadres, and with Iranian backing as an Islamic movement protesting against social and political conditions. Over the years 1984/5 to 1991, Hizbullah became a full-pledged social movement in the sense of having a broad overall organization, structure, and ideology aiming at social change and social justice, as it claimed. Starting in 1992, it became a mainstream political party working within the narrow confines of its pragmatic political program. The line of argument in this book is that Hizbullah has been adjusting its identity in the three previously mentioned stages by shifting emphasis among its three components: (1) from propagating an exclusivist religious ideology; (2) to a more encompassing political ideology; and (3) to a down-to-earth political program.

In these three stages, however, Hizbullah's identity as an Islamic *jihadi* (struggle) movement remained as one of its *thawabit* (immutable set of values), but the justifications of Islamic principles, in particular, *jihad* altered. The important shifts in Hizbullah's ideology in the three stages tackle the following topics: *wilayat al-faqih* (guardianship of the jurisprudent or jurisconsult); oppressors and oppressed, with special focus on the US and Israel; *jihad* and martyrdom; Islamic state; Hizbullah's relations with the Lebanese Christians; and Lebanonisation or *infitah* ("opening up").

1.1   Wilayat al-Faqih

In stages one and two, Hizbullah argued that during the formation and early stages, it needed a unifying religio-political ideology, rather than an elaborate political program. So Hizbullah based itself on *wilayat al-faqih* and regarded Imam Khumayni as the jurisconsult of all the Muslims.[1] In stage

one, Hizbullah was almost ideologically completely dependent on Khumayni. In stage two the dependency witnessed some leeway in the sense that
Hizbullah did not blindly follow Iran; rather it had some specificity, since
in his capacity in determining the legitimacy, Khumayni highlighted certain precepts, however, he left their implementation to Hizbullah's discretion. Thus, although Hizbullah was ideologically dependent on Iran, it had
some room to manoeuvre in its decisions pertaining to Lebanese domestic issues, at least in some cases. Although the multiplicity of marja's and
marja'iyya (religious authority/ies) among the Shi'ites continued after Imam
Khumayni's death; however, in Hizbullah's case the issue of marja'iyya has
been determined on the doctrinal-ideological basis of following the official
marja' al-taqlid (authority of emulation) in Iran. Thus, Hizbullah's religious
authority was, is, and will always be the Iranian faqih. This made the transition after Khumayni's death smoother in the end of the second stage and
the third stage, especially since Khamina'i was appointed by Khumayni as
Hizbullah's godfather since its early beginnings. That being said, Hizbullah
from a religious and an ideological stance used to fully abide by the ideas
and opinions of Imam Khumayni as communicated by Khamina'i. Hizbullah clarified that from the stance of religious ideology, it regarded highly
Imam Khumayni, and after his death the same allegiance was accorded to
Khamina'i.

A shift occurred in the third stage when Hizbullah argued that it does
not consider the regime in the Islamic Republic of Iran is the jurisconsult
of *all* the Muslims, and in consequence, not all Islamic movements have to
abide by the orders and directives of the faqih or the regime.[2] Another shift
occurred in stage three, when, in May 1995, Khamina'i nominated Sayyid
Hasan Nasrallah, Hizbullah's Secretary general, and Shaykh Muhammad Yazbik, Hizbullah's Shura Council member, as his representatives in Lebanon.
This led to more Lebanese authenticity in line with the specificities and particularities of the Lebanese society, rather than blind adherence to Iran. Thus,
Hizbullah moved from complete ideological dependency on Khumayni in
the first stage, to less dependency after his death in the second stage, and
finally in the third stage Hizbullah has had more independence in decision-
making, not only in practical political issues, but also in doctrinal issues, to
the extent that one can purport that Hizbullah exercised almost independent decision-making, at least in some cases. For instance, in the summer of
2005, Hizbullah secured the legitimacy to participate in the Lebanese cabinet, for the first time in its history, from Shaykh 'Afif al-Nabulsi, the head of
the Shi'ite religious scholars of Jabal 'Amil of south Lebanon. Thus, Hizbullah

heeds to Lebanese religious authority in addition to the Iranian one. There-fore, Hizbullah's participation in the Lebanese cabinet, which ideologically requires the *shar'i* (religious) judgment and legitimacy of the *faqih*, has been relegated to an administrative matter that Hizbullah's leadership is capable of taking a decision on, exercising independent decision-making. And so, Hizbullah joined the cabinet and proliferated in Lebanese state institutions and administrative structure at a time when the conservative Iranian presi-dent, Mahmud Ahmadi Nejad, and his government came to power in Iran.

Many argue that since the death of Imam Khumayni, there seems to be a discernable change in Hizbullah's political relationship with Iran stress-ing that the liberalization process in Iran might have had its toll on Hizbullah and have influenced its policies towards moderation.[3] However, the reform-ers in Iran do not drastically affect Hizbullah's external and internal poli-cies since its main relationship is with the official *marja'* and Iranian state institutions. That is why the shifting of the presidency from the reformist Khatami to the conservative non-*'alim* (non-cleric)[4] Mahmud Ahmadi Nejad does not alter Hizbullah's relationship with Iran. Hizbullah clarified during its August 2005 visit to Tehran, that contrary to the common perception that categorizes Iran as being torn between the reformists and conservatives, it regards Iran as a monolithic order, rather than two competing powers. Indeed, the previous presentation points to a shift in Hizbullah's relations with Iran, which arguably are moving towards more and more independ-ence, autonomy in decision-making, Lebanese authenticity, and Lebanese particularities, specificities, and interests irrespective of the person of the *faqih* or the president.

It is worth mentioning that until now, Hizbullah's religious ideology continues to play a significant role simply because it is difficult to separate Hizbullah from religious concerns, since it is a religiously based party. How-ever, religion no longer constitutes the sole ideological justification and legitimisation of Hizbullah's behaviour since its usage is nominally based upon the moral claims of Shi'ite Islam, rather than on an uncompromising religious-ideological dogmatic basis, as it where in the first stage. Based on inside sources and my fieldwork observations, it could be fairly stated that the majority of Hizbullah's cadres consider disagreements in religious and political opinions and viewpoints of the leaders to be a true phenomenon, which represents a healthy "democratic" atmosphere. However, strict obe-dience and discipline prevents disagreements from festering into discord, al-Tufayli's case being an exception.

1.2 Oppressors and oppressed, with special focus on the US and Israel

In the first two stages, Hizbullah's use of oppressors and oppressed took another twist in practical terms since it regarded the political Maronites, Israel, France, and the US as the oppressors and all third-world countries as the oppressed. In stage two, Hizbullah employed in political-ideological terms specific Islamic expressions or Qur'anic terminology against the West such as oppressors, oppressed, Great Satan, Little Satan[5], etc. As such, Hizbullah legitimised the distinction between oppressors and oppressed on the basis of the Qur'an (34: 31-33) offering an Islamic theory of oppression. Grounding itself on a host of Qur'anic verses (28:5-6); (8:26); and (42:39), Hizbullah argued that oppressed is a Qur'anic concept that came to prominence with the advent of the Islamic Revolution; as such it has nothing to do with Marxism or Liberation theology, which are deemed completely un-Islamic by Hizbullah. Fadlallah stressed that the Qur'an distinguishes between two groups of the oppressed: the negligent, who practice *taqiyya* (expedient dissimulation) and refuse to migrate, and the committed, who engage in *ta'bi'a* (mobilization) to change their lot (4:97-99). Hizbullah's political ideology emphasizes the all-encompassing nature of the Qur'anic concept of oppression that does not discriminate between race, religion, class, gender, or cultural background.

This translated itself in practical political-ideological terms as a face off with both the East and the West, upholding only Islam (24:35). Hizbullah's reference to the Qur'anic verse on East and West gets another touch since its original use, as a mystical interpretation, is different from the East and West of the cold war. It seems that in stages one and two, Hizbullah's ideology of "No East, no West, rather only Islam" resulted in a substantial following to Iranian foreign policy objectives[6] with regard to the international community and the West. It is most likely that Hizbullah had adopted the Iranian framework of identity. However, Hizbullah replaced Persian nationalism with Arab nationalism. In conformity with Iran's third component of its identity, namely, anti-imperialism, Hizbullah's political ideology preached hostility towards the United States, France, and Israel. This could be seen as a wider symbolic extension of the Iranian revolutionary struggle against foreign intervention and colonialism. Hizbullah's ruling elite viewed its revolutionary struggle in Lebanon through the political-ideological prism of anti-imperialism, anti-colonialism, and pan-Islamism; this was reflected through the linkage of Hizbullah's activity with Iran's foreign policy within Lebanon.

In spite of the aforementioned, xenophobia or antipathy to the West is not rooted in Hizbullah's political ideology of anti-imperialism. Rather Hizbullah's attitude to the West could be viewed from the stance of Westoxification since Hizbullah's anti-imperialism is directed mainly against the political and cultural hegemony of the "Great Satan" (US) and the "Small Satan" (Israel). As such, Hizbullah's political ideology conveys that its animosity is towards the US Administration, not the US people, while in Israel's case Hizbullah's animosity is both towards the Israeli Administration and the Israeli citizens.[7] In short, in stage one, Hizbullah practiced xenophobia; in stage two it shifted to exercise Westoxification; and in stage three less Westoxification, mainly against the US and Israel, while at the same time opening up to European countries, including France and Britain, and international NGOs.

Thus, in the third stage, both Hizbullah's conception and perception towards the oppressed did not change since it still applied the same categorisation as in stages one and two. Although Hizbullah's conception towards the oppressors remained the same, Hizbullah's perception towards the oppressors witnessed some changes. Domestically, the Lebanese state and political Maronism ceased to be regarded as oppressors; on the contrary, Hizbullah co-opted and cooperated with the Lebanese state and participated in the parliamentary and municipal elections, and it even joined the cabinet legitimising that from the stance of its *shar'i* responsibility towards the oppressed people. Regionally and internationally, Hizbullah's animosity towards France – equating it with the Great Satan and the Small Satan – was completely dropped, mainly due to its improved relations with Iran in the 1990. However, Hizbullah's enmity and ideological stance towards Israel and the US remained the same.

Nevertheless, an important policy shift could be noticed. Instead of using Trad Hamadé as a channel of communication, Hizbullah aspires for and wants direct contact and dialogue with the US, as proposed by Hamadé during his talks with the US Administration in June 2005. Nawwaf al-Musawi's meeting with Graham Fuller in March 2005 is a step in that direction. Hizbullah's position presents an ideological shift towards the US. In May 2001 Nasrallah claimed that the US Administration is doing its best to establish contact with Hizbullah. However, according to him, Hizbullah is refusing that from the perspective of its political-ideological stance, power politics, and the interest of the stronger party. He added that the stick and carrot as well as rationalization policies employed by the US Administration to contain and curtail Hizbullah's activities are to no avail.[8]

In stages one and two Hizbullah directed its revolution against political and social injustice and oppression, but did not offer a political program that constructively deals with pressuring socio-economic matters. Hizbullah's call for *hakimiyya* (God's governance) lacked a socio-economic vision, something that would only materialise in the third stage. In the third stage, Hizbullah's parliamentary, municipal, and governmental work was not at the expense of its welfare programs. On the contrary, boosting political work was concomitant with boosting social work. In its political program, Hizbullah stresses its abidance by the International Bill of Human Rights as well as the UN Charter. Hizbullah's assertion of cooperation with local and international voluntary welfare and development associations, including the UNICEF and the UNDP, presents an overhaul to Hizbullah's earlier policies and stands in sharp contrast to its earlier view in the Open Letter regarding international organizations, which were accused of serving Western interests at the expense of the oppressed.[9]

1.3   *Jihad* and martyrdom

Smaller and greater jihad

In the three stages, Hizbullah engaged in smaller military *jihad* by sacrificing the self and possessions as an act of defensive *jihad* against the Israeli forces occupying south Lebanon and the *Biqa'*. In stages one and two, Hizbullah did not have the time to engage in the greater *jihad* of reforming the political system, or in participating in the municipal and parliamentary elections, and governmental and administrative work in order to ward off corruption; rather this is a trait of the third stage. In fact, in stages one and two, Hizbullah engaged in the greater *jihad* of refining and reforming the self through a spiritual-transcendent process that aims at building a coalescent human being. Only then, can the Hizbullahis engage in smaller military *jihad*. Also in these two stages Hizbullah employed greater *jihad* in its *ta'tir* (screening) and recruitment policies as well as its mobilization strategies, through *intizam* (spiritual-religious indoctrination, self-discipline) and *ta'a* (obedience) to God and the *faqih*. Without inculcating this method of Islamic mobilization in the psyche of every Hizbullah member, engagement in smaller military *jihad* and martyrdom was prohibited. In stage two, Hizbullah amplified greater *jihad* to encompass all stages of membership in Hizbullah's activity. Although in these two stages Hizbullah condemned the corrupt practices of the Lebanese state and its sectarian-confessional nature, Hizbullah did not justify its discourse by recourse to greater *jihad*.

196

In stage three, for the first time since its birth, Hizbullah engages in greater *jihad*, by integrating in the Lebanese public sphere through its *infitah* ("opening up") policy. Thus, Hizbullah's greater *jihad* did not remain confined to the theoretical (political-ideological) dimension of membership in the party rather transcended it to the practical political implication of fighting corruption in the Lebanese political and administrative system. The reason behind that might be that after it achieved liberation, it turned a large portion of its resource mobilization inward through an *infitah* policy in the domestic Lebanese public sphere. Its aim has been to prove that it is the largest political force in Lebanon. Thus, its transnational identity of pan-Islamism dwindled at the expense of its integration in Lebanese domestic affairs.[10]

It seems that Hizbullah also adapted and applied its *infitah* policy to *jihad*. Hizbullah specifically stated that engaging in greater *jihad* is hundred times more difficult than practicing smaller military *jihad*. Another ideological shift is that Hizbullah did not conduct any martyrdom operation after the nearly complete Israeli withdrawal in May 2000. Thus, it is most likely that the meaning and application of *jihad* and martyrdom changed from smaller military *jihad* in the battlefield to the greater *jihad* in participating in internal-domestic democratic processes.

Hizbullah witnessed ideological discursive shifts after the liberation. Hizbullah stated that its greater *jihad* and dedication to addressing the socio-economic plight of the Lebanese oppressed populace does not contradict or compromise its priority of smaller military *jihad* for the sake of liberation of occupied land. Indeed, Hizbullah's priorities and discourse changed before the liberation from saliency of the resistance, to the prominence of its socio-economic program after the liberation. The reason might be that in the context of national liberation struggle against non-Muslim rule, Islamic movements almost purely function in a nationalist fashion. Only after the attainment of the goal of national liberation do Islamic movements shift their attention to domestic reform issues pertaining to individual and social morality as well as to good governance. This has translated itself into Hizbullah's intensified focus on the social-economic reconstruction of the liberated areas and other deprived areas as indicated in its comprehensive socio-economic program.

Suicide and martyrdom

Concerning the time frame of the martyrdom operations, it seems as if Hizbullah divided them evenly in the following fashion: four in the era of the dominance of the religious ideology; four in the period of the political ideology; and four in the phase of the political program. In stage one, building on its religious ideological justifications of martyrdom, Hizbullah explicitly identified the suicide bombers as being inspired by and emulating Imam Husayn's martyrdom in *Karbala'*. However, in all three stages, Hizbullah did not distinguish between dying on the battlefield with bullets, or blowing oneself up with explosives; both actions amount to an act of martyrdom as long as they are sanctioned by the religious authorities.

In stage two, Hizbullah considered martyrdom as the key or ticket to Heaven but its explanations, ideological justifications, and rationalizations were couched more in political terms such as Hizbullah's identification with pan-Arabism, pan-Islamism, anti-Zionism, anti-imperialism, in short with the oppressed against the oppressors, colonizers, and "rapists" of the land. And so, Hizbullah shifted its religious-ideological justification of *jihad* and martyrdom to a political-ideological justification.

The first stage's prohibition on conducting martyrdom operations unless each operation leads to at least thirty Israeli soldiers dead, was given up in stages two and three. Nevertheless, martyrdom was sanctioned in all three stages in case Hizbullah was facing a superior military, such as the Israeli army, and the conventional ways of smaller military *jihad* proved totally ineffective. As such Hizbullah stressed that martyrdom is the most efficient means available for the Islamic Resistance to fight an outnumbered and well-equipped occupation force.

In all three stages Hizbullah did not engage in any suicide operation against Israeli civilians in its 18-year struggle with the Israeli forces occupying south Lebanon since (1) suicide is completely prohibited in Islam, and (2) Hizbullah's religious ideology, political ideology, and political program prohibit targeting Israeli civilians in its war of attrition against the occupying Israeli forces. Rather, all its field and martyrdom operations targeted Israeli military and intelligence personnel occupying Lebanese soil. In fact, "During the course of Hezbollah's 17-year struggle with Israel along the Lebanese/Israeli frontier in southern Lebanon, it has never been established by any party directly involved (including the United Nations contingent on the ground) that the Party of God has perpetuated a single terrorist attack against Israeli civilians… Hezbollah made an early strategic decision to exclude terrorist tactics from its *jihad* against Israeli occupation and stuck to it".[11]

It is interesting to note that in stage three, Hizbullah included a nation-alistic justification for martyrdom operations in its political program, in addition to its earlier religious and political-ideological justification in stages one and two. The discursive shift in Hizbullah's justification of martyrdom suggests that it evolved from a religious-ideological justification, to a political-ideological justification, and finally to a nationalistic-secular justification. It seems that the motivation for Hizbullah and secularist resistance movements to conduct martyrdom operations was in order to uphold the honour, pride, and dignity of the "nation" ('izzat wa karamat al-umma). The common ground for both Islamic and nationalistic/secularist movements is the agreement that living under occupation is tantamount to disgrace and humiliation, as such it is respectively a religious and nationalistic duty to end the occupation using all possible means, including martyrdom operations. Thus, it is most likely that martyrdom operations – whether carried out by Islamic movements or resistance movements – are altruistic, self-sacrificial operations legitimised by upholding the honour and dignity of the nation.[12]

In stage three, on the whole, Hizbullah's official pronouncements on *jihad* and martyrdom seem to suggest that Hizbullah also adapted and applied its infitah policy to *jihad* and martyrdom. Thus, it seems that the meaning and application of *jihad* and martyrdom changed from the battle-field to the elections and dealing with internal-domestic issues. Hizbullah's greater *jihad* was directed towards more integration in the Lebanese political system and state institutions. Arguably this move is in accordance with Hizbullah's resistance identity (smaller *jihad*) and is a basic technique of the party's survival by trying to integrate its identity within the Lebanese state's sovereignty, while trying to keep its regional commitments intact.

In other words, Hizbullah was founded as an Islamic *jihadi* Movement. The initial meaning of *jihad* since its founding denoted smaller military *jihad*. The important shift to notice after two decades is that this smaller *jihad* was transformed into greater *jihad*: *jihad* in the elections, fighting corruption, joining the cabinet, and in integrating in state institutions as well as the Lebanese public sphere at large.

1.4   Islamic State

In the first and second stages Hizbullah's Islamic current considered that the Qur'an is the constitution of the Islamic *umma*, and Islam is both *din wa dawla* (a religious and a governmental order). Hizbullah enjoined the Muslims to strive using all legitimate means in order to implement the

Islamic order, wherever they are. Hizbullah based its argument in the Lebanese context on demographic realities (the fact that the Muslims constitute the majority of the population) and proposed that Lebanon become part of the over-all encompassing Islamic state. Hizbullah's cadres argued for the necessity of establishing an Islamic order, stressing that social change must begin from the top by changing the political system and annihilating the ruling elite through a top-down revolutionary process.

In stages one and two, Hizbullah considered the Lebanese political system, which is dominated by the political Maronites, as a *jahiliyya* (pre-Islamic pagan) system. The same would apply to any non-Islamic system, be it patriotic, democratic, or nationalist, even if it were to be governed by Muslims. In other words, in the first and second stages Hizbullah pursued the establishment of an Islamic state respectively from the perspective of a religious ideology and a political ideology. Religious ideology, as Hizbullah's leading cadres argued, to instate God's sovereignty and divine governance on earth through *hakimiyya* and the execution of God's law by the establishment of an Islamic order as *taklif shar'i* (a religious and legal obligation). As a political ideology, Hizbullah did not want to impose the Islamic order by force; rather only if an overwhelming majority of Lebanese voted, by way of a referendum, in its favour. This should be taken with a grain of salt since Hizbullah's rhetoric, in stages one and two, was different from what it was actually doing in reality, in the sense of being actively engaged in preparing the ground for establishing an Islamic order, at least in the areas it wielded power in or controlled.

In stage one, Hizbullah wanted to forcefully impose the Islamic order. In stage two, Hizbullah argued that it would apply the Islamic order only by the consent of the majority of the Lebanese, claiming that they are longing for it. In the third stage, Hizbullah's pragmatic and realistic approach reigned, making it concede that the majority of the Lebanese would say no to its Islamic order. Therefore, it not only vacated its call to establish it, but also totally dropped it from all of its election programs. In stage three Hizbullah did not blast political Maronism, rather its current political equivalent: "political sectarianism", in which both Sunnis and Shi'ites participate. Hizbullah called for reforming the political system along the lines of the abolishment of political sectarianism, as Lebanon's new 1990 constitution stipulated. Basing itself on its demographic strength, Hizbullah called for changing the electoral system to proportional representation. Thus, the shift from blasting "political Maronism" in stages one and two, to censuring "political sectarianism" could be seen as a rhetorical shift, rather than a genuine policy shift since its *infitah* policy does not warrant anymore its earlier criticism of political Maronism.

Hizbullah argues that it benefits from its jurisprudential vision that believes in the doctrine of *wilayat al-faqih*, which legitimises it having a political program in a multi-cultural, multi-religious country, which is also characterized by pluralist groupings and forces, without encroaching upon its doctrinal-ideological, Islamic-religious convictions.[13] Employing this logic, Hizbullah reformulated what it meant by an Islamic state by making a categorical distinction between its *al-fikr al-siyasi* (political ideology) and its *al-barnamaj al-siyasi* (political program). From an ideological perspective Hizbullah is committed to an Islamic state, and it will not be dropped as a legal abstraction. However, Hizbullah's political program has to take into account the political status quo and the overall functioning of the Lebanese political system. Hizbullah characterises the Lebanese political situation as a complicated mould of sectarian-confessional particularities and specificities that prohibit the establishment of an Islamic state, not only from a practical perspective, but also from a doctrinal one. Hizbullah's political ideology stipulates that an Islamic state should be established on solid foundations having full legitimacy and sovereignty from the people. Since the general will of the Lebanese people is against the establishment of an Islamic state, then it is not plausible to establish one.[14]

Other Hizbullah cadres argued that founding an Islamic state in Lebanon has been an ideological project (political ideology) rather than a political one (political program). The Islamic state has been part of Hizbullah's *adabiyyat* (culture), and has been debated in the domain of its political ideology, but was never a part of its political program.[15] Hizbullah distinguishes between the "ideological vision" (political ideology) and the "practical application" (political program). Hizbullah's ideological vision (political ideology) not only calls for the establishment of an Islamic state but also encourages others to accept it, since it leads to "man's felicity". Nevertheless on the practical level (political program), this needs the "proper base" that accepts the establishment of such an (Islamic) state; the proper base being the populace who have the right to choose which system should govern them.[16]

In short, Hizbullah stressed that its religious and political ideologically defends the establishment of an Islamic state, but as a political program it is not practical because of confessionalism and sectarianism and because of opposition from the majority of the Lebanese, both Christians and Muslims. In other words, Hizbullah put its political ideology in the drawer and practiced a down-to-earth pragmatic political program. Thus, in conformity with its political program, Hizbullah moved from Islamiziation in the narrow sense of establishing an Islamic state to Lebanonisation and *infitah* policy. Although in the third stage Hizbullah has vacated its call for the implantation of the Islamic state in Lebanon from all its election programs and political declarations, a discrepancy could be noticed between Hizbullah's political program and the discourse of its leaders. Hizbullah's public discourse reiterated its earlier position of no imposition of the Islamic state by force and its implementation only if the majority of the Lebanese Christians and Muslims consent to it. Hizbullah shifted its position by its acceptance and engagement in the democratic process under a sectarian-confessional political and administrative system. More dramatically, Hizbullah's political program modified its demand from the abolishment of political sectarianism, to adopting the political Maronite discourse of the abolishment of political sectarianism in the mentality, before abolishing it in the texts. It seems Hizballah is moving ever closer to being a full participant in "normal" Lebanese politics – with the limitations that implies – merging into the Lebanese sectarian-confessional, corrupt political system that it abhorred in stages one and two.

1.5   Hizbullah's relations with the Lebanese Christians

In stages one and two Hizbullah vehemently opposed to being ruled by the "crusader" Christians. As such, Hizbullah considered it a religious injunction to bar the Christians from participating in the Islamic order by precluding them from any political freedom. Rather, as *dhimmis* ("people of the Book"), only their social and religious freedom was upheld. In stage three, the Christians were no longer regarded as *dhimmis*, rather partners in government, which represents a complete overhaul of Hizbullah's views and of its total rejection of being ruled by Christians in the previous two stages.

In the third stage, Hizbullah's discourse signified a shift from blaming its misfortunes on the conspiracy theory to its dialogue with and *infitah* to the Christians along the lines of the Papal Guidance, vacating its earlier exhortation to convert them to Islam. Contrary to its earlier policy of excluding Christians with blatant connections with Israel from dialogue (i.e. the political Maronites and the Phalangists), Hizbullah affirmed that it did not in principle have a problem with the Christians; rather its problem was with those who acted to promote Israel's policies in Lebanon. However, Hizbullah has embarked on conducting dialogue with them on the basis of transparency in order to reach common grounds (3:64) without encroaching upon the specificity of every sect or community. In fact, Hizbullah broadened the horizon of its dialogue with the Christians to include almost the entire grouping that comprise the Lebanese myriad. Hizbullah stressed that political dialogue also includes socio-economic and civil society issues. Therefore in stage three, Hizbullah tried to portray itself as a big Muslim-Christian co-existence promoter. As has been the common practice since 1992, Hizbullah included Christians, including Maronites, in its parliamentary elections lists. Hizbullah also shared municipal council seats with the Christians.

1.6   Lebanonisation or *infitah*

In the first two stages Hizbullah viewed it as its mission to liberate Lebanon from the shackles of political Maronism and the Lebanese sectarian-confessional political system that is based upon positive (man-made) laws and legislations (*al-qawanin al-wad'iyya*) such as state constitutions, and establish instead the *shari'a* (Islamic law and legislation), which could only be instated by *hakimiyya* through a pure and uncompromising Islamic order, system, or mode of government, be it an Islamic government, state, or republic. Hizbullah argued that abiding by *al-qawanin al-wad'iyya* instead of Islamic *shari'a* is entirely prohibited both from a religious and political ideological perspective. The major shift in the third stage is that Hizbullah became satisfied with *al-qawanin al-wad'iyya* and even contributed to their legislation through its MPs in the parliament. Hizbullah argued that the *shari'a*, as a socially constructed phenomenon, is flexible and can account for all the complicities of modern life.

The shift that happened in the third stage could be attributed to the transformation of Iranian politics after the death of Imam Khumayni as well as to a change in Hizbullah's own internal dynamics. For instance, there was a clear alteration in the Iranian stance from Imam Khumayni's 1986 *fatwa* (religious edict) – which stipulated that the Lebanese system is illegitimate and criminal and Khamina'i's argument for the necessity of the Muslims to rule Lebanon since they comprise the majority of the population[17] – to Khamina'i's 1992 ruling in favour of participation in the parliamentary elections, which Hizbullah interpreted as its unequivocal right to proliferate in the Lebanese political system as a whole, including state institutions and administration. Another ideological shift in the third stage is that Hizbullah put its political ideology in the drawer making compromises on doctrinal issues by allying itself, on the same election slate, with former foes and engaging in negotiations and bargaining with a wide spectrum of groups across the Lebanese myriad.

In the third stage, Hizbullah faced the problematic of reconciling its political ideology with reality, Hizbullah shifted from a *jihadi* perspective to a flexible *shari'a* perspective. So Hizbullah portrayed a distinguished flexibility in its political program in an attempt to reconcile, as much as possible, among its principles, aims, and political ideology, on the one hand, and the circumstances and its objective capabilities, on the other hand, by heavy reliance on the jurisprudential concepts of necessity, vices, and interests as a kind of Islamic prima facie duty. This is how Hizbullah's pragmatism was conducive in forging a marriage of convenience between political ideology and reality to the extent that Hizbullah was willing to place its political ideology on the shelf and pursue a policy of *infitah* as sanctioned by its political program. Thus, the logic of operating with the bounds of the Lebanese state prevailed over the logic of the revolution. Hizbullah justifies and legitimises its political program and pragmatism by resorting to Qur'anic and jurisprudential bases. In fact, Shi'ite religio-political heritage conferred upon Hizbullah all the authenticity it needed in order to derive from it a political program based on flexibility and pragmatism.

Although Hizbullah is still primarily an Islamic movement, it displays, more and more, the characteristics of a nationalist-patriotic political party pursuing *al-waqi'iyya al-siyasiyya* (*realpolitik*), when and if this is required by the circumstances. Like any political party, Hizbullah has an overall grasp of the political system, acting, more or less, rationally and weighing the advantages (interests) and disadvantages (vices) of every decision and action it embarks upon. In order to keep its Islamic identity intact while functioning within the domain of Lebanese state sovereignty, Hizbullah conferred a de facto recognition of Lebanese state, but not a de jure one. In other words, Hizbullah's adherence to democratic principles and politics is not based on political-ideological grounds since its political ideology anathematised the Lebanese political system, rather on advancing *al-masalih* (interests) and warding off *al-mafasid* (vices). Hizbullah does legitimise its participation in the democratic process on the basis of the flexibility of the *shari'a* and its jurisprudential stipulations as well as Qur'anic concepts of *shura* (consultation), *ikhtilaf* (pluralism), *al-huquq al-shar'iyya* (human or 'legal' rights), and *ijtihad* (independent reasoning).

Although most of the maxims Hizbullah mentions are given in the classical books of jurisprudence, and even though Hizbullah's arguments are quite familiar and echo the Islamists justifications for participation in secular politics with an Islamist objective, one can notice two main shifts. First, these principles are now applied to politics, and politics becomes now state centred with lawmaking as its own activity. Historically, the state or the Imam were conceived more as a person, rather than an institution. Sunnis and Shi'as alike mistrusted the ruling Imams. The Sunnis hesitated to allow the Imam the right to legislate. The Shi'as differentiated between the true Imam and the ruler. Now both realise the significance and necessity of the state and its legislative role. It is admirable how this shift is made, quite convincingly, by semantics and hermeneutics between the classical concepts and terms with modern meaning. Second, it seems that the role of *al-waliyy al-faqih* or Khamina'i is absent in this regard. Hizbullah took the decision and legitimatised its participation in democratic processes by recourse to jurisprudential maxims and principles made by legislators such as Muhammad Ra'd, common Muslims such as Bilal N'im, and leaders of Muslim opinion such as Shaykh 'Afif al-Nabulsi. Even though the notion of *maslaha* (interest) has a negative connotation in Middle Eastern societies on a popular level, the same notion has gained a positive reception by religio-political ideologies, especially that one advocated by Imam Khumayni. Khumayni stipulated that the *maslaha* of the Islamic state or its agencies gains priority over any other principle in the social and political affairs. With Hizbullah's "modern" usage, *maslaha* has not only gained a positive sense, but is also regarded as a core Islamic political concept.

6 **Epilogue**
Conclusion and Implications

Hizbullah did not start from scratch, but its evolution was always a sequence of gradual stages of development, in relation to what directly preceded it. In fact, many foundations of Hizbullah's thought, doctrines, and policies – especially its *infitah* ("opening up") policy – were already laid down by Imam Musa al-Sadr and the 1969 program of the Islamic Shi'ite Higher Council. No wonder Musa al-Sadr is considered as one of Hizbullah's ideologues.

Musa al-Sadr, a charismatic, veteran, and distinguished leader, mobilized the Lebanese Shi'a in the 1960s and 1970s and was able to channel their grievances into political participation.[1] Although al-Sadr built on Shi'ite popular heritage and religious history, he perceived his mission in Lebanon predominately in secular and integrative terms through a search of the identity of the Shi'ites and their mobilization for political, social, and economic advancement.[2] Thus, building on his religious knowledge and charisma, al-Sadr was a pioneering figure in modern Lebanese history to promote religion as an idiom of opposition.[3] Al-Sadr never called for an Islamic state, rather for equality and social justice among the various denominations within the Lebanese multi-confessional system. Out of these circumstances Hizbullah emerged and formulated its religious ideology.

In 1978 Israel launched its first invasion of Lebanon; in the same year, Imam al-Sadr disappeared in Libya in mysterious circumstances. A year later, in 1979, Imam Khumayni announced the victory of the Islamic Revolution and the creation of the Islamic Republic in Iran. These catalysts were aggravated by the second Israeli invasion of 1982, which resulted in the occupation of one-third of Lebanon, including Beirut. The 1982 Israeli invasion, with all of its appalling multi-sided consequences to the Lebanese populace and different ramifications, has acted as a direct accelerator for the emergence of Hizbullah, a new resistance movement – having a religious background, with Islam serving as the backbone of its ideology and principles – against the occupation. Many already existing Islamist Shi'ite groups, as well as independent active Islamist figures and clerics joined ranks and established Hizbullah as an Islamic *jihadi* movement. These groups came together in fighting the Israeli occupation and built the backbone of the party, most importantly its "resistance identity".

With the unprecedented accomplishments they achieved in directing several blows to the Israelis, these groups gained a wide reputation in their constituencies and garnered an unshakable credibility as a party renowned for fighting Israel and what was seen as aggression against the Lebanese. Their later achievements in addressing the socio-economic grievances, resulting from the Israeli aggression, gained the party a solid ground among the grassroots. This prompted its leadership in 1985 to found its political constitution, manifesto, or "Open Letter", in which it declared its political ideology, thus engaging directly in Lebanese political life after operating clandestinely for some years.

From 1985 to 1990, Hizbullah emerged as a strong internal organization with limited following. Al-Tufayli's firm, uncompromising political discourse and his repeated references to the establishment of an Islamic state in Lebanon, which is unprecedented in Lebanese political discourse, backfired domestically alienating the party from other political and social movements, and from the Lebanese public sphere to a great extent. Thus, Hizbullah's policies were counterproductive, leading to the failure of integration in Lebanese political life, especially after Hizbullah's vehement criticisms against the Ta'if Agreement, Lebanon's new constitution.

Since the end of the Civil War in 1990, Hizbullah has been confronting major developments in Lebanon: prominently, the emergence of a pluralist public sphere and increasing openness toward other communities, political parties, and interest groups in the Lebanese myriad. This resulted in a change in Hizbullah's discourse and priorities. The mixed confessional space in Lebanon led Hizbullah to move from marginalisation to *infitah*, by which the party became a major player in the Lebanese public sphere, thus altering its stance and changing the political rules from Islamisation to Lebanonisation by propagating a down-to-earth political program. Thus, since the 1990s, Hizbullah gradually evolved into a mainstream political party having an extensive network of social services (accorded to Muslims as well as to Christians), and participated in parliamentary, municipal, and governmental work.

Some changes that took place in the Lebanese system illustrate the growing importance of Hizbullah in the Lebanese political arena. Hizbullah's integration in the Lebanese public sphere through electoral politics sheltered it with additional political legitimacy and a wider following. Hizbullah seems to have realized from the Iranian experience, as well as from the internal dynamics of the Lebanese milieu, that electoral politics (parliamentary elections, especially municipal ones) is the cornerstone of democratic practice. Thus, Hizbullah's participation in the elections could be considered as a pivotal event in shaping its current identity.

In summary, in its successive political programs from 1992 to 2005, and in addition to calls for upholding resistance and liberation as well as enhancement of the Lebanese state's foreign policy, Hizbullah stressed the following: (1) the establishment of civil peace; (2) the founding of the state of law and institutions; (3) the promotion of political participation; (4) political, administrative, social, and economic reforms; (5) upholding 'public freedoms'; (6) *infitah* and dialogue among all the Lebanese; (7) addressing demands dealing with health, educational, environmental, and cultural issues; (8) and the achievement of social justice through the following measures: (a) dealing with the serious and pressuring socio-economic and financial crisis by finding the proper balance between material resources and human resources; (b) attaining and realizing socio-economic development by developmental projects targeting the deprived and dispossessed areas in order to reach balanced development; (c) defending and protecting the "downtrodden" and oppressed grassroots.

Islamist identity and state sovereignty

Equating Hizbullah's political ideology with its political program leads to a quandary in the understanding of Hizbullah's role as a political party in the third stage. What adds to the confusion is that Hizbullah states in its Open Letter, "we in Lebanon are neither a closed organisational party nor a narrow political framework. Rather, we are an *umma* tied to the Muslims in every part of the world by a strong ideological-doctrinal, and political bond, namely, Islam". This seems to imply that Hizbullah abides by Imam Khumayni's theory that considers political parties in the Islamic context as a Western phenomenon.[4] Thus, in its political ideology, Hizbullah clearly states that it is not a political party, yet it developed a political program and participated in the national elections. Based on this, one needs to consider the time and the causes for this change.

The aura and stereotyped notion of Hizbullah's advocacy of an Islamic state seems to hamper or, at least, downplay, Hizbullah's political program of *infitah* or integration in the Lebanese public sphere. In other words, the claim of an Islamic state seems to boost Hizbullah's religious credentials at the expense of its political credentials. It has been demonstrated that, in stages one and two, Hizbullah pursued the establishment of an Islamic state both from a political ideology and a political program perspective through a top-down process. However, as has been already clarified in stage three, Hizbullah's Islamic state remained a political ideology, rather than a political program.

Since the early 1990s Hizbullah started promoting its Islamic identity and agenda by following a pragmatic political program, mainly to lull Christians and other Muslims who were opposed to the Islamic state. In the meantime, Hizbullah remained faithful to its Shi'ite constituency by employing a bottom up Islamisation process through working within the Lebanese state's political and administrative structures, while, at the same time establishing Islamic institutions within the civil society.

Shift in Syrian-Lebanese relations: Hizbullah's benefits after the Syrian withdrawal

A major shift is the relations between Lebanon and Syria occurred after Hariri's assassination, which gradually led to the waning of Syrian influence in Lebanon. This calls into question the degree to which the Lebanese government is practicing its right in taking domestic, regional, and international decisions, especially in the wake of UN Resolution 1559. It also poses questions on the overall strategy in Lebanon's foreign policy. In spite of that, there has not been a significant change in Hizbullah's political relationship with Syria before and after the Syrian withdrawal in April 2005. Nevertheless, Hizbullah's leaders and cadres concede that the Syrian withdrawal hastened its joining the cabinet and proliferation in the Lebanese public life and state institutions.

Hizbullah's political victories in 2005 – its winning of 14 seats in the parliament and fielding two ministers in the cabinet – portrayed more the patriotic-nationalistic character of this mainstream political party that is not only supported by its major Shi'ite constituency, but also by many Sunnis, Druz, and Christians.[5] Based on its demographic strength and massive following, Hizbullah aimed to portray itself as the biggest political force in Lebanon.

Although two ministers cannot veto the cabinet's decisions, it seems that Hizbullah gave up its older argument of refusing to be represented in the cabinet because it rejected to hold responsibility for any dire decisions or unfavourable actions adopted by a 2/3-majority vote by the cabinet. Previously, Hizbullah argued that its prospective representatives in the cabinet could do nothing to alter these decisions. However, in the parliament and in municipality councils, Hizbullah's members can voice their opinion freely and act in favour of the masses or the social base that they represent. Those municipal councils, which are controlled by Hizbullah, act as advocacy groups, employing a kind of empowerment mechanism, in order to lobby the government to pursue a course of balanced development as well as to live up to its promises and perform its developmental projects. Hizbullah's enrolment in the cabinet calls into question the extent to which the party is willing to be co-opted into the Lebanese political system and its state institutions.

Hizbullah is reputed in public to keeping its promises. This explains way people overwhelmingly voted for the party after it has proven its determination in aiding them, and not only spreading verbal promises. The condition of some other parties was the opposite due to their poor municipal performance that was based on impromptu work. One can argue that the municipal councils, which are controlled by Hizbullah, act as advocacy groups, employing a kind of empowerment mechanism, in order to lobby the government to pursue a course of balanced development as well as to live up to its promises and perform its developmental projects. In general, the results of the elections are indicative of the likelihood of Hizbullah's successful resource mobilization that showered it with mass appeal, particularly at the local grassroots level, and made it a major player in the Lebanese public sphere, thus substantiating and consolidating its claims of being a Lebanese patriotic-nationalistic political party. This implies that Hizbullah has accommodated its position in such a way as to demonstrate its full acceptance of the Lebanese political system and its techniques, but with a reservation when it comes to the doctrinal principles dealing with religion and its identity of resistance towards Israel.

Although parliamentary and municipal elections are not always considered as a true measure of democracy (being a necessary rather than a sufficient condition), the municipal elections could be, to a certain extent an indicator of democracy because they reflect the grassroots' voice. Unlike the parliamentary elections law, the municipal elections law is not drawn along sectarian lines, which leaves a large room for the grass roots to voice their opinion in the ballot and make their subaltern voices heard. Thus, municipal elections reflect, more the less, Hizbullah's real support base in society. The municipal elections dwell on developmental issues *par excellence* seeking balanced development among the different constituencies and districts, thus giving Hizbullah the chance to reap more legitimacy for its socio-economic work. The 2004 municipal elections and the 2005 parliamentary elections conveyed Hizbullah's ability to employ its resource mobilization in order to boost its support base domestically, regionally, and internationally. Domestically, voter's turnout was remarkably high in Hizbullah's main constituencies and strongholds in comparison to other constituencies.[6] Regionally and internationally, Hizbullah gave a strong message to its foes – especially Israel, the US, and France – through its strong show-out in the elections and through the massive following it enjoys.

The new role of Hizbullah's religious legitimisation

Even though Hizbullah seems categorically against secularism as such[7], it is forced, due to changing circumstances, to approach some secular aspects of society and politics, but without adopting secularisation as an objective or strategy. It is interesting to note that, although Hizbullah participated in the parliamentary elections that follow western models, it could not distance the religious element from what is supposed to be free and democratic elections. The fact that Hizbullah used the notion of *taklif shar'i* (religio-legal obligation) in directing the votes of its voters, deprived Hizbullah's involvement in the electoral system from true democracy. In this way, for devout believers, elections became an act of obedience to religious authorities, rather than an expression of free political will. However, it should be noted here that Hizbullah's use of religious influence on its public, is not necessary for religious ends in all cases. In the last parliamentary elections, the *taklif shar'i* method[8] was used by Hizbullah in support of its Druz and Christian political allies against its political opponent Michel 'Aun who endorses the 1559 UN resolution.

Hizbullah is referring more to the problems of society from a civil perspective stressing issues such as democracy, human rights, the rule of law, accountability, transparency, meritocracy, weeding off corruption, stamping out favouritism and nepotism, finding a conducive solution to the socio-economic problems, etc. These are not only the demands of the poor grass-roots, but also the liberals, the secular middle class, educated professionals, technocrats, etc. Hizbullah is employing a pragmatic-liberal approach simply because the running of a modern state is a natural process of civil development. It seems that Hizbullah has been forced to abandon a lot of its religious ideological dogma and discourse in order to enlarge its constituency and engage in more inclusive-pluralist discourse, and thus including Christians and Sunnis in its electoral lists. Most likely Hizbullah has been forced by political experience to put less emphasis on moral and religious issues and discourse, and as a matter of political expediency to concentrate on worldly affairs that concern the general public. Through this process of disenchantment Hizbullah has been able to create a balance between its Islamic identity and nationalist-patriotic dimension. This is why Hizbullah was not only able to retain its voting base, put also expand it since voters judge how convincingly its performance is by assessing if it delivers its promises and services or not. In this case, moralizing-religious discourse is not enough to attract voters if it does not have practical implications. However, Hizbullah kept this moral-religious discourse as an umbrella, but not as a religiously dogmatic prescription, which excludes participation in an open system. In spite of the aforementioned, it seems that the changes that are occurring within Hizbullah has made some scholars to go as far as saying that Hizbullah has been "secularised by the process of politicisation".[9] This, of course, is debatable if all the factors that have been mentioned earlier are taken into consideration.

This analysis falls in line with the earlier argument in the preface, which says that a social movement must, in order to mobilize resources, appeal to a broad constituency. In other words, Hizbullah must focus on things that a lot of people are concerned about. This might explain why Hizbullah's political program dropped the notion of Islamic state and concentrated on addressing broad problems and concerns that are deeply embedded in society and that worry the majority of the voters irrespective of their denomination or political orientation. It is most likely that Hizbullah was able, by this move, to reap more political and socio-economic legitimacy, not only from its major constituencies, but also from other consistencies as well. This proves that Hizbullah is not detached from the concerns that occupy the general public in Lebanon.

The so-called "secularisation" trend has even caused some shifts in Hizbullah's *thawabit* (immutable set of values), the only constants have been: Hizbullah as an Islamic *jihadi* movement and safeguarding the Resistance. Some of the earlier *thawabit* in stages one and two that shifted in stage three are the following: (1) From anathematising the Lebanese state and regarding the regime as an infidel, to upholding the sovereignty and territorial integrity of Lebanon, which bears a striking resemblance to the Lebanese Forces' slogan of the 10, 425 square kilometre Lebanon. (2) From censuring the Ta'if Agreement to safeguarding it. (3) From calling for the establishment of an Islamic state to working within the narrow confines of the Lebanese sectarian-confessional political and administrative system, etc.

Hizbullah's future

Hizbullah made it clear, as early as 2002, that its Resistance identity is a strategic choice, rather than a means for the liberation of a few meters of land.[10] Hizbullah declares that it would remain on guard and would not allow Israel to enforce its hegemony on the Middle East as it pleases. Hizbullah stresses that it did not come into being just to perform for a short while, or to execute a specific project, or to be a tool of policy to regional or international actors; rather, it originated from an immutable belief in God, Almighty, and from the stance of its *taklif*, which made it incumbent upon it to pursue its continuous *jihadi* mission of reforming this world till the end of time. As such, Hizbullah would remain "as long as heaven and earth exist"[11], according to a chief leader in the party. Such statements are often considered as rhetoric or propagandist statements. However, it can reflect the mentality that directs the decisions made by Hizbullah, which can be categorised as extremist, aiming at political gains.

Another Hizbullah cadre tries to highlight the humanistic dimension of Hizbullah's future. Basing himself on Hizbullah's NGOs and welfare institutions, he argues that the party has a strong social base and is investing its legitimacy for the establishment of social justice. According to him, although Hizbullah is a logical-rationalistic party, this does not mean that it does not have a project, which longs to cross the limitations of its natural boundaries. He claims that Hizbullah carries on its shoulders the message of organising society in such a way as to safeguard the humanism of the individual in all respects. He clarified that Hizbullah's ideology is being constructed within the *thawabit*, while at the same time observing progress and development. According to him, Hizbullah was not only founded to fight Israel nor is it an introvert party; its *infitah* policy is a witness to the contrary. He seems to complement the earlier analysis by stressing that even if the struggle against Israel were put to a halt, Hizbullah would direct its resource mobilization from the regional dimension towards the domestic dimension[12].

Although *al-Aqsa Intifada* provided Hizbullah with the opportunity to market its model of resistance abroad, Nasrallah employed his cautious approach: "If we were allowed to head to Palestine [Israel], then we would do it. However, if our going [to Israel] leads to problems, then simply we would not go".[13] Nasrallah clarified that Hizbullah's banner of liberating Jerusalem and Palestine does not mean that the party wants to ignite a war in the Middle East. Rather, he stresses that the Palestinian populace is capable of liberating its own land with the support of Hizbullah, the populace of the Middle East, and the free world. Nasrallah adds, "We do not need a regional war to regain occupied land; we just need to liberate Lebanese occupied land [*Shib'a* Farms] and free our remaining prisoners of war… If this could be accomplished by recourse to the international community and international relations, then we welcome that".[14]

For the first time, Nasrallah spelled out clearly that after Israel withdraws from the Shib'a Farms, Hizbullah is ready to put down its arms after receiving assurances and guarantees, from the international community and leading world powers, that Israel would not "aggress" against Lebanon again.[15] Although this development is too recent to warrant sufficient commentary and analysis, it seems to be a rhetorical shift rather than a real policy shift since no one in the international community can forcefully give these assurances and guarantees. Further, Hizbullah does not seem to be satisfied with these assurances. One can notice that Nasrallah's reasoning runs totally against Hizbullah's theory of "calculated ambiguity". It seems that after the Israeli withdrawal, Nasrallah undermined the taboo of the "if theory". This change led to stay away from pre-anticipation in order to keep Israel in the dark as far as Hizbullah's plans.[16] Thus, Hizbullah has frozen its political ideology of the liberation of Jerusalem and is currently pursuing a realistic political program that gives primacy to Lebanese domestic affairs.

It has been demonstrated that Hizbullah's resistance identity is there to stay. One could argue that, in this context, resistance identity corresponds to Hizbullah's "model of resistance". Thus, Hizbullah's role does not end with the end of the Arab-Israeli conflict; the party would remain an active social movement and a mainstream political party after that. Bearing this in mind, it seems that Hizbullah's *infitah* policy is gradually transforming the party into a viable mainstream political party with the following traits:

1. Hizbullah's progressive views on the Islamic state and its dialogue, not only with the Christians, but also with all the Lebanese confessions, resulted in multi-confessional parliamentary and municipal representation aimed at fostering pluralism and national unity.
2. Its pragmatic political program: the flexibility of its jurisprudential stipulations and *shari'a*, which justify participation in secular politics with an Islamic objective based upon *maslaha* (interest) as a core Islamic political concept. Through the power of its religious identity, Hizbullah was able to shift from the restrictive politics of a narrow exclusive identity (*wilayat al-faqih*) to the more encompassing identity based upon the mobilization of its intellectual and cultural resources. This new jurisprudence leads to dramatic transformations

that translate themselves into an Islamic identity that function within Lebanese state sovereignty.

3. Hizbullah's holistic vision materialised in substantial financial resources that granted it the ability to found a comprehensive socio-economic program; wide-ranging civil institutions and NGOs, including its think tank CCSD; far-reaching al-Manar[17] satellite TV, which remains a precedent in the Middle East among Islamic movements; and *al-Nour* satellite radio station.[18] Indeed, since Khamina'i appointed Nasrallah and Yazbik as his religious deputies in 1995, the huge financial resources of the *khums* (one-fifth religious tax), *zakat* (alms giving), and *shar'i* (religious) donations – from the Lebanese Shi'ite diaspora who follow Khamina'i – poured directly to Hizbullah, instead of being channelled through him, as was the case before the appointment.

4. Throughout its history, Hizbullah's identity has been permanently under construction, both concretely and on a symbolic level.[19] This is substantiated by the continuously revised and updated versions of its self-descriptions and political programs since the propagation of its Open Letter.[20] This last point illustrates Hizbullah's employment of resource mobilization beyond the survival strategy level, aiming at continuous development and progress in a dynamic world that is in constant flux.

Hizbullah seems to be accommodating its identity within the *thawabit* in order to accompany progress and development, thus constructively working within its humanistic agenda, which allows it to legitimise itself through accumulation and transformation of its socio-economic legitimacy into a political legitimacy and vice versa. It is most likely that after every parliamentary or municipal election, Hizbullah earns more and more political legitimacy and it spends it by investing it more and more into socio-economic legitimacy in line with its "civilizational mission" of accomplishing social justice. Nevertheless, Hizbullah's *infitah* policy is not only confined to its Lebanese domestic and regional sphere but it is also employing some of its resource mobilization to openness and to seriously conduct a constructive dialogue with the EU, in particular, and the West, in general. The following meetings seem to suggest this trend: meetings between Hizbullah cadres, on the one hand, and the Friedrich Ebert Foundation, the German Orient Institute, University of Birmingham[21], the International Crisis Group, the UK government[22], and numerous Western NGOs, on the other hand, as well as the meeting between Nasrallah and Patrique Renault, the EU ambassador,[23] and meetings with the members of the US Administration such as Dibble's watershed gathering with Trad Hamadé, and Graham Fuller's groundbreaking meeting with Nawwaf al-Musawi. Therefore, the indicators of Hizbullah's *infitah* are not only domestic and regional, but also international, in the sense of Hizbullah's gradual opening up to the West.

Final word

It has been argued that the causes behind the shifts in Hizbullah's ideology are due to the alterations in the local Lebanese domestic dimension, as well as the regional and international dimensions. Hizbullah's own internal dynamic changed, Iranian politics shifted, and the international situation has been transformed.

Hizbullah relies on the balance between the actual and the possible, altering its stance from rejectionism and opposition (religious and political ideology strategies) to accommodation and conformity (political program policies). Hizbullah modified its position from branding the Lebanese state with unrighteousness and infidelity, thus shunning the public sphere, to Lebanonisation and integration in the public sphere, participating actively in the political system through contestation, cooptation, and empowerment. Usually, this makes it shift its strategies from hawkish (religious and political ideology discourse) to dovish policies (political program discourse) according to altering political circumstances. While keeping its doctrinal principles in sight, Hizbullah is persistent in honouring its overall political program. Thus, from time to time and as opportunities arise, Hizbullah might put aside, temporarily, its ideological program by leading a dynamic program without specifying a rigid political program. Hizbullah favours the incremental model of decision-making and employs piecemeal social engineering that requires a thorough discussion, by the Hizbullah leadership, of each issue at a time. Although it seems that Hizbullah does not have a ready-made formula to deal with all problems and possibilities that might arise, Hizbullah's *Shura* Council makes readily available answers to all questions. However, since its enemies, especially Israel, might benefit from this information, Hizbullah reserves the right of not disclosing these alternatives and contingency measures to the public.

Although Hizbullah dwells on its religious legitimacy, its political program deals realistically with the particularities of the Lebanese public sphere. Indeed, Hizbullah's *taklif* is not confined only to religious legitimacy; rather it transcends it to deal, not only with all local Lebanese domestic socio-economic and political concerns, but also foreign issues such as continuing the resistance till the evacuation of the last Israeli soldier from the *Shib'a* Farms. However, after the Israeli withdrawal in May 2000, Hizbullah knows that the legitimacy it derives from its Resistance and military operations in *Shib'a* is marginal and minimal, while it realizes that the part and parcel of its legitimacy is based on a balance between both its socio-economic and political work. In spite of the fact that Hizbullah's NGOs are flourishing, Hizbullah is still pressuring the government to pursue a course of balanced development in order to alleviate the "relative deprivation" that its main constituencies are suffering from. It seems that the integration of Islamic movements into the political process is not only plausible, but is also the best alternative that serves their overall interests.

Regarding Hizbullah's future in Lebanon as a viable Lebanese nationalistic political party, one should be cautious not to read too much into the results of the municipal and parliamentary elections as well as its joining the cabinet. It is interesting to note, here, that since the cabinet reflects the power balances in the parliament, it is obvious that any dismay by the parliament will always be extended to the cabinet and vice versa. However, Hizbullah's infusion into the Lebanese public sphere suggests that the party has been able to win the "hearts and minds" of many Lebanese voters, especially in its major Shi'ite constituencies, thus confirming the efficiency of its *infitah* policy in the Lebanese public sphere by agreeing to participate in a sectarian-confessional political process, while earning a reputation of probity, transparency, accountability, and integrity in its political and socio-economic work. Through its civil institutions and NGOs, Hizbullah has triumphantly portrayed itself as a Lebanese nationalist political party working in favour of the "wretched of the earth", the relatively deprived, irrespective of their communal identity, political affiliation, or sectarian-confessional belonging.

Rafiq Hariri's assassination along with the Syrian withdrawal and its aftermath played a major role in accelerating the political changes within Hizbullah. Thus, being disarmed and becoming an "ordinary" political party, would not cause its demise; rather, it would boost its domestic role, causing it to democratise and liberalise more in order to enhance its stance as one of the key players in the Lebanese milieu. Nevertheless, Hizbullah could not have faired so well in Lebanese domestic affairs without its two regional backers, Syria and Iran.

Hizbullah's political program sanctioned its *infitah* while, at the same time, stressed consolidating its regional and transnational ties with Syria and Iran. Despite the withdrawal of their supposed Syrian patron, Hizbullah remains a strong political actor with the avowed intent of "safeguarding the

Resistance". Although Hizbullah cautiously straddled the fence during the "Cedar Revolution", it has arguably benefited from Syria's departure more than the erstwhile Lebanese opposition through its infusion in the Lebanese public sphere and its firm grip on Lebanon's foreign policy in relation to its resistance identity and keeping up its arms. It could be argued that the strategic and political alliance between Iran and Syria has been to Hizbullah's advantage not only because Iranian weapons and material aid to Hizbullah passed through Damascus, but also because Damascus benefited and used the Hizbullah card and Hizbullah's Resistance as a bargaining chip against Israel. However, the transnational-ideological nexus between Hizbullah and Iran should not be construed as undermining the regional political-strategic link between Hizbullah and Syria, but ought to be regarded as a complementary phenonenon.

In addition to investing in its domestic image, Hizbullah has exerted efforts in portraying its international image as a pan-Arab, pan-Islamic movement with ties with Syria and Iran. The former is in conformity with Hizbullah's political program, whereas the latter agrees with its political ideology. It could be argued that Hizbullah is practicing authenticity politics in a religious garb, which is typical of Islamic discourse when it operates in secular politics while upholding its Islamic objective. Hizbullah translates this into practice by basing its relations with Iran on political-ideological, strategic-policy terms (pan-Islamism), while its relations with Syria on a common ethno-national identity (pan-Arabism).

Of course, anyone who follows Hizbullah's rhetoric knows that the statements released by its leaders are always exposed to change as circumstances change, a precept that is sanctioned by the jurisprudential theory of *maslaha*. This political mentality reflects, to a large extent, Iranian political thinking, where alteration leads to genuine *maslaha*. Keeping in mind that there is no *salafism* (extremely militant Sunni fundamentalism) in Shi'ite Islam since emulating a dead *marja'* is not fully endorsed, Iran employed the logic of *maslaha* in order to safeguard its society from *salafism*, which currently informs the ideology of *al-Qa'ida*. Based on the Middle Eastern theory which says: "the enemy of my enemy is my friend", it seems that Iran is serving the interests of the US by warding off and curbing Sunni Islamists through stopping the diffusion of the *salafist* Bin Ladenist-Zarqawi fundamentalism. Although the US Administration seems adamant in enforcing its policy of disarming the Lebanese Hizbullah, one might consider a different perspective which leads to thinking that the US policy might prefer that Hizbullah keeps up its arms in order to perform a similar job as Iran, namely, to protect Lebanese society and American interest there from the resurgence of Sunni fundamentalism. Thus, by following their own *maslaha*, both Iran[24] and Hizbullah are indirectly serving the *maslaha* of the US without consciously intending to do so.

7 **Appendices**

A   *Map of Lebanon*

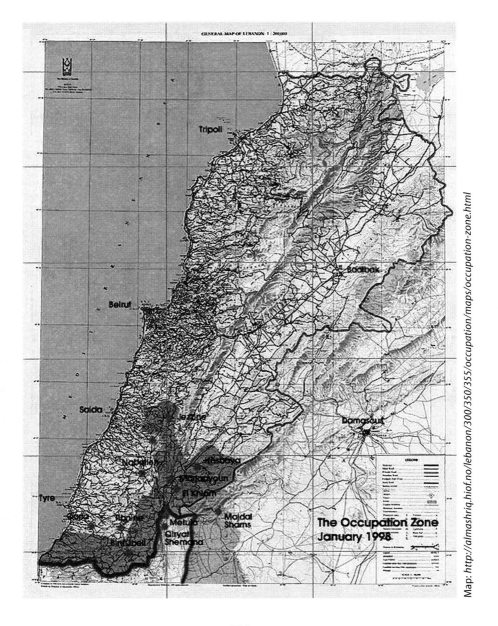

Map: *http://almashriq.hiof.no/lebanon/300/350/355/occupation/maps/occupation-zone.html*

Appendixes B, C, and D intend to convey how Hizbullah's ideological shifts are taking place.[1]

B   Hizbullah Statements

1.   **The text of the Open Letter[2] addressed by Hizbullah to
      the oppressed in Lebanon and the world**
      February 16, 1985

The cover page of the Manifesto opens with the following Qur'anic quote:
"Whoever takes Allah, His Apostle and those who believe as friends [must
know] that Allah's party [Hizbullah] in indeed the triumphant". (5:56)

Dedication

- To the torch that increased in light and brightness, so that it lit, to the oppressed
  in Lebanon, the path to a free dignified life, and burned, with its pure glittering
  blood [*jihad* and martyrdom], the strength of the "Zionist Entity" [Israel] and its
  myth.

- To the leader who confided in and trusted his folk and was the lead for them in
  jihad [Shaykh Raghib Harb]. He sacrificed his soul and died as a martyr or was
  martyred in order to grant them victory[3], and as a witness to the tyranny and
  oppression of the world oppressors.

- To the emblem of the victorious Islamic Resistance, and the great uprising
  (*Intifada*) that our people are still underlining with it the greatest Husayni[4]
  epics in the South and Western *Biqa'*.

- To the one who shattered the American dream in Lebanon and fought (resisted) the Israeli occupation, raising the banner of action according to the *wilayat
  al-faqih*, the leader, who liked to be addressed/characterized as the prince of
  the Muslims, Abdallah (the servant of God) al-Khumayni...

- We [Hizbullah] dedicate this, "Open Letter to the oppressed of the world", to
  the Shaykh of the martyrs, Raghib Harb (may God's blessings be upon him),
  consolidating between its lines the Islamic revolutionary-political path that
  was personified by our happy martyr, with his brothers the martyrs, so that
  he will become a leading example [to emulate] and a clear guide to all the
  freedom fighters (*mujahidin*) in Lebanon... We ask God, Glory be to Him and

highly exalted, to endow us with patience, consolidate our grounds, and make us victorious over the oppressors (al-qawn al-zalimin).[5]

The main text of the Manifesto opens with the following Qur'anic substantiation:

"And say: 'The truth is from your Lord. Whoever wishes, let him believe; and whoever wishes, let him disbelieve'. We have prepared for the wrongdoers a Fire whose canopy encompasses them all. If they call for relief, they will be relieved with water like molten brass which scars the faces. Wretched is the drink and wretched is the resting-place!" (18:29).[6]

1. Who are we, and what is our identity?

We, the son's of Hizbullah's umma, whose vanguard God has given victory in Iran and which has established the nucleus of the world's central Islamic state, abide by the orders of a single wise and just command represented by the guardianship of the jurisprudent (waliyy al-faqih), currently embodied in the supreme Ayatullah Ruhallah al-Musawi al-Khumayni... who has detonated the Muslim's revolution, and who is bringing about the glorious Islamic renaissance.

Therefore, we in Lebanon are neither a closed organisational party nor a narrow political framework. Rather, we are an umma tied to the Muslims in every part of the world by a strong ideological-doctrinal, and political bond, namely, **Islam**, whose message God completed at the hands of the last of His prophets, Muhammad... God has established Islam as a religion for the world to follow... Therefore, what befalls the Muslims in Afghanistan, Iraq, the Philippines, or elsewhere befalls the body of our Islamic nation of which we are an indivisible part and we move to confront it out of a "religious duty" (wajib shar'i) primarily and in light of a general political visualisation decided by the leader waliyy al-faqih.

The main sources of our culture are the venerable Qur'an, the infallible Sunna, and the rules and religious edicts made by the jurist (faqih), the authority of emulation. These sources are clear, uncomplicated, and accessible to all without exception and they need no theorisation or philosophy. All they need is abidance and application.

... Each of us is a combat soldier when the call of **jihad** demands it and each of us undertakes his task in the battle in accordance with the "legitimate and religious responsibility" (taklif shar'i) of the **Wilayat al-Faqih**, the leader. God is behind us with His care, putting fear in our enemies' hearts, and giving His dear and resounding victory against them. (Bold is mine). [7]

224

2. The "Oppressors" are in concordance in fighting us

The US has tried, through its local agents, to persuade the people that those who crushed their arrogance in Lebanon and frustrated their conspiracy against the oppressed (*mustad'afin*) were nothing but a bunch of fanatic terrorists whose sole aim is to dynamite bars and destroy slot machines. Such suggestions cannot and will not mislead our *umma*, for the whole world knows that whoever wishes to oppose the US, that arrogant superpower, cannot indulge in marginal acts which may make it deviate from its major objective. We combat abomination and we shall tear out its very roots, its primary roots, which are the US. All attempts made to drive us into marginal actions will fail, especially as our determination to fight the US is solid.[8]

3. America is behind all our catastrophes

We are dedicated to fighting and uprooting the vice... The first root of vice is America [the US]... All endeavours to push us into marginal action would be of no avail if measured in relation to our face off with America...

Imam Khumayni has stressed time and again that America is behind all our catastrophes, and it is the mother of all vice... When we fight it, we only exercise our legitimate right of defending our Islam and the dignity of our *umma*.[9]

We declare openly and loudly that we are an *umma* which fears God only and is by no means ready to tolerate injustice, aggression and humiliation. America, its Atlantic Pact allies [NATO], and the Zionist entity in the holy land of Palestine [Israel], attacked us and continue to do so without respite. Their aim is to make us eat dust continually. This is why we are, more and more, in a state of permanent alert in order to repel aggression and defend our religion, our existence, our dignity. They invaded our country, destroyed our villages, slit the throats of our children, violated our sanctuaries and appointed masters over our people who committed the worst massacres against our *umma*. They do not cease to give support to these allies of Israel, and do not enable us to decide our future according to our own wishes.

In a single night the Israelis and the Phalangists executed thousands of our sons, women and children in Sabra and Shatila. No international organization protested or denounced this ferocious massacre in an effective manner, a massacre perpetrated with the tacit accord of America's European allies, which had retreated a few days, maybe even a few hours earlier, from the Palestinian camps. The Lebanese defeatists accepted putting the camps under the protection of that crafty fox, the US envoy Philip Habib.[10]

"You shall find the most hostile people to the believers to be the Jews and the polytheists"(5: 82)[11]

4 & 5 We have no choice except confrontation, Zionist-Phalangist coordination/coalescing

We have no alternative but to confront aggression by sacrifice. The coordination between the Phalangists and Israel continues and develops.

A hundred thousand victims – this is the approximate balance sheet of crimes committed by them and by the US against us. Almost half a million Muslims were forced to leave their homes. Their quarters were virtually totally destroyed in *Nab'a*, my own Beirut suburb, as well as in *Burj Hammud, Dekonaneh, Tel Zaatar, Sinbay, Ghawarina* and *Jubeil*[12] – all in areas controlled today by the 'Lebanese Forces'[13]. The Zionist occupation then launched its usurpatory invasion of Lebanon in full and open collusion with the Phalanges. The latter condemned all attempts to resist the invading forces. They participated in the implementation of certain Israeli plans in order to accomplish its Lebanese dream and acceded to all Israeli requests in order to gain power.

And this is, in fact, what happened. Bashir Jumayyel[14], that butcher, seized power with the help also of OPEC countries and the Jumayyel family. Bashir tried to improve his ugly image by joining the six-member Committee of Public Safety presided over by former President Elias Sarkis[15], which was nothing but an American-Israeli bridge borrowed by the Phalangists in order to control the oppressed. Our people could not tolerate humiliation any more. It destroyed the oppressors, the invaders and their lackeys. But the US persisted in its folly and installed Amin Jumayyel[16] to replace his brother. Some of his first so called achievements were to destroy the homes of refugees and other displaced persons, attack mosques, and order the army to bombard the southern suburbs of Beirut, where the oppressed people resided. He invited European troops to help him against us and signed the May 17th, [1983] accord with Israel making Lebanon an American protectorate.[17]

6 & 7 Our main enemies, and our objectives/goals in Lebanon

Our people could not bear any more treachery. It decided to oppose infidelity – be it French, American or Israeli – by striking at their headquarters and launching a veritable war of resistance against the Occupation forces. Finally, the enemy had to decide to retreat by stages.

Let us put it truthfully: the sons of Hizhallah know who are their major enemies in the Middle East – the Phalanges, Israel, France and the US. The sons of our *umma* are now in a state of growing confrontation with them, and will remain so until the realization of the following three objectives:

    a. To expel the Americans, the French, and their allies definitely from Lebanon, putting an end to any colonialist entity on our land;

    b. To submit the Phalanges to a just power and bring them all to justice for the crimes they have perpetrated against Muslims and Christians;

    c. To permit all the sons of our people to determine their future and to choose in all the liberty the form of government they desire. We call upon all of them to pick the option of Islamic state, which alone, is capable of guaranteeing justice and liberty for all. Only an Islamic state can stop any further tentative attempts of imperialistic infiltration into our country.[18]

8.   Our Friends

These are Lebanon's objectives; those are its enemies. As for our friends, they are all the world's oppressed peoples. Our friends are also those who combat our enemies and who defend us from their evil. Towards these friends, individuals as well as organizations, we turn and say:

Friends, wherever you are in Lebanon... we are in agreement with you on the great and necessary objectives: destroying American hegemony in our land; putting an end to the burdensome Israeli Occupation; beating back all the Phalangists' attempts to monopolize power and administration.

Even though we have, friends, quite different viewpoints as to the means of the struggle, on the levels upon which it must be carried out, we should surmount these tiny divergences and consolidate cooperation between us in view of the grand design...[19]

You convey ideas that do not originate from Islam... and this does not preclude cooperation with you in order to achieve these goals... especially since we feel that the motives, which exhort you to struggle, are Muslim motives in the first place, originating from the oppression and tyranny that has been practiced and imposed upon you ... even if these motives were formed by un-Islamic ideas, they have to converge back to the essence of Islam. Then, you witness that revolutionary Islam spearheads the struggle to confront tyranny and oppression...[20]

9.   We are committed to Islam, but we do not impose it by force

We are an *umma*, which adheres to the message of Islam. We want all the oppressed to be able to study the divine message in order to bring justice, peace and tranquillity to the world: "There is no compulsion in religion; true guidance has become distinct from error. Thus he who disbelieves in the Devil and believes in Allah grasps the firmest handle [bond] that will never break. Allah is All-Hearing, All-Knowing. Allah is the Supporter of the believers. He brings them out of darkness into light. As for those who disbelieve, their supporters are the devils who bring them out of light into darkness. Those are the people of the Fire in which they shall abide forever" (2:256-7).

This is why we don't want to impose Islam upon anybody, as much as we don't want others to impose upon us their convictions and their political systems. We don't want Islam to reign in Lebanon by force, as is the case with political Maronism today.[21]

We stress that we are convinced of Islam as an ideology, doctrine, political order, and mode of governance. We call all the populace to be conversant with it and its religious imperatives/injunctions. We also call upon the populace to adhere to its teachings at the individual, political, and social levels. If our populace could freely choose the system of government in Lebanon, then they would definitely opt for Islam. From this perspective, we call for the implementation of an Islamic order on the basis of direct and free choice as exercised by the populace, and not on the basis of force, as others might entertain…[22]

10.   The bare minimum of our aspirations in Lebanon

This is the minimum that we can accept in order to be able to accede by legal means to realize our ambitions, to save Lebanon from its dependence upon East and West, to put an end to foreign occupation [Israeli occupation] and to adopt a regime freely wanted by the people of Lebanon.[23]

11.   Why do we confront the existing regime?

This is our perception of the present state of affairs. This is the Lebanon we envision. In the light of our conceptions, our opposition to the present system is the function of two factors; (1) the present regime is the product of arrogance so unjust that no reform or modification can remedy it. It should be changed radically, and (2) World Imperialism which is hostile to Islam.[24]

"Whoever does not judge according to what Allah has revealed, those are the evildoers!" (5:45).[25]

12. Our stance towards the opposition (to the Lebanese political system[26])

We consider that all opposition in Lebanon voiced in the name of reform can only profit, ultimately, the present system. All such opposition, which operates within the framework of the conservation and safeguarding of the present constitution without demanding changes at the level of the very foundation of the regime, is hence, an opposition of pure formality, which cannot satisfy the interests of the oppressed masses. Likewise, any opposition, which confronts the present regime but within the limits fixed by it, is an illusory opposition, which renders a great service to the Jumayyel system. Moreover, we cannot be concerned by any proposition of political reform, which accepts the rotten [Lebanese political] system actually in effect. We could not care less about the creation of this or that governmental coalition or about the participation of this or that political personality in some ministerial post, which is but a part of this unjust regime.[27]

13. Words to the Christians in Lebanon

The politics followed by the chiefs of political Maronism through the 'Lebanese Front'[28] and the 'Lebanese Forces' cannot guarantee peace and tranquillity for the Christians of Lebanon, whereas it is predicated upon 'asabiyya (narrow-minded particularism), on confessional privileges and on the alliance with colonialism and Israel. The Lebanese crisis has proven that confessional privileges are one of the principal causes of the great explosion, which ravaged the country. It also proved that outside help was of no use to the Christians of Lebanon, just when they need it most. The bell tolled for the fanatic Christians to rid themselves of denominational allegiance and of illusion deriving from the monopolization of privileges to the detriment of other communities. The Christians should answer the appeal from heaven and have recourse to reason instead of arms, to persuasion instead of sectarianism.

If you review your calculations and know that your interest lies in what you decide, by your own free will, not what is imposed upon you, then we renew our call to you: "Say: 'O People of the Book, come to an equitable world between you and us, that we worship none but Allah, do not associate anything with Him and do not set up each other as lords besides Allah' " (3:64).

If you, Christians, cannot tolerate that Muslims share with you certain domains of government, Allah has also made it intolerable for Muslims to participate in an unjust regime, unjust for you and for us, in a regime which is not predicated upon the prescriptions (*ahkam*) of religion and upon the basis of the Law (the *shari'a*) as laid down by Muhammad, the Seal of the Prophets. If you search for justice, who is more just than Allah? It is He who sent down from the sky the message of Islam through his successive prophets in order that they judge the people and give everyone his rights. If you were deceived and misled into believing that we anticipate vengeance against you – your fears are unjustified. For those of you who are peaceful, continue to live in our midst without anybody even thinking to trouble you.

We don't wish you evil. We call upon you to embrace Islam so that you can be happy in this world and the next. If you refuse to adhere to Islam, we would not force you to do otherwise, rather we just expect you to respect and honour your covenants with the Muslims and not to aggress against them. Free yourselves from the consequences of hateful confessionalism. Banish from your hearts all fanaticism and parochialism. Open your hearts to our Call (*da'wa*), which we address to you. Open yourselves up to Islam where you'll find salvation and happiness upon earth and in the hereafter. We extend this invitation also to all the oppressed among the non-Muslims. As for those who belong to Islam only formally, we exhort them to adhere to Islam in religious practice and to renounce all fanaticisms, which are rejected by our religion.[29]

14. Our story with the world oppressors

We reject both the USSR and the US, both Capitalism and Communism, for both are incapable of laying the foundations for a just society.

With special vehemence we reject UNIFIL[30] as they were sent by world arrogance to occupy areas evacuated by Israel and serve for the latter as a buffer zone. They should be treated much like the Zionists. All should know that the goals of the Phalangist regime do not carry any weight with the Combatants of the Holy War [jihad], i.e., the Islamic resistance. This is the quagmire, which awaits all foreign intervention.

There, then, are our conceptions and our objectives, which serve as our basis and inspire our march. Those who accept them should know that all rights belong to Allah and He bestows them. Those who reject them, we'll be patient with them, till Allah decides between us and the people of injustice.[31]

15. Israel must be completely obliterated/wiped out of existence

We see in Israel the vanguard of the United States in our Islamic world. It is the hated enemy that must be fought until the hated ones get what they deserve. This enemy is the greatest danger to our future generations and to the destiny of our lands, particularly as it glorifies the ideas of settlement and expansion, initiated in Palestine, and yearning outward to the extension of the Great Israel, from the Euphrates to the Nile.

Our primary assumption in our fight against Israel states that the Zionist entity is aggressive from its inception, and built on lands wrested from their owners, at the expense of the rights of the Muslim people. Therefore our struggle will end only when this entity is obliterated. We recognize no treaty with it, no cease-fire, and no peace agreements, whether separate or consolidated.

We vigorously condemn all plans for negotiation with Israel, and regard all negotiators as enemies, for the reason that such negotiation is nothing but the recognition of the legitimacy of the Zionist occupation of Palestine. Therefore we oppose and reject the Camp David Agreements, the proposals of King Fahd, the Fez and Reagan plan, Brezhnev's and the French-Egyptian proposals, and all other programs that include the recognition (even the implied recognition) of the Zionist entity.[32]

We condemn all perverted countries and organizations, which are running after recapitulative solutions with the enemy and that agree to the principle of 'land for peace', and we consider that as a blatant betrayal to the blood of the Palestinian-Muslim people and the holy Palestinian cause.[33]

16. Escalation in the operations of the Islamic resistance (against the Israeli forces)

The dignified Islamic Resistance, which has underscored and still is underscoring the best epics of heroism against the occupying Zionist forces [Israeli Army], has destroyed, with the religious belief of its fighters, the myths of the invincible Israel. It has put the "Rapist Entity" [Israel] in real trouble due to the daily war of attrition it waged against its military as well as human and economic resources, which has led its leaders to concede to the severity of the confrontation they are facing at the hands of the Muslims [Hizbullahis]…This Islamic Resistance is destined to continue and grow, God willing. It is expecting from all Muslims in the world all the support and backing in order to uproot the "Cancerous Gland" [Israel] and wipe it out of existence. In conformity with realism, we [Hizbullah] insist and stress the Islamic character of our Resistance, which is concomitant with its nationalist-patriotic nature.[34]

231

17. Appeal for broad Islamic participation

We take the opportunity to call on all the Muslims in the world to share, with their brothers in Lebanon, the honour of fighting against the occupying Zionists, either directly or by supporting the *mujahidin* (Hizbullah's freedom fighters) because it is the responsibility of all the Muslims to do so, and not only the residents of *Jabal 'Amil* and Western *Biqa'* (which were the areas under Israeli occupation).

The Islamic Resistance was able, with the blood of its martyrs and the jihad of its heroes, to force the enemy [Israel], the first time in the history of struggle against it, to take the decision and withdraw from Lebanon[35] without any American influence. On the contrary, the [Israeli] decision to withdraw led to a real American concern, and it resulted in a historical overturn in the history of the struggle against the "rapist Zionists".

Hizbullah's freedom fighters have proven that the *umma*, if left alone to conduct its own affairs freely, is capable of making miracles, and change the illusionary predestination [of defeat].[36] It is worth mentioning that The Islamic Resistance is not only composed of young men whose weapon is the rifle and a religiously strong will, but also of women, children, and elderly.[37]

18. The mercenary politics of the (Lebanese) government and its treacherous negotiations

We grant little attention to the occasional boasting of the Lebanese government, which attempts to delude people that it is supporting the Resistance against the occupation...

We overtly declare that the [alleged] verbal and media support is a source of contempt to our populace... Even if some declarations have emanated from some members of the ruling elite, our informed public cannot be deceived by these declarations because they do represent the official stance of the Lebanese government, especially since it is unwilling to deploy the [Lebanese] Army in order to participate in the honour of liberating occupied land...

The contended financial support to the resistance is useless if the money does not reach Hizbullah's freedom fighters *(al-mujahidin)* and is not used to buy ammunition, weaponry, and the like...

Our populace rejects the mercenary policies [the Lebanese government is engaged in] at the expense of the Resistance. There will come a day, when all of those – who debased and "traded" with the blood of the heroic martyrs and built for themselves glories at the expense of the *mujahidin*'s wounds – will be brought to justice.

We can only assert that the policy of negotiations with the enemy [Israel] is a grave treason towards the Resistance that the Lebanese state contents to stand by and support... The insistence of the Lebanese government to join the negotiations with the enemy can only be regarded as a conspiracy aiming at acknowledging the Zionist occupation and according it legitimacy as well as privilege on the crimes it had committed against the oppressed in Lebanon...

The Islamic Resistance, which has openly declared its unwillingness to abide by any result/consequence emanating from the negotiations, stresses the continuity of *jihad* until the Zionists evacuate the occupied lands, which is seen as a step in the right direction to obliterate them from the face of the earth.[38]

19. International forces and their suspicious role

The International Forces that the world oppressors are trying to deploy on Muslim lands – in the areas that the enemy withdraws from, so that it makes up a security barrier that protects Israel and shelters its occupying forces derailing the movements of the Resistance –are totally rejected being indulged conspirators with Israel... we might be compelled to treat it as we engage with the Zionist occupying forces...

May everyone know that the commitments of the Phalangist regime [to Israel] are totally rejected and are unbinding, in any way whatsoever, on the freedom fighters of the Islamic Resistance [who wash their hands from these commitments]... These countries [which sent its forces to Lebanon] has to deeply think before it indulges into the quagmire or quicksand that Israel has drowned itself into.[39]

20. Defeatist Arab Regimes

Concerning the Arab regimes which are running after reconciliation with the Zionist enemy, these regimes are impotent and short sighted in accompanying the ambitions and aspirations of the *umma*... These regimes cannot think of confronting the Zionist entity that raped Palestine because they were founded under colonial guardianship, which had a great role in the shaping of these rusty regimes...

Some reactionary rulers, especially those in the oil producing countries, do not hesitate to make of their countries military bases for America and Britain. They are not ashamed in being dependent on foreign experts whom they appoint in official high places. They abide by and execute what the "White House" dictates to them, especially the policies of getting out the natural resources and the riches [of their countries] and distribute it on the colonizers, using all possible means [to accomplish that]...

Some of those who claim to be the guardians of the Islamic *shari'a* [The Saudi regime] employ this claim to cover up their treason as well as to find a pretext for their yielding to the US Administration. At the same time, they [The Saudi regime] vehemently ban and prohibit any revolutionary Islamic book… [A reference to Imam Khumayni's books]

As a result of the defeatist policy employed by these reactionary regimes towards Israel, the latter was able to convince a lot of them that it has become fait accompli and that there is no way out save to recognize it and concede the need to providing security for it…

This policy of yielding encouraged the deceased Sadat to commit a grave treason by reconciling with Israel and signing a disgraceful peace treaty with it… This policy of yielding governs and constrains the movement of the Gulf Cooperation Council (GCC), and the Jordanian-Egyptian axis, Iraq, and the Arafati Organization [i.e. the PLO]…

The defeatist policy in front of America directs the attitude of the reactionary rulers concerning the aggressive war imposed on the Islamic Republic of Iran… It stands behind the unlimited financial, economic, and military support the agent Saddam [Husayn] is showered with. They [the US] think that the Takriti [Tikrit is Saddam's hometown] Zionist regime can annihilate the Islamic Revolution and can stop the emanation of its revolutionary light and ideals.

This defeatist policy pushes reactionary regimes to make the people ignorant; to brain wash them and make their Islamic personality wither away; to repress any Islamic mobilization that is against America and its allies in these countries. The defeatist policy also makes the reactionary governments fearful of the vigilance of the oppressed, banning them from interfering in its political affairs because it posses a grave danger on the survival of these regimes, especially since the populace is aware of the corruption of its governments and its suspected relations/linkages [with other states], as well as the sympathy this populace shows towards liberation movements in all parts of the Islamic world as well as the world at large…

We find in these reactionary Arab regimes an impediment against the increase in conscious raising and unity of the Islamic populace. We consider them [reactionary Arab regimes] responsible in stalling the attempts to keep the wound open and the struggle with the Zionist enemy going on…

We have a big hope in the Muslim populace that started to clearly complain, in most Islamic countries, and was able to benefit from the revolutionary world, especially the victorious Islamic Revolution… The day will come when these barely standing regimes will fall under the fist of the oppressed, as has the thrown of despotism collapsed in Iran.

We are fighting a ferocious battle against America and Israel and their plans for the region [Middle East]. We warn these reactionary [Arab] regimes from working against the dominant reformist current in the *umma*, which is against colonialism and Zionism. These [reactionary Arab regimes] have to learn from the Islamic resistance in Lebanon grand lessons in the persistence in fighting the enemy in order to completely defeat it.

We warn these regimes from being engaged in new defeatist projects, or in aggressive projects targeting the young Islamic Revolution... because that will lead these regimes to the same fate that was accorded to Anwar al-Sadat, and before him Nur al-Sa'id.[40]

21. *International front for the oppressed*

We turn our attention to all the Arab and Muslim populace in order to declare to them that the experience of the Muslims in Islamic Iran, does not leave a pretext to anyone, because it has proven beyond the shadow of a doubt, that bear chests that are driven by a faithful volition, with the great aid of God, was able to break all the iron [power] of the tyrannical regimes...

That is why, we call upon these populace to unify their ranks, plan their objectives, mobilize to break the chains that engulf its volition, and to over through the despotic collaborating governments [with the 'enemy'].

We exhort all the oppressed in the world to the necessity of forming an international front comprised of all their liberation movements in order to fully coordinate among themselves so that an efficient action will transpire, thus concentrating on the Achilles heals of the enemies...

So if the colonizing countries and regimes have shown a consensus on fighting the oppressed... so the oppressed must bond together in order to face the conceit of the world oppressors.

All the oppressed populace, especially the Arab and Islamic ones, should understand that only Islam is capable of becoming the intellectual foundation or thinking that is capable of resisting and confronting the aggression because all situational/positive (man made) ideologies have been disbanded forever in the interest of the deterrence among the Americans and the Soviets as well as others.

The time has come to be cognizant of the fact that all foreign ideas, concerning the origin of man and his instinct, are incapable of answering his ambitions or saving him from the darkness of ignorance and waywardness...

Only Islam leads to man's reform, progress, and creativity because "It is kindled from a blessed olive tree, neither of the East nor the West. Its oil will almost shine, even if no fire has touched it. Light upon light, Allah guides to His light whomever He pleases..." (24:35).[41]

22.   God is with the unity of the Muslims

A call on the Muslim populace:

Be aware of the malignant colonial discord [*fitna*] that aims at rupturing your unity in order to spread sedition among you and enflame Sunni-Shi'a sectarian feelings.

Be knowledgeable that colonialism was not able to control the natural resources and riches of the Muslims except after breaking up their unity... inciting Sunnis against the Shi'as and vice versa. Later on the colonizer left this mission of spreading dissention among the Muslims to its collaborators, be it the governing elite, the corrupt Muslim religious scholars (state jurists), or the feudal leaders (*zu'ama*).

God is with the unity of the Muslims... It is the rock that breaks all the conspiracies of the oppressors; it is the hammer that crushes the evil schemes of the oppressors...

Do not allow the policy of "divide and rule" to be practiced among you; rather fight it by recourse to the Qur'an:

"And hold fast to Allah's bond [His religion], all of you, and do not fall apart. And remember Allah's grace upon you; how you were enemies, then He united your hearts [by becoming Muslims] so that you have become, by His grace, brethren. You were on the brink of the pit of Fire, but He saved you from it". (3:103).

"Those who have made divisions in their religion and become sects, thou art not of them in anything" (6:159).[42]

23.   (An appeal/call on the) 'ulama of Islam

You Muslim 'ulama,

You have a grave responsibility, as grave as the calamities that strike the Muslims... You are the best in conducting your duty of leading the *umma* towards Islam... And in alerting it to what the enemies are plotting in order to control and enslave it as well as rob it of its treasures...

No wonder you are conversant that the Muslims look upon you as bearers of the Prophet's trust (*amana*) in your capacity as successors to the prophets and messengers... So be the hope and the good lead in overtly calling for right and standing up against the tyrants and despots. Be the lead in austerity, the passion to [go to] Heaven, and martyrdom in the way of God…

You have the good lead of Prophet Muhammad who used to share hunger and satisfaction with the people; he used to lead the prayer at the Mosque; he used to lead the populace in *jihad*…

He used to guide the people in missions; they used to get warmth from his guidance and in being around him; they followed him being assured and comforted…

You Muslim *'ulama*,

Imam Khumayni repeatedly stressed the need to rectify, reform, and refine the self, before rectifying reforming, and refining others and the world at large. He said in more than one occasion that if people knew that a shop owner is dishonest and immoral, then they say that Mr. X is dishonest and immoral; if they found out that a trader is cheating then, then they say that Mr. X is a cheater; however, if they knew that a Muslim religious scholar *('alim)*, God forbid, is not upright, then they would generalize and say that all religious scholars are not upright (perverted) and the religion (Islam) as a whole is not upright.[43]

You Muslim *'ulama*,

For this and other reasons… You have a grave responsibility, so invoke God in order to be able to conduct it in a proper way, and invoke Him with the calling of Imam 'Ali: "God, we do not ask you [to take] a small burden, rather we ask you to be a strong bulwark supporting us". Then the *umma* will respond to your call, guidance, and leadership.

Be knowledgeable about the importance of your position in the *umma* because the colonizer has known its importance. That is why the colonizer has vehemently targeted the *'ulama al-mujahidin*… so the colonizer prepared a devilish conspiracy to conceal Imam Musa al-Sadr after recognizing him as an impediment hurdling his aggressive plans… The colonizer killed the Islamic philosopher Ayatullah Murtada Mutahhari… and executed the grand Islamic *marja'* Ayatullah Sayyid Muhammad Baqir al-Sadr[44] because the colonizer felt the danger of his stance, which was personalized in these words: "Melt in Imam Khumayni as Islam has melted in you". That is why the colonizer is stalking and ambushing every religious scholar who is accomplishing his Islamic duty to the best of his knowledge.

From another perspective, the colonizer started to penetrate the Muslims with state jurists who do not fear God. They make religious edicts *(fatwas)* where there is no place for *fatwas*; therefore they sanction peace with Israel, prohibit fighting it, and find excuses for the treason of tyrant rulers…

The colonizer would not have done that without [knowing] the important impact a religious scholar has on the people...

That is why, one of your most important responsibilities, you Muslim *'ulama*, is to raise up/rear the Muslims to abide by the religious injunctions, to clarify to them the righteous political path that they should follow, and to lead them to glory and honour... Also you take care of the religious seminaries so that the *umma* can graduate leaders who are faithful to God and who are committed to the victory of the religion and the *umma*[45] (My emphasis).

24.   A final word regarding international organizations

Finally, there is a need for a few words concerning international organizations such as the UN, the Security Council and others...

We note that these organizations do not constitute a podium for the oppressed nations, and in general, they remain ineffective and inefficient due to the procedural hegemony and domination of the world oppressors on its decisions...

The veto right, which is accorded to some countries, is a testimony to what we say...

From this perspective, we do not predict these organizations to issue anything serving the interests of the oppressed. We call on all the countries, which respect themselves, to adopt a resolution banning the right of veto, which is accorded to the oppressor countries...

We also call on all countries to adopt a resolution to fire Israel from the UN because it is an illegitimate-rapist entity, which is opposed to humanity at large.

You free oppressed...

These are our visions and goals, and these are the basic regulations that guide our path...

There are those who have wholeheartedly and righteously accepted us [our discourse], God is the only Truth; and there are those who have contested our views. We patiently wait till God has judged between us, and the oppressors (al-*qawn al-zalimin*).

May God's blessings and peace be upon all of you,

Hizbullah[46]

2. **Hizbullah: Views and Concepts, Manar TV, Beirut,**
June 20, 1997[47]

Introduction

Freedom, right, justice and peace are essential values for any society to rise and develop. Freedom is the basis for this rise, while justice cannot be applied without right and peace is inaccessible with the exclusion of justice.

Adopting and practicing these human values require commitment and credibility, for they make one importable whole; freedom can not be enjoyed by one group and denied to another, right should not prevail here and be paralyzed there; if abated, justice turns into injustice; peace can not be achieved unless it is comprehensive.

These values have been established by the divine religions, the clearest and most comprehensive of which has been Islam, whether in theoretical or practical conception.

Hizbullah-Lebanon

Hizbullah-Lebanon is an organized striving current that has been established on the basis of its commitment to the above-mentioned values, seeking, with its noble religious and national struggle to achieve these values in Lebanon and the region and to eliminate all the artificial barriers that would obstruct that purpose.

Hizbullah has faithfully, courageously and persistently resisted the Zionist invasion of Lebanon and prevented it from achieving its political objectives that were represented at that time by dominating this small country and establishing a political regime whose decision was to be controlled by the desires of the racist Zionist Jews.

In order to liberate the occupied land, maintain the national dignity and materialize these values, Hizbullah has sacrificed hundreds of martyrs, injured and disabled as an act of faith in the legitimacy of its resistance against the usurping invaders.

Hizbullah between Peace and Violence

Hizbullah has a strong belief in the necessity of achieving the security and peace that are based on right and justice in Lebanon, the region and the world. Consequently, it rejects all forms of aggression and terrorism; at the same time Hizbullah views the Zionist Jews' occupation of Palestine, displacing its people and establishing the entity of Israel on its usurped land as the living materialization of the most hideous kinds of aggression and organized terrorism that is supported by the USA, the sponsor of international terrorism, and some other states that claim to be democratic and protecting human rights whilst they support Israel that was founded on invasion, killing and blood-shed, besides its daily violations of human rights in Lebanon and Palestine.

Hizbullah does not believe it is right for some people in the world to view the Zionist Jewish occupation as accepted violence and terrorism, while they condemn the counter-violence, which is a natural human reaction to the Zionist violence and terrorism.

Hizbullah and the Resistance

Hizbullah has benefited from the experiences of the nations and peoples of the world and read the history of the French people's resistance against the Nazi occupation, and the resistance of the American people against the colonialists as well; It saw how the free world countries and the peoples of the world respect these resistances and annually commemorate their memory because they had expressed the will of freedom and the longing for right, justice and peace.

When Hizbullah resists in Lebanon against the Zionist Jewish occupation lying heavily on its soil in the South and West Bekaa, it is exercising its legitimate and sacred right that was once exercised by the French and American peoples.

Considering Hizbullah's resistance to the Zionist Jewish occupation as "terrorism" is a kind of injustice, discrimination besides being a renunciation of the Bill of Human rights and the Charter of the United Nations.

Therefore, we call on the peoples of the world to distinguish between aggression, which is none other than terrorism, and the honest resistance that is the only way to deter the aggression and confront the terrorism resulting from that aggression. Israel is an aggressive entity that practices terrorism; occupation is one of the forms of terrorism. Hizbullah of Lebanon is a popular resisting trend against occupation and terrorism.

Hizbullah and Dialogue

Hizbullah observes the creed of the genuine Muhammadan Islam and the sublime human values emanating from it. This observance arises from ideological conviction that is established with proofs and evidence and does not originate from emotional liking or sectarian, denominational or racial group spirit. Since reason is the source of this observance, Hizbullah has always been ready to have dialogue with others over its convictions and creeds or even its method and positions; Hizbullah does not seek to impose its convictions on anyone, as it does not like anyone to impose their convictions on it. It is attached to have mutual understanding with the others. It does not think of annulling anyone, as it does not accept anyone to annul

240

it. Therefore, continuing and incessant dialogue is the best way to rectify visions and positions; it is also a feature of Hizbullah.

Hizbullah and the Political System in Lebanon

Lebanon's political system which is based on the principle of political confessionalism can never achieve justice or realize right and peace. Perhaps one of the most important reasons of the civil war that broke out in 1975 lies within the confessional tendency that had been established by the political system.

The Taif Charter of National Reconciliation did not resolve this dilemma, but rather established it and re-distributed the sectarian quotas anew. This implies a foundation for a future crisis.

That document, nevertheless, is viewed by Hizbullah as a bridge to transfer Lebanon from the stage of bloody conflicts to a new stage of internal peace that we, in Hizbullah, very strongly and definitely desire.

In spite of that, it never calls off our looking forward to more change and development in the Lebanese political system in order to abolish the abhorred sectarian discrimination and achieve justice among the citizens.

Hizbullah and Human Rights

It is axiomatic to say that Hizbullah considers, as its religious task, serving human beings, protecting their rights, maintaining their interest, and exerting effort to provide them with the requirements of a dignified living and developing their society.

If the existing regimes remiss in fulfilling their duties toward that human being, Hizbullah has efficiently contributed in providing humanitarian services to the citizens in various Lebanese areas without discrimination between one citizen and another, or one sect and another.

These services have included many domains; some of them are restoring damaged buildings, farming guidance, providing utilities for the least cost prices and sometimes for free, providing medical care and hospitalization at the health care centers that are distributed in the areas and in private hospitals, providing primary and intermediate schooling, providing the needy students with scholarships to continue their college schooling plus providing them with scientific orientation, and securing fresh water to the neighborhoods that the public water network does not reach.

However, the most important human right that Hizbullah sacrifices blood and lives in order to maintain is the right of the Lebanese human beings in their land and in determining the political system they desire.

241

3.   Statement of Purpose: Hizbullah Press Office
March 20, 1998 [48]

Hizbullah is an Islamic freedom fighting movement founded after the Israeli military seizure of Lebanon in 1982, which resulted in immediate formation of the Islamic resistance units for the liberation of the occupied territories and for the expulsion of the aggressive Israelis forces.

In addition to shouldering the burden of resisting the Israelis occupation as it is stated by the International Bill of Human Rights, Hizbullah is also concerned about the presentation of Islam which addresses the mind and reason. Hizbullah is concerned about presenting Islam that is confident of its fundamentals, its highly civilized understanding of man, life and the universe, Islam as being self-assured about its capability to achieve the basis of right and justice. We are anxious to present Islam as being open hearted to all nations their various political and cultural trends and their numerous experiences, away from subjection or bewilderment. We are anxious to present Islam as being the guardian for human rights defining choices, adopting convictions and expressing them, socially. We opt for the formation of political pressure in education, pedagogy, medical care and other social benefits announced in the Bill of Human Rights. We are anxious to define the priorities for our cultural project that utilizes persuasiveness and polarization through the civilized and the human methods confirmed by the Bill of the Human Rights. Away from evidence force, and coercion: We are anxious to offer a model of performance in struggling targeting the enemy that represents a challenge for the existence of the whole nation along with its regimes and people. We also circumvent conflicts that do not serve the main aim, fighting the enemy, or that could create discord at the front, which is to be unified around the common interests. The hope is to rid of the pressuring threats practiced by the foreign Zionist Entity, which has been thrust upon the Islamic, and the Arab contemporary nation. It should be clear that the kind of Islam we want is a civilized endeavour that rejects injustice, humiliation, slavery, subjugation, colonialism and blackmail while we stretch out our arms for communication among nations on the basis of mutual respect. The Islam we mean is the religion that never accepts control or delegation by others for the sake of manipulating the rights and the interests of the nation. The Islam we mean is the religion that recommends communication among civilization and rejects divisive collision between those civilizations. An Islam that believes in cultural communication among nations and refuses setting up barriers and embargos and sees that it is our right to remove those barriers by the diplomatic means, however, when others intend to launch wars against it, Hizbullah finds it a natural right to defend itself representing its supporters and their achievements [sic].

242

Islam that we understand is a message that aims at establishing justice, security, peace and rights for all people no matter what nation, race or religion they belong. We don't have any complex toward others, but we feel the responsibility toward them, to make them understand the essence of our religion away from obligation and fanaticism.

We don't seek the application of Islam by force or violence but by peaceful political action, which gives the opportunity for the majority in any society to adopt or reject it. If Islam becomes the choice of the majority then we will apply it, if not, we will continue to coexist and discuss till we reach correct beliefs.

We hereby affirm that our Islam rejects violence as a method to gain power, and this should be the formula for the non-Islamists as well.

4.   Hezbollah: Identity and goals [49]
(August 2004)

Hezbollah is an Islamic struggle (jihadi) movement. Its emergence is based on an ideological, social, political and economical mixture in a special Lebanese, Arab and Islamic context.

As a result of this background Hezbollah went through various decisive moments in its history. With the most important moment being in 1982 the year of the Zionist invasion of Lebanon. This invasion led to the occupation of the capital Beirut making it the second Arab capital to be occupied during the Arab-"Israeli" conflict, with Jerusalem being the first. This crossroad speeded up the presence of Hezbollah as a struggle movement that is totally affiliated in the long complicated and complex fight against the Zionist enemy. The starting point of that struggle being the Zionist occupation of Palestine, and then to many of the Arab lands in Egypt, Syria and Jordan leading up to Lebanon. All that led to the establishment of the identity of Hezbollah as a struggle movement against the Zionists. Add to that many social, economical, political and cultural ideals of the Shiaa in Lebanon. Another very important factor that developed Hezbollah was the establishment of the Islamic Revolution in Iran that was led by the late Imam Khomeini. This revolution consolidated new concepts in the field of Islamic thought mainly the concept of Willayat Al-Faqih. The revolution also generalized Islamic expressions against the west such as arrogance, the great Satan, hypocrites and the oppressed.

With this crossroad and with the historic tie between the Shiaas in Lebanon and in Iran, which is a doctrinal tie. As well as of the reason that Iran hosts the second most important religious school of the Shiaa in Qom with the second being the Al-Najaf school in Iraq. But because of many obvious reasons Qom has occupied the number one Shiaa school in the world today.

Due to that it was only normal for the ideological doctrine in Iran to take root in Lebanon. This tie was very quickly translated on the ground by direct support from the Islamic Republic of Iran through its revolutionary guards and then to Hezbollah that was resisting the "Israeli" occupation.

This religious and ideological tie between Hezbollah and Iran following the revolution with its stance towards the Zionist entity had a great effect on releasing vital material and moral support to Hezbollah. This support speeded up the acknowledgement of making Hezbollah one of the leading struggle movements against the Zionists. But during and after 1985 Hezbollah was the only such movement in this field.

It was not by cheer coincidence that Hezbollah turned into a struggle movement against the "Israeli" occupation. Because Hezbollah's ideological ideals sees no legitimacy for the existence of "Israel" a matter that elevates the contradictions to the level of existence. And the conflict becomes one of legitimacy that is based on religious ideals. The seed of resistance is also deep in the ideological beliefs of Hezbollah, a belief that found its way for expression against the Zionist occupation of Lebanon. And that is why we also find the slogan of the liberation of Jerusalem rooted deeply in the ideals of Hezbollah. Another of its ideals is the establishment of Islamic Republic[50].

The Islamic Resistance was able to direct very painful blows to the Zionist enemy forcing them to withdraw step by step. One of the principal withdrawals is that of 1985 leading up to the withdrawal from the Christian area Jezzine. And finally, leaving the enemy with no choice but to withdraw completely as a final solution to their problems.

Hezbollah also used one of its own special types of resistance against the Zionist enemy that is the suicide attacks. These attacks dealt great losses to the enemy on all thinkable levels such as militarily and mentally. The attacks also raised the moral across the whole Islamic nation.

It is also vital to state here, that the resistance gained high credibility amongst the people and in all official statuses, both locally and internationally. The US also once stated that the resistance is a justified movement in facing the "Israeli" occupation.[51]

The resistance also established an internal national axis in a way that was never witnessed in Lebanon before. This matter is of vital interest when we notice how Lebanon is divided into various religions, sects, ideologies, societies, cultures etc.

Today, Hezbollah is one of the most prominent Lebanese political parties that has its presence in the parliament (with 8 MPs).

Hezbollah today also commands respect politically after it proved its powerful presence through a high level of efficiency measured by rationalism, steadfastness, and high moral values aimed at respecting the values of others. This made Hezbollah inaugurate innovate political process.

Hezbollah also sees itself committed in introducing the true picture of Islam, the Islam that is logical. Committed to introduce the civilized Islam to humanity.

Hezbollah also sees itself committed in introducing the Islam that is confidant in achieving justice, as well as introducing the Islam that protects all human rights. Introducing the Islam that supports education, the Islam that offers medical support. Hezbollah also has its own cultural plan to attract and convince through civilized and humanitarian means as specified in the human rights laws, far from any use of violence or coercion.

It should also be clear that the kind of Islam that Hezbollah seeks is a civilized one that refuses any kind of oppression, degradation, subjugation and colonization. Hezbollah also stretches its arm of friendship to all on the basis of mutual self-respect.

The Islamic path that Hezbollah follows is one of a message that aims to establish peace and justice to all humanity whatever their race or religion. Hezbollah does not have a problem with anyone, but it feels responsible towards him or her to clarify the true Islam far away of any fanaticism.

Hezbollah does not wish to implement Islam forcibly but in a peaceful and political manner, that gives the chance to the majority to either accept or refuse. If Islam becomes the choice of the majority only then will it be implemented. If not it will then continue to co-exist with others on the basis of mutual understanding using peaceful methods to reach peaceful solutions. And that is how the case should be to the non-Islamists as well.

C   *Parliamentary Elections Programs*

1.   **Hizbullah's 1992 Parliamentary Elections Program**[52]
     (My translation)

In the name of God, the Merciful, the Compassionate

"Those who, if we establish them firmly in the land, will perform the prayer, give the alms, command the good and prohibit evil. To Allah belongs the outcome of all affairs" (22:41).

From the stance of our legal *(shar'i)* responsibility towards our oppressed people in Lebanon that gives due concern to the populace's grand destining causes and its neglected daily demands; in light of a deep-conscientious reading to the nature of the degrading situation in Lebanon, and the changes in the international arena and their domestic impact, and the need to stand up against conspiracies that are being contrived against the land, rights, and dignities of our populace; based on a realistic diagnosis of the clear and possible dangers as well as the opportunities available to the Islamists in order to take a leading role, while avoiding slippery slopes, in the path to fortify the Islamic project, and consolidate its steps and fruits; in harmony with the jurisprudential *(fiqhi)* stipulations that, for us, act as a guide and an authority of emulation *(marja')*…

In conveying our gratitude to the righteous expression of our populace's aspirations, pains, hopes, and aspirations; from the stance of the people's trust in Hizbullah's integrity and its great sacrifices, and its vigilance for public interest, and its principled stance.

We [Hizbullah] made up our mind, relying on God, and decided to participate in electoral politics on the basis of a comprehensive political program, in which our candidates are obliged to do their utmost best to put it [political program] into operation, asking our populace to support it and follow up on it.

The dignified Lebanese,

The loyal oppressed,

In this sensitive and grave period of the history of our wounded country; in the midst of grand international changes that ravaged out existence and led to the collapse of regimes and changed the features of policies and alliances; at the time when the Zionist enemy [Israel] is still occupying a beloved section of our country, the South and the *Biqa'*, portraying the ugliest pictures of conquest and extortion, while the project of the oppressors, spearheaded by the US, continues its bet on subduing Lebanon and the region [Middle East] in order to seal the deal of recognition in the legitimacy of the Zionist Entity, and normalise relations with it, thus melting/fusing the *cultural identity* of the people of the region and tying its destiny to the [market] economy and Western mode of production and what it leads to in the sense of plundering riches and natural resources, the imposition of regimes, and the execution of programs [policies and plans].[53]

In these circumstances, Lebanon is embarked upon the preparation for the first parliamentary elections in twenty years. The Lebanese are facing an enormous historical eventuality that will paint the future picture of the general political situation in the country, be it on the level of the building a new [political] system, or on the level of its role, performance, and relations.

And if it assumed that the performance of the parliamentary elections will be conducive to finding a new formula for the [political] system that repels political sectarianism and builds the foundations of a state that personifies the will of the Lebanese people, then Hizbullah's decision to participate, with its brothers and friends, in these elections is based on perpetual principled political convictions, enforced by the blood of its martyrs, and the suffering and pain of its prisoners of war, detainees, wounded, families of the martyrs, and the oppressed; Hizbullah has sacrificed for these [principles and convictions] its best cadres and holy warriors *(mujahidin)*, led by the leader of the martyrs of the Islamic resistance, Sayyid Abbas al-Musawi and his wife and child, and the Shaykh of the martyrs, Shaykh Ragib Harb, and Al-Sayyid the martyr Abdulatif al-Amin, and the Shaykh of the prisoners of war and the detainees, Shaykh AbdulKarim 'Ubayd, and others from the heroes of the caravan of martyrdom and resistance who expelled the Zionist Occupation[54] and enforced on it defeat and withdrawal, without any conditions, setting a precedent in the history of conflict against it, thus regaining to the *umma* the hope of victory and confidence in itself. It also gave Lebanon a chance to catch its breath and solve its plight away from direct Zionist [Israeli] intervention.

These convictions became embedded in our peoples' souls, rendering them [i.e. convictions] a daily *jihadi* and political path, which revolves on two basic objectives:

1. Lebanon's liberation from the Zionist occupation and from the oppressors' influence and following.

2. The abolishment of political sectarianism

Hizbullah had a leading role in accomplishing important steps towards the realisation of these two goals. And Hizbullah has to continue, with the cooperation of other faithful [dedicated people], the necessary step in order to achieve total liberation [the total withdrawal of the Israeli army from Lebanon] and strengthen the path to domestic peace, on the basis of political consensus, away from the despicable sectarian strife and narrow zealous partisanship and fanaticism; the removal of the traces of the devastating [civil] war, and objectively, constructively, and responsibly address its causes and consequences so that no party can feel duped, and so that privileges will not be accorded to any group [at the expense of another].

Today as Hizbullah embarks on participating in the parliamentary elections in Lebanon, it [Hizbullah] is trying to elevate the level of political work by selecting its nominees for the elections both on the basis of merit and a political program that is dedicated, in full honesty and seriousness, to address and solve people's problems. Hizbullah's responsible performance materialises in paying perpetual attention to accord the best care to the interests and the causes of the people, from the stance of its [Hizbullah's] integrity in [honouring] word and deed as well as fidelity in following up people's rights and defending their rights, honour, and dignity.

Hizbullah's nominees have no desire to compete with others over power, wealth, or material possessions; rather to be dedicated to a religious duty *(taklif shar'i)* in front of God, in order to preserve the country, uphold the interests of the people, and achieve the objectives that the holy warriors and the martyrs fought for.

From this stance, they [Hizbullah's nominees] are committed to perpetual, industrious work, both within the confines of the parliament and outside it, in order to achieve the following objectives in the different domains:

On the general political stance:

1. The Resistance

The conservation of a unified Lebanon, and its belonging to the civilised world, especially its Islamic-Arab milieu, dictates on us [Hizbullah] the serious commitment to the Resistance as an alternative against the Zionist occupation until the liberation of all the occupied soil, especially after it has been proven on the ground that the Resistance is capable of foiling the conqueror's [Israeli] plans, which aim at imposing a political reality that is against the interest of Lebanon and the Lebanese. After it became crystal clear that the Resistance is the only choice that is capable of standing out against the enemy and its extortions. In addition the Resistance stands for the right way of liberating Lebanon and upholding its unity and the unity of its people.

This choice [of Resistance] requires endeavouring to achieve the following:

A. Being committed to the alternative of Resistance by supporting the fighters, backing up their ways of *jihad*, and embracing them and granting them popular and governmental support.

B. Put up programs that direct the capabilities in order to defend our populace and erect a withstanding *resistance society (mujtama' al-muqawama)*[55] on all levels and domains, especially in the South and Western *Biqa'* [the occupied areas at the time].

C. The Lebanese state, with all its institutions, especially the army, should contribute in the operation of liberation and the defence of the land, the people, and the dignities.

D. According serious and practical attention to the occupied "Security Zone", and take all necessary measures in order to foil the Zionist normalisation project.

E. Exhort the Lebanese government to secure the lives of the families that have either lost their breadwinners or whose breadwinners have became permanently handicapped, in the detention camps or as a result of Zionist aggressions.

F. Standing up firmly and condemning every attempt of normalisation of relations or establishing peace with the "Zionist Entity", which, in the first place, is found upon aggression and raping other people's land.

2.   The abolishment of political sectarianism

Political sectarianism is one of the gravest ills for the corruption of the system in Lebanon. It is also the result behind all cultural, political, security, social, and developmental misfortunes and disasters that have plagued the Lebanese people. It also offered the malignant entry to the oppressive greedy forces to interfere in domestic Lebanese issues and jeopardise Lebanon's future and destiny. The first duties of Hizbullah's nominees is to follow up the conducive efforts, in cooperation with all friends and loyal ones, to abolish it [political sectarianism], during the first constitutional cycle of the new parliament.

3.   The electoral law

Amending the electoral law so that it will be more representative of the populace, by adopting the following two measures:
- Lebanon as one election district.
- Reducing the age of voting to 18.

4.   Political and media freedoms

- Secure the freedom of belief and practicing religious rituals and rites, as well as respecting the sanctity of Abrahamic religions.
- Enact laws that guarantee the freedom of political work.
- Organise the media within the following framework:

A. Harmonisation between the media mediums, on the one hand, and Lebanon's [Arab-Muslim] cultural identity, on the other.
B. Abiding by the sanctity of public conduct and morals.
C. Preserving the right of private media [institutions] to work within the above-suggested points [A and B], without any guardianship [censorship] from the government

5.   The nationality

- Enacting a modern naturalisation law based on meritocracy, rather than sectarianism and favouritism.

- Granting the nationality to the residents of the "Seven Villages" and the Arabs of Wadi Khaled.[56]

6. The displaced

- Secure the comprehensive return of all the displaced.[57]
- Find [conducive] solutions to the displaced of the "Security Zone".
- Set up a comprehensive developmental plan targeting all the geographical areas where the displaced are present in.

7. Administrative, social, and educational issues

The need to fix and reform the infrastructure of the country in the administrative, educational, social, and developmental domains. In addition to constructively addressing many pressing issues along these lines; issues which call for a convergence of efforts in order be accomplished.

1. At the administrative level
   A. Abolish the sectarian factor in public and private jobs and appointments.
   B. Merit and open examinations should be used as a basis for selecting employees instead of favouritism.
   C. Periodic rehabilitation of employees according to the demands of technological advancement.
   D. Increase the effectiveness of administrative inspection.

2. On the developmental level
   A. Protect the domestic produce; support the agricultural and industrial sectors by developing individual capabilities and providing external markets.
   B. Develop the infrastructure of the oppressed [deprived] areas; enhance the lines of transportation, communication, electricity, and water.
   C. Secure job opportunities for all the Lebanese and protect the working force.
   D. Support animal produce, help fishermen, and encourage handicrafts.
   E. Agricultural guidance; the inauguration agricultural centres, cooperatives, and laboratories.
   F. Develop deprived areas in order to reach the level of flourishing areas in Lebanon; after accomplishing that balanced development.

3.   On the educational and cultural levels

A.   Reinforce public education in all its stages and sectors, especially vocational education.

B.   Realisation of mandatory education, at least, till the middle level [preparatory for high school].

C.   Buttress the Lebanese University, in particular the faculties of applied sciences.

D.   Sponsor those who excel, and consolidate research at the [Lebanese] University.

E.   Rewriting the history [school] books based on an objective curriculum, and be committed to the standards of the cultural belonging of Lebanon to its Arab and Islamic milieu.[58]

F.   Reinforce and protect religious education.

G.   Re-stimulate the teacher's education and rehabilitation centres, across the education spectrum or levels.

H.   Strengthen the teachers' financial conditions as well as their educational, and scientific qualifications.

I.   Arabisation of the academic curriculum.

4.   On the social level

−   Enact a law so that all Lebanese, including self-employed and daily workers, can benefit from social security, social and health benefits, and an old-age retirement plan.

−   Reform [governmental] institutions that are responsible for social and health benefits and insurance [social security].

−   Erect public hospitals and public medical centres in all Lebanese areas.

Based on this program, Hizbullah, through its nominees, presents itself to the parliament, while being resolute in protecting the interests of the oppressed in Lebanon, invoking God Almighty for acceptance and success. Hizbullah hopes to achieve victory, honour, glory, and progress (towards the better). God is All-Hearing and All-Responding.

Peace be upon you, God's Mercy and Blessings
Hizbullah
July 1992

2. Hizbullah's 1996 Parliamentary Elections Program[59]

In His Name Be He Exalted

The Electoral Program of Hizbullah, 1996

And those who strive [jahadu] in our (cause), we will certainly guide them to our paths[60] for verily Allah is with those who do right.

(Holy Koran)

Faithful Lebanese

In persistence with our political course that is based on divine values,

In commitment to our vast cultural affiliation with all its diversity, richness and sublimation of human value, within a framework of integration and unity,

On the basis of our firm pledge of the Lebanese people's interests in liberating our land in the South and West *Bekaa*, of maintaining our security and right in a decent life and an honorable living besides their looking forward to a political society of more balance and justice, a society more capable of understanding the internal flaw points and confronting the foreign challenges and a more stable society,

We continue the unlimited course of giving, the giving of blood, the honesty of stand, the courageous word, and the political behavior that aims at changing instead of submitting to the status quo, overcomes balances instead of falling because of them and seeks a nation beyond sectarianism, a state with no monopolization or absorption, a state of development with no discrimination and participation with no exclusion or elimination.

In the light of a conscious reading of the magnitude of the perils and challenges that overwhelm the regional situation due to the policies of American hegemony and Zionist terrorism,

Out of the position of deep realization of the historic stage through which our country is passing,

Under the staggering production of a sound political life and the disappointing results of the state institutions' performance and their alleged attempts of development,

Before the regression of the state situation due to a combination of many factors surging out of the unbalanced nature of the Lebanese political system and the wrong practices by the authority men that led to deepening the status of corruption, favoritism and migration of qualifications, besides establishing the sectarian, confessional and regional divisions,

In the light of all that, and after four years, during which we had the honor of contribution in serving the Lebanese from the parliamentarian post, we run with you for the scheduled parliament elections with established responsibility and greater insistence on shouldering the trust that our dear Lebanese people made us carry to complete the course of all the noble martyrs who died while defending our sacred soil and the dignity, freedom, future and welfare of our people, on top of whom the Master of the Islamic Resistance martyrs Sayyed Abbas Mussawi and Sheikh of its martyrs Sheikh Ragheb Harb (May Allah be pleased with them).

As it has always been, Hizbullah will continue to be, with greater drive and increasing responsibility, the party of Resistance and Liberation, the party of steadfastness and construction and the party of change to a better status, according to the following program:

1. Resisting the occupation

Through its liberating and striving course and its field and political achievement, the most distinguished of which were the steadfastness and victory in two large-scale wars, July 1993 and April 1996, the Islamic Resistance has affirmed its being the only option towards a dignified liberation with no conditions or prices that would[61] damage the sovereignty, resources and right; it has also affirmed its being an element of unity and dignity for the Lebanese and a major guarantor for their security and their regional and international presence. Therefore, we confirm the following:

- We will work on the strong and efficient continuation of the Resistance until our occupied land is completely liberated and restored to the national sovereignty, until our people in the occupied strip are released and able to secure a free honorable decent living away from any direct or indirect presence of the usurping Zionists. We will also work on confronting the logic of the theatrical negotiations that seek to establish Israel's position at the expense of the people of the land.

- Protecting the Lebanese civilians will remain essential in the Resistance performance, due to its being a major objective and main role performed by the Resistance with wisdom, awareness and responsibility.

- We will seek with all carefulness that the Lebanese people with all its sects, categories and individuals, remain the Resistance's embracer and base from which it derives strength and presence. The sought-after liberation – Allah willing-will only be a gift to all the Lebanese and a major contribution in constructing a country with complete sovereignty and a state of consideration and estimation in the arena of regional and international conflict.

- We will continue seeking to achieve more effective state involvement in the operation of liberation and embracing the Resistance men, and the prisoners, detainees and martyrs' families plus providing the steadfastness requirements through establishing and developing foundations for these ends, besides supporting any action that assists in fighting normalization and cultural invasion along with rejecting any form of reconciliation with the enemy.

2.   Achieving Equality and Establishing the Just State

Achieving justice and equality among the Lebanese is considered one of the main bases for establishing a stable dignified and prosperous country in which all the Lebanese engage in the process of construction with drive and solidarity under equality of opportunities, equality of all, individuals, classes and areas, in rights and duties, whether political, economical or social. Consequently we will seek to continue working until we achieve:

- Abolishing political sectarianism that represents the center of the essential flaw in the formula of the Lebanese political system and its social structure, besides being what secretes most of the domestic instability features, the fertile soil for the disturbance that marks the authority institutions and the inter-confessional relations.
- A just and balanced electoral system that treats all the Lebanese even-handedly, allows for real representation, and leads towards developing the Lebanese political status through the approbation of Lebanon as one constituency with a proportional representation system.
- Establishing real political institutions that can not be summarized in individuals, nor emptied by the dominance of parties or groups, or employed to serve the "favorites" and "guys". The most dangerous thing that confronts the state and topples its logic is politicizing the administration and linking it to political loyalties away from the criteria of qualification and equality.
- Applying the principle of administration decentralization through a consistent and proportionate law that guarantees achieving administrative divisions capable of accomplishing efficient development in the various areas besides reviving the municipal and mayor councils to allow for real participation by the civil society in running its development and social affairs.

3. At the Economical Level

We will work on making the state adopt economical policies that give priority to achieving integral human development instead of being confined to imported economical policies that do not consider in their priorities the economical and social particularities discharged by the war and that led to increasing the rates of poverty, unemployment, and the evanescence of the middle class that is considered the scales of economical justice. Moreover, we will work on realizing justice in the distribution of taxes and charges among citizens according to their capabilities.[62]

What is required is the rearrangement of development priorities and subsidizing the sectors of industry, agriculture, animal breeding and fishery, plus providing loans and production requirements, protection, and marketing, in addition to supporting all forms of craftsmanship.

The state's role in the economical operation must be based on a delicate harmonization between the necessity of activating the public sector, prosperity of its movement and investments, on one hand, and the necessity of not deserting the state's responsibilities towards the citizens and the public utilities, especially what concerns supporting the steadfastness of the areas confronting the Zionist occupation.

4. At the Educational and Syndical [Syndicate] levels

- The chronic demand of enhancing and reforming public schooling has not taken its implementation course seriously and effectively until today, therefore; it is vital to seek enhancing and developing public schooling, as schools, teachers and administrations. Furthermore, the development of the educational structure must be followed by the policy of reestablishing and modernizing the curriculums in harmony with the modern necessities, besides accomplishing the history book drafting on objective basis and working on increasing the interest in vocational education, taking into account the necessity of linking it to the Lebanese market needs.

Uplifting the Lebanese University is a vital demand that we will work on achieving through modernizing its curriculums, uniting the branches of the capital and the surrounding areas, enhancing the branches of the areas, reviving specialization scholarships and sponsoring top students and strengthening research methods to get out of the currently-adopted dictation method and allow for developing talents and qualifications.

Reinforcing the labor movement and the syndical frameworks is a civil and political must; that ought to be away from pressure, straitening and harassment that are being practiced by the authority at times of crises and critical phases. Moreover, justice to teachers and university professors in achieving their various demands, without procrastination and postponement is an urgent measure for the stability of these two sectors. Therefore, Hizbullah affirms its persistence on staying in the stand of supporting the syndical movement and supplying it with political, and popular support and power.

5.   At the Social and Health Levels

–   We affirm the importance of the role of the youth in constructing their country and the necessity of providing them with the essentials for strengthening their personalities and filling their times with constructive activities.

–   The woman's role is based on her being the other half that raises and is effective in all the political, educational, social, cultural and economical life. Women must not be treated as supplements nor as commodities of advertisement.

–   Enhancing and maintaining the unity of the family that is the cornerstone in building a good society and providing all the educational and social conditions to establish this direction.

–   The completion of resolving the two issues of naturalization and the displaced so as those who have the right to the nationality obtain it and all the displaced return to their houses or villages in dignity, plus giving the displaced of the occupied strip a special priority attention and consideration.

–   Completing the task of improving public hospital and health clinics with the required equipment, spreading these health centers all over the country especially in remote areas and the steadfast and resisting areas in the South and West *Bekaa*, in addition to making health security accessible to all the sectors of the Lebanese society.

–   Developing the social welfare foundations, supporting the social care institutions, adopting old-age pension, and establishing institutes specialized in treating the various social problems and perversions.[63]

–   The necessity of reforming and developing prisons, establishing reformations for juvenile delinquents in all the Lebanese provinces.

–   Activating the foundations and legislative laws that protect the public resources and the environment, adopting a forestry policy that would restore the balance to the Lebanese environment, protect it from the jeopardy of aridity, maintain the water resources, set projects to be used in all the Lebanese areas and reclaim the lands in order to increase the arable areas.

- Making serious plans that secure a gradual resolution for the housing problem in Lebanon, plus considering this issue one of the great challenges that confront the Lebanese society and have negative social results at numerous levels.

6. Safeguarding Public Freedoms

- To work carefully and persistently on safeguarding public freedoms, i.e. the freedom of belief, freedom of syndical [syndicates] and political activity, freedom of practicing religious rituals and schooling, in addition to accomplishing the regulation of the media without abating the freedom of press, on one hand, but while preserving the maintenance of the identity, public ethics and morals on the other.

7. Foreign Policy

- Adherence to maintaining the Lebanese-Syrian relations, being the practical application of Lebanon's Arab affiliation and since these relations represent a major element of inaccessibility and fortification for Lebanon before the attempts of isolating it under the regional challenges. Furthermore, the previous years have proven that these relations comprise factors of stability for the uneasy Lebanese formula.
- To work on cementing the Lebanese stand in the face of the American pressure policies which are being practiced against Lebanon politically and economically, to reject the continuous American interference in its internal affairs and to deal with the American policy on the grounds of its being identical to and supportive for the positions of the Israeli enemy that occupies our land, kills our children and targets our villages with its incessant daily aggressions.
- The necessity of adopting serious policies and efficient plans to communicate with the Lebanese communities in the countries of expatriation; sponsoring the frameworks that organize those communities' existence; protecting them from attempts to expose them, weaken them or damage their economical presence (as has been the case in more than one African country); working effectively and persistently on rehabilitating the Lebanese expatriate existence

and precluding its being vulnerable and without political protection before the challenges and plots it confronts.

- To emphasize building normal and balanced relations with the Arab and Islamic countries and all the countries of the world on the basis of independence and strengthening the ties that assist in confronting the plots of the American arrogance and allow for honorable and constructive cooperation.

Dear Lebanese People,

From the position of representing the people, with all its implications of religious, national and ethical dimensions and responsibilities, and with our full realization of the magnitude of the complications and obstacles that our Lebanese society is experiencing and with our realization of the long time needed to achieve all what our people anticipates, Hizbullah confirms its candidates' observance and their doing their utmost to put into effect this electoral program that will formulate the framework for the political-legislative role of Hizbullah's parliamentarian bloc.

Success is Granted by Allah

Hizbullah
Summer 1996[64]

3. Hizbullah's 2000 Parliamentary Elections Program[65]
(My translation)

The elections offer a chance to participate in the parliamentary life in order to continue defending the rights of our people, country and causes.

We work for the continual readiness of the [Islamic] Resistance, the populace, and the official stance of defending the country.

The unique relations with Syria are an element of strength for Lebanon and Syria in facing the challenges.

Alleviating the economic problem needs extraordinary efforts by propagating a general reformist economic plan.

Giving due care to the deprived areas, especially the Biqaʿ and Akkar, and allocating to them the necessary attention in order to develop them.

In the name of God, the merciful, the compassionate

"But seek, thanks to what Allah gave you, the Hereafter, and do not forget your portion of the here below [the present world]. Be charitable, as Allah has been charitable to you, and do not seek corruption in the land; for Allah does not like the seekers of corruption" (28:77).

Our loyal Lebanese populace:

Based on the experience that we provided [through our work in] the Lebanese political life, and using as a point of departure our immutable and clear intellectual-political curriculum, which is based upon our civilizational belonging and commitment that makes religious norms the fulcrum of human life, and which aims at providing felicity to man in conjunction with upholding his/her dignity and elevating his/her status… we continue the road to offering, giving, sacrifice, and *ithar* or "preference" in all positions and domains, putting our mind on continuing to defend our people's and country's rights and causes. [We] face the dangers and challenges that target our *umma*, primarily the "Zionist" conquest and US hegemonic projects.

[We] stress national unity, and we uphold national coexistence with all the religious denominations in Lebanon.

From this perspective, our engagement in the elections constitutes an opportunity for us to take part in Lebanese parliamentary life in order to continue our course in defending our people's and country's rights and causes.

1.   Resistance and liberation

The Resistance has proven over the course of the past 18 years of continuous sacrifice and *jihad*, and through the blood of its dignified martyrs, that it is the only road to deter [Israeli] aggression and face "Zionist" greed, uphold the security and dignity of our people, [achieve] the liberation of our land and a true national unity based upon a national consensus in rejecting the occupation and its corroborators, and in buttressing the resistance.

- The Resistance was able to regain occupied Lebanese land and enforce its stance in the regional and international equation, forcing the Zionist enemy to capitulate and withdraw in humiliation, a precedent that the region [Middle East] has never experienced in the history of struggle against the "Zionist Entity". Moreover, the resistance has proven its salient civilizational [cultured] behaviour during the liberation, that it is up to the grand national responsibility, and its upholding of the security of all the citizens, without any discrimination among their groups and sects, and the country. This great achievement [liberation] has been accomplished by the cooperation of the public government, and the Lebanese army. This was conducive to the creation of a general positive atmosphere, which has shielded the victory [liberation].
- The Resistance imposed itself as a serious option that could be bet upon in order to regain the rights and liberate occupied land, without any conditions or dictated peace treaties. It [the Resistance] became a model to emulate and to adopt by all the people in the region, especially the oppressed Palestinian people inside Palestine [Occupied Territories].
- That is why, it is a duty to consolidate and generalise the experience of the Islamic Resistance in Lebanon [Hizbullah's model], in order to awaken and elevate the *umma* as well as to strengthen the stances of its rulers and regimes, and to stop normalization with the Zionist enemy. This will lead to inflicting a "retreat" on the US-Israeli project, which aims at imposing their hegemony on the region and imposing their dictates forcing its people to grant them concessions.

- We work to continuously keep on guard the Resistance and the readiness of the populace as well as the official [Lebanese] stance to defend our country against any aggression or "Zionist" threat. [This is in line with] our continued convictions and belief in facing the Israeli enemy in order to prevent its schemes and dangerous projects from materialising in the region [Middle East].

In order to continue the path and aims of liberation we stress the following:
- Exhort the government to decree and execute a *developmental-service oriented socio-economic program* for the liberated areas and their peripheries, and work on the reconstruction and development of human resources, the economic cycle, and the return of all the displaced, without discriminating against them and giving their cause the appropriate care without humiliating them and forcing them to seek favours[66]. (Italics are added for emphasis).
- The continuation of different and rapid efforts in order to liberate the prisoners of war, detainees, and the purified bodies of the martyrs. The activation and development of the necessary social care for the families of the martyrs, the liberated prisoners of war and detainees, and the wounded and handicapped of the Resistance.
- Being cautious on safeguarding our total rights and national interests in order to accomplish a total liberation of Lebanese soil, and expropriating our total sovereignty on our land, water rights, and security rights, without giving in any part of it, especially those aspects (points) of disagreement[67] and the *Shib'a Farms*.
- Resisting normalization [of relations with Israel], opposing the cultural conquest, refusing coexistence with the Zionist invaders [by not] giving legitimacy to their "Rapist Entity", and refusing the naturalization [of the Palestinians living in Lebanon][68] and insisting on their right of return to all their land in Palestine.

2. *Lebanese foreign policy*

- Work on consolidating the Lebanese stance in the face of the US aggressive policy, which is always biased towards and supportive of the "Zionist Entity", covering up all its crimes, aggressions, and terrorism against our people. Reject the continuous US interference in Lebanese domestic affairs, which is against all norms and diplomatic standards.
- Consider the special and destined relations with Syria as an element of force for both Lebanon and Syria in order to confront the challenges facing them, especially the dangers posed by the "Zionist Entity".

- Follow a governmental policy towards taking care of the matters and causes of the Lebanese expatriates and diaspora in order to make it as an element of force for Lebanon abroad (in the international domain) as well as an element of economic support for the Lebanese residing inside the country.
- Aspire for consolidating Lebanon's relationships with the Arab and Islamic countries as well as other friendly countries in the world of nations.
- Fortify interests and complimentarily with the Arab nations economically.
- Develop the relations with the Islamic Republic of Iran, which has always been a staunch supporter of Lebanon.

3. *Socio-economic problem*

- The aggravation of the social problem reached a serious level making most Lebanese suffer from poor living standards, which are marked by severe shortages. This calls for exercising extraordinary efforts in order to solve the problem by propagating a general economic reform plan that aims at materializing the following:
- Treating the budget deficit by adopting a general and balanced economic-developmental plan among the different sectors in order to increase revenues, decrease expenses, and increase the levels of growth.
- Austerity in expenditure, dealing with the public debt, and reducing its burdens.
- Follow homogeneous fiscal, monetary, and economic policies, which aim at developing economic growth, increasing employment, and encouraging investment.
- Energise the national productive sectors of industry and agriculture by increasing government spending on these sectors and by following stimulating policies and animating procedures.
- Protect local production; be committed to the principle of [fair] competition, increase the ability to compete in foreign markets, and protect the interests of the consumer.
- Develop the sectors [material resources] and human resources by adopting up to date plans and programs aimed at rehabilitation, organisation, and guidance.
- Taking due care of the deprived areas, especially in the *Biqa'* and *Akkar*, and allocate to them due attention in order to develop them, especially the agricultural sector and work on accomplishing the following:

1. Find a plan to buttress agricultural products.
2. Make available agricultural loans and ensure investment.
3. Begin actual work in the Public Foundation for Alternative Agricultural products in the *Biqa'* region, and place a time-schedule suitable in dealing with the grave catastrophe that has ravaged this struggling, productive area.
4. Engage in a continual effort in order to make available the necessary funding required for alternative agricultural products.
5. Decrese the middleman role between the farmer and the consumer by activating the role of cooperative agricultural farms.
6. Fortify the interest of domestic products and protecting it by contracts and agreements.
7. Reduce the cost of insecticides, fertilisers, electricity, and water.
8. Give due attention to natural resources, and prepare the ground for exploiting them, and looking for them, especially oil and water.

4. The building of the state of law and institutions, and the promotion of political participation

From the stance of our concern: with the development of political life and the establishment of social justice among all the Lebanese without any discrimination; the building a stable country; of a fruitful future that offers equal opportunities to all individuals, groups, and geographical areas, and where all people are equal in rights and duties, we [Hizbullah] will continue to work so that the following will materialise:

- Establish the "National Body for the Abolishment of Political Sectarianism".
- Accord special attention to the youth in order to activate their role in the public and political life, and founding specialised centres in order to rehabilitate them on different levels or scales.
- Strengthen the role of women and open the doors for them to participate in the building and activation of public life.
- Enact an election law that is conducive to the development of political life and which gives chance to be a better representation that is based on political programs according to proportional representation, and reduce the voting age [from 21] to 18 in order to offer the opportunity for the youth to express their genuine nationalistic choices.
- Strengthen the role of political parties, the institutions of civil society, and the associations and syndicates [that are engaged in] the public life.
- Develop surveillance and accountability bodies, and activate their role away from the politics of arbitrary decisions and the centres of power.

265

- Accomplish administrative and political reform, and fight and prevent corruption and waste.
- Accomplish an administrative decentralisation law.
- Accomplish a new and modern naturalisation law.

5. *Educational [Pedagogical] and cultural issues*

- Strengthen public education and increase the efficiency in the teachers' roles; furnish the schools with the necessary equipment in order to be able to cope with the implementation of the new educational curricula; make the educational opportunity available to all walks of life, especially the poor and deprived; give the proper attention and care to the deprived areas in this respect.
- Accord serious attention to vocational education according to market demand.
- Develop the Lebanese University and activate its role; encourage specialised scientific studies and research.
- Enact [a law making] religious education an obligatory subject in both public and private schools.
- Reactivate the National Union of the Students of the Lebanese University.

6. *Social and health issues*

- Put a just end to the displaced file or dossier, with particular attention to the special circumstances of the displaced in light of the [Israeli] occupation and "Zionist" attacks.
- Develop and activate the institutions of social care that all strata of society are in need of, especially social security; reconsider and re-evaluate social security's legislations in order to increase the benefits and the circle of the services so that they extend to all Lebanese strata [and not only those registered in social security] and contribute with the available social security's money to economic development and addressing the housing problem.
- Increase and expand social benefits and public services based on a well-studied plan in order to help the families residing in Lebanon, because 40% of these families are poor or deprived and live below the poverty line. That is why it is incumbent upon [the state] to provide a dignified way of living for these families.

- Constructively remedying the social problem according to a general developmental-economic vision in order to root it out.
- Put into practice the old-age retirement plan, and improve it for the benefit of the citizen.[69]
- Develop the state hospitals, and extend social security to cover all hospitalisation cases pertaining to the poor strata.
- Continue to deal with the loopholes that resulted from the naturalisation decree.
- Reform and develop the prisons, and establish and universally introduce rehabilitation centres; place mandatory safeguards in order to uphold ethical norms, moral values, and public mores, in all domains, especially in the media; launch national conscious-raising campaigns aimed at reducing the crime rate.
- Work on placing practical plans, which are conducive in solving the difficult and severe housing problem.
- Place the necessary programs and plans aimed at providing total, safe, and real care for the children.
- Encourage private initiate and work; ensure the availability of work for Lebanese manual labour; work for putting an end to the aggravated unemployment problem.

7. Environmental issues

- Develop and organise recycling plants for sanitary sever water, and continue the installation of sanitary sewer networks.
- Put accurate, scientific plans in order to deal with the issue of "solid" garbage.
- Work on preserving forestry; launch a campaign to plant trees in all geographical areas in order to face desertification; legislate the necessary laws in order to protect forestry and establish natural conservations.
- Activate the role of municipalities in the environmental activities.
- Universally introduce a general guided program for the planning gravel and rock excavation and appropriation.
- Activate the institutions that cater for consumer protection through increased control and supervision on domestic and imported goods in order to ensure their validity and quality.
- Increase supervision and control the way factories dispose their chemical waste; legislate laws that protect the environment, especially the rivers, sea, and underground waterbeds, from the dangers of pollution.

Dear dignified Lebanese,

By counting on you, and with our confidence in the loyalty and consciousness of our populace that has given and sacrificed a lot, we boldly embark upon [participate in] the elections, renewing the oath to dispense all efforts and potentials [do our best] within the narrow confines of the parliament and outside it, in every place and domain, "to serve you with our eyebrows" – as the leader of the martyrs of the Islamic Resistance, al-Sayyid Abbas al-Musawi, may God have mercy on his soul – and to continue, with you, our march in order to achieve all our goals that we all aspire for, our election program, as an avant-garde.

God is behind the intention.

Hizbullah.

4. **Hizbullah's 2005 Parliamentary Elections Program**[70]
   (My translation)

1. Safeguard Lebanon's independence and protecting it from the Israeli menace by safeguarding the (Islamic) Resistance, Hizbullah's military wing, and its weapons in order to accomplish total liberation of Lebanese occupied land (a reference to the *Shib'a* farms).

2. Facilitate the mission of the UN investigating team into Hariri's assassination.

3. Take practical measures to organize a special relationship between Lebanon and Syria.

4. Reject any foreign tutelage or intervention in Lebanese domestic affairs under any pretext or form.

5. Contest the parliamentary elections with the mentality of achieving the broadest and most encompassing national and populist representation in order to come up with an efficient parliament that protects the established national set of values *(thawabit wataniyya)*.

6. Affirm the recourse to the constitutional apparatus and state institutions, while urging the employment of a national discourse through openness and dialogue in a national-comprehensive framework.

7. Stress the need for establishing a comprehensive socio-economic program aimed at stamping out poverty by boosting productive sectors such as agriculture, industry, and trade that are conducive to rendering basic services to the Lebanese citizens.

D   Municipal Election Program

Hizbullah's 2004 Municipal Election Program[71]
(My translation)

1. Hizbullah's principles dictate that the populace constitute the main pillars behind its movement. From this perspective, Hizbullah is under a responsibility to fend off all oppression and injustice in order to serve them and protect their dignity.
2. One of Hizbullah's aims is to adopt the plight of the oppressed and the disenfranchised populace by protecting them and actively working for putting an end to oppression and discrimination towards the deprived areas in order to raise its standards (of living) in all respects.[72]

1.   Core Program

1.1   *Administration and organization*
- find a unified internal order for the employees which takes into account the development of the need of municipal work;
- be strict in enforcing remuneration and punishment as well as a rotation policy targeting the appraisal of employees by developing a special magnetic card for that purpose;
- consider the service of the citizen as a legal and ethical obligation;
- employ state of the art communication and technology as well as rehabilitate, train, and modernize the administrative cadre in order to efficiently render services to the citizens;
- apply accountability, objectivity, and transparency in dealing with the citizens in taking decisions and on a procedural basis;
- regularly publish a brochure, which clearly indicates the accomplishments of the municipalities and its activities as well as a detailed appraisal of the employees and their responsibilities in front of the municipal councils, in order to build a two way street with the public and keep it informed.[73]

1.2   *The efficiency of the municipal council and boosting the confidence of the citizens in it*
- make sure that the members of the municipal councils are conversant with the municipal and administrative rules and regulations;

- erect efficient municipal committees, composed of specialized and authoritative individuals that could be chosen from outside the municipal council, according to a promulgated internal order, specifying its role and jurisdiction, making sure that the same person can not participate in more than two committees;
- layout an annual plan, which is adopted by the municipal council, and followed up by regular appraisal sessions;
- building good relations with the authority of administrative surveillance and public institutions;
- building good relations with the deputies of the region and cooperate with them in order to effectively follow up people's administrative transactions or "dossiers" (mu'amalat) and the developmental projects;
- establishing dialogue sessions, between the municipal council and the citizens, which include debating the projects and submitting a summary of the municipal achievements as well as the impediments facing it. Also, listening to the problems and complaints of the citizens;
- launch campaigns that encourage the submission of innovative projects accompanied by valuable financial prizes to these projects;
- sponsoring conflict resolution by peaceful means between the feuding families;
- establish a special "complaint box", and respond in an efficient way to the complaints of the people;
- follow transparency and accountability in executing promises;
- establish committees from the people in order to react and interact with the municipal work;
- erect big bulletin boards in the centre of the towns and villages and place on them the decisions and news of the municipal councils.[74]

1.3   *Expand the financial revenues of the municipalities*
- specifying in detail the expenditures and the incomes that the municipalities incur;
- incomes are divided along the following lines: the money that the municipality derives directly from the people as well as the money that the state levies on behalf of the municipalities, which is distributed accordingly among them.[75]

1.4   *Developmental projects*

A. Guiding plans;
–   study the possibility of redefining the municipal enclosures or boundaries with respect to the projects and studies of every town;
–   form specialized committees by the central committees in various districts or areas;
–   lay out "guided planning" *(mukhatat tawjihi)* in conformity with the demographic, social, and touristic stance of the towns concerned, in such a way that takes into consideration the present situation and the benefit of each and every town. Also, activate the role of the municipality by voicing its opinion during the propagation of studies and guided planning by the official governmental institutions;
–   supervise (public) works taking place within the municipal domain;
–   work on detailing the "guided planning" for each municipality, dividing the projects with specifying the technical and financial needs for every project, and the time needed to executed it;
–   divide the town according to the deprivation index, (level of) oppression, different walks of life (social, economic, and touristic). Also, setting priorities in order to take proper care of the various areas according to the recommendations of the proposed studies;
–   prepare topographies and computerized maps that clearly indicate real estate, roads, planned projects in order to make use of them in all engineering, developmental, and financial studies for the town.[76]

B. Specific projects
–   study and execute sanitary sewer and drainage network for all the streets that are included within the municipal domain, and seriously thinking for establishing a recycling factory in conjunction with the neighbouring municipalities;
–   erect central water tanks in the municipalities and villages in order to make use of rain or ground water. Also constructing dams and asking the Ministry of Water and Energy to help find other sources of water and construct water networks in the towns and villages lacking it;
–   organize garbage collection without resorting to containers placed on the streets; rather working hard in order to establish garbage recycling factories;
–   supply streets and internal allies with lights;
–   build bridges for pedestrians above the main roads and highways, especially at the entrance of villages and towns;
–   encourage agriculture and the free reclamation of barren land to make it agriculturally productive. Rehabilitate and secure irrigation networks, ponds, and

dams as well as constructing agricultural roads and encouraging the erection of cooperatives and establishing seminars and special guidance sessions;

- construct markets (groceries, fish, meat) or reorganize what is available according to the stipulated requirements;
- build and rehabilitate shelters in a good manner, especially in the southern areas adjacent to the "occupied lands" (Palestine) by the "Zionist Entity" (Israel);
- put an end to building violations (mukhalafat al-bina') and being sever towards handling encroachments on public and private property;
- building parking lots and making use of unused land as well as constructively working on solving the traffic problem;
- building care and recreational centres for ages ranging between 65-75 in order to find good substitutes for what is presently available;
- work on executing the modal street and taking proper care of ruins;
- helping private companies in constructing housing complexes for low income people in an attempt to help the youth[77] to get married and solve the escalating problem of housing.[78]

1.5 *Giving importance to environmental conditions within the municipal jurisdiction*

- regular check up of the state of the environment in order to determine the polluters in sanitary sewers, drinking water, air, garbage, etc., while keeping in touch with private companies, local ministries, and foreign associations that are all specialized in executing projects capable of fighting pollution, while being strict in regular follow up inspection and supervision;
- be strict in spreading environmental awareness;
- planting trees and various plants as well as establishing public gardens and greenhouses;
- putting temporary solutions as well as long term ones in order to get rid of all kinds of garbage and polluters to the environment, in coordination with the concerned ministries as well as competent international associations;
- preservation of the environmental and national heritage;
- encouraging/motivating private initiatives aiming at establishing model/exemplar neighbourhoods;
- be strict in giving permits that might affect the environment;
- conduct efficient health inspection on restaurants, slaughter houses, and food factories;
- regular medical examination and check up on school pupils;
- cleaning and protecting beaches and river banks.[79]

1.6   *Social care*

A. Consolidating the *resistance society* (in order to substantiate the already exist-
     ing "resistance identity")

–   naming the streets within the municipal jurisdiction in such a way as to reflect
     the identity of the village, town, or city (article 49 of the municipal law);

–   erecting monuments (article 62 of the municipal law);

–   protecting the youth from the causes of immorality or vices (article 62 of the
     municipal law) by erecting gyms, public gardens, children playgrounds as well
     as helping in ridding society from social problems;

–   caring for the oppressed families (article 49 of the municipal law);

–   support and encourage clubs and associations working within the geographi-
     cal areas of the municipalities (article 49 of the municipal law);

–   helping in building mosques and *husayniyyat;*

–   according special attention to religious occasions and public holidays through
     decoration and congratulatory call on feast days;

–   consolidating commendable societal customs and habits;

–   erecting a special praying place *(musalla)* in the town hall so that people can
     pray at the stipulated times;

–   exhort the citizens to form special committees, under the jurisdiction of the
     law, in order to deal with procedural matters concerning their dwelling facili-
     ties;

–   regulate and strictly observe, within the narrow confines and the jurisdiction
     of the municipal law, media and information activities situated within the con-
     fines of the municipalities.[80]

B. Caring for the youth

–   appointing a committee, headed by one of the members of the municipal
     council, in order to follow up on the matters or affairs of the associations, thus
     rendering a variety to youth activities such as scouts, athletics, and cultural
     activities. Also it would lead to the erection of clubs aiming at attracting the
     highest possible number of youth;

–   setting up handicraft, vocational, athletic, scientific, mathematical and cultural
     training courses in cooperation with the specialized ministries, UN programs,
     and local associations, which are concerned with the youth's welfare and their
     (scientific) development;

–   encourage the youth to acquire scientific and cultural education by helping
     them in pursuing higher education in their own fields of specialization;

- stimulate the successful, creative, innovative youth by organizing an annual celebration in their honour;
- doing their utmost best in creating job opportunities and establishing athletic playgrounds and well-equipped facilities for the youth;
- encourage the youth to visit holy places by organizing competitions and offering them prizes;
- establishing a monthly or seasonal journal or brochure specifically for the youth.[81]

C. Children, motherhood, old age, and handicap (disability)[82]
- collect information and data on the orphans, old people, working children and handicapped children, so that it could be studied and evaluated in order to find the appropriate ways to deal with it;
- fighting illiteracy in society and establishing pedagogical and educational training courses;
- reducing child labour and dealing with difficult cases through guidance, rehabilitation, and effectively working for finding them schools;
- establishing training and vocational courses for mothers in order to help them to perform their role in a satisfactory way by helping them raise more income for their families. Also, finding or building day care centres (for children) in order to help working women;
- upgrading contact with specialized international associations in order to guide the nursing mother and afford her with what she needs;
- constructing gardens for children and the old aged;
- helping, as much as possible, the poor, especially the elderly in order to pay state and municipal taxes;
- making health and social care available for the elderly, orphans, handicapped and the needy through municipal associations and other governmental and private institutions;
- commemorating the grandfather, grandmother, mother, and child day and honouring the eldest man or woman by special celebrations and meetings, or according them media coverage.[83]

D. Pedagogical care
- honouring the directors, faculty, and educational staff;
- setting up educational training courses and reinforcements for the public degree;
- celebrating the "Day of Victory and Resistance" (May 25) in the domain of the municipality school;

- celebrating "Teachers day" at schools located inside the municipality;
- working on rehabilitating public schools located within the municipal domain
- adopting (as a course of action) and encouraging the holding of cultural and technical fairs;
- working on the erection of a public library and cultural centre.[84]

1.7 The domestic, regional, and international resources that the municipalities benefit from

- local or domestic institutions: The Ministry of Social Issues, The Ministry of Health, The Ministry of Environment, The Ministry of Public Works, The Ministry of Energy and Waterworks, The Institution of Civil Planning/Organization; and the Lebanese Army;
- regional and international institutions and organizations: UNICEF, UNDP, (Iranian) Jihad Al-Bina', etc.[85]

2 Recommendations

1. according special attention to the Lebanese diaspora[86] and encourage them to invest their capital in developmental projects within the municipal domain;[87]
2. the relationship between the municipalities and Hizbullah and its civil institutions and NGOs should be one of coalescence in such a way that it ought to serve the objectives of the party, which are the same as the objectives of municipal work, since the latter aims at actively working in order to redress deprivation at the level of the municipalities, which ultimately leads to a constructive political society;[88]
3. organize detailed studies targeting the following:
- establishing a union of municipalities in order to evaluate things and address obstacles/impediments;
- twin ship programs;
- a new municipal elections law;
- the jurisprudence of municipal work (the religious safeguards, dawabit shar'iyya, for municipal work and municipal decisions);
- a general evaluation of municipal work in every municipality with specific mention of the weaknesses in order to constructively address them.[89]

E   Chronology of events (1975-2005)

1975

- April 13 witnessed the beginning of the 16-year old Lebanese civil war

1976

- In response to an official request by the Lebanese government, on July 20, the Syrian army entered Lebanon as a contingent to the *Quwat Al-Rad' Al-'Arabiyya* (Arab Deterrent Forces) in order to help the Lebanese government enforce law and order in the civil war torn Lebanon.

1978

- Hizbullah came into being in 1978 when Sayyid Abbas al-Musawi, one of its primary founders and its second secretary general, came back from *Najaf* to Lebanon and established in the *Biqa'*, along with other Lebanese and Iranian clergy and cadres, the religious and ideological foundations of the party. Sayyid Abbas established religious seminaries *(hawzas)* and started his Islamic propagation or call *(da'wa)*, in B'albak, in the *Biqa'*. This also coincided with the arrival of dissident Iranian clergy and military personnel (most notably Ali Akbar Muhtashami and Mustafa Shamran) who established religious and military training centres with substantial material and spiritual backing from Imam Khumayni who was himself banished in *Najaf* for a period of 13 years.
- On March 14 Israel launched "Operation Litani" by invading Lebanon and eventually occupying a 500-squared kilometre "Security Zone", which included 61 cities and villages. On March 19, the UN Security Council issued resolution 425 calling for the unconditional withdrawal of the Israeli forces from Lebanon, a resolution that fell on deaf ears. In order to help restore the Lebanese state's sovereignty to the border, the UN established the UNIFIL, a 5000 interim peace-keeping force, which was sent to Lebanon as of March 23. However, Israel did not allow the UNIFIL to deploy all the way to the border.
- On August 31, Imam Musa al-Sadr, the leader of the Lebanese Shi'a community and the head of the Islamic Shi'ite Higher Council, disappeared in Libya in mysterious circumstances. All of these factors were conducive to the emergence of Hizbullah's rudimentary foundations that crystallized in the birth of its religious ideology.

1979

- On February 1, Imam Khumayni landed in Tehran, thus ushering the victory of the Islamic Revolution in Iran on February 11. Many Lebanese Shi'ites were inspired by Imam Khumayni's revolutionary ideology, which led them to actively mobilize and struggle for a more active role in the Lebanese political system. Thus, after the victory of the Islamic Revolution, Sayyid Abbas Al-Musawi along with his students and other leading 'ulama officially founded "The Hizbullah of Lebanon".

1982

- At a time when the Arabs and the international community were preoccupied with the Iraq-Iran war, on June 6 Israel invaded Lebanon for a second time through its "Peace for Galilee" operation. From 8 to 13 June, the Khaldé battle (which was spearheaded by many of Hizbullah's founding cadres, many of whom were wounded) heralded the initiation of Hizbullah's military wing, the "Islamic Resistance". Khaldé, a small town near Beirut, was the only location that the Israeli invasion was temporary halted because of the stiff resistance it met, a resistance that resulted in heavy Israeli casualties (16 dead and 176 wounded) and led the Israelis to change their military strategy and tactics.
- As early as July, the political framework of Hizbullah was embarked upon, a task that passed through different stages, most notably in 1984-85.
- On August 23, Bashir Jumayyel, the head of the Phalangist Christian militia, was elected president.
- On August 21, the Multi-National Forces, made up of contingents of US, French, UK, and Italian forces, landed in Beirut in order to supervise the implementation of the agreement between the PLO and Israel. The agreement dictated the withdrawal of PLO fighters, cadres, and leaders from Beirut, including Yasser Arafat who left Beirut on August 30.
- In Tyre, in south Lebanon, on August 31 during the fourth anniversary of the disappearance of Imam Musa al-Sadr, a massive popular uprising, in the hundreds of thousands, paid allegiance to al-Sadr avowing that Israel will remain the enemy, shouting: "Israel is the absolute evil, and dealings with it are religiously prohibited (haram)". This event culminated in violent confrontations with the Israeli forces in Jibshit, in south Lebanon.
- On September 3, PLO fighters left Beirut, thus ending a military presence that lasted decades.
- After 83 days of besieging it, Israeli army entered Beirut on September 14 in the wake of the assassination of president elect Bashir Jumayyel by a car bomb.

- September 15-17 witnessed the massacres of the Palestinian civilians in the *Sabra* and *Shatila* refugee camps.
- On September 23, Amin Jumayyel, Bashir's brother, was elected as president of the Lebanese Republic.
- On September 28, the Israeli army withdrew from Beirut.
- On November 11 Ahmad Qasir, Hizbullah's first suicide bomber ("martyr"), detonated his car in the Israeli headquarters in *Tyre* killing around 76 soldiers and military personnel and wounding 20.
- Thus, the military birth of Hizbullah, as an Islamic *jihadi* (resistance/struggle) movement, was a direct result of the Israeli invasion – in which Israel killed around 20,000 people (mostly Lebanese and Palestinian civilians, but also some Lebanese, Palestinian, and Syrian fighters) as well as occupied almost one-third of Lebanon (3560 squared kilometres) including 801 cities and villages.

1983

- January witnessed the first massive launch of Katyusha rockets at Israel's northern settlements as well as the capture of the first Israeli soldier by the Islamic Resistance. The Israeli soldier died suffering from wounds during his abduction, and his body was left behind.
- In March Shaykh Raghib Harb, the leader of the popular uprising in the south, was captured by Israeli forces.
- On April 13, Hizbullah conducted its second martyrdom operation when 'Ali Safiyyeddine detonated his car into an Israeli convey in *Dayr Qanun al-Nahr* killing 6 soldiers and wounding 4 others.
- On April 18 the US Embassy in West Beirut was targeted by a suicidal attack resulting in the death of 63 people, out of whom 17 were Americans, including the entire Middle East contingent of the CIA.
- On May 17, Israel and the Lebanese government signed a peace agreement.
- In July Israel withdrew from Mount Lebanon to the *Awwali* River, near *Sidon*, in the south. October witnessed the *'Ashura* uprising in *Nabatiyyé*, in the south, in response to Israeli's defilement of the ritual. On October 14 Hizbullah conducted its third martyrdom operation when Ja'far Al-Tayyar blew himself in an UNIRWA building in *Tyre* housing Israeli soldiers, killing 29 soldiers by the concessions of the Israelis themselves. On October 23 the "Islamic Jihad" committed twin-suicidal attacks against the Marines barracks and the French paratroopers, which resulted in the death of 241 American and 58 French soldiers respectively.

- Hizbullah put a lid on its aborted double suicidal (martyrdom) operation when the car of the two suicide bombers got blown prematurely on its way to Tyre.
- In November the Israeli air force started targeting Hizbullah's training bases in the *Biqaʿ*. On November 23 the Israelis released 4,500 Lebanese and Palestinian detainees from the *Ansar* detention camp (in southern Lebanon) and 63 other Palestinians in exchange for the release of one Israeli pilot and six soldiers.

1984

- Hizbullah's *Shura* Council, or main decision body, passed through different stages from 9 members to 5 and was finalized to 7 as of 1984. Hizbullah released several political declarations bearing its name and established its politburo.
- In March the Lebanese parliament abrogated the May 17, 1983 agreement with Israel.
- On June 18 Hizbullah's mouthpiece and weekly newspaper *Al-ʿAhd* came to light.
- On February 16 Saykh Raghib Harb, Hizbullah's most influential resistance leader in the south, was assassinated by the Israeli forces.
- On September 20 the US Embassy in East Beirut was targeted by a suicide operation.

1985

- On February 16 Hizbullah published its "Open Letter" or Political Manifesto, ushering the birth of its political ideology. The Open Letter officially announced the establishment of Hizbullah, and its military wing, the Islamic Resistance. The Open Letter was read by Sayyid Ibrahim Amin Al-Sayyid, its spokesman at that time. In February Israel withdrew from Sidon.
- In March Israel blew the *Husayniyya* (religious gathering place) of *Maʿraké* and assassinated two leading Hizbullah cadres.
- In April Israel withdrew from *Nabatiyyé* and *Tyre*.
- The *Jalil* Operation on May 20 between the General Command of the Popular Front for the Liberation of Palestine (PFLP) and the Israeli government resulted in the release of 1,150 Lebanese and Palestinian detainees from the *Atlit* detention camp in Israel, in exchange for three Israeli soldiers.
- In June the Israeli Army announced that it has finalised its withdrawal and established an 1100-squared kilometre "Security Zone", which included 168 cities and village. The "Security Zone" comprised around 15% of Lebanese territory along Lebanon's southern border with Israel that is reminiscent of the 1978 invasion, which aimed at creating a similar security arrangement in order

to protect the northern Israeli settlements from missile attacks across the Lebanese border.

1986

- On February 16 the Islamic Resistance captured two Israeli soldiers in an operation in the *Kunin* area of *Bint Jubayl*. Israel launched a limited incursion in 17 villages for six consecutive days in order to retrieve the two soldiers, but with no avail. The Islamic Resistance waged a relentless war against the SLA posts aiming at occupying them and destroying them, killing and detaining all members, then blowing the entire post.
- In October an Israeli jet fighter was downed, and Ron Arad, the assistant pilot was captured.
- Hizbullah standardised the practice of videotaping military operations against Israeli forces in order to convey the exact number of the Israeli dead and wounded to the Israeli public, thus belying Israeli claims of low casualties.

1987

- On June 15, the Lebanese government issued the official double annulment of the May 17, 1983 Agreement and the November 3, 1969 Cairo Agreement.
- Nasrallah assumed the newly established "chief executive officer" post, in addition to being a member of the Consultative Council, which is Hizbullah's highest leading panel.[90] This year witnessed the reinvigoration of the war of attrition against SLA posts in an unprecedented manner. December marked the beginning of the first Palestinian *Intifada* (popular uprising).

1988

- The first major military encounter and direct confrontation took place between the Islamic Resistance and the Israeli Army, in an Israeli attack on *Maydun*, in the Western *Biqa'*. On March 11 Hizbullah conducted its fifth martyrdom operation when 'Amer Kalakish blew himself in an Israeli convoy near the *Mtulé* settlement at the Lebanese border killing 12 Israeli soldiers and wounding 14 others.
- The *AMAL*-Hizbullah control war – secular Shi'ites against Islamist Shi'ites – started in on April 5 in the South and spread to the *Dahiya* on May 6, which led to the ousting of AMAL fighters from the Dahiya. This control war ended more than 2 years later in November 1990.
- The Consultation Centre for Studies and Documentation (CCSD), Hizbullah's think tank, was created. In May Hizbullah's *al-Nour* radio station started broadcasting. On August 19 Hizbullah conducted its sixth martyrdom operation

when Haytham Dbuq blew himself in an Israeli convoy on the *Marji'yun* road killing one Israeli soldier and wounding three others according to Israeli military sources. The seventh operation occurred on October 19 when Abdallah 'Atwi blew himself near the Fatima Gate on the border between Lebanon and Israel killing eight soldiers and wounding another eight by the concession of the Israelis.

- The tenure of the then Lebanese President Amin Jumayyel ended without electing a successor by the Lebanese parliament. (It is worth mentioning that Jumayyel was "voluntarily" banished to France from 1988 till 2000). So, on September 23, 1988, Jumayyel appointed General Michel 'Aun, the Lebanese Army Commander, to head a military government composed of 3 Christians and 2 Muslims. Deeming the appointment unconstitutional, Muslim spiritual leaders met and issued a *fatwa* banning any Muslim from participating in the military government. So General 'Aun virtually ruled the Christian areas in East Beirut and Mount Lebanon, while the rest of the country was under the mandate of prime minister Salim Al-Hoss, who formed a second government in West Beirut. Thus, at that time, Lebanon had 2 governments, a situation that lasted for almost 2 years.

1989

- Hizbullah held its first conclave and revealed the identity of its leaders and cadres. The conclave resulted in the creation of the post of the secretary general and the election of Shaykh Subhi al-Tufayli as Hizbullah's first secretary general.
- On July 28 the Israeli army abducted Shaykh AdbulKarim 'Ubayd, a leading Hizbullah cadre, from his hometown, *Jibshit*.
- In an attempt to drive the Syrian Army out of Lebanon, on March 14, General Michel 'Aun, waged a "Liberation War" against the Syrian forces present in Lebanon since 1976.
- On August 9 Hizbullah conducted its eighth martyrdom operation when Shaykh As'ad Birru blew himself in an Israeli convoy across the *Marji'un* road killing five soldiers and wounding five others according to Israeli military sources.
- The Ta'if Agreement, a "bill of rights" or a blueprint for national reconciliation and reform aimed towards a more equitable political system for all sectarian-confessional groups, was drafted and ratified between the 30th of September and the 22nd of October in Ta'if, Saudi Arabia. On Saturday, October 22 at 10:45 pm, it was officially announced, from the Palace of Conventions at Ta'if, that the civil war ended. 'Aun issued a decree dissolving the parliament, but it fell on deaf ears.

1990

- The proposed changes in the Ta'if Agreement were officially written into the Constitution in August and September 1990. The final document is known as "The Constitution of Lebanon after the Amendments of August 21".
- October 13 witnessed the actual ending of the 16-year civil war by the ousting of General Michel 'Aun and banishing him to France.
- On November 9 the 2 and a half-year AMAL-Hizbullah war ended by a final accord brokered between the warning factions through intensive Syrian and Iranian pressure.

1991

- In line with the Ta'if Agreement, in March the Lebanese government officially declared the dissolution of the militias. The end of April was set as a deadline for the militias to hand in their heavy weapons and to close their military and training centres. Hizbullah was a notable exception, and to a lesser extent *AMAL*.
- Starting May 22, Hizbullah held its second conclave and elected Sayyid 'Abbas Al-Musawi as its second Secretary General. Unlike the first conclave in which the seven-member *Shura* Council were nominated, in the second conclave they were elected. On June 3 Hizbullah's *Al-Manar* TV station was created.
- The first swap operation between Hizbullah and Israel, which was brokered by UN[91], took place took place, on three instalments, between September 11 and December 1. Israel released 91 Lebanese detainees (one from Israeli prisons and 90 from the *Khyam* detention camp, including ten women), and the remains of nine fighters in exchange for information about two Israeli soldiers who were detained by Hizbullah on February 16, 1986.

1992

- February 16 witnessed the assassination of Sayyid Abbas al-Musawi, his wife, and his son, by an Israeli helicopter. Two days later, Sayyid Hasan Nasrallah, Hizbullah's third Secretary General, was elected as well as Shaykh Na'im Qasim as Deputy Secretary General. Both Nasrallah and Qasim retain their posts till the current day.
- Israel attacked the two villages of *Kafra* and *Yatir*, an act that is met with forceful resistance from Hizbullah fighters.
- Hizbullah started employing the Katyusha weapon as a deterrent strategy to protect Lebanese civilians from Israeli aggressions.
- Hizbullah launched its political program as a distinct manifestation (or extension) of its political ideology. Hizbullah participated and won 12 seats in the

first parliamentary elections, which were frozen for a period of 20 years due to the Lebanese civil war.

- On September 21 Ibrahim Dahir conducted Hizbullah's ninth martyrdom operation when he targeted an Israeli convoy on the *Jarmaq* road, killing and wounding 25 according to Hizbullah.

1993

- In its third conclave, Hizbullah re-elected Sayyid Hasan Nasrallah as its Secretary General, and Shaykh Na'im Qasim as Deputy Secretary General. It is important to note that the Islamic Resistance was rewarded by electing Hizbullah's "Central Military Commander", Hajj Muhsin Al-Shakar, as one of the seven-member Shura Council.
- July 23 till 31: "The seven days war" or the Israeli "Operation Accountability" erupted as a direct result of the Islamic Resistance's killing of seven Israeli sol-diers. "The seven days war" led to the death of 130 people, mostly Lebanese civilians, and it displaced around 300,000. "Operation Accountability" resulted in an *unwritten* agreement between Hizbullah and Israel to sideline the civilians on both sides of the border. (Italics added for emphasis).
- On September 13, when Hizbullah was protesting peacefully against the Oslo Agreement, the Lebanese Army and ISF (Police) killed 13 Hizbullah supporters – including two women – and wounded 40 because they took to the streets when the Hariri government imposed a ban on demonstrations.

1994

- April 21: the Lebanese state jailed Samir Geagea, the leader of the right wing Christian Lebanese Forces (LF), and banned the LF.
- In October the Islamic Resistance stormed the Israeli post of *Dabshé*. Hizbullah exploited the camera as a primary weapon in its psychological warfare against Israel by airing, through its *al-Manar* TV, details of the operation and the Israeli casualties.
- On 31 May an Israeli commandos unit abducted Hajj Mustafa al-Dirani, an Islamic *AMAL* leading cadre, from his hometown, *Qsarnaba*, in the *Biqa'*.

1995

- On May 17 Imam Khamina'i appointed Sayyid Hasan Nasrallah, Hizbullah's Secretary general, and Shaykh Muhammad Yazbik, Hizbullah's *Shura* Council member, as his religious deputies *(wakilayn shar'iyyan)* in Lebanon "in the *hisbi* domain and *shar'i* issues, taking over from him the religious duties and dispos-ing them to the benefit of the Muslims; warding off oppression and injustice;

conducting *shar'i* reconciliations for the *khums* people; and appointing their own deputies".[92]

- On April 25 Salah Ghandur conducted Hizbullah's tenth martyrdom operation when he blew himself in an SLA post in *Bint Jubayl* wounding eleven according to Israeli military sources.

- Hizbullah's fourth conclave was held in July. The Secretary General and his deputy were re-elected. Some of the basic organizational changes that Hizbullah made were the following: (1) The Politburo was renamed as the "Political Council" and its jurisdiction was enlarged; (2) The creation of the "*Jihadi* Council", headed by Sayyid Hashim Safiyyeddine, the only new member of the *Shura* Council; (3) The "Executive Council" replaced the "Executive *Shura*" with, more or less, the same jurisdictions; (4) In order to evaluate Hizbullah's experience in the parliament, the party formed a new body called the "Parliamentary Block Council".

1996

- On March 20 'Ali Ashmar conducted Hizbullah's eleventh martyrdom operation in the Town of *Rub Thalathin* in *al-'Daysé* killing two according to Israel military sources. From April 11 till 18, the Israeli military operation of the "Grapes of Wrath" ended with the *Qana* massacre, where more than 100 Lebanese civilians, seeking shelter in a UN complex, where killed by Israeli shelling. The Israeli aggression resulted in what became known as "April 1996 Understanding/ Agreement" that protected both Israeli and Lebanese civilians from military operations. The UN, France, Syria, and the US brokered the April 26 *written* Agreement between Israel and Hizbullah, which established the "Monitoring Group for the Understandings of Operation Grapes of Wrath". The "Grapes of Wrath" led to the death of more than 150 Lebanese civilians and displaced around half a million others. (Italics added for emphasis).

- Under German sponsorship, on July 21 Hizbullah exchanged the bodies of 2 Israeli soldiers (kidnapped on February 16, 1986) and 17 SLA collaborators, for 45 Lebanese detainees and 123 remains.

- In the 1996 parliamentary elections of this year, Hizbullah managed to keep 11 seats.

1997

- In February, while attempting to avoid being spotted by Hizbullah, 73 Israeli soldiers were killed on board of two helicopters, which collided into each other while they were on a mission aimed at deploying troops in south Lebanon.

- On April 7 a swap operation between Hizbullah and Israel resulted in the exchange of three Lebanese detainees for the body of a dead SLA sergeant.

- Conflict between Hizbullah's identity and the Lebanese state sovereignty: on May 4, Shaykh Subhi al-Tufayli founded the "Revolution of the Hungry", and on 4 July he called for civil disobedience against the Lebanese government, which culminated in blocking roads on October 26.
- On September 5 the Israeli operation of *al-Ansariyyé* resulted in the death of 12 high-ranking officials of an elite Israeli military commandos while not a single member of the resistance was injured.
- On September 12, Sayyid Hadi Nasrallah, Sayyid Hasan Nasrallah's son, died in a confrontation with the Israel soldiers in southern Lebanon.
- On November 3, Hizbullah formed *Al-Saraya Al-Lubnaniyya Li-Muqawamat Al-Ihtilal Al-Israeli* or the Multi-confessional Lebanese Brigades to fight Israel (Lebanonisation of the resistance).

1998

- Shaykh Subhi al-Tufayli was officially expelled from Hizbullah by a political declaration issued on January 24. On January 30 a violent military confrontation erupted between the Lebanese army and al-Tufayli's supporters, who occupied by military force Hizbullah's religious seminary in 'Ayn Burday, near B'albak. The bloody face off ended with the destruction of Tufayli's headquarters and the Lebanese state's issuing of an arrest warrant against him. However, till this day, Tufayli is still at large. After solving the internal discord problem, Hizbullah held its fifth conclave between June 20 and the end of July. Nasrallah was elected for a third term. For this move to be made, Hizbullah had to amend its internal bylaws by deleting the stipulation that the secretary general cannot serve for more than two consecutive terms.
- The May-June 1998 municipal elections – that reflect true populace representation and which had not been carried out since 1963 – were carried out only after pressure and lobbying from Hizbullah. The Lebanese government used the pretext of lack of financial and technical resources and manpower, but Hizbullah insisted on the reactivation of the elections. Eventually, Hizbullah won a landslide victory in its main constituencies (with the exception of the B'albak district), including electoral districts that were supported by the Lebanese government and its candidates.
- On 26 June, by mediation of the Lebanese government, the remains of an Israeli soldier, who died during the *Ansariyyé* battle of Sept. 1997, were exchanged for 60 detainees (10 of whom were detained in Israel) and the remains of 40 Lebanese resistance fighters, including Hadi Nasrallah.

- On September 13 Israel released Suha Bshara (who 10 years ago attempted to take the life of the SLA leader, Antoine Lahd) after 10 years of imprisonment and torture at the notorious Khyam prison.

1999

- On February 28 the Islamic Resistance blew the convoy of the Israeli Brigadier-General in Lebanon, Erez Gerstein, which resulted in his immediate death. Gerstein was the highest-ranking Israeli soldier to be killed in 17 years.
- In early June Israeli forces and SLA withdrew from *Jezzin* (a predominantly Christian enclave) that comprised around 6% of the "Security Zone", thus reducing the total size of the "Security Zone" to 9% of the Lebanese territory.
- Through German mediation, Israel released, on two instalments, 13 Lebanese freedom fighters, five of whom were released on December 26 from the Israeli *Ayalut* detention camp, in exchange for a promise from Hizbullah to help track the missing Israeli pilot, Ron Arad, whose plane was downed over south Lebanon in 1986.
- On December 30 'Ammar Husayn Hammud conducted Hizbullah's twelfth martyrdom operation on the road to *al-Qlay'a* killing 7 Israeli soldiers and wounding seven others according to Hizbullah, while according to Israeli military sources the operation resulted in no Israeli casualties due to premature denotation on behalf of the suicide bomber.[93]

2000

- In February the Islamic Resistance blew the farm of the SLA's second man in rank, 'Aqil Hashim, who died in the blast.
- On April 19 Israel released 13 Lebanese detainees from the Israeli *Ayalut* detention camp.
- On 24 May Israel withdrew from southern Lebanon after 22 years of occupation. (Israel failed to relinquish the Lebanese *Shib'a* farms, which are a bone of contention between Israel and Lebanon).
- On 28 September the second Palestinian *Intifada* was inaugurated in the wake of Sharon's visit to the Dome of the Rock *(al-Masjid al-Aqsa)*.
- Hizbullah won 12 seats in the parliamentary elections held in the summer.
- On October 7 Hizbullah captured 3 Israeli soldiers from the Lebanese *Shib'a* farms. On 15 October Hizbullah lured and apprehended, at Beirut, a retired Israeli Mossad colonel.

2001

- In Hizbullah's sixth conclave that ended on July 30, 2001, Nasrallah was re-elected for life, and Sayyid Ibrahim Amin Al-Sayyid and Hajj Jawad Nureddine replaced Hajj Muhammad Ra'd and Hajj Muhsin Shakar in the *Shura* Council. Hizbullah placed its media institutions under the direct command of Nasrallah aided by the head of the Political Council and that of the Executive Council. This was done in order to upgrade the role of Hizbullah's media, and pursue its ideological hegemony. Also, Hizbullah abolished its "Central Planning Council", and strengthened internal audit and accountability mechanisms. From this perspective, the roles and duties of the municipal councils were expended (horizontally) and upgraded (vertically).

2002

- On March 27-28 the Arab Summit was held in Beirut and the Arab initiative of ending the Israeli-Palestinian conflict was propagated.
- In late March, early April, the Israeli army conducted a deadly incursion into the West Bank. Hizbullah's responded by 12-day military operations in the *Shib'a* farms in order to buttress the *Intifada*.
- On June 10, in light of the revival of the prisoner-swap negotiations and as a good well gesture towards Hizbullah, Israel released Muhammad al-Birzawi, a Hizbullah fighter, who has been detained since 1987.

2003

- On August 21 Israel returned the remains of two Hizbullah fighters in return for a meeting between the detained Mossad colonel and the German mediator.
- In response to a suicide operation in Israel a day earlier, in which 19 Israeli civilians died, on December 5 Israeli jets violated Lebanese airspace and bombed an alleged Palestinian training camp near Damascus. This was the first Israeli air strike on Syria in 30 years, since the end of the October 1973 war.

2004

- On January 19 Hizbullah destroyed an Israeli military bulldozer after it crossed the "Blue Line". Hizbullah targeted it by firing an anti-tank rocket when it was 26 meters inside Lebanese territory by the concession of the UNIFIL. 1 Israeli soldier was killed, and another was seriously wounded. This confrontation came at a time when the prisoner exchange negations between Israel and Hizbullah were at a their peak/ reached a climax. This exemplifies Hizbullah's 2-track policy: military confrontation and negotiations.

- On January 29-30, Hizbullah and Israel conducted the first phase of a watershed prisoner exchange deal after 4 years of negotiations brokered by Germany. Hizbullah released the Israeli colonel and the bodies of three Israeli soldiers captured in October 2000 in return for 400 Palestinians, 23 Lebanese and Arabs (including two Hizbullah senior cadres: Shaykh AbdulKarim 'Ubayd and Hajj Mustafa Al-Dirani), and the remains of 59 Lebanese guerrilla fighters, 11 of whom belonged to Hizbullah. It was a watershed operation since it was the first time that Israel acquiesced to Hizbullah's demands and released Palestinians, setting a precedent and bestowing Hizbullah an unprecedented role in the Intifada, thus regionalizing the conflict. By this move, Israeli granted Hizbullah a de facto recognition as a legitimate resistance movement.
- On May 7 an Israeli incursion reminiscent of *Ansariyyé* occurred after the elite Israeli Egoz commandos unit crossed the "Blue Line". Hizbullah fighters ambushed it, killed one soldier and wounded 5 others, by the concession of the Israel's themselves. Unlike the precedent set by *Ansariyyé* and in spite of Hizbullah's intensive firing power, the Israeli's were able to evacuate their dead and wounded, but they left behind a dead dog.
- Between the 2nd and 30th of May the second municipal elections were held after a lapse of 6 years. Hizbullah achieved a landslide victory in Beirut (100%), the *Biqa'* (almost 95%), and the south (almost 61%).[94]
- May 21: Hizbullah held a big demonstration to protest the desecration of the holy sites in Iraq. Around half a million Hizbullah supporters wearing white burial shrouds chanted "death to Israel" and "death to America". This show of force came 2 days before the municipal elections in the South, which was considered an *AMAL* den and strong constituency.
- May 27: Events reminiscent of Sept. 13, 1993 occurred: *licensed* demonstrations spread over the country in protest for the pressing socio-economic situation triggered by a severe hike in fuel prices. In *Hayy al-Sulum*, in *Dahiya*, the Lebanese Army fired at the demonstrators who where throwing rocks at it, killing 5 and wounding several others. As a result, riots spread in the *Dahiya* and the demonstrators burned the first floor of the Ministry of Labour.
- May 29: Nasrallah held a news conference in which he accused the US Embassy in Beirut of infiltrating the demonstrators and perpetrating the violence, thus giving weight to the hidden hand explanation or the conspiracy theory. He called on the cabinet and parliament to hold emergency sessions to discuss the issue, and he called on the government to launch an investigation about what has happened.

291

- May 30: Hariri visited Nasrallah and conducted a meeting with him in the house of the latter's political advisor/aide.
- May 31: Conceding to Nasrallah's demands, the Lebanese cabinet held an urgent meeting in which it vehemently condemned the May 27 shootings and offered, as blood money, around $33,000 to the family's victims. The cabinet asked the Justice Minister and the Defence Minister to conduct an investigation into the unrest and report directly to it.
- Between June and August 16, Hizbullah held its seventh conclave. *Shura* Council members retained their same functions. *Sayyid* Hasan Nasrallah, Hizbullah's Secretary General became the head of the *Jihadi* Council. The most salient administrative amendment was Hizbullah's division of the South into two geographical areas: the first south of the *Litani* river, and the second to its north. Both function under the auspices of one central organisational leader in order to secure organisational structures that are capable of improving local administration and activate polarisation. In addition, Shaykh Karim 'Ubayd was appointed as the head of Hizbullah's social institutions. Shaykh Hasan Izzeddine, Hizbullah's spokesman at the Central Press Office, was appointed as Hizbullah's political representative in the South, and Nasrallah's media aide or advisor, the engineer Hajj Muhammad Afif, replaced him.
- September 2: The UN Security Council issued Resolution 1559 censuring Syrian intervention in Lebanese affairs and criticising both Syria and Lebanon for the intended constitutional amendment that will extend president Lahud's tenure for three more years, till November 2007. Among other things, Resolution 1559 called on the Lebanese government to disband and disarm Lebanese militias, which is a direct reference to Hizbullah since it is the only Lebanese political party that still bears up arms.
- September 3: The Lebanese parliament amended the constitution, thus allowing president Lahud to remain in office for a second half-tenure, or a three-year term.
- October 1: A failed assassination attempt targeted MP Marwan Hamadé in West Beirut and left his bodyguard dead and wounded his driver.
- November 11: On Hizbullah's Martyr's day, the party set a precedent in its "balance of terror" with Israel. For the first time since its founding, Hizbullah flew an unmanned drone, which is a small spying plane supplied with state of the art cameras and is capable of carrying 40 to 50 kilograms of explosives and can be programmed to hit any target, for 14 minutes over Israel. It took pictures of the northern Israeli settlement of Keryat Shmona. Israel confirmed the flight and claimed the drone flew over Israel for 5 minutes. The Israeli government issued a statement condemning the act a serious breach of Israeli sovereignty

forgetting the 9400 breaches Israel conducted to Lebanese sovereignty, by air and sea, since its nearly complete withdrawal in May 2000.[95]

- November 30: Around 250,000 Lebanese people, one-third of whom were Hizbullahis, demonstrated against resolution 1559. All the participants carried out Lebanese flags including Hizbullahis. It was the fist time that Hizbullah participates in a demonstration without portraying flags, banners, and special slogans. The only two features that pointed out at Hizbullah were (1) the chanting of "death to Israel" and "death to America" and (2) the Hizbullahi veiled women who outnumbered Hizbullahi men by a great margin. Some of the banners raised by the Hizbullahis were the following: "Unity, unity in Lebanon so that we can defend our country"; "We do not want democracy American style".

- In the beginning of December and in light of the decisions taken in Hizbullah's seventh conclave, Hizbullah, for the first time in its history, has appointed the head of Hizbullah's Women's Organization, Rima Fakhry, as a member of its 18-member Political Council (Politburo). Also, Hizbullah appointed Wafa' Hutayt, the person responsible for political programs in al-Nour radio, as deputy of Hizbullah's Central Information Office.

- December 13: France banned Hizbullah's satellite TV, al-Manar, from broadcasting to France and other EU countries. Hizbullah abided by the ruling and al-Manar voluntarily stopped transmission. However, al-Manar continued to broadcast from six other satellites covering most of the globe, including three in Europe, which do not fall under France's jurisdiction.

- December 17: the US followed suit and banned al-Manar classifying it as a "terrorist organization".

2005

- January 29: Hizbullah's first annual celebration of the "Day of Freedom" marking the watershed prisoner release operation a year ago.

- February 14: ex-PM Rafiq al-Hariri was assassinated by a suicidal massive truck bomb.

- March 8: Hizbullah organized a pro-Syrian demonstration. Around half a million Hizbullahis along with their supporters and sympathizers filled the streets of the capital carrying Lebanese flags. Nasrallah delivered a speech calling for national unity, dialogue, and coexistence.

- March 14: The "Cedar Revolution": one million people took to the streets in Downtown Beirut to demand Syrian troops withdrawal and the truth about Hariri's assassination.

- April 19: Omar Karami's government resigned and Nagib Miqati's 14-member Cabinet took office. The cabinet included Trad Hamadé, a Hizbullah affiliated sympathizer (non official member), for the first time in its history.
- April 26: Syria ends its military presence in Lebanon after all its remaining 14,000 soldiers along with its intelligence personnel leave Lebanon after a 29-year presence.
- May 23: The UN verified the Syrian military pullout from Lebanon.
- 29 May-June 19: first parliamentary elections after the Syrian withdrawal. Sa'd Hariri's camp won 72 seats out of the 128. Hizbullah won 14 seats, adding 2 seats to its previous gains.
- June 27: Trad Hamadé signed a memo allowing the Palestinians who were born in Lebanon to work.
- Early July: Syrian trade embargo begins; a de facto economic embargo.
- July 18: 100 MPs voted for the parole of Samir Geagea – the leader of the right-wing outlawed Christian Lebanese Forces (LF), who has been serving a jail sentence for 11 years – and the Sunni Islamists who served a 5-year jail sentence.
- July 19: Fa'ud al-Sanyura forms the first cabinet after Syrian withdrawal, where Hizbullah joins with an official member, MP Muhammad Fnaysh, and an ally, Trad Hamadé.
- July 22: Condoleezza Rice visits Lebanon, the first visit of a Secretary of State since Collin Powell's visit in May 2003.
- July 30: Sanyura's cabinet wins a parliamentary vote of confidence of 92 votes.
- July 31: Sanyura visited Syria in an attempt to end the Syrian economic embargo.
- August 1: Syria partially lifted its economic embargo and opened its border to Lebanese transit trucks.
- 31 July-August 6: Nasrallah along with members of the *Shura* Council visited Tehran in order to attend the inauguration of the newly elected president Mahmud Ahmadi Nejad on August 3 as well as conduct meetings with him, Imam 'Ali Khamina'i, and other Iranian officials. The Iranian leadership assured Hizbullah that disarming it is a mirage.
- August 17: Israel relinquished the Gaza strip after 38 years of occupation and starts evacuating its settlers. Nasrallah termed this eventuality as the send victory for the model of resistance in five years: "The choice of resistance liberates Gaza". He added that this constitutes further proof for the utility of holding on to the weapons of the Hizbullah's Islamic Resistance.
- September 12: Israel officially ended its occupation of Gaza after the complete withdrawal of its military.

- October 21: Detlev Mehlis, the head of the UN investigation team into Rafiq Hariri's assassination, presented a legally inconclusive, but politically powerful report that implicated high-ranking Syrian and Lebanese officials in the assassination.
- October 24: *AMAL* and Hizbullah released a joint declaration blasting the Mehlis report for failing to convey the truth, sided with the Syrian regime in its face off with the international community, but endorsed the Lebanese government's decision to extend Mehlis' mandate till December 15.

F   Glossary

Ajr
remuneration
'Amma
ordinary people
Arkan al-Islam
the five pillars of Islam: al-shahada-tayn (Muslim credo: Testimony that there is no god but Allah (God), and that Muhammad is His Prophet), prayer, fasting, hajj (pilgrimage to Mecca), and zakat (alms giving)
'Awliya'
saints
Batin
esoteric
Dahiya
the southern suburb of Beirut that houses around 850,000 Shi'ites
Din
religion
Faqih
jurisprudent or jurisconsult: an authority or expert in fiqh; in Shi'ism faqih is synonymous with mujtahid
Fara'id
religious duties
Fatwa
a guiding, non-binding religious edit
Fiqh
religious jurisprudence, elucidation, and application of shari'a
Fitna
discord, internal strife
Fuqaha'
jurists
Hadi
Guide

Hadith
traditional accounts of the sayings and actions of Prophet Muhammad, which became an important source for determining Islamic law. They are made up of two parts: the names of the transmitters (isnad); and the text (matn)
Al-hala al-Islamiyya
Islamic Milieu/Islamic Current
Halal
religiously sanctioned
Haqiqat
truth
Haram
religiously prohibited
Hikma
divine wisdom
Hisbi
(Obeying) the religious and moral instructions of Islam. It could also cover a wide range of financial, administrative, political, and social matters. In short, hisbi matters are things that God does not allow that we forsake
Hizbullah
"Party of God"
Hizbullahi
A member or follower of Hizbullah
Hujja
Apodictic Proof
Husnayayn
outcomes or rewards of jihad (martyrdom and victory)
Ijtihad
making religious decisions on the basis of independent reasoning

Ilgha' al-ta'fiyya al-siyassiyya fi al-nufus, qabla al-nusus
the abolition of political sectarianism in the mentality, before abolishing it in the texts

'Ilm
religious knowledge

Al-'ilm al-muhit or al-ihatah fi al-'ilm
the Imam is the most learned in all branches of religious knowledge

Infitah
"opening-up" or Hizbullah integration in the Lebanese public sphere

'Isma (ma'sum)
entails impeccability, sinlessness, and infallibility of the Imams

Al-istikhlaf bi al-nass wa al-ta'yyin
the Shi'ites consider the Imamate a divine appointment

Al-istikhlaf bi al-shura wa al-bayy'a
the Sunnis consider the Caliphate as political process that is the product of consensus

Istishhad
martyrdom

Jahiliyya
pre-Islamic pagan period in Arabia from 500 to 610 AD

Al-Jihad al-asghar (smaller *jihad*)
struggle (holy war) against the enemies of Islam

Al-Jihad al-akbar (greater *jihad*)
struggle against the self (*jihad al-nafs*) or individual's service for the cause of religion

Juhhal
ignorant people

Kafir
infidel

Khass wa 'amm
private and public

Khums (one-fifth)
a religious tax comprising 20% on a person's surplus of income over necessary living expenses. Half is paid to the *marja'* as the representative of the Imam (*sahm al-Imam*), and half to the Sayyids

Khususiyyat
specificities or particularities

Kitman
concealment

Lebanonisation
Hizbullah's enrolment in Lebanese domestic political life

Ma'nawi
moral influence

Madad
support and reinforcement

Marja' al-taqlid/muqallad
The supreme Islamic legal authority to be emulated or accepted for emulation by the majority of the Shi'a in matters of religious practice and law

Marja'iyya
religious authority

Al-mas'uliyya al-shar'iyya
legitimate and religious responsibility to the *marja'* or *muqallad*

Al-mas'uliyya al-shar'iyya wa al-taklif al-shar'i al-Ilahi (*taklif*)
is loosely translated as "legitimate and religious responsibility"

Mubaya'a
homage and pledge of allegiance, usually to God

Mujahidin
those who carry out *jihad* or freedom fighters

Mujtahid
a *'alim* or a high ranking Shi'ite jurist who exercises *ijtihad* or independent reasoning

Muqalidin
followers of the *muqallad* in law and ritual

Muqallad
see *marja' al-taqlid*

Murshid ruhi
spiritual guide or leader

Mustad'afin
oppressed

Mustakbirin
oppressors

Nass (textual designation)
refers to the specific designation of an Imam by the preceding Imam

Al-qada
leaders
Rahbar
leader of the Islamic Revolution.
This title was assumed by
Khumayni, and after his death, it
was accorded to Khamina'i when
he became the official *marja' al-
taqlid* in 1995
Fi sabili Allah
in the way of God
Shahada
martyrdom
Shahid
martyr
Shari'a (divine or Islamic law)
The whole set of norms, morals,
and laws derived from the Islamic
sources (mainly Qur'an and *hadith*)
pertaining to the various aspects
of life of individual Muslims and
the Muslim *umma*
Al-Sirat al-Mustaqim
Straight Path or the path of the
righteous
Al-ta'a
strict obedience and discipline,
which conveys a religious connotation
Ta'bi'a
mobilization
Tafsir
textual, literal, or scriptural interpretation of the Qur'an
Tahkim
arbitration
Taklif
religious-legal obligation
Al-taklif al-shar'i al-Ilahi
delegated responsibility/obliga-
tion of the *muqalidin* towards the
muqallad

Taqiyya
expedient dissimulation
Taqlid
emulation
Taqwa
piety
Ta'wil
Shi'ite hermeneutics or allegorical
interpretation of the Qur'an
Thawabit
immutable principles, established
set of values and norms
'Ulama
Muslim religious scholars
Umma
the entire community of Muslims
'Urfan
Shi'ite theosophy
Wajib
religious duty or obligation
Wakilayn shar'iyyan
religious deputies
Wilaya
spiritual guidance
Wilayat al-Faqih
governance of the jurisprudent or
jurisconsult
Wilayat al-umma 'ala nafsiha
the governance of the *umma* by
itself
Yaqin
strong conviction
La yughsl wa la yukaffan
neither washed nor wrapped in a
burial shroud
Yutashhad/ istashhadu
martyred
Zahir
exoteric
Zu'ama
feudal leaders

G   Selected Bibliography⁹⁶

Al-'Abd, 'Arif. (2001). *Lubnan wa Al-Ta'if: Taqatu' Tarikhi wa Masar Ghatr Muktamil [Lebanon and the Ta'if: A Historical Crossroad and an Unfinished Trajectory]*. Beirut: Markaz Dirasat Al-Wihda Al-'Arabiyya.

Abdelnour, Ziad K. (January 2003). "The Lebanese-Canadian Crises", *Middle East Intelligence Bulletin*. 5.1 http://www.meib.org/articles/0301_l3.htm

Abdul-Jabar, Faleh (Ed). (2002) *Ayatollahs, Sufis and Ideologues: State, Religion and Social Movements in Iraq*. London: Saqi books.

Abramamian, Ervard. (1993). *Khomeinism: Essays on the Islamic Republic*. London: I.B. Taurus and Co. Ltd.

Abu Khalil, As'ad. (1999). *Historical Dictionary of Lebanon*. London: Scarecrow Press.

—— (March 1997). "Change and Democratization in the Arab World: The Role of Political Parties". *Third World Quarterly*. 18.1: 149-163.

—— (1994). "The Study of Political Parties in Lebanon: Toward a Typology". In Frank Tachau. (Ed.). *Political Parties of the Middle East and North Africa*. London: Mansell Publishing Limited, 297-368.

—— (Autumn 1994). "The incoherence of Islamic Fundamentalism: Arab Islamic Thought at the End of the 20th Century." *Middle East Journal*. 48.4: 677-694.

—— (July 1991). "Ideology and Practice of Hizbollah in Lebanon: Islamization of Leninist Organizational Principles". *Middle Eastern Studies*. 27.3: 390-403.

—— (1985). "Druze, Sunni and Shi'ite Political Leadership in Present-Day Lebanon." *Arab Studies Quarterly* 7.4: 28-58.

Abu-Rabi', Ibrahim M. (1996). *The Intellectual Origins of Islamic Resurgence in the Modern Arab World*. Albany, N.Y.: State University of New York.

Abun-Nasr, Fadeel M. (2003). *Hizbullah: Haqa'iq wa Ab'ad [Hizbullah: Facts and Dimensions]*. Beirut: World Book Publishing.

Ajami, Fouad. (1986). *The Vanished Imam: Imam Musa al-Sadr and the Shi'a of Lebanon*. London: Cornell University Press.

Alagha, Joseph. (Winter 2005). "Hizbullah After the Syrian Withdrawal". *Middle East Report*. 237: 34-39.

—— (Forthcoming). "Hizbullah's Gradual Integration in the Lebanese Public Sphere", in: *Approaching Public Spheres: Theory, History, Gender, Conflict*. SSRC⁹⁷ publication. (Completely different in content and orientation than my first published article).

—— (March 2004). "Hizbullah and Martyrdom". *ORIENT: German Journal for Politics and Economics of the Middle East*. 45.1: 47-74.

—— (September 2003). "Hizbullah, Terrorism, and Sept. 11" *ORIENT: German Journal for Politics and Economics of the Middle East*. 44.3: 385-412.

—— (January 2002)."Hizbullah, Iran and the *Intifada*". *ISIM Newsletter* 9: 35.

—— (July 2001). "Successen Hezbollah bij 'kleine oorlog' om Shib'a [Hizbullah's Successes in the Small War in Shib'a]". *Soera: Midden-Oosten Tijdschrift*. 9.2: 34-38.

—— (2001). "Hizbullah's Gradual Integration in the Lebanese Public Sphere". *Sharqiyyat: Journal of the Dutch Association for Middle Eastern and Islamic Studies*. 13.1: 34-59.

Algar, Hamid. (June 1988). "Development of the Concept of the Concept of *velayat-i faqih* since the Islamic Revolution in Iran". London: Paper presented at Conference on Wilayat al-faqih.

—— Trans. (1980). *Constitution of the Islamic Republic Of Iran*. Berkeley, C.A.: Mizan Press.

The Constitution of the Islamic Republic Of Iran. (1406 AH). Tehran: Ministry of Islamic Guidance.

Ali, A. Yusuf. (1993). *The Holy Qur'an: Translation and Commentary.* Fourth printing. Lahore: Islamic Propagation Center.

Anderson, Benedict. (1991). *Imagined Communities: Reflections on the Origin and Spread of Nationalism.* London: Verso.

Anderson, Sean, and Stephan Sloan. (1995). *Historical Dictionary of Terrorism.* London: The Scarecrow Press.

Antoun, Richard T. (2001). *Understanding Fundamentalism: Christian, Islamic, and Jewish Movements.* Oxford: Altamira Press.

—— (1989). *Muslim Preacher in the Modern World: A Jordanian Case Study in the Comparative Perspective.* Princeton, New Jersey: Princeton University Press.

Appleby, R. Scott. (Ed). (1997). *Spokesmen for the Despised.* Chicago: The University of Chicago Press.

Arberry, Arthur J. (Ed). (1964). *The Koran Interpreted.* Oxford: Oxford University Press.

Ayubi, Nazih. (1991). *Political Islam: Religion and Politics in the Arab World.* London: Routledge.

Aziz, Talib. (2001). "Fadlallah and the Remaking of the Marja'iyya". In Linda S. Walbridge. (Ed.). *The Most Learned of the Shi'a: The Institution of Marja' Taqlid.* Edited by. Oxford: Oxford University Press, 205-215.

Balqaziz, Abd Al-Ilah. (2000). Al-Muqawama wa Tahrir Al-Janub: Hizbullah min Al-Hawza Al-'Ilmiyya ila Al-Jabha [The Resistance and the Liberation of the South: Hizbullah from the Religious Seminary to the Battle Front]. Beirut: Markaz Dirasat Al-Wihda Al-'Arabiyya.

Al-Bahadli, Ali Ahmad. (1993). *Al-Hawza Al-'Ilmiyya fi Al-Najaf: Ma'alimuha wa Harakatuha Al-Islahiyya (1920-1980) [The Religious Seminary in Najaf: Features and Reformist Trends].* Beirut: Dar Al-Zahra'.

Barakat, Halim. (1993). *The Arab World: Society, Culture, and State.* Oxford: University Press of California.

—— (Ed). (1988). *Toward A Viable Lebanon.* London: Croom Helm.

Barker, Benjamin. J. (1995). *Jihad vs. McWorld.* New York: Times Books.

Barker, Chris and Dariusz Galasinski. (2001). *Cultural Studies and Discourse Analysis: A Dialogue on Language and Identity.* London: Sage Publications.

Batatu, Hanna. (Autumn 1981). "Iraq's Underground Shia Movements: Characteristics, Causes and Prospects", *Middle East Studies*, 35.

Baudrillard, Jean. (1994). "The Masses: The Impulsion of the Social in the Media". In *The Polity Reader in Cultural Theory.* Cambridge: Cambridge University Press, 111-118.

Baumann, Gerd. (1996). *Contesting Culture: Discourses of identity in multi-ethnic London.* Cambridge: Cambridge University Press.

Bayat, Asef. (2005). (26 April 2005). *Islam and Democracy: Perverse Charm of an Irrelevant Question.* Leiden: ISIM Inaugural Lecture.

—— (2000). *Social Movements, Activism, and Social Development in the Middle East.* Geneva: UNRISD.

—— (1998). *Street Politics: Poor People's Movement in Iran.* Cairo: The American University in Cairo Press.

Beauchamp, Tom L. (1991). *Philosophical Ethics: An Introduction to Moral Philosophy.* Second edition. New York: McGraw-Hill, Inc.

Blanford, Nicholas. (14 September 2004). "Hizballah and Syria's 'Lebanon Card'". *MERIP.* http://www.merip.org/mero/mero091404.html

—— (28 April 2003). "Hizballah in the Firing Line". *MERIP.* http://www.merip.org/mero/mero042803.html

Bluhm, William T. (1978). *Theories of the Political System*. Englewood Cliffs, New Jersey: Prentice-Hall, Inc.

Blum, William. (2000). *Rogue State: A Guide to the Word's Only Superpower*. Monroe, ME: Common Courage Press.

Bourdieu, Pierre. (1994). *Language and Symbolic Power*. Oxford: Polity Press.

—— (1994). "Structures, Habitus, and Practices" in *The Polity Reader in Cultural Theory*. Cambridge: Cambridge University Press, 95-110.

—— (1993). *The Field of Cultural Production*. Cambridge: Polity Press.

—— (1990). *In Other Words: Essays Towards a Reflexive Sociology*. Cambridge: Polity Press.

—— (1991). "Genesis and Structure of the Religious Field". *Comparative Social Research*. 13: 1-44.

—— (1980). *The Logic of Practice*. Cambridge: Polity Press.

—— (1971). "Genèse et structure du champ religieux", *Revue française de sociologie*, 12: 295-334.

Brunner, Rainer and Werner Ende. (Eds.). (2001). *The Twelver Shia in Modern Times: Religious Culture & Political History*. Leiden: Brill.

Buchta, Wilfried. (2000). *Who Rules Iran? The Structure of Power in the Islamic Republic*. Washington, DC: The Washington Institute for Near East Policy and the Konrad Adenaueur Stiftung.

Bulliet, Richard W. (1994). *Islam: The View from the Edge*. New York: Colombia University Press.

Burke, Peter. (1992). *History and Social Theory*. New York: Cornell university Press.

Byers, Ann. (2003). *Lebanon's Hezbollah (Inside the World's Most Infamous Terrorist Organizations)*. London: Rosen Publishing Group.

Byman, Daniel. (November/December 2003). "Should Hezbollah Be Next?" *Foreign Affairs*. 82.6: 54-66.

Chandhoke, Neera. (1995). *State and Civil Society: Explorations in Political Theory*. London: Sage Publications.

Calhoun, Craig. (Ed.). (1994). *Social Theory and the Politics of Identity*. Oxford. Blackwell.

Castells, Manuel and Martin Ince. (2003). *Conversations with Manuel Castells*. Cambridge: Politiy Press.

Castells, Manuel. (2000). *The Rise of the Network Society. (The Information Age: Economy, Society, and Culture, Volume I)*. Second edition. Oxford: Blackwell Publishers Ltd.

—— (2004). *The Power of Identity. (The Information Age: Economy, Society, and Culture, Volume II)*. Second edition. Oxford: Blackwell Publishers Ltd.

—— (2000). *End of Millennium. (The Information Age: Economy, Society, and Culture, Volume II)*. Second edition. Oxford: Blackwell Publishers Ltd.

Chamie, Joseph. (1977). *Religion and Population Dynamics in Lebanon*. Ann Arbor, MI: Population Studies Center of the University of Michigan.

Cobban, Helena. (1986). "The Growth of the Shi'i Power in Lebanon and its Implications for the Future". In Juan Cole and Nikki Keddie. (Eds.). *Shi'ism and Social Protest*. New Haven: Yale University Press, 137-155.

—— (1985). *The Shia Community and the Future of Lebanon*. Washington, D.C.: American Institute for Islamic Affairs.

—— (1985). *The Making of Modern Lebanon*. London: Hutchinson.

Dahl, Robert A. (1971). *Polyarchy: Participation and Opposition*. New Haven: Yale University Press.

Davies, James. (Ed). (1971). *When Men Revolt and Why?* New York: The Free Press.

Davis, Joyce M. (2003). *Martyrs: Innocence, Vengeance and Despair in the Middle East*. New York: Palgrave Macmillan.

Deeb, Marcus. (1984). "Lebanon: Prospects for National Reconciliation in the mid-1980s". *Middle East Journal*, 38: 268-273

—— (1980). *The Lebanese Civil War*. New York: Preager Publishers.

Deeb, Yusuf. (February 2001). *Mazari' Shib'a: Dirasa Watha'qiyya Li-Marahil Al-Ihtilal wa Al-Iqtila' wa Al-Atma' wa Ta'kid Al-Haq Al-Lubnani [Shib'a Farms: Documented Research on the Stages of the Occupation, the Withdrawal, the Greed, and the Insistance on the Lebanese Right (of Ownership)]*. Beirut: Lebanese Parliament.

Dekmejian, Hrair R. (1985). *Islam in Revolution: Fundamentalism in the Arab World*. New York: Syracuse University Press.

Dishum, Ramzi and Muhammad Jarbu'a. (2001). *Al-'Amama Al-Sawda': Hizbullah wa Al-Mu'adala Al-Iqlimiyya [The Black Turban: Hizbullah and the International Equation]*. Beirut: Al-Nida' lil Nashr wa Al-Tawz'i.

Duverger, Maurice. (1978). *Political Parties: Their Organization Activity in the Modern State*. London: Methuen and Company, Ltd.

Eckstein, Harry. (1971). "On the Etiology of Internal Wars". In Clifford Paynton. (Ed.). *Why Revolution*. Massachusetts: Schenkman Publishing Co., Inc.

Eickelman, Dale F. and James P. Piscatori. (2004). *Muslim Politics*. Second edition NJ.: Princeton University Press.

Eickelman, Dale F and Jon W. Anderson. (Eds). (2003). *New Media in the Muslim World: The Emerging Public Sphere*. Second edition. Bloomington, IN: Indiana University Press.

Enayat, Hamid. (1983). "Iran: Khumayni's Concept of the 'Guardianship of the Jurisconsult.'" In J.P. Piscatori. (Ed.). *Islam in the Political Processes*.Cambridge: Cambridge University Press.

—— (1982). *Modern Islamic Political Thought*. Austin, Texas: University of Texas Press.

Esposito, John L. and R.K. Ramazani. (Eds.). (2001). *Iran at the Crossroads*. (New York: Palgrave.

Esposito, John L. (1998). "Shii Politics in Lebanon". In John Esposito. (Ed). *Islam and Politics*. Syracuse: Syracuse University Press.

—— (Ed). (1990). *The Iranian Revolution: Its Global Impact*. Miami: Florida International University Press.

El-Ezzi, Ghassan. (1998). *Hizbullah: Min Al-Hulm Al-Aydiyuluji ila Al-Waqi'iyya Al-Siyasiyya [Hizbullah: From Ideological Dream to Political Realism]*. Kuwait: Qurtas Publishing.

Fadlallah, Hadi. (1999). *Fikr al-Imam Musa al-Sadr al-Siyasi wa al-Islahi [The Political and Reformist Thought of Imam Musa al-Sadr]*. Beirut: Dar al-Hadi.

Fadlallah, Hasan. (2001). *Suqut al-Wahim: Hazimat al-Ihtilal wa Intisar al-Muqawama fi Lubnan [The Fall of the Illusion: The Defeat of the Occupation and the Victory of the Resistance in Lebanon]*. Beirut: Dar al-Hadi.

—— (1998). *Harb al-Iradat: Sira' al-Muqawama wa al-Ihtilal al-Isra'ili fi Lubanan [The war of Volitions: The Struggle of the Resistance and the Israeli Occupation Forces in Lebanon]*. Beirut: Dar al-Hadi.

—— (1994). *Al-Khiyar al-Akhar: Hizbullah: al-Sira al-Zatiyya wa al-Mawqif The Other Choice: Hizbullah's Autobiography and Stance]*. Beirut: Dar al-Hadi.

Fadlallah, Ayatullah Al-Sayyid Muhammad Husayn. (2001). *Al-Haraka Al-Islamiyya: Humum wa Qadaya [The Islamic Movement: Worries and Causes]*. Fourth edition. Beirut: Dar Al-Malak.

—— (2001). *Fiqh Al-Shari'a [The Jurisprudence of the Shari'a]*. Volume I, fifth edition. Beirut: Dar Al-Malak.

—— (2000). *Iradat Al-Quwwa: Jihad al-Muqawama fi Khitab al-Sayyid Fadlallah. [The Will to Power: The Jihad of the Resistance in Fadlallah's Discourse]*. First edition. Beirut: Dar Al-Malak.

—— (17 June 1995). *"Fi Hiwar Al-Din wa Al-Mar'a wa Al-Siyasa wa al-Mufawadat [Dialogue on Religion, Women, Politics, and the Peace Talks]"*. *Al-Majalla*: 23-26.

—— (1994a). *Al-Ma'alim Al-Jadidat lil-Marja'iyya Al-Shi'iyya [The New Features of the Shi 'ite Religious Authority]*. Compiled by Salim Al-Husayni. Third Edition. Beirut: Dar Al-Malak.

—— (1994b). *Al-Marja'iyya wa Harakat Al-Waqi' [Religious Authority and the Contemporary World Transformation]*. Beirut: Dar Al-Malak.

—— (1985). *Al-Islam wa Mantiq al-Quwwa [Islam and the Logic of Power]*. Third Edition. Beirut: Dar Al-Malak.

Fakhry, Majid. (1998). *The Qur'an: A Modern English Version*. Reading, UK: Garnet Publishing.

Fayyad, Ali. (22 November 1999). *"Al-Saraya Al-Lubnaniyya Limuqawamat Al-Ihtilal Al-Israeli: Al-Tarkiba Al-Ijtima'iyya-Al-Siyassiyya wa Afaq Al-Dawr* ["Lebanese Multi-Confessional Brigades: The Socio-political Makeup and Future Role]". Beirut: CCSD.

Fidda, Rafiq Sulayman. (n.d.) *Athar Al-Imam Al-Khymayni ala Al-Qadiyya Al-Filastiniyya [Imam Khymayni's Impact on the Palestinian Cause]*. Beirut.

Finkelstein, Norman. (2000). *The Holocaust Industry: Reflections on the Exploitation of Jewish Suffering*. London: Verso.

Fisk, Robert. (1992). *Pity the Nation: The Abduction of Lebanon*. Second edition. London: Oxford University Press.

Fuller, Graham E. (2003). *The Future of Political Islam*. New York: Palgrave, Macmillan.

Fuller, Graham E. and Rend Rahim Francke. (1999). *The Arab Shi'a: The Forgotten Muslims*. New York: St. Martin's Press.

Foucault, Michel. (1972). *Power/Knowledge*. C. Gordon. (Ed.). New York: Pantheon.

Fukuyama, Francis. (2004). *State-Building: Governance and World Order in the 21st Century*. Ithaca, N.Y.: Cornell University Press.

—— (1993). *The End of History and the Last Man*. New York: Avon Books.

Garaudy, Roger. (2000). *The Founding Myth of Modern Israel*. Orange County, Southern California: Institute for historical review.

—— (1997). *Founding the Myth of Israeli Policy*. Madison, WI: IPP publishers.

Gellner, Ernest. (1992). *Postmodernism, Reason, and Religion*. London: Routlegde.

—— (1983). *Nations and Nationalism*. Oxford: Basil Blackwell.

—— (1981). *Muslim Society*. Cambridge: Cambridge University Press.

Glahn, Gerhard von. (1996). *Law among Nations: An Introduction to Public International Law*. Seventh edition. Boston: Allyn & Bacon.

Giddens, Anthony. (2001). *Sociology*. Fourth Edition. Cambridge: Polity Press.

Glock, Charles and R. Stark. (1971). *"On the Origins and Evolution of Religious Groups"*. In: Kenneth Thompson and Jeremy Tunstall. (Eds.). *Sociological Perspectives*. London: Penguin, 392-407.

Goethe, J.W. von. (1983). *Faust*. Baltimore, MD: Penguin Books.

Goldstein, Joshua S. (2003). *International Relations*. Fifth Edition. New York: Longman.

Greene, Thomas. (1990). *Comparative Revolutionary Movements*. New Jersey: Prentice-Hall International, Inc.

Gunaratna, Rohan. (2003). *"Suicide Terrorism: A Global Threat"*. In Pamela L. Griset and Sue Mahan. *Terrorism in Perspective*. London: Sage Publications, 220-225.

Habermas, Jürgen. (1989). *The Structural Transformation of the Public Sphere: An Inquiry into a Category of Bourgeois Society*. Cambridge: Polity Press.

—— (1987). *Theory of Communicative Action*. 2 Vols. Cambridge: Polity Press.

—— (1979). *Communication and the Evolution of Society*. Boston: Beacon Press.

—— (Fall 1974). "The Public Sphere". *New German Critique*. 1.3: 49-55.

Hagopian, Eliane C. (Ed.). (1985). *Amal and the Palestinians: Understanding the Battle of the Camps*. Mass.: The Association of Arab-American University Graduates, Inc.

Halawi, Majed. (1992). *A Lebanon Defied: Musa al-Sadr and the Shi'a Community*. Boulder: Westview Press.

Hall, Rodey Bruce. (1999). *National Collective Identity: Social Constructs and International Systems*. Colombia: Colombia University Press.

Hamade, Shaykh Hasan. (2001). *Sirr Al-Intisar: Qira'a fi Al-Khalfiyyah Al-Imaniyya Al-Jihadiyya li Hizbullah [The Secret of Victory: A Reading in the Religious, Jihadi Background of Hizbullah]*. Beirut: Dar al-Hadi.

—— (2000). *Ayyam Al-Intisar [Days Of Victory]*. Beirut: Dar Al-Hadi.

Hamzeh, Nizar A. (2004). *In the Path of Hizbullah*. Syracuse: Syracuse University Press.

—— (October 2000) "Lebanon's Islamists and Local Politics: A New Reality". *Third World Quarterly*. 21.5: 739-759.

—— (1998). "The Future of Islamic Movements in Lebanon". In Ahmad S. Moussalli. (Ed.). *Islamic Fundamentalism: Myths or Realities*. Reading, UK: Ithaca Press, 249-274.

—— (1997). "The Role of Hizbullah in Conflict Management within Lebanon's Shi'a Community". In Paul Salem. (Ed) *Conflict Resolution in the Arab World: Selected Essays*. Beirut: American University of Beirut, 93-118.

—— (September 1997). "Islamism in Lebanon: A Guide to the Groups". *Middle East Quarterly*: 47-54.

—— (1993). "Lebanon's Hizbullah: From Islamic Revolution to Parliamentary Elections". *Third World Quarterly* 14. 2: 321-337.

Hanf, Theodor. (1993). *Coexistence in War Time Lebanon: Decline and Rise of a Nation*. Oxford: The Centre of Lebanese Studies.

Harik, Judith Palmer. (2004). *Hezbollah: The Changing Face of Terrorism*. London: I.B. Tauris.

—— (March 1996). "Between Islam the System: Sources and Implications of Popular Support for Lebanon's Hizballah". *Journal of Conflict Resolution*. 40. 1: 41-67.

—— (July-September 1997). "Syrian Foreign Policy and State/Resistance Dynamics in Lebanon". *Studies in Conflict & Terrorism*. 20. 3: 249-265.

—— (September 1994). *The Public and Social Services of the Lebanese Militias*. Papers on Lebanon: 14. Oxford: Centre for Lebanese Studies.

Held, David. (1990). *Introduction to Critical Theory: Horkheimer to Habermas*. Cambridge: Polity Press.

Henslin, James M. (2003). *Sociology: A Down-To-Earth Approach*. New York: Allyn and Bacon.

Hinnebusch, Raymond and Anoushiravan Ehteshami. (Eds.). (2002). *The Foreign Policy of Middle Eastern States*. Boulder, Co.: Lynne Rienner Publishers.

Hiro, Dilip. (1985). *Iran Under the Ayatollah*. First edition. London: Routledge and Kegan Paul.

Hitti, Nassif. (1993). "Lebanon in Iran's Foreign Policy: Opportunities and Constraints". In Hooshang Amirahmadi and Nader Entessar. (Eds.). *Iran and the Arab World*. London: Macmillan, 180-197.

Hizbullah's Central Press Office. (16 July 2002). *Mu'tamar Al-Baladiyyat Al-Awwal [The First Municipal Conference/Convention]*. Beirut: Hizbullah's Central Press Office.

—— (2000). *Malahim Al-Butula: 'Amaliyyat Al-Muqawama Al-Islamiyya Al-Naw'iyya [Heroic Epics: The Islamic Resistance's Major Operations]*. (A Videotape and a CD). Beirut: Hizbullah's Central Press Office.

—— (1992-2000). *Safahat 'Izin fi Kitab Al-Umma: 'Ard wa Tawthiq Li-'Amaliyat Al-Muqawama Al-Islamiyya [Pages of Dignity in the Book of the Nation: Portrayal and Documentation of the Islamic Resistance's Operations]*. Beirut: Hizbullah's Central Press Office.

—— (1998). *Kawkab Al-Shahada: Sirat, Hayat, wa Jihad Sayyid Al-Muqawama Al-Islamiyya, Al-Sayyid Abbas Al-Musawi [The Planet of Martyrdom: Biography, life, and Jihad of the Leader of The Islamic Resistance, Al-Sayyid Abbas Al-Musawi]*. Beirut: Hizbullah's Central Information Office.

—— (October 1998). *Sjil Al-Nur: Qanadil Ila Al-Zaman Al-Akhar [Al-Nur's Record: Lanterns to the Hereafter]*. Beirut: Hizbullah's Central Press Office.

Hizbullah's Central Internet Office. (2002). *Saykh Al-Shuhada': Raghib Harb [The Shaykh of Martyrs: Raghib Harb]*. CDROM.

—— (2001). *Fajr Al-Intisar [The Dawn of Victory]*. (Documents the Israeli Withdrawal). CDROM.

—— (2001) *Mu'taqal Al-Khiam [Al-Khiam Detention Centre]*. CDROM.

—— (2000). *Wa Kanat Al-Bidaya: Imam Musa Al-Sadr [And It was the Beginning: Imam Musa Al-Sadr]*. CDROM.

—— (2000). *Tahrir Asra Mu'taqal Al-Khiyam [The Liberation of the Khiam Detainees]*. CDROM.

Hizbullah's Politburo: The Committee of Analysis and Studies. (1989). *Wathiqat Al-Ta'if: Dirasat fi Al-Madmun [The Ta'if Document: A Study in its Content]*. First edition. Beirut.

"Hizbullah: Identity and Role". (24 September 1998). In "Hot Spot" (*Nuqta Sakhina*). AL-JAZEERA TV.

Hollis, Rosemary, and Nadim Shehadi. (Eds). (1996). *Lebanon on Hold: Implications for Middle East Peace*. London: Royal Institute of Middle East Affairs.

Hohendahl, Peter. (Fall 1994) "Introduction to Habermas". *New German Critique*. 1.3: 45-48.

Huntington, Samuel. (1996). *The Clash of Civilizations and the Remaking of World Order*. New York: Simon and Schuster.

—— (Summer 1993). "The Clash of Civilizations". *Foreign Affairs*. 72. 3: 22-49.

—— (1968). *Political Order in Changing Societies*. New Haven: Yale University Press.

Husem, Eric. (2002). *The Syrian Involvement in Lebanon: An analysis of the role of Lebanon in Syrian regime security, from Ta'if to the death of Hafiz al-Asad (1989-2000)*. Kjeller, Norway: Norwegian Defence Research Establishment.

Al-Hurr Al-'Amili, Al-Shaykh Muhammad Bin Al-Hasan. (1993). *Wasa'il Al-Shi'a [Shi'ite Rituals]*. Beirut: Mu'assat Al-Hulul, Bayt Ihya' Al-Turath.

Ibrahim, Fu'ad. (1998). *Al-Faqih wa Al-Dawla: Al-Fikar Al-Siyasi Al-Shi'i [The Jurisprudent and the State: Shi'ite Political Thought]*. Beirut: Dar Al-Kunuz Al-Adabiyya.

Idris, Nisreen, (2001). *'Irs Aylul:Qissat al-Shahid Hadi Hasan Nasrallah [September's Wedding: The Story of the Martyr Hadi Hasan Nasrallah]*. Beirut: Dar Al-Amir.

Jaber, Hala. (1997). *Hezbollah: Born with a Vengeance*. New York: Colombia University Press.

Jafri, S. Husain M. (1979). *Origins and Early Development of Shi'a Islam*. London: Longman Group Ltd.

Jahanbakhsh, Forough. (2001). *Islam, Democracy and Religious Modernism in Iran (1953-2000)*. Leiden: Brill.

Jorisch, Avi. (2004). *Beacon of Hatred: Inside Hizballah's Al-Manar Television*. Washington, D.C.: Washington Institute for Near East Policy.

Al-Jam'iyya Al-Ijtima'iyya Al-Thaqafiyya Li-Abna' Al-Qura Al-Sabi'.(November 2003). *Al-Qura Al-Sabi' Al-Lubnaniyya Al-Muhtalla: Dirasa Qanuniyya-Ijtima'iyya [The Seven Lebanese Occupied Villages: A Legal-Social Study]*. First edition. Beirut: Al-Markaz Al-Istishari Lil-Dirasat.

Kader, Haytham A. (1990). *The Syrian Social Nationalist Party: Its Ideology and Early History*. Beirut: Dar Fikr.

Kadivar, Shaykh Muhsin. (2000). *Nazariyyat Al-Dawla fi Al-Fiqh Al-Shi'i: Buhuth fi Wilawat Al-Faqih [The Theory of the State in the Shi'ite Jurisprudence: Research in the Rule of the Religious Jurist].* Beirut: Dar al-Jadid.

Kane, Ousmane. (2003). *Muslim Modernity in Postcolonial Nigeria: A Study of the Society for the Removal of Innovation and Reinstatement of Tradition.* Leiden: Brill.

Karmon, Ely. (December 2003). *Fight on all Fronts: Hizballah, the War on Terror, and the War on Iraq.* Policy Focus, no. 46. Washington, DC: The Washington Institute for Near East Policy.

Kashshafat Al-Imam Al-Mahdi. (2003). *Sayyid Shuhada Al-Muqawama, Abbas Al-Musawi: Nash'tahu, Jihadahu, Shahadatahu [The Leader of the Martyrs of the Resistance, Abbas Al-Musawi: His Childhood, Jihad, and Martyrdom].* Beirut: Kashshafat Al-Imam Al-Mahdi.

Katzenstein, Peter. J. (Ed.). (1996). *The Culture of National Security: Norms and Identity in World Politics.* Colombia: Colombia University Press.

Kaufman, Asher. (Autumn 2002). "Who Owns the Shebaa Farms? Chronicle of a Territorial Dispute". *The Middle East Journal.* 56.4: 576-595.

Keddie, Nikki, and Juan Cole. (Eds). (1986). *Shi'ism and Social Protest.* New Haven: Yale University Press.

Kepel, Gilles. (2002). *Jihad: The Trial of Political Islam.* Translated by Anthony F. Roberts. London: I.B. Tauris Publishers.

Khalidi-Beyhum, Ramla. (1999). *Economic and Social Commission for Western Asia, Poverty Reduction Policies in Jordan and Lebanon: An Overview.* Eradicating Poverty Studies (Series number 10). New York: United Nations.

Al-Khamina'i, Al-Imam. (2002). *Al-Sira wa Al-Masira [Biography and Path].* Beirut: Al-Dar Al-Islamiyya.

—— (2001). *'Itr Al-Shahada [The Perfume of Martyrdom].* Beirut: Al-Dar Al-Islamiyyah. (A series of lectures delivered by Khamina'i before the victory of the Islamic Revolution in 1979 and in the early years of the Iraq-Iran war).

—— (2000). *Al-'Awda ila Nahj Al-Balagha [The Return to the Peak of Eloquence].* Beirut: Markaz Baqiyyat Allah.

—— (2000). *Al-Wilaya [Guardianship].* Beirut: Dar Al-Hadi.

—— (1999). *Al-Imama wa Al-Wilaya: Qiyadat Al-Mjtama' Al-Islami wa Mas'uliyyat Al-Muslim [The Imamate and Guardianship: The Leadership of the Muslim Community and the Responsibilities of the Muslim].* Beirut: Markaz Baqiyyat Allah. (A series of lectures delivered by Khamina'i before the victory of the Islamic Revolution in 1979, collected and published in 1980).

—— (1999). *Shams Al-Wilaya [The Sun of Guardianship].* Beirut: Markaz Baqiyyat Allah.

—— (1998). *Al-Khutut Al-'Amma lil Fikr Al-Islami [The General Guidelines of Islamic Thought].* Beirut: Markaz Baqiyyat Allah.

—— (1997). *General Concepts of Islam in the Quran.* Tehran: Department of Translation and Publication, Islamic Culture and Relations Organization.

—— (1995). *Al-Hukuma fi Al-Islam [Islamic Government].* Translated by Ra'd Hadi Jaber. Beirut: Dar Al-Rawda. (A series of lectures delivered during Friday prayers by Khamina'i between 1983 and 1995 during his appointment by Imam Khumayni as the leader of prayers in Tehran University).

Khatami, Muhammad. (2000). *Madinat Al-Siyasat: Fusul min Tatawwur Al-Fikr Al-Siyasi fi Al-Gharb [The City of Politics: Sections in the Development of Political Thought in the West].* Beirut: Dar al-Jadid.

—— (1999). *Al-Islam wa al-'Alam [Islam and the World].* Cairo: Maktabat al-Shuruq.

—— (1998a). *Mutala'a fi al-Din wa al-Islam wa al-'Asr [A Reading inReligion, Islam, and Modern Times].* Beirut: Dar al-Jadid.

—— (1998b). *Bim Muj [In the Commotion].* Beirut: Dar al-Jadid.

Al-Khatib, Munif. (2001). *Mazari' Shib'a: Haqa'iq wa Watha'iq [Shib'a Farms: Facts and Documents]*. Beirut: Sharikat Al-Matbu'at Lil-Tawzi' wa Al-Nashr.

Khatun, Al-Shaykh Muhammad Ali. (2002). *Amir Al-Qafila: Al-Sira Al-Zatiyya Li-Sayyid Al-Muqawama Al-Islamiyya, Al-Sayyid Abbas Al-Musawi [The Autobiography of the Leader of The Islamic Resistance, Al-Sayyid Abbas Al-Musawi]*. Introduction by Sayyid Hasan Nasrallah. Beirut: Dar Al-Wala.

El-Khazen, Farid. (2003). "The Postwar Political Process: Authoritarianism by Diffusion". In Thoedor Hanf and Nawaf Salam. (Eds.). *Lebanon in Limbo: Postwar Society and State in an Uncertain Regional Environment*. Baden Baden: Nomos, 53-74.

—— (Autumn 2003). "Political Parties in Postwar Lebanon: Parties in Search of Partisans". *Middle East Journal*. 57.4: 605-624.

—— (2000). *The Breakdown of the State in Lebanon: 1967-1976*. London: I.B. Tauris Publishers.

—— (2000). *Intikhabat Lubnanma Ba'd Al-Harb:1992, 1996, 2000: Dimuqratiyya Bila Khiyar [The Lebanese Elections After the War: 1992, 1996, 2000: Democracy without Choice]*. Beirut: Dar Al-Nahar.

—— (Spring 1992). "Lebanon's Communal Elite-Mass Politics: The Institutionalization of Disintegration". *Beirut Review*. 3. http://www.lcps.org.lb/

Khumayni, Ruhallah. (1996). *Al-Hukumah Al-Islamiyyah [The Islamic Government]*. Tehran: The Institute of Coordinating and Publishing Imam Khumayni's Heritage.

—— (1996). *Al-Imam Al-Khumayni wa Thaqafat 'Ashura [Al-Imam Al-Khumayni and 'Ashura Culture]*. Tehran: The Institute of Coordinating and Publishing Imam Khumayni's Heritage.

—— (1992). *Kashf al-Asrar [The Revelation of Secrets]*. Beirut: Dar wa Maktabat Al-Rasul Al-Akram.

—— (1992). *Al-Istiqama wa Al-Thabat [Straightforwardness and Steadfastness]*. Translated by Qazim Yasim. Beirut.

—— (1989). *Sahifat Al-Thawra Al-Islamiyya: Nass Al-Wasiyya Al-Siyasiyya Al-Ilahiyya Lil-Imam Al-Khumayni, Qa'id Al-Thawra Al-Islamiyya [The (Religious) Book of the Islamic Revolution: The Text of the Political-Divine Will of Imam Khumayni, the Leader of the Islamic Revolution]*. Beirut: Iranian Cultural Centre.

—— (1981). *Tahrir Al-Wasila*. Volume 1. Beirut: Dar Al-Ta'aruf. *Tahrir Al-Wasila* is Imam Khumayni's practical treatise (*risala 'amaliyya*).

—— (1981). *Islam and Revolution: Writings and Declarations*. Translated by Hamid Algar. Berkeley, CA: Mizan Press.

—— (1980). *Al-Jihad Al-Akbar [Greater Jihad]*. Translated by Husayn Kurani. Tehran: Islamian Grand Library.

—— (n.d). *Al-Kalimat Al-Qisar: Al-Islam wa A'malina [Short Words: Islam and our Works]*. Beirut.

Al-Kurani, 'Ali. (1985). *Tariqat Hizbullah fi Al-'Amal Al-Islami [Hizbullah's Method of Islamic Mobilization]*. Tehran, Maktab Al-I'lam Al-Islami: Al-Mu'assa Al-'Alamiyya.

Khuri, Fouad. (1990). *Imams and Emirs: State, Religion, and Sects in Islam*. London.

Khosrokhavar, Farhad. (2002). *Les Nouveaux Martyrs D'Allah [God's New Martyrs]*. Paris: Flammarion.

—— (2000) "Le Hezbollah, de la Société Révolutionnaire a la Société Post Islamiste [The Hizbullah: From a Revolutionary Society to a Post-Islamist Society]". CURAPP, *Passions et Sciences humaines*, PUF, 129-144.

—— (1995). *L'Islamisme et la Mort: Le Martyre Revolutionnare en Iran [Islamism and Death: The Revolutionary Martyrs in Iran]*. Paris: L'Harmattan.

Kohlberg, Etan. (1997). "Medieval Muslim Views on Martyrdom" in: *Mededeelingen der Koninklijk Akademie van Wetenschappen, Afdeeling Letterkunde; dl. 60, nr. 7*. Amsterdam: KNAW publications, 281-307.

Kramer, Martin. (1997). "The Oracle of Hizbullah". In R. Scott Appleby. (Ed.) *Spokesmen for the Despised*. Chicago: The University of Chicago Press, 83-181.

—— (1997). *The Islamism Debate*. Tel Aviv: The Moshe Dayan Center for Middle Eastern and African Studies.

—— (1993). "Hizbullah: The Calculus of Jihad". In *Fundamentalisms and the State: Remarking Polities, Economics, and Militance*. Vol. III. Chicago: The University of Chicago Press, 539-56, via the Internet at: http://www.martinkramer.org/pages/899528/index.htm

—— (Autumn 1991). "Sacrifice and 'Self-Martyrdom' in Shi'ite Lebanon". *Terrorism and Political Violence*. 3.3: 30-47, via the Internet at: http://www.geocities.com/martinkramerorg/Sacrifice.htm

—— (1990). "Redeeming Jerusalem: The Pan-Islamic Premise of Hizbullah". In David Menashri. (Ed.). *The Iranian Revolution and the Muslim World*. Boulder, 105-130.

—— (1989). *Hizbullah's Vision of the West*. Washington: Washington Institute for Near East Policy.

—— (Ed.). (1987). *Shi'ism, Resistance and Revolution*. Boulder: Westview Press.

—— (August 1987). *The Moral Logic of Hizbullah*. The Dayan Center for Middle Eastern and African Studies. Occasional Papers. 101: 1-28. Tel Aviv University: The Shiloah Institute.

Krayyem, Nayef. (1997). *Hawla Al-Dawla Al-Mansuba li Hizbullah [On Hizbullah's Alleged State]*. Beirut: Hizbullah's Educational Mobilization Unit.

The Lebanese Council of Muslim 'Ulama. (2002). *Masa'il Jihadiyya wa Hukm Al-'Amaliyat Al-Istishhadiyyah [Jihadi Issues and the Judgment of Martyrdom Operations]*. Beirut: Dar Al-Wihda Al-Islamiyya.

Lebret, Louis Joseph. (1963a). *Le Liban Face à son Développement*. Beyrouth: Institut de Formation en vue du Développement Etudes et Documents.

—— (1963b). *Le Liban au Tournant*. Beyrouth: Institut de Formation en vue du Développement Etudes et Documents.

Leenders, Reinoud. (30 July 2003). "Hizbullah: Rebel Without a Cause?" *ICG Middle East Briefing Paper*. http://www.crisisweb.org/projects/middleeast/arab_ israeliconflict/reports/A401070_30072003.pdf

Levitt, Mattew A. (August-September 2003). "Hezbollah's West Bank Terror Network". *Middle East Intelligence Bulletin*, 5.8-9. http://www.meib. org/articles/0308_I3.htm

Lynch, Mark. (1999). *State Interests and Public Spheres*. New York: Colombia University Press.

Al-Madini, Tawfiq. (1999). *Amal wa Hizbullah fi Halabat al-Mujabahat al-Mahaliyya wa al-Iqlimiyy [Amal and Hizbullah in the Arena of Domestic and Regional Struggles]*. Damascus: Al-ahli.

Mackey, Sandra. (1989). *Lebanon: Death of a Nation*. New York: Congdon and Weed Inc.

Malik, Habib C. (1997). *Between Damascus and Jerusalem: Lebanon and Middle East Peace*. Washington, DC: Institute for Near East Policy.

Mallat, Chibli. (1996). *The Middle East into the First Century: Studies on the Arab-Israeli Conflict, the Gulf Crisis and Political Islam*. UK: Garnet Publishing Limited.

—— (1993). *The Renewal of Islamic Law*. Cambridge: Cambridge University Press.

—— (1988). *Shi'i Thought from the South of Lebanon*. Papers on Lebanon: 7. Oxford: Oxford University Press.

Malraux, André. (1990). *Man's Fate*. New York: Vintage Books.

Al-Manar. (2003). *Shu'a' Al-Nasr [The Bean of Victory: A Collection of Works in Support of the Intifada and the Palestinian People]*. Beirut: Dar Al-Manar Li-Intaj Al-Mar'i wa Al-Tawzi'. (A videotape).

—— (2003). *Amir Al-Qafila [The Autobiography of the Leader of The Islamic Resistance, Al-Sayyid Abbas Al-Musawi]*. Beirut: Dar Al-Manar Li-Intaj Al-Mar'i wa Al-Tawzi'. (A videotape).

—— (2002). *Al-Harb Al-Sadisa: Al-Ijtiyah Al-Sahyuni Li-Lubnan 1982 [The Sixth War: The Zionist Invasion of Lebanon 1982]*. Beirut: Dar Al-Manar Li-Intaj Al-Mar'i wa Al-Tawzi'. (Two videotapes).

—— (2001). *Qudwat Al-Tha'rin [The Leaders of the Revolutionaries]*. Beirut: Dar Al-Manar Li-Intaj Al-Mar'i wa Al-Tawzi'. (A videotape).

—— (2000). *'Urs Al-Nasr: Tahrir Qura Al-Janub wa Al-Biqa 'Al-Gharbi wa Dahr Al-Ihtilal Al-Sahyuni [The Wedding of Victory: The Liberation of the South and the Western Biqa' and the Defeat of the Zionist Occupier]*. (Documents the Israeli Withdrawal in May 2000). Beirut: Dar Al-Manar Li-Intaj Al-Mar'i wa Al-Tawzi'. (A videotape and 3 CDROMs).

Manashri, David. (Ed.) (1990). *The Iranian Revolution and The Muslim World*. Boulder, CO: Westview Press.

Markaz Baqiyyat Allah. (1999). *Al-Jihad wa Khisal Al-Mujahidin [Jihad and the Martyrs' Traits]*. Beirut: Markaz Baqiyyat Allah.

Martin, Gus. (2003). *Understanding Terrorism: Challenges, Perspectives, and Issues*. London: Sage Publications.

Marty, Martin E., and R. Scott Appleby (Eds). (1995). *Fundamentalisms Comprehended*. Vol. V. Chicago: The University of Chicago Press.

—— (1994). *Accounting for Fundamentalism: The Dynamic Character of Movements*. Vol. IV. Chicago: The University of Chicago Press.

—— (1993). *Fundamentalisms and the State: Remarking Polities, Economics, and Militance*. Vol. III. Chicago: The University of Chicago Press.

—— (1993). *Fundamentalisms and the Society: Reclaiming the Sciences, the Family, & Education*. Vol. II. Chicago: The University of Chicago Press.

—— (1991). *Fundamentalisms Observed*. Vol. I. Chicago: The University of Chicago Press.

Masri, Shafiq. (Winter 2002). "*Al-Irhab fi Al-Qanun Al-Duwali [Terrorism in International Law]*". *Shu'un al-Awsat*. 105: 46-56.

Mervin, Sabrina. (2003). *Harakat Al-Islah 'Inda Al-Shi'a [The Reformist Movement among the Shi'a]*. Beirut: Al-Nahar.

—— (2000). *Un réformisme chiite. Ulémas et lettrés du Jabal 'Âmil (actuel Liban-Sud) de la fin de l'Empire ottoman à l'indépendance du Liban*. Paris: Karthala-CERMOC-IFEAD.

Momen, Moojan. (1999). *The Phenomenon of Religion: A Thematic Approach*. Oxford: Oneworld Publications.

—— (1985). *An Introduction to Shi'i Islam: The History and Doctrines of Twelver Shi'ism*. New Haven: Yale University Press.

Moore, Brooke Noel and Richard Parker. (1998). *Critical Thinking: Evaluating Claims and Arguments in Everyday Life*. Fifth Edition. CA: Mayfield Publishing Company.

Morris, Brian. (1987). *Anthropological Studies of Religion: An Introductory Text*. Cambridge: Cambridge University Press.

Moussalli, Ahmad S. (2001). *The Islamic Quest for Democracy, Pluralism, and Human Rights*. Gainesville, FL: University Press of Florida.

—— (1999). *Moderate and Radical Islamic Fundamentalism: The Quest for Modernity, Legitimacy, and the Islamic State*. Gainesville, FL: University Press of Florida.

—— (1999) *Historical Dictionary of Islamic Fundamentalist Movements in the Arab World, Iran, and Turkey*. MD.: Scarecrow Press Inc.

—— (Ed). (1998). *Islamic Fundamentalism: Myth and Realities*. Reading, UK: Ithaca Press.

Al-Muqawama Al-Wataniyya Al-Lubnaniyya. (1985). *Al-'Amaliyyat Al-Istishadiyya: Watha'iq wa Suwar [Martyrdom Operations: Documents and Pictures] (1982-1985)*. Damascus: Al-Markaz Al-'Arabi li al-Ma'limat.

Mustapha, Amin. (2003). *Al-Muqawama fi Lubnan [The Resistance in Lebanon] (1948-2000)*. Beirut: Dar Al-Hadi.

NBN. (21, 28 July and 4 August 2002). *Ahzab Lubnan: Hizbullah: Al-Jiz' Al-Awwal [Lebanese Parties: Hizbullah, Parts I, II, III]*. (3 Videotapes).

Al-Nabulsi, Al-Saykh Al-'Allama 'Afif. (2003). *Mushahadat wa Tajarib: Laqatat mi Sirat Al-Imam Al-Sadr [Sightings and Experiences: Glimpses from Imam Al-Sadr's Biography]*. Beirut: Dar Al-Mahajja Al-Bayda'.

Nasr, Seyyed Hossein, Hamid Dabashi, and Seyyed Vali Reza Nasr. (Eds.). (1988). *Shi'ism: Doctrines, Thought, and Spirituality*. New York: State University of New York Press.

—— (1989). *Expectation of the Millennium: Shi'ism in History*. New York: State University of New York Press.

Nasrallah, Fida. (1992). *Prospects for Lebanon: The Questions of South Lebanon*. Oxford: Centre for Lebanese Studies.

Norton, Augustus R. (January 2002) "America's Approach to the Middle East: Legacies, Questions, and Possibilities". *Current History*. 101.651: 3-7.

—— (February 2000). "Hizballah of Lebanon: Extremist Ideas vs. Mundane Politics. *Council on Foreign Relations*. Via the Internet at: http://www.foreignrelations.org/public/resource. cgi?pub!3586

—— (January 1998). "Hizballah: From Radicalism to Pragmatism." *Middle East Policy Council*. 5. 4. www.mepc.org/journal/9801norton.html

—— (Ed). (1995, 1996). *Civil Society in the Middle East*. Volumes I and II. Leiden: E.J. Brill.

—— (Summer 1991). "Lebanon After Ta'if: Is the Civil War Over?" *The Middle East Journal*. 45. 3: 457-473.

—— (1992). "Breaking through the Wall of Fear in the Arab World". *Current History*. 91: 37-41.

—— (1990). "Lebanon: The Internal Conflict and the Iranian Connection". In John Esposito. (Ed.). *The Iranian Revolution: Its Global Impact*. Miami: Florida University Press, 116-137.

—— (1987). *Amal and the Shi'a Struggle for the Soul of Lebanon*. Austin: University Press of Texas.

Olmert, Joseph. (1987). "The Shi'is and the Lebanese State". In: Martin Kramer (Ed.). *Shi'ism, Resistance, and Revolution*. Boulder, CO.: Westview Press.

Picard, Elizabeth. (1993). *The Lebanese Shi'a and Political Violence*. UNRISD: Discussion Paper 42.

—— (1986). "Political Identities and Communal Identities: Shifting Mobilization Among the Lebanese Shi'a Through Ten Years of War, 1975-1985". In: Dennis L. Thompson and Dove Ronen. (Eds.) *Ethnicity, Politics and Development*. Boulder, Colorado: Lynne Riener Publishers, 157-78.

Piscatori, James. (2000). *Islam, Islamists, and the Electoral Principle in the Middle East*. Leiden: ISIM.

Qasim, Na'im. (2002). *Hizbullah: Al-Manhaj, Al-Tajriba, Al-Mustaqbal [Hizbullah: The Curriculum, the Experience, the Future]*. Beirut: Dar Al-Hadi.

Interview with Na'im Qasim. (25 January 2003). "*Salun al-Sabt [Saturday's Saloon]*", Sawt Lubnan.

Qasir, Ali. (13 February 2004). "Lebanese-Iranian Relations: Cooperation, Coalescing, and Partnership Visions". *Al-Intiqad* 1044.

Ranstorp, Magnus. (Summer 1998). "The Strategy and Tactics of Hizbullah's Current 'Lebanonization Process' ". *Mediterranean Politics*. 3.1: 103-134.

—— (1997). *Hizb'allah in Lebanon: The Politics of the Western Hostage Crises*. London: Macmillan Press Ltd.

Reuter, Christoph. (2004). *My Life as a Weapon: A Modern History of Suicide Bombing*. Translated from German by Helena Ragg-Kirkby. Princeton, NJ: Princeton University Press.

Rizq, Hiyan. (2002). *Sayyid Al-Qada: Qissat Sayyid Shuhada Al-Muqawama Al-Islamiyya [The Leader of the Leaders: the Story of the Leader of The Islamic Resistance]*. Beirut: Dar Al-Amir.

Rizq, Imad. (2003). *Al-Sharq Al-Awsat fi Mizan Al-Ru'b [The Middle East in the Balance of Terror]*. Beirut: Naufal Group.

Rodinson, Maxime. (1983). *Cult, Ghetto, and State: The Persistence of the Jewish Question*. London: Al Saqi Books. [Translated from French by Jon Rothschild]

Rosenau, James N. (1997). *Along the Domestic-Foreign Frontier: Exploring Governance in a Turbulent World*. Cambridge: Cambridge University Press.

Roy, Olivier. (2004). *Globalised Islam: The Search for A New Umma*. Revised and updated edition. London: Hurst and Company.

—— (August/September 2001) "Les islamologues ont-ils invente L'islamisme? [The Islamologists, Did They Invent Islamism?]" *Esprit*. 277: 116-138.

—— (Spring 1999). "The Crisis of Religious Legitimacy in Iran". *Middle East Journal*. 53. 2: 201-216.

—— (Summer 1998). "Tensions in Iran: The Future of the Islamic Revolution". *Middle East Report* 28. 2: 38-41.

—— (1994). *The Failure of Political Islam*. Translated by Carol Volk Cambridge: Harvard University Press.

Al-Ruhaimi, Abdul-Halim. (2002). "The Da'wa Islamic Party: Origins, Actors and Ideology", in: *Ayatollahs, Sufis and Ideologues: State, Religion and Social Movements in Iraq*. Edited by Faleh Abdul-Jabar. London: Saqi books, 149-160.

Ruhani, Muhammad Mahdi. (2002). *Thawrat Al-Faqih wa Dawlatuhu: Qira'at fi 'Alamiyyat Madrasat Al-Imam Al-Khumayni [The Revolution of the Jurisprudent and his Government: Readings in the Global Nature of Imam Khumayni's School]*. Second edition. Compiled by. Beirut: Mu'assat Al-Balagh.

Russett, Bruce, Harvey Starr and David Kinsella. (2000). *World Politics: The Menu for Choice*. New York: Bedford/St. Martin's.

Schirazi, Asghar. (1997). *The Constitution of Iran: Politics and the State in the Islamic Republic*. London: I.B. Tauris.

Saad, Abdo. (2005). *Al-Intikhabat Al-Niyabiyya li-'Am 2005: Qira'at wa Nata'ij [The Parliamentary Elections of 2005: Readings and Results]*. Beirut: Markaz Beirut lil Abhath wa Al-Ma'lumat (The Beirut Center for Research and Information).

Saad-Ghorayeb, Amal. (September 2003). "Factors Conducive to the Politicization of the Lebanese Shi'a and the Emergence of Hizbu'llah". *Journal of Islamic Studies*. 14.3: 273-307.

—— (2002). *Hizbu'llah: Politics and Religion*. London: Pluto Press.

Sachedina, Abdulaziz. (2001). "The Rule of the Religious Jurist in Iran". In John L. Esposito and R.K. Ramazani. (Eds.). *Iran at the Crossroads*. New York: Palgrave, 123-147.

—— (1991). "Activist Shi'ism in Iran, Iraq and Lebanon." In Martin E. Marty and Scott R. Appleby. (Eds). *Fundamentalism Observed*. Vol. I. Chicago: The University of Chicago Press, 403-56.

—— (1980). *Islamic Messianism: The Idea of Mahdi in Twelver Shiism*. Alabany, NY.: State University of New York Press.

Hayy'at Nasrat Al-Imam Al-Sadr wa Rafiqayh. (2003). *Qalu fi Al-Imam Al-Sadr [What Has Been Said About Al-Imam Al-Sadr]*. Beirut: Dar Al-Mahajja Al-Bayda'.

Al-Sadr, Imam Musa (1969). *Minbar wa Mihrab [A Podium and a Shrine]*. Beirut: Dar Al-Arqam.

Salman, Talal. (June 2000). *Sira Dhatiyya li Haraka Muqawina 'Arabiyya Muntasira: Hizbullah [An Autobiography of a Victorious Arab Resistance Movement: Hizbullah]*. Beirut: Al-Safir. http://www.nasrollah.org /arabic/hassan/ sera/about002.htm

Schaumann, Christoph. (2001) "The Generation of Broad Expectations". *Die Welt Des Islams.* 41.2: 174-205.

Schaefer, Richard T. and Robert P. Lamm. (1998). *Sociology.* New York: McGraw-Hill, Inc.

Shami, Hajj Husayn. (Fall 1997). *"Hizbullah In Haka* [Hizbullah Speaks Out]". *Hurriyat* (CRED, Beyrouth). 9: 34- 41.

Shamran, Mustapha. (2004). *Qudwat Al-Qada [The Lead of the Leaders].* Beirut: Al-Mustashariyya Al-Thaqafiyya Lil-Jumhuriyya Al-Islamiyya Al-Iraniyya fi Lubnan.

Shanahan, Rodger. (June 2004). "The Islamic *Da'wa* Party: Development and Future Prospects". *MERIA JOURNAL.* 8.2. Via the Internet at: http://meria.idc.ac.il/journal/2004/issue2/jv8n2a2. html#Dr.%20Rodger

Sharafeddine, Hasan. (1996). *Al-Imam Al-Sayyid Musa Al-Sadr, Mahatat Tarikhiyya: Iran, Al-Najaf, Lubnan [Al-Imam Al-Sayyid Musa Al-Sadr, Historical Moments: Iran, Al-Najaf, Lebanon].* Beirut: Dar Al-Arqam.

Sharara, Waddah. (1997). *Dawlat Hizbullah: Lubnan Mujtama'an Islamiyyan [The State of Hizbullah: Lebanon as an Islamic Society].* Second edition. Beirut: Al-Nahar.

Shatz, Adam. (29 April 2004). "In Search of Hezbollah". *The New York Review of Books.* 51.7 http:// www.nybooks.com/articles/17060?email

Shay, Shaul. (2005). *The Axis of Evil: Iran, Hizballah, and the Palestinian Terror.* London: Transaction Publishers.

—— (2004). *The Shahidas: Islam and Suicide Attacks.* Translated by Rachel Lieberman. London: Transaction Publishers.

Al-Shira'. (1984). *Al-Harakat al-Islamiyya fi Lubnan [Islamic Movements in Lebanon].* Beirut.

Singer, Peter. (1999). *Practical Ethics.* Second edition. Cambridge: Cambridge University Press.

Skocpol, Theda. (1979). *States and Social Revolutions: A Comparative Analysis of France, Russia, & China.* Cambridge: Cambridge University Press.

Smit, Ferdinand. (2000) *The Battle for South Lebanon: The Radicalisation of Lebanon's Shi'ites (1982-1985).* Amsterdam: Bulaaq.

Sobelman, Daniel. (January 2004). *Rules of the Game: Israel and Hizbullah After the Withdrawal from Lebanon.* Memorandum No. 69. Tel Aviv university: Jaffee Center for strategic Studies. http://www.tau.ac.il/jcss/memoranda/memo69.pdf

Sorensen, Georg and Robert Jackson. (2003). *Introduction to International Relations: Theories and approaches.* Second Edition. Oxford: Oxford University Press.

Swartz, David. (1997). *Culture and Power: The Sociology of Pierre Bourdieu.* Chicago: The University of Chicago Press.

Tachau, Frank. (Ed). (1994). *Political Parties of the Middle East and North Africa.* Conn.: Greenwood Press.

Taheri, Amir. (1985). *The Spirit of Allah: Khomeini and the Islamic Revolution.* London: Hutchinson.

Taqi-ud-Din Al-Hilali, Muhammad and Muhammad Muhsin Khan. (1420 A. H., 1999 A.D). *Translation of the meanings of The Noble Qur'an in the English Language.* Madinah: King Fahd Complex for the Printing of The Holy Qur'an.

Tarrow, Sidney (1994). *Power in Movement: Social Movements, Collective Action and Politics.* Cambridge: Cambridge University Press.

Telhami, Shibley and Michael Barnett. (Eds.) (2002). *Identity and Foreign Policy in the Middle East.* Ithaca: Cornell University Press.

Thompson, John. (1995). *The Media and Modernity: A Social Theory of the Media.* Cambridge: Polity Press.

—— (1994). "Social Theory, Mass Communication and Public Life" in *The Polity Reader in Cultural Theory.* Cambridge: Cambridge University Press, 24-37.

—— (1994). "The Theory of the Public Sphere: A Critical Appraisal" in *The Polity Reader in Cultural Theory*. Cambridge: Cambridge University Press, 91-99.

Thompson, Kenneth and Jeremy Tundestall. (Eds.). (1971). *Sociological Perspectives*. England: Penguin Books, Ltd.

Victor, Barbara. (2003). *Army of Roses: Inside the World of Palestinian Women Suicide Bombers*. PA: Rodale Press.

Viotti, Paul and Mark Kauppi. (1997). *International Relations and World Politics: Security, Economy, Identity*. New Jersey: Prentice-Hall.

—— (1993). *International Relations Theory: Realism, Pluralism, Globalism*. (Second Edition). Boston: Allyn and Bacon.

Walbridge, Linda S. (Ed.). (2001). *The Most Learned of the Shi'a: The Institution of Marja' Taqlid*. (Oxford: Oxford University Press.

Walker, Iain and Heather J. Smiths. (Eds.). (2002). *Relative Deprivation: Specification, Development and Integration*. Cambridge: Cambridge University Press.

Waltz, Kenneth N. (2001). *Man, the State and War: A theoretical Analysis*. (New edition with a new introduction). New York: Colombia University Press.

Warm, Mats. (May 1999). *Staying the Course: the "Lebanonization" of Hizbullah; -the integration of the Islamist movement into a pluralist political system*. Stockholm University: Department of Political Science. www.almashriq.hiof.no/lebanon/300/320/324/324.2/hizballah/warn2/index.html

—— (May 1997). *A Voice of Resistance: the Point of View of Hizbullah;-perceptions, goals and strategies of an Islamic movement in Lebanon*. Stockholm University: Department of Political Science: Advanced Course in Political Science. www.almashriq.hiof.no/lebanon/300/320/324/ 324.2/ hizballah/warn/

Wasfi, Muhammad Rida. (2000). *Al-Fikar Al-Islami Al-Mu'asir fi Iran: Jadaliyyat Al-Taqlid wa Al-Tajdid [Contemporary Political Thought in Iran: the Dialectics of Traditionalism and Innovation]*. Beirut: Dar Al-Jadid.

Weber, Marx. (1976). *The Protestant Ethic and the Spirit of Capitalism*. London: Allen and Unwin.

—— (1963). *The Sociology of Religion*. Boston, Mass.: Beacon.

Wendt, Alexander. (1999). *Social Theory of International Politics*. New York: Cambridge.

—— (June 1994). "Collective Identity Formation and the International State". *American Political Science Review*. 88.2: 384-396.

—— (1992). "Anarchy Is What States Make of It: The Social Construction of Power Politics". *International Organization*. 46.2: 391-426.

Wensinck, A. J. "The Oriental Doctrine of the Martyrs". In: *Mededeelingen der Koninklijk Akademie van Wetenschappen, Afdeeling Letterkunde; dl. 53, nr. 6*. Amsterdam: Koninklijk Akademie van Wetenschappen (KNAW publications), 1922, 147-174.

Whittier, Nancy. (1995). *Feminist Generations: The persistence of Radical Women Movements*. Philadelphia: Temple University Press.

Wiktorowicz, Quintan. (Ed). (2004). *Islamic Activism: A Social Movement Theory Approach*. Bloomington: Indiana University Press.

Wilson, Bryan. (1982). *Religion in Sociological Perspective*. Oxford: Oxford University Press.

Winslow, Charles. (1996). *War and Politics in a Fragmented Society*. New York: Routledge.

Wright, Robin. (1988). "Lebanon". In Shireen T. Hunter. (Ed.) *The Politics of Islamic Revivalism*. Indianapolis: Indiana University Press.

Yamak, Labib Z. (1966). *The Syrian Social Nationalist Party: An Ideological Analysis*. Harvard: Center for Middle Eastern Studies.

Z'aytir, Muhammad. (1988). *Nazra 'ala Tarh Al-Jumhuriyya Al-Islamiyya fi Lubnan [An Outlook at the Proposal of the Islamic Republic in Lebanon]*. Beirut: Al-Wikala Al-Sharqiyya lil-Tawzi'.
—— (1986). *Al-Mashru' Al-Maruni fi Lubnan: Juzuruhu wa Tatawwuratuhu [The Maronite Project in Lebanon: Roots and Development]*. Beirut: Al-Wikala Al-'Alamiyya lil-Tawzi'.
Zisser, Eyal. (1997). "Hizballah in Lebanon- At the Cross Roads". In Maddy-Wietzmann, Bruce and Efraim Inbar. (Eds.). *Religious Radicalism in the Greater Middle East*. London: Frank Cass.

Notes

Notes Prologue

1. From the creation of the "Greater Lebanon" in 1920 till 1975, Lebanon witnessed at least two serious civil unrests in 1958 and 1961.
   2. Hizbullah neither clashed with the Christian militias nor kidnapped, car bombed or sniped at Lebanese civilians.
3. "Identity and Goals" is Hizbullah's latest self-description. See http://www.hizbollah.org/english/frames/index_eg.htm. (Last accessed: August 2004).
4. See section 1 of the Open Letter and Na'im Qasim, *Hizbullah: Al-Manhaj, Al-Tajriba, Al-Mustaqbal [Hizbullah: the Curriculum, the Experience, the Future]*. Beirut: Dar Al-Hadi, 2002, 25-78.
5. Neera Chandhoke, *State and Civil Society: Explorations in Political Theory*. London: Sage Publications, 1995, 24.
6. Qasim, op. cit., 286, 294, 320, 327.
7. Chris Barker and Dariusz Galasinski, *Cultural Studies and Discourse Analysis: A Dialogue on Language and Identity*. London: Sage Publications, 2001, 30-31.
8. Manuel Castells, *The Power of Identity. (The Information Age: Economy, Society, and Culture, Volume II)*. Oxford: Blackwell Publishers Ltd., 1998, 3.
9. Richard T. Schaefer and Robert P. Lamm, *Sociology*. Sixth Edition. New York: McGraw-Hill, Inc., 1998, 584-5.
10. Chandhoke, op. cit, 230.
11. Ibid., 233.
12. Graham E. Fuller, *The Future of Political Islam*. New York: Palgrave, Macmillan, 2003, 24.
13. Ibid., 193. (Italics in the original; my underlining)
14. *Al-Mustashariyya Al-Thaqafiyya Lil-Jumhuriyya Al-Islamiyya Al-Iraniyya fi Lubnan.*
15. See Appendixes A, B, and C.

Notes Chapter 1

1. My aim is just to give a brief impression of what preceded the formation of Hizbullah. There are ample books and articles that deal with the history of the Shi'ites in Lebanon. See for instance Sabrina Mervin, *Un réformisme chiite. Ulémas et lettrés du Jabal 'Âmil (actuel Liban-Sud) de la fin de l'Empire ottoman à l'indépendance du Liban [The Reformist Movement among the Shi'a in South Lebanon]*, Paris: Karthala-CERMOC-IFEAD, 2000; Amal Saad-Ghorayeb, "Factors Conducive to the Politicization of the Lebanese Shi'a and the Emergence of Hizbu'llah", *Journal of Islamic Studies*, 14 (September 2003), 3, 273-307; Graham E. Fuller and Rend Rahim Francke, *The Arab Shi'a: The Forgotten Muslims*. New York: St. Martin's Press, 1999; Majid Halawi, *A Lebanon Defied: Musa al-Sadr and the Shi'a Community*. Boulder: Westview Press, 1992; Augustus Richard Norton, *Amal and the Shi'a Struggle for the Soul of Lebanon*. Austin: University Press of Texas, 1987; Fouad Ajami, *The Vanished Imam: Musa al-Sadr and the Shia of Lebanon*. Ithaca: Cornell University Press, 1986.

2. For a geographical description of the boundaries *Jabal 'Amil*, see Chibli Mallat, *Shi'i Thought from the South of Lebanon*. Papers on Lebanon: 7. Oxford: Centre for Lebanese Studies, 1988, 3.

3. Helena Cobban, "The Growth of the Shi'i Power in Lebanon and its Implications for the Future", in: Juan Cole and Nikki Keddie (eds.), *Shi'ism and Social Protest*. New Haven: Yale University Press, 1986, 138; Halawi, op. cit., 20-21, 30ff; Ajami, op. cit., 62. See also Imam Musa al-Sadr, *Minbar wa Mihrab [A Podium and a Shrine]*. Beirut: Dar Al-Arqam, 1969, 187.

4. Joseph Olmert, "The Shi'is and the Lebanese State", in: Martin Kramer (ed.), *Shi'ism, Resistance, and Revolution*. Boulder, CO.: Westview Press, 1987, 189.

5. Fuller and Francke, op. cit., 231.

6. It is worth mentioning that al-Karaki (1465-1533), better known as *al-Muhaqqiq al-Thani* laid the foundation of the guardianship of the jurisprudent doctrine (*Wilayat al-Faqih*) because he pioneered the suggestion that the Muslim religious scholars were the general deputies of Imam al-Mahdi. See Moojan Momen, *An Introduction to Shi'i Islam: The History and Doctrines of Twelver Shi'ism*. New Haven: Yale University Press, 1985, 190.

7. Al-Shaykh Muhammad Bin Al-Hasan Al-Hurr Al-'Amili, *Wasa'il Al-Shi'a [Shi'ite Rituals]*. Beirut: Mu'assat Al-Hulul, Bayt Ihya' Al-Turath, 1993. Al-Hurr Al-'Amili died in 1104 AH/1692 AD.

8. According to Deeb their leadership remained till the mid-1980s. See Marius Deeb, "Lebanon: Prospects for National Reconciliation in the mid-1980s", *Middle East Journal*, 38 (1984), 268-273.

9. Halawi, op. cit., 19-42.

10. On the emigration of the *'Amili ulama* and Iran, cf. Mervin, op. cit., 30-33 and the indicated references.

11. Ali Qasir, "Lebanese-Iranian Relations: Cooperation, Coalescing, and Partnership Visions". *Al-Intiqad* 1044 (13 February 2004). Currently there are a lot of Lebanese families from Iranian origins. Some of these are the following: Al-Asfahani, Al-'Ajami, Al-Shirazi, Al-Hamadani, Al-Mirza, Al-Musawi, Al-Husayni, Maktabi, Agha, Al-Sadr, and many others. Among the most salient Iranian families who bear a Lebanese name are the Sadr 'Amili family. According to Muhammad Rida Wasfi also the reverse trend is of considerable importance since about 1.5 million Iranian families are of Lebanese origin; these families constitute an "ideological army". However, these are not totally Shi'ites. Even Lebanese prominent Christian families such as Jumayyel and Akhawan have immigrated to Iran and contributed to its cultural recovery. (Personal interview in Beirut, 18 July 2002). Wasfi is an Iranian researcher in Christian-Muslim Studies and an advisor to the International Centre of the Dialogue of Civilizations in Tehran.

12. Halawi, op. cit., 39-40.

13. Joseph Chamie, *Religion and Population Dynamics in Lebanon*. Ann Arbor, MI: Population Studies Center of the University of Michigan, 1977, 113-118.

14. Olmert, op. cit., 189-200.

15. Norton, op. cit., 6ff.

16. Cobban, op. cit., 139-140.

17. Halawi, op. cit., 39.

18. Most notably, Michael Shiha and Petro Trad.

19. Momen, op. cit., 265.

20. Elizabeth Picard, "Political Identities and Communal Identities: Shifting Mobilization Among the Lebanese Shi'a Through Ten Years of War, 1975-1985", in: Dennis L. Thompson

and Dove Ronen (eds.), Ethnicity, Politics and Development (Boulder, Colorado: Lynne Riener Publishers, 1986), 162ff.

21. John L. Esposito, "Shii Politics in Lebanon", in: John L. Esposito, *Islam and Politics*. Syracuse: Syracuse University Press, 1998, 274ff. It is worth mentioning this formula has survived over the years and it still hold in spite of the Ta'if Agreement, which was drafted as Lebanon's new constitution in 1990. See also "Constitutional Texts" in: The Committee of Analysis and Studies of Hizbullah's Politburo, *Wathiqat Al-Ta'if: Dirasat fi Al-Madmun [The Ta'if Document: A Study in its Content]*. First edition. Beirut: 1989, 63-67.

22. Helena Cobban, *The Making of Modern Lebanon*. London: Hutchinson, 1985, 24ff.

23. Amended by a constitutional law issued on November 9, 1943.

24. Hizbullah's Politburo, *Wathiqat Al-Ta'if...*, 67.

25. As'ad Abu Khalil, "The Study of Political Parties in Lebanon: Toward a Typology", in: Frank Tachau, (ed.), *Political Parties of the Middle East and North Africa*. London: Mansell Publishing Limited, 1994, 299-300.

26. Picard, op. cit., 162.

27. Halawi, op. cit., 49-77.

28. Picard, op. cit., 163.

29. Cf. section 1.1.3 "Perenniality" in Chapter 2.

30. Olmert, op. cit., 197.

31. David McDowall, *Lebanon: A Conflict of Minorities*. London: Minority Rights Group no. 61, 1983, 3-17.

32. International Institute of Research and the formation of Educational Development. See http://www_old.coordinationsud.org/coordsud/membres/irfed.html IRFED was founded in 1958 by Louis Joseph Lebret.

33. See Louis Joseph Lebret, *Le Liban Face à son Développement*, and *Le Liban au Tournant*. Beyrouth: Institut de Formation en vue du Développement Etudes et Documents, 1963. For example, even till today, the *'Akkar* district in the North has only one hospital with 38 beds.   .

34. Lebret, Ibid. The socio-economic factors Lebret highlighted were not the only causes of the civil war. For instance Farid el-Khazen argues that these factors would not have caused armed clashes were it not for the external dimensions of the conflict. *The Breakdown of the State in Lebanon: 1967-1976*. London: I.B. Tauris Publishers, 2000. Ayatullah Muhammad Husayn Fadlallah characterises the civil war as "the war of others on Lebanese soil". Personal Interview 14 December 2005.

35. Interview conducted on 28 July 1998 at Hizbullah's Central Press Office in *Haret Hurayk*, *Dahiya* (Beirut's southern suburb). Al-Musawi is a media cadre who is an *al-Manar* TV editor and *al-Intiqad* weekly newspaper columnist. Al-Musawi reiterated the same argument in a talk given at the German Orient Institute in Beirut (OIB) on 9 December 2005. See also http://almashriq.hiof.no/lebanon/300/320/324/324.2/hizballah/.

36. See El-Khazen, op. cit., 132-133.

37. See also http://almashriq.hiof.no/lebanon/300/350/355/occupation/israeli-terror-in-lebanon.html.

38. Cobban, "The Growth of the Shi'i Power...", 141.

39. Not all the Lebanese sided with the Palestinians –the Phalangists, for example, fiercely opposed Palestinian armed attacks from Lebanese territory.

40. Augustus Richard Norton, "Hizballah of Lebanon: Extremist Ideas vs. Mundane Politics", *Council on Foreign Relations*, (February 2000), (via the Internet), 25.

41. See "Exodus and Proletarianization" in Halawi, op. cit., 68-74.

42. The spark that started the civil war was the *'Ain Al-Rimané* incident in Christian East Beirut. Unknown militia fighters, presumed PLO fighters, fired at a Maronite Church killing four people including two Maronite members of the Phalangist Christian militia. On the same day, the Phalangists retaliated by ambushing a bus passing through *'Ain Al-Rimané* and fatally shooting 27 Palestinians on board. Later on, left wing Lebanese political parties joined the war to the side of the Palestinians. See for instance, As'ad Abu Khalil, *Historical Dictionary of Lebanon*. London: Scarecrow Press, 1999 and "The Study of Political Parties in Lebanon", 297-368; 647. Norton, *Amal and the Shi'a*...; Halawi, op. cit.; and Ajami, op. cit.

43. The Christian Militias used the word *tathir*, which is equivalent to "cleansing" or "purging" the area from the Muslims and Palestinians. For instance, after two months of besieging the *Tal al-Za'tar* camp, the Christian militias raided the camp on August 12, 1976 killing around 1,600 persons. *Al-Nahar* 13 August 1976. It is worth noting that not only the Christians, but also almost all the warring factions in Lebanon pursued these strategies at moments, failing to prevent their members from committing crimes to similar effect.

44. Cobban, "The Growth of the Shi'i Power...", 141-143.

45. Momen, op. cit., 268.

46. For instance, see Ramla Khalidi-Beyhum, *Economic and Social Commission for Western Asia, Poverty Reduction Policies in Jordan and Lebanon: An Overview*. Eradicating Poverty Studies (Series number 10). New York: United Nations, 1999. On July 17, 2004, Elie Yashu'i, a Lebanese economic expert and the dean of the business school at Notre Dame University (NDU), affirmed that 90% of the Lebanese live below the poverty line. (See Lebanese daily newspapers of 19 July 2004). See also "The diaspora: Lebanon's secret weapon against economic collapse ", *Agence France-Presse (AFP)*, 20 July 2004.

47. See Lebanese daily newspapers the next day.

48. See Augustus Richard Norton, "Hizballah: From Radicalism to Pragmatism", *MiddleEast Policy Council*, 5 (January1998), 4, 7. Via the Internet at: *www.mepc.org/journal/9801norton. html*

49. See Adam Shatz, "In Search of Hezbollah", *The New York Review of Books*, 51 (29 April 2004), 7, 2. Via the Internet at: http://www.nybooks.com/articles/17060?email

50. My estimates are based on the Ministry of Interior, October 2005. Only the bearers of the Lebanese passport, to the exclusion of all other passports, were counted. On August 26, 2005, Sayyid Hasan Nasrallah, Hizbullah's current Secretary General, affirmed that the late ex-PM Rafiq Hariri told him – during the weekly meetings that were held between them before his assassination on February 14, 2005 – that the Lebanese Muslims constituted 70% to 75% of the population, while the Christians were estimated to comprise from 20% to 25%. Nasrallah added that independent research centres estimate the Christians to number from 17% to 20%. (See Nasrallah's interview with *Al-Ra'i Al-'Am* Kuwaiti newspaper, as reported by the Lebanese National News Agency and the Lebanese daily newspapers of 29 August 2005). Jaber estimated the number of the *Dahiya* residents to be 800,000. (See Hala Jaber, *Hezbollah: Born with a Vengeance*. New York: Colombia University Press, 1997, 1). On March 24, 2001 the U.S. Embassy in Beirut declared that the percentage of Christians in Lebanon is 25%, which is a substantial decrease to President Chirak's statistics in his April 1996 visit to Lebanon when the French estimated that number to be 36.6%. (See *LBCI* 24 March 2001 and *Daily Star* 25 March 2001). It is worth mentioning that as early as November 5, 1975 *al-Nahar* estimated the Christians to comprise 38.4% of the population.

51. According to Lebanese law, a mother cannot grant her children the Lebanese nationality.

52. Halawi, op. cit., 124-126.

53. On December 30, 1957, the representative of the Lebanese Shi'ite community, Sayyid Abd al-Husayn Sharafeddine died. It is note worthy to mention that the Mufti of the Lebanese Republic was, and still is, a Sunni, even though, currently, the majority of the Lebanese are Shi'ites.

54. On the link between the Sadr family and *Jabal 'Amil*, see Mervin, op. cit., 437-439.

55. Dilip Hiro, *Iran Under the Ayatollah*. First edition. London: Routledge and Kegan Paul, 1985, 345-246.

56. One-fifth: a religious tax comprising 20% on a person's surplus of income over necessary living expenses. Half is paid to the *marja'* (religious authority) as the representative of the Imam (*sahm al-Imam*), and half to the Sayyids.

57. Personal interview with Muhammad Rida Wasfi conducted in Beirut, 18 July 2002. See also his book entitled *Al-Fikar Al-Islami Al-Mu'asir fi Iran: Jadaliyyat Al-Taqlid wa Al-Tajdid [Contemporary Political Thought in Iran: the Dialectics of Traditionalism and Innovation]*. Beirut: Dar Al-Jadid, 2000, especially part one: "The Formation of Collective [Shi'ite] Identity through the Fusion of Political and Religious Authorities", 23-48.

58. Halawi, op. cit., 147-148ff, 187.

59. One of his most famous sayings in this regard is: "Muslim-Christian coexistence is a treasure that should be safeguarded at all costs". AMAL's banners and posters portrayed this slogan.

60. *Al-Harakat al-Islamiyya fi Lubnan [Islamic Movements in Lebanon]*. Beirut: *al-Shira'*, 1984, 33-34.

61. Tawfiq Al-Madini, *Amal wa Hizbullah fi Halabat al-Mujabahat al-Mahaliyya wa al-Iqlimiyya [Amal and Hizbullah in the Arena of Domestic and Regional Struggles]*. Damascus: Al-Ahli, 1999, 85, 90.

62. The three would later become Hizbullah's leading cadres, and Tufayli its first Secretary General.

63. Hizbullah considers both Imam Musa al-Sadr and Sayyid Muhammad Baqir al-Sadr among its ideologues.

64. Both books published by Dar Al-Hadi, Beirut, (various editions).

65. Sharif al-Husayni, "*Hizbullah: Haraka 'Askariyya am Siyasiyya am Diniyya?* (Hizbullah: A Military or Political or religious Movement?)". Beirut: *Al-Shira'* (17 March 1986), 16.

66. Dissident Iranians also received military help from the Palestinian camps in Lebanon.

67. In the beginning of the Iraq-Iran war he died on board of an Iranian military plane that was downed by the Iraqis.

68. Amir Taheri. *The Spirit of Allah: Khomeini and the Islamic Revolution*. London: Hutchinson, 1985, 193. Shamran had a Ph.D. in electro mechanics and plasma physics from the university of California in the US. In addition to taking part in the founding of the Movement of the Deprived and AMAL with Imam Musa al-Sadr, in Iran he held prominent positions such as the deputy of the prime minister for the revolution issues (*shu'un al-thawra*), and was also Imam Khumayni's representative in the Higher Defence Council. See Mustapha Shamran, *Qudwat Al-Qada [The Lead of the Leaders]*. Beirut: Al-Mustashariyya Al-Thaqafiyya Lil-Jumhuriyya Al-Islamiyya Al-Iraniyya fi Lubnan, 2004.

69. See Amin Mustapha, *Al-Muqawama fi Lubnan: 1948-2000 [The Resistance in Lebanon: 1948-2000]*. Beirut: Dar Al-Hadi, 2003, 572-574.

70. Ibid., 270-271.

71. Al-Madini, op. cit., 78, 89.

72. Cobban, "The Growth of the Shi'i Power...", 143-144. Halawi, op. cit., 136-137; 155-157. It is worth mentioning that Shaykh Na'im Qasim, Hizbullah's current deputy secretary general,

actively worked with Imam Musa al-Sadr in the founding of *Harakat Al-Mahrumin*. See http://www.naimkassem.org/materials/serathateya/sera.htm

73. Elizabeth Picard, *The Lebanese Shi'a and Political Violence*. UNRISD: Discussion Paper 42, 1993, 13. See also her article entitled Picard, "Political Identities…", 157-78.

74. Saad-Ghorayeb, op. cit., 295-298.

75. Farid El-Khazen, "Lebanon's Communal Elite-Mass Politics: The Institutionalization of Disintegration". *Beirut Review* 3 (Spring 1992), 15.

76. El-Khazen argues *AMAL* is the military wing of *Harakat Al-Mahrumin*. El-Khazen, *The Breakdown…*, 306. Also Shamran claims the same thing in *Qudwat Al-Qada…*, 16.

77. *Al-Nahar* 30 June 1975.

78. Al-Madini, op. cit., 35-39; 49-60. See also Abd Al-Ilah Balqaziz, *Al-Muqawama wa Tahrir Al-Janub: Hizbullah min Al-Hawza Al-'Ilmiyya ila Al-Jabha [The Resistance and the Liberation of the South: Hizbullah from the Religious Seminary to the Battle Front]*. Beirut: Markaz Dirasat Al-Wihda Al-'Arabiyya, 2000, 43-46. For the exact number of killed and wounded, see Halawi, op. cit., 217.

79. Ajami, op. cit., 43. See also Saad-Ghorayeb, op. cit., 295-298.

80. According to al-Sadr "Israel is the absolute evil, and dealings with it are *haram* (religiously prohibited)". See Halawi, op. cit., 147.

81. El-Khazen subscribes to this view. El-Khazen, *The Breakdown…*, 306.

82. Halawi, op. cit., 206-207.

83. Judith Palmer Harik, *Hezbollah: The Changing Face of Terrorism*. London: I.B. Tauris, 2004, 22. See also Robin Wright, "Lebanon", in: Shireen T. Hunter (ed.), *The Politics of Islamic Revivalism*. (Indianapolis: Indiana University Press, 1988), 63.

84. Husayn al-Husayni was *AMAL*'s secretary general at that time. He served in his post till April 4, 1980, the date of the election of his deputy Nabih Berri, who is till now *AMAL*'s leader and the speaker of the parliament. See *al-Madini*, op. cit., 75.

85. Waddah Sharara, *Dawlat Hizbullah: Lubnan Mujtama'an Islamiyyan [The State of Hizbullah: Lebanon as an Islamic Society]*. Second Edition. Beirut: Al-Nahar, 1997, 117.

86. Rodger Shanahan, "The Islamic Da'wa Party: Development and Future Prospects". *MERIA JOURNAL* 8 (June 2004), 2. Via the Internet at: http://meria.idc.ac.il/journal/2004/issue2/ jv8n2a2.html#Dr.%20Rodger; and Hanna Batatu, "Iraq's Underground Shia Movements: Characteristics, Causes and Prospects", *Middle East Studies*, 35 (Autumn 1981), 4.

87. Juan R. I. Cole and Nikki R. Keddie (eds.), *Shiism and Social Protest*. New Haven, CT.: Yale University Press, 1986, 191. See also Abdul-Halim Al-Ruhaimi, "The Da'wa Islamic Party: Origins, Actors and Ideology", in: *Ayatollahs, Sufis and Ideologues: State, Religion and Social Movements in Iraq*. Edited by Faleh Abdul-Jabar. London: Saqi books, 2002, 149-160.

88. In 1975 Nasrallah became *AMAL*'s organizational officer in the *Bazuriyé* village, near Tyre in south Lebanon. In 1979, he became the political officer of the *Biqa'* in addition to being an *AMAL* politburo member. See http://www.nasrollah.org/english/hassan/sera/sira.htm (Last accessed April 2004).

89. Nassif Hitti, "Lebanon in Iran's Foreign Policy: Opportunities and Constraints", in: Hooshang Amirahmadi and Nader Entessar (eds.), *Iran and the Arab World*. London: Macmillan, 1993, 182-3.

90. El-Khazen, *The Breakdown…*, 44-45.

91. Hizbullah ironically notes that the name "IDF" is itself a euphemism since the "aggressor" is being labelled as the "defender". By Hizbullah, I mean Hizbullah's official policy – as conveyed by its "Central Press Office" and media institutions – which is usually based on the discourse and policy of its leaders.

92. Daniel Sobelman, *Rules of the Game: Israel and Hizbullah After the Withdrawal from Lebanon*. Memorandum No. 69. Tel Aviv university: Jaffee Center for strategic Studies, January 2004, 45, at: http://www.tau.ac.il/jcss/memoranda/memo69.pdf. Author's own observations attest to this claim. For instance, in the predominantly Muslim West Beirut, Israeli soldiers were given *Baklawa* (Arabic sweets) right after their Mirkava tank flattened all the cars in the street.

93. For a detailed presentation and analysis of the Palestinian resistance in Lebanon, see Mustapha, op. cit., 245-306.

94. See *Al-Harb Al-Sadisa: Al-Ijtiyah Al-Sahyuni Li-Lubnan 1982 [The Sixth War: The Zionist Invasion of Lebanon 1982]*. Vol. I, Episode 3. Beirut: Dar Al-Manar Li-Intaj Al-Mar'i wa Al-Tawzi', 2002. See also Na'im Qasim, *Hizbullah: Al-Manhaj, Al-Tajriba, Al-Mustaqbal [Hizbullah: The Curriculum, the Experience, the Future]*. Beirut: Dar Al-Hadi, 2002, 24, note 1.

95. Ethical deprivation, which "refers to value conflicts between the ideals of society and those of individuals or groups", might explain this move. Thus, "current theories of revolution specify that there must be a deflection from the ranks of the elite in order that direction and leadership be provided for lower class discontent, if revolution is to occur". Charles Glock and R. Stark, "On the Origins and Evolution of Religious Groups", in: Kenneth Thompson and Jeremy Tunstall (eds.), *Sociological Perspectives*. London: Penguin, 1971, 397.

96. Other leaders or cadres who did the same are the following: Subhi al-Tufayli (the first Secretary General of Hizbullah), Muhammad Yazbik (one of the deputies of Imam Khamina'i in Lebanon and the head of Hizbullah's Religio-Judicial Council); Husayn Khalil (Nasrallah's "Political Aide" or political advisor); Na'im Qasim (Hizbullah's Deputy Secretary General); Muhammad Ra'd (Hizbullah's head of the parliamentary bloc entitled "Loyalty to the Resistance"); 'Abbas al-Musawi (Hizbullah's second Secretary General); Husayn al-Musawi (AMAL's deputy president at that time; he founded Islamic *AMAL*, which later became part of Hizbullah. Currently, he serves as Nasrallah's Executive Aide for Municipal Issues); and Ibrahim Amin al-Sayyid (AMAL's representative in Tehran; he moved to Hizbullah in 1982. Currently, he is Hizbullah's head of the Political Council).

97. Elite fragmentation can be cited as another provocation to revolution, since a divided elite is perceived as both incompetent and illegitimate by an already discontented populace. (Thomas H. Greene, *Comparative Revolutionary Movements*. New Jersey: Prentice Hall, 1990, 144). The incoherence of an elite facilitates revolution by allowing insurgent groups to gain the favour of certain members of the elite who in turn possess the necessary leadership skills and political expertise needed by inexperienced insurrectionists. (Harry Eckstein, "On the Etiology of Internal Wars," in: Clifford Paynton (ed.), *Why Revolution*, Massachusetts: Schenkman Publishing Co., Inc., 1971, 143-144). Thus, "[R]evolutions are explained as basically due to the occurrence in a society of widespread, intense, and multifaceted relative deprivation that touches both masses and elite aspirants. For if potential leaders and followers alike are intensely frustrated, then both broad participation in, and deliberate organization of, political violence are probable, and the fundamental conditions for internal war are present". (Theda Skocpol, *States and Social Revolutions: A Comparative Analysis of France, Russia, & China*. Cambridge: Cambridge University Press, 1979, 9-10).

98. This and the following statement are not new. Berri has already uttered these statements as early as the mid-1980s when *AMAL* was stronger and more popular than Hizbullah. The author has also proven that most of Hizbullah's leading cadres originated from *AMAL*.

99. Thana' 'Atwi, "The Shi'ite Conclave in Tyre Gives Importance to Denying the Background of the Meeting ", Al-Safir 20 August 2004.

100. Established in 1966. See Sharara, op. cit., 87ff. It is worth mentioning that Shaykh Na'im Qasim was one of its leading founding members. See http://www.naimkassem.org/ materials/serathateya/sera.htm

101. Talal Salman, *Sira Dhatiyya li Haraka Muqawina 'Arabiyya Muntasira: Hizbullah [An Autobiography of a Victorious Arab Resistance Movement: Hizbullah]*. Beirut: Al-Safir, June 2000, 7. See the following web page: http://www.nasrollah.org/arabic/hassan/sera/ about002.htm

102. Compiled from *Kawkab Al-Shahada: Sirat, Hayat, wa Jihad Sayyid Al-Muqawama Al-Islamiyya, Al-Sayyid Abbas Al-Musawi [The Planet of Martyrdom: Biography, life, and Jihad of the Leader of The Islamic Resistance, Al-Sayyid Abbas Al-Musawi]*. Beirut: Hizbullah's Central Information Office, 1998; Hiyan Rizq, *Sayyid Al-Qada: Qissat Sayyid Shuhada Al-Muqawama Al-Islamiyya [The Leader of the Leaders: the Story of the Leader of The Islamic Resistance]*. Beirut: Dar Al-Amir, 2002; Al-Shaykh Muhammad Ali Khatun, *Amir Al-Qafila: Al-Sira Al-Zatiyya Li-Sayyid Al-Muqawama Al-Islamiyya, Al-Sayyid Abbas Al-Musawi [The Autobiography of the Leader of The Islamic Resistance, Al-Sayyid Abbas Al-Musawi]*. Introduction by Sayyid Hasan Nasrallah. Beirut: Dar Al-Wala, 2002, and a videotape bearing the same title, Beirut: Dar Al-Manar Li-Intaj Al-Mar'i wa Al-Tawzi', 2003; A Videotape entitled *Qudwat Al-Tha'rin [The Leader of the Revolutionaries]*. Beirut: Dar Al-Manar Li-Intaj Al-Mar'i wa Al-Tawzi', 2001; and *Sayyid Shuhada Al-Muqawama, Abbas Al-Musawi: Nash'tahu, Jihadahu, Shahadatahu [The Leader of the Martyrs of the Resistance, Abbas Al-Musawi: His Childhood, Jihad, and Martyrdom]*. Beirut: Kashshafat Al-Imam Al-Mahdi, 2003.

103. Talib Aziz, "Fadlallah and the Remaking of the Marja'iyya", in: *The Most Learned of the Shi'a: The Institution of Marja' Taqlid*. Edited by Linda S. Walbridge. Oxford: Oxford University Press, 2001, 207. Muhtashami was an advisor and political aide to the ex-president Khatami. He is also the secretary-general of the International Committee for the Support of the Palestinian *Intifada* (popular uprising).

104. Sharara, op. cit., 269, 375.

105. Ibid., 254.

106. Ibid., 100, 109, 269.

107. According to Nabih Berri. See "In the Commemoration of Shamran's Anniversary, Berri Stresses *AMAL*'s Commitment towards the Continuation of the Resistance", *al-Safir* 22 July 2004.

108. According to Mahdi Shamran, Mustapha's brother. (Ibid.).

109. Saad-Ghorayeb, op. cit., 303.

110. Al-Madini, op. cit., 172. Al-Madini refers to an original Hizbullah document in order to substantiate his argument.

111. Saad-Ghorayeb, op. cit., 306.

112. It seems that Husayn al-Musawi is employing an aposteriori discourse, which assumes, at that time, Khumayni was a leading *marja'* for the Lebanese.

113. *Al-Harb Al-Sadisa…*,Vol. I, Episode 3.

114. Sharara, op. cit., 315.

115. Contrary to Hizbullah's consistent policy of denying receiving military aid from Iran, Nasrallah concedes that it *does*. See Nasrallah's interview with *al-Safir* 28 June 2001.

116. The author only adumbrated the initial characterisation of Iran's purported influence on Hizbullah. Throughout the course of the dissertation, this characterisation would be examined systematically.

117. "Identity and Goals" is Hizbullah's latest self-description, which could be considered as an abridged, updated, and modified version of Hizbullah's 1985 "Open Letter" or "Political Manifesto". See http://www.hizbollah.org/english/frames/index_eg.htm (Last accessed April 2004).

118. See the program entitled "Ahzab Lubnan: Hizbullah: Al-Jiz' Al-Awwal [Lebanese Parties: Hizbullah, Part I]" (1979-1989), NBN, 21 July 2002.

119. See Nasrallah's speech on December 28, 2000, in the "Jerusalem Day Celebration".

120. Based on Israeli press and media reports as cited in: Al-Harb Al-Sadisa...,Vol. II, Episode 6.

121. The issue zero of al-'Ahd "The Voice of the Islamic Revolution in Lebanon" dated 18 Ramadan 1404 AH/ 18 June 1984 was distributed free of charge. The right side depicted a picture of Imam Khumayni and the left side showed the Hizbullah logo, on top (5:56) "The part of God are victorious" and on the bottom, "The Islamic Revolution in Lebanon". To the right of the logo the following statement was written: "It is incumbent upon each and everyone of us to mobilize in order to uproot Israel from existence".

122. For instance, Magnus Ranstorp, Judith Miller, Mary-Jane Deeb, Gabriel Almond, Emmanuel Sivan, Fouad Ajami, Scott Appleby, Graham Fuller, James Piscatori, and Ann Byers contend that Fadlallah is Hizbullah's spiritual leader (guide) or Hizbullah was his brainchild, while Hala Jaber, Chibli Mallat, Augustus Richard Norton, Judith Palmer Harik, and Daniel Sobelman deny this claim. (See Amal Saad-Ghorayeb, Hizbullah: Politics and Religion. London: Pluto Press, 2002), 6. As an update to Saad-Ghorayeb's list, I have added Ajami, Fuller, Piscatori, Byers, Norton, Harik, and Sobelman, and removed Nizar Hamzeh whom she erroneously included in her first list of names. Ajami claims that Fadlallah "became the 'spiritual guide' of groups such as the Party of God". See Ajami, op. cit., 213. Fuller argues, "Sayyid Husayn Fadlallah, spiritual mentor to Hizballah...". See Fuller and Francke, op. cit., 28, 212. Piscatori asserts, "But its [Hizbullah's] spiritual guide, Muhammad Husayn Fadlallah..." See James Piscatori, Islam, Islamists, and the Electoral Principle in the Middle East. Leiden: ISIM, 2000, 27. Byers claims Fadlallah is Hizbullah's "spiritual leader", while Nasrallah is its "operational leader". See Ann Byers, Lebanon's Hezbollah (Inside the World's Most Infamous Terrorist Organizations). London: Rosen Publishing Group, 2003, 16. Norton argues, "Fadlallah – somewhat inaccurately who is if widely depicted as the 'spiritual guide,' or al-murshid al-ruhi of Hizballah". Norton, "Hizballah of Lebanon...", 26; Harik subscribes to the view that "Fadlallah never formally associated himself with Fadlallah". See Harik, op. cit., 61; Sobelman writes, "Fadlallah, who is sometimes referred to – albeit incorrectly –as Hizbollah's official spiritual leader". See Sobelman, op. cit., 49; "Sayyid Muhammad Husayn Fadlallah, who erroneously has been called al-murshid al-ruhi (spiritual guide) of Hizbullah". See A. Nizar Hamzeh, In the Path of Hizbullah. Syracuse: Syracuse University Press, 2004, 35.

123. Personal Interviews, 27 December 2001 and 14 December 2005. This statement is not new. It has been repeatedly stated by Fadlallah as of the early 1980s, especially after his failed assassination attempt on March 8, 1985, which killed 92 (mostly women), and wounded around 250 others. See al-Husayni, "Hizbullah: Haraka 'Askariyya..., 20; Ghassan El-Ezzi. Hizbullah: Min Al-Hulm Al-Aydiyuluji ila Al-Waqi'iyya Al-Siyasiyya [Hizbullah: From Ideological Dream to Political Realism]. Kuwait: Qurtas Publishing, 1998, 57; Al-Madini, op. cit., 175.

124. Personal interview 14 December 2005.

125. See "Fi Hiwar Al-Din wa Al-Mar'a wa Al-Siyasa wa al-Mufawadat [Dialogue on Religion, Women, Politics, and the Peace Talks]", Al-Majalla, 17 June 1995, 23-26. For an insider's view on the relationship between Ayatullah Fadlallah and Hizbullah refer to: Hasan

Fadlallah, *Al-Khiyar al-Akhar: Hizbullah: al-Sira al-Zatiyya wa al-Mawqif [The Other Choice: Hizbullah's Autobiography and Stance]*. Beirut: Dar al-Hadi, 1994, 83-89.

126. http://www.nasrollah.org/ (Last accessed April 2005).

127. This is elaborated later in chapter three, "Section III", entitled, "Fadlallah's possible contribution to Hizbullah's ideology and thinking".

128. *Al-Nahar* 19 January 1983.

129. *Al-Nahar* 21 March 1985. In fact, Hizbullah's "Open Letter" stipulates that Islam should not be imposed by force, but should be the result of a consensus among the Lebanese.

130. On Friday 3 *Jamadi al-Thani* 1405 AH (22 February 1985), pages five to eight. It was read one week earlier, on Saturday, February 16, by Hizbullah's spokesman at the time Sayyid Ibrahim Amin al-Sayyid. In addition to publishing its Open Letter in *al-'Ahd*, Hizbullah's mouthpiece, the Manifesto was also published three days later on the 25th of February 1985 on the second page of *Al-Safir*, a Lebanese daily that is owned by a Shi'ite and has a leftist orientation; its motto, "The voice of those who have no voice", supports the oppressed, subaltern voices. Maybe the reason for that might be Hizbullah's aim to acquire more readership since *al-'Ahd* was not that known, and had limited circulation and readership. This analysis has been substantiated by an interview conducted by the author on 18 November 2005 with Imad Mrmal, *al-Safir* columnist and *al-Manar* political talk show presenter.

131. See http://www.nasrollah.org/english/hassan/sera/sira.htm (Last accessed April 2005).

132. See Lebanese daily newspapers of 8 February 1988.

133. He was "voluntarily" banished to France from 1988 till 2000.

134. Before his death, Khumayni appointed Ayatullah Muntazari as his successor. However, due to the latter's criticisms on *wilayat al-faqih* doctrine, he was alienated and put in house arrest. At the time of the appointment of 'Ali Khamina'i as Khumayni's successor, Khamina'i was not the most learned in all branches of religious knowledge (*a'lamiyya*), not even an Ayatullah (i.e. he did not satisfy the necessary qualifications to be classified as a *marja'*). The Islamic Republic's constitution was amended in 1989 in order to make it possible for Khamina'i to become *al-waliyy al-faqih*. (See Ervad Abrahamian, *Khomeinism: Essays on The Islamic Republic*. London: I.B. Taurus, 1993, 34; Abdulaziz Sachedina, "The Rule of the Religious Jurist in Iran" in: John L. Esposito and R.K. Ramazani (eds.), *Iran at the Crossroads*. New York: Palgrave, 2001, 139). Thus, it is quite possible that during the selection process of a successor other factors enter into consideration other than the criteria stipulated by the *wilayat al-faqih* doctrine.

135. See Paul Salem, *The Beirut Review*, Beirut: Lebanese Center for Policy Studies (LCPS), 1, 1 (Spring 1991), 119-120. See also, Hizbullah's Politburo, *Wathiqat Al-Ta'if...*, 69-78. For a detailed study and analysis on the Ta'if, see for instance: 'Arif Al-'Abd, *Lubnan wa Al-Ta'if: Taqatu' Tarikhi wa Masar Ghatr Muktamil [Lebanon and the Ta'if: A Historical Cross-Road and an Unfinished Trajectory]*. Beirut: Markaz Dirasat Al-Wihda Al-'Arabiyya, 2001.

136. See William W. Harris, *Faces of Lebanon: Sects, Wars, and Global Extensions*. Princeton, NJ.: Markus Wiener Publishers, 1996, 243-278.

137. See Lebanese daily newspapers of 14 August 1989.

138. *Al-Safir* 6 October 1989.

139. Hizbullah's Politburo, *Wathiqat Al-Ta'if...*, 5-62.

140. See the preamble of the Lebanese constitution pertaining to the need to liberate all Lebanese territory from foreign occupation.

141. Under "Establishing the state's authority on all Lebanese territory", the first article stipulates, "The announcement of disbanding all Lebanese and non-Lebanese militias,

and the submittal of their weapons to the Lebanese Army, six months after ratification of the Ta'if Agreement". Hizbullah's Politburo, *Wathiqat Al-Ta'if...*, 76.

142. Hizbullah's Central Press Office.

143. Hasan Fadlallah, op. cit., 137.

144. See Nasrallah's speech in the fifth day of *Muharram*, 1425 A.H., 24 March 2004.

145. The last parliamentary elections before the eruption of the civil war on April 13, 1975, were held in April 1972.

146. For details, see Chapter 4: Political Program.

147. It seems that one cannot sideline Iran in this respect because it is a major player in Hizbullah's ideology, policies, and decision-making, even in mundane political issues. Thus, it seems that ideology can interfere in practical decision-making.

148. It is worth mentioning that the abolition of political sectarianism is stipulated in article 95 of the Ta'if Agreement.

149. See Hizbullah's detailed 1992 election program in "Appendix B".

150. Fadeel M. Abun-Nasr, *Hizbullah: Haqa'iq wa Ab'ad [Hizbullah: Facts and Dimentions]*. Beirut: World Book Publishing, 2003,131.

151. *Al-'Ahd* no. 441.

152. Qasim, op. cit., 294-295.

153. Ibid., 295-297.

154. Interview with *Al-Bilad* 12 October 1994.

155. Actually, for any established *marja'* it is possible and normal to have more than one representative.

156. *Al-Safir* 18 May 1995.

157. See Augustus R. Norton, "Hizbullah and the Israeli Withdrawal from Southern Lebanon", *Journal of Palestine Studies,* 30 (Autumn 2000), 1, 27. See also Hasan Fadlallah, *Harb al-Iradat: Sira' al-Muqawama wa al-Ihtilal al-Isra'ili fi Lubanan [The War of Volitions: The Resistance's Struggle and the Israeli Occupation in Lebanon.* Beirut: Dar al-Hadi, 1998, 181-202

158. See Hizbullah's detailed 1996 election program in "Appendix B".

159. He's most probably referring to the "Grapes of Wrath" and its aftermath.

160. Abun-Nasr, op. cit., 131-132.

161. It is worth mentioning that the naming has a religious/Qur'anic connotation. When the Prophet participated in a battle, it was called a *ghazwa*; when he did not, it was called a *sariyya*, singular of *saraya*. This is another indication of the importance of Hizbullah's religious ideology.

162. Lebanonisation or *infitah* policy refers to Hizbullah's integration policy in the Lebanese public sphere in the 1990s. See Qasim, op. cit., 286, 294, 320, 327.

163. The following social indicators are telling: 24.3% of the LMCB were between 20-25 years old, 46.1% between 25-and 30, and 29.3% older than 30. 17.2% had elementary education, 24.3% had intermediate education, 35.7% had secondary education, 35.7% had high school education, 16.9% had university education, and 5.9% had MAs and PhDs. 69% were bachelors, 25.8% married with children, and 5.2% married without children. The following political indicators are telling: 51% were ex-political parties' members, 6.8% were affiliated with various political parties, and 42.2% were non-members of political parties. Further 38% were Sunni, 25% Shi'a, 25%, Druz 20%, and 17% Christians. In addition, 40% came from Beirut, 20.6% from the North and *Kisirwan* (predominantly Christian areas), *Biqa'* 13.4%, Mount Lebanon 8.6%, and the South and *Iqlim al-Karrub* 17.4%. See Ali Fayyad,"*Al-Saraya Al-Lubnaniyya Limuqawamat Al-Ihtilal Al-Israeli: Al-Tarkiba*

Al-Ijtima'iyya-Al-Siyassiyya wa Afaq Al-Dawr ["Lebanese Multi-Confessional Brigades: The Socio-Political Makeup and Future Role]". Beirut: CCSD, 22 November 1999.

164. Unlike the parliamentary elections law, the municipal elections law is not drawn along sectarian lines, which leaves a large room for the grass roots to voice their opinion in the ballot and make their subaltern voices heard.

165. Hamzeh based himself on al-'Ahd issues during the election period. See Nizar Hamzeh, "Lebanon's Islamists and local politics: a new reality", Third World Quarterly 21 (October 2000), 5, 745.

166. For an accurate tabulation of the election results, see Hamzeh, "Lebanon's Islamists...", 751-755. See also Reinoud Leenders, "Hizbullah's Baalbek Reversal", Middle East International, 577 (19 June 1998), 8.

167. See "Hizbullah: Identity and Role" in "Hot Spot" (Nuqta Sakhina) on Al-Jazeera TV, 24 September 1998. The entire episode is based upon interviews with Hizbullah's leading cadres, rank, and file as well as journalists and political analysts considered close to the party. The above-mentioned statement was made by Nasrallah and commented upon by Ibrahim al-Amin of al-Safir.

168. Sobelman, op. cit., 47-48.

169. Norton, "Hizbullah of Lebanon...", 27.

170. Norton, "Hizbullah and the Israeli Withdrawal...", 27.

171. Israel withdrew from the town of Shib'a, but not its farms. Hizbullah continued its resistance and military operations in the Lebanese Shib'a Farms, a small strategic strip of land – bordering Lebanon, Israel, and Syria – situated near the Golan Heights. See my article entitled: "Successen Hezbollah bij 'kleine oorlog' om Shib'a [Hizbullah's Successes in the 'Small War' in Shib'a]", Soera 9,2 (July 2001), 34-38.

172. Norton added that "Hizballah forces displayed impressive discipline" when they took over Lebanese territories evacuated by the IDF during the withdrawal from Southern Lebanon. (Norton, "Hizbullah and the Israeli Withdrawal", 32). For more details and analysis see my article entitled "Hizbullah, Terrorism, and September 11", ORIENT: German Journal for Politics and Economics of the Middle East 44 (September 2003), 3, 393.

173. See Munif Al-Khatib, Mazari' Shib'a: Haqa'iq wa Watha'iq [Shib'a Farms: Facts and Documents]. Beirut: Sharikat Al-Matbu'at Lil-Tawzi' wa Al-Nashr, 2001; Yusuf Deeb, Mazari' Shib'a: Dirasa Watha'qiyya Li-Marahil Al-Ihtilal wa Al-Iqtila' wa Al-Atma' wa Ta'kid Al-Haq Al-Lubnani [Shib'a Farms: Documented Research on the Stages of the Occupation, the Withdrawal, the Greed, and the Insistance on the Lebanese Right (of Ownership)]. Beirut: Lebanese Parliament, February 2001; and Mazari' Shib'a: Al-Siyada wa Al-Haq Al-Qanuni [Shib'a Farms: Sovereignty and Legal Right]. Second edition. Beirut: CCSD, 2002.

174. The UN sent a UNIFIL contingent to southern Lebanon and the Biq'a in order to monitor and act as a disengagement force between the Israeli and Lebanese sides.

175. Israel started its withdrawal on May 21, 2000 and ended it on May 24, 2000. The Lebanese government observes May 25, the day of "Liberation and Resistance", as an official holiday.

176. See Nasrallah's Bidnayyel's Speech 20 May 2001.

177. Lebanese National News Agency.

178. Interview with CNN, 17 April 2002. In this connection, James Abu Rizq, an ex-US Senator, accused the US media of hiding the truth about the Shib'a Farms affirming that it is Lebanese, not Syrian. He decried the US policy that supports Israel; Rizq conceded that Hizbullah played a positive role in Lebanon. (Al-Nour, 13 GMT News, 13 June 2002; al-Safir and Daily Star, 13 and 14 June 2002).

179. See Ha'aretz 25 June 2002, quoted by al-Safir 26 June 2002, and Daily Star 28 June 2002. Kaufman is a professor at the Truman Institute at Jerusalem Hebrew University. Mirroring Ha'aretz the Daily Star wrote, " 'all the documents found by Kaufman from the period of the French Mandate over Syria and Lebanon, and which was supposed to mark the border between Lebanon and Syria back up the Lebanese argument'... The documents, mostly French maps and arbitration documents from the period, position the Shebaa Farms 'about a kilometer or two inside Lebanon'... the evidence suggests that locals in the area during the period consistently fell under the jurisdiction of Lebanese authorities". For more details see Kaufman's article entitled "Who Owns the Shebaa Farms? Chronicle of a Territorial Dispute", The Middle East Journal, 56 (Autumn 2002), 4, 576-595.

180. See also the report by the "Lebanese Association for Democratic Elections" on the issue.

181. As reported by the Syrian media and press, Kan'an, the ex-head of the Syrian Intelligence in Lebanon (1982-2002) and the Minister of Interior as of 2004, committed suicide on October 12, 2005.

182. New TV (Lebanon), News Bulletin, 11 October 2005. This is questionable since dividing Beirut into three electoral districts disadvantages Hariri in favour of traditional Sunni leaders such as the then PM Salim al-Hoss, and the ex-MP Tamman Salam, who both failed to be re-elected.

183. See Hizbullah's detailed 2000 election program in "Appendix B".

184. See Farid El-Khazen, Intikhabat Lubnanma Ba'd Al-Harb:1992, 1996, 2000: Dimuqratiyya Bila Khiyar [The Lebanese Elections After the War: 1992, 1996, 2000: Democracy without Choice]. Beirut: Al-Nahar, 2000.

185. Abun-Nasr, op. cit., 132.

186. Interview with Abun-Nasr, op. cit., 216.

187. Hizbullah's is careful to clarify that its animosity is towards the US Administration, and not the US people. (This seems to be in conformity with Khumayni's discourse on hakimiyyat Allah or "God's Sovereignty", which is tolerant towards the populace, but not the ruling elite. This stands in sharp contrast to Bin Laden's nihilist discourse that does not distinguish between the two).

188. See Nicholas Blanford, "Hizbullah to issue updated version of manifesto: New 'Open Letter' will reflect changes", Daily Star (28 October 2002), 2.

189. Hizbullah annually celebrates the 29th of January as the "Day of Freedom".

190. I was told by Hizbullah cadres that this is an edited and appended version of the 1998 municipal election program after the recommendations of Hizbullah's "First Municipal Conference". See Mu'tamar Al-Baladiyyat Al-Awwal [The First Municipal Conference/ Convention]. Beirut: Hizbullah's Central Press Office, 16 July 2002. (See "Appendix C").

191. It is worth mentioning that these points have been outlined, before, during, and after the elections, but not in considerable detail, in the following al-Intiqad issues: 1054 (23 April 2004); 1055 (30 April 2004); 1056 (7 May 2004); 1057 (14 May 2004); 1058 (21 May 2004); 1059 (28 May 2004); 1060 (4 June 2004).

192. However, also other factors account for electoral results: (1) Generally the taboo to vote against the Resistance regardless of party program; (2) Lebanon's winner-takes-all majority electoral system pushing out even serious contenders; (3) Syrian influence forcing Hizbullah to leave seats to AMAL; (4)Hizbullah's own strategy to not claim all seats in districts even if it could in order to control guarantee a degree of integration into the Lebanese political system congruent with Resistanceoperations.

193. Al-Intiqad 1057 (14 May 2004), 4-10. In Beirut and Tripoli voter turnout was around 20% and 30% respectively. This is significant because it is much lower than Hizbullah's constituencies, most notably the Biqa' and the South.

194. *Al-Intiqad* 1059 (28 May 2004), 4-9.

195. Compiled from Lebanese daily newspapers and *al-Intiqad* issues: 1054 (23 April 2004); 1055 (30 April 2004); 1056 (7 May 2004); 1057 (14 May 2004); 1058 (21 May 2004); 1059 (28 May 2004); 1060 (4 June 2004).

196. Two leading cadres in the Islamic Resistance were assassinated by blowing up their cars: Ghalib Awali on July 19, 2004 and Ali Husayn Salih on August 2, 2003. The Lebanese government and Hizbullah accused Israel of being behind these assassinations; Israel repeatedly denied any involvement or responsibility in these attacks.

197. Sayyid Fadlallah is the local Lebanese *marja'* who has following among the Shi'ite community in Lebanon and still wields power and influence over *al-hala al-Islamiyya*, being its godfather. Many consider him Hizbullah's spiritual leader, a charge which he persistently denies. It is interesting to note that Fadlallah's declaration of *'id al-fitr* at the end of Ramadan in 2002, which coincided with that of the (Sunni) Mufti of the Lebanese Republic, split the *Dahiya*, Hizbullah's main constituency in Beirut, between Hizbullah's adherents of the Iranian religious authority and Fadlallah's followers who celebrated the *'id* a day before the Hizbullahis. Such eventualities increase the tensions between Hizbullah and the Iranians, on the one hand, and Fadlallah and his followers, on the other hand.

198. See " *'Abna' Al-Tufayli' Yuhajimun Nasrallah* [Tufayli's Followers Chastise Nasrallah]", *Al-Safir* 5 July 2004.

199. Compiled from *Al-Safir* 17 and 18 August 2004; Lebanese daily newspapers of 18 August 2004; and "Hizbullah's Seventh Conclave: Vivid Organization, Stability of Leadership, and A follow up on Recent Events", *Al-Intiqad* 1071 (20 August 2004).

200. See http://www.un.org/News/Press/docs/2004/sc8181.doc.htm

201. This number stands in sharp contrast to the 2000 Christian students who, on November 19, 2004, demonstrated against Syrian presence and domination, calling for the implementation of 1559.

202. It is worth mentioning that on May 21, 2004 Hizbullah alone was able to mobilize half a million to participate in its demonstration.

203. At the time of the appointment, Rima Fakhry was a 38-year old mother of four. She has been a Hizbullah member since the age of 18. She also holds a BS in Agriculture from the American University of Beirut. *Al-Safir* 5 January 2005; *Daily Star* 6 and 7 January 2005; *al-Intiqad* 1091 (7 January 2005).

204. This seems to suggest, more and more, the credibility of Hizbullah's *infitah* policy.

205. An unknown group by the name of "The Organization for Victory and *Jihad* in the Levant" claimed responsibility.

206. See Nasrallah's speech on 8 March 2005.

207. Hamadé is not an organizational member of Hizbullah; rather he is affiliated with the party intellectually and politically. He cooperates with many of Hizbullah's intellectual and media organizations such as CCSD, *al-Intiqad* and academic colleges and universities.

208. Hamadé has also repeatedly met with Jeffrey Feldman, the US Ambassador to Lebanon. *Al-Safir* 19 July 2005.

209. "The Story of US Contacts with Hizbullah: Unofficial Dialogue for Years in Arab and European Capitals", *Al-Mustaqbal* 1982 (19 July 2005), 3.

210. See, for example, the interview with Qasim in *al-Intiqad* 26 April 2005.

211. For instance, Hizbullah's MP Muhammad Fnaysh received 154,056 votes, while Anwar Yasin, the liberated detainee who ran on the communist party ballot, received only 18,244 votes. There was a boycott from some Christian villages in *Jizzin* where the turn out was 23%: *Sidon* (2 Sunni MPs): 43%; *Tyre*: 47%; *Zahrani*: 53%; *Nabatiyyé*: 55%; *Hasbayya*: 42%;

Bint jubayl 47% (in spite of the Christian villages boycott); *Marj'yyun*: 45%. *Al-Nour* 1:00 GMT 6 June 2005. Lebanese daily newspapers the next day.

212. See Abdo Saad, *Al-Intikhabat Al-Niyabiyya li-'Am 2005: Qira'at wa Nata'ij [The Parliamentary Elections of 2005: Readings and Results]*. Beirut: *Markaz Beirut lil Abhath wa Al-Ma'lumat* (The Beirut Centre for Research and Information), 2005. Hajj Abdo Saad is the election and political analyst of the party and the head of this independent research centre.

213. Press conference, Hizbullah's Central Press Office 15 June 2005.

214. Hariri's bloc won 36 seats proper, while its allies appropriated the rest.

215. By way of clarification, it is worth noting that Syria's so-called 'faithful allies' appropriated, in the new parliament, a total of 35 seats made up of the following: Hizbullah (14 seats), AMAL (15 seats), the SSNP (2 seats), the Lebanese Ba'th Party (1 seat), Paqraduni's Phalangists (1 seat), Nicholas Fattush (1 seat), and Michel al-Murr (1 seat).

216. Here is a list of the 14 names with (O) and (N) beside the names to denote old and new respectively: Muhammad Ra'd (O); Muhammad Fnaysh (O); Muhammad Haydar (N); Hasan Fadlallah (N); Hasan Huballah (N); Amin Sherri (N); Ali Ammar (O); Pierre Serhal, Maronite (N); Isma'il Sukariyyé, Sunni (N); Kamel al-Rifa'i, Sunni (N); Ali al-Miqdad (N); Husayn al-Hajj Hasan (O); Jamal al-Taqsh (N); Nawwar al-Sahili (N).

217. *Al-Liwa'* 21 June 2005.

218. See Hizbullah's "Weekly Stand" on 14 June 2005 entitled, "The Islamic view towards tactical political slogans", at: http://arabic.bayynat.org/ahdathwakadaya/ahd14062005.htm.

219. Personal interview 14 December 2005.

220. He reiterated the same stance is a dialogue program at *Sawt Lubnan* (Voice of Lebanon), 23 October 2005.

221. Interview with Brent Sadler, CNN 20 June 2005.

222. These claims have been substantiated by Sa'd Hariri during his interview with CNN, and subsequently with the local press and media.

223. See his speech in the fifth anniversary of the "Liberation" (the Israeli withdrawal from Lebanon) on May 25, 2005. *Al-Intiqad* 1111 (27 May 2005).

224. See *al-Intiqad* 1115 (24 June 2005), entitled, "Expectations after the Elections: Lebanon's Confrontation of (Foreign) Tutelage".

225. Interview with *Al-Safir* 29 July 2005.

226. *Al-Intiqad* 1121 (5 August 2005), 4.

227. Interview with *al-Safir* 29 July 2005.

228. *Al-Intiqad* 1123 (19 August 2005), 6.

229. See *al-Safir* 7 June 2005.

230. See Lebanese daily newspapers the next day.

231. *Al-Safir* 17 August 2005.

232. It was the first time since Lebanese independence that an appointed prime minister gets a high percentage of votes. In a symbolic gesture, the ex-Speaker Husayn al-Husayni as well as Usama Sa'd, an anti-Hariri Sidon MP, abstained.

233. See Joseph Alagha, "Hizbullah and Martyrdom", *ORIENT: German Journal for Politics and Economics of the Middle East*, 45 (March 2004), 1, 63-64.

234. *Al-Nour* 10:00 GMT 15 July 2005.

235. *Al-Nahar* 21 July 2005.

236. All vehemently condemned by Hizbullah.

237. On the results of the elections of the parliamentary committees, see Lebanese daily newspapers of 19 October 2005.

238. *Al-Nour* 13:00 GMT 22 July 2005.

239. 14 deputies voted against; there were 2 abstentions and 20 absentees including 'Aun, Strida Geagea, who was abroad, and most notably Sa'd Hariri and Walid Jumblatt, for security reasons.
240. See *al-Intiqad* 1123 (19 August 2005). In harmony with Hizbullah's leaders, Imam Khamina'i reiterated, during his August 19 Friday sermon, that the *jihad* and resistance of the Palestinian people liberated Gaza. He added that negotiations during the past 70 years did not liberate one iota of Palestinian land. (*Mahr*).
241. Rami Khouri, "The Mehlis Report: Legally Inconclusive, Politically Powerful", *DailyStar* 22 October 2005.
242. *Al-Intiqadnet* and Lebanese National News Agency.

Notes Chapter 2

1. By Shi'ites is meant Twelver Shi'ites who, by the most generous estimates, currently comprise around 16% of the Muslims in the Islamic world. Others argue that they comprise between 10-15%. Graham E. Fuller and Rend Rahim Francke, *The Arab Shi'a: The Forgotten Muslims*. New York: St. Martin's Press, 1999, 12.
2. See section 1 of the Open Letter and Na'im Qasim, *Hizbullah: Al-Manhaj, Al-Tajriba, Al-Mustaqbal [Hizbullah: the Curriculum, the Experience, the Future]*. Beirut: Dar Al-Hadi, 2002, 25-78. Na'im Qasim, Hizbullah's current Deputy Secretary General, is the main ideologue and drafter of Hizbullah's political ideology.
3. Testimony that there is no god but Allah (God), and that Muhammad is His Prophet/Messenger.
4. One-fifth: a religious tax comprising 20% on a person's surplus of income over necessary living expenses.
5. Muhammad Jawad Maghniyyé, *Al-Shi'a wa Al-Hakimun [The Shi'ites and the Rulers]*. Beirut: Al-Maktaba Al-Ahliyya, 1966, 7; Shaykh Muhammad Mahdi Shamseddine, *Nizam Al-Hukum wa Al-Idara fi Al-Islam [The Order of Governance and Administration in Islam]*. Seventh edition. Beirut: Al-Mu'assasa Al-Dawliyya lil Dirasat wa Al-Nashr, 2000, 105; 382. See also Moojan Momen, *An Introduction to Shi'i Islam: The History and Doctrines of Twelver Shi'ism*. New Haven: Yale University Press, 1985, 175-180.
6. Said Amir Arjoumand, "Political Theory and Practice" in: Seyyed Hossein Nasr, Hamid Dabashi, and Seyyed Vali Reza Nasr (eds.), *Expectation of the Millennium: Shi'ism in History*. New York: State University of New York Press, 1989, 110ff.
7. Muhammad Hasanayn Haykal, *Madafi' Ayatullah: Qissat Iran wa Al-Thawra [Ayatullah's Canons: The Story of Iran and the Revolution]*. Cairo: Dar Al-Shuruq, 1982, 105-108.
8. Shamseddine, op. cit., 105-136.
9. Sayyid Husain M. Jafri, *Origins and Early Development of Shi'a Islam*. London: Longman Group Ltd., 1979, 290.
10. Momen, op. cit., 154.
11. Jafri, op. cit., 291.
12. Enayat, op. cit., 22.
13. Jafri, op. cit., 312.
14. James Wilson Morris, "Taqiyah", in: Mircea Eliade (ed.), *The Encyclopedia of Religion*, Vol. VII. (New York: Macmillan Publishing Co., 1987), 317.
15. Shamseddine, op. cit., 380-382.
16. Momen, op. cit., 148-49; 151.
17. Arthur J. Arberry, ed., *The Koran Interpreted*. Oxford: Oxford University Press, 1964, 430.

18. Shamseddine, op. cit., 263.

19. Momen, op. cit., 155.

20. Muhammad Jamal Barut, *Al-Harakat Al-Islamiyya Al-Rahina [Contemporary Islamic Movements]*. Beirut: Riyyad Al-Rayyes Publishing House, 1994, 49-58.

21. Ibn Babawayh Al-Qummi is the author of *Man La Yahduruhu Al-Faqih*, one of the four Shi'ite authoritative collections of *hadith*.

22. See the article entitled: "*Al-'Iqqda Al-Shi'iyya wa Zaman Al-Intiqal ila Al-Aydiulujiyyat Al-Tai'fiyya* (The Shi'ite Complex and the Era of Moving to Sectarian Ideologies)". Beirut: Marasil Al-Anba', 26-27 December 1980.

23. Muhammad Al-Sadr, "Tarikh Al-Ghayba Al-Sughra (The History of the Smaller Occultation)", in: *Mawsu'at Al-Imam Al-Mahdi [The Encyclopaedia of Imam Al-Mahdi]*. Volume I. Beirut: Dar Al-Ta'awun, 1992, 324-341.

24. Muhammad Al-Sadr, "Tarikh Al-Ghayba Al-Kubra (The History of the Greater Occultation)", in: *Mawsu'at Al-Imam Al-Mahdi [The Encyclopaedia of Imam Al-Mahdi]*. Volume II. Beirut: Dar Al-Ta'awun, 1992, 19-45.

25. See Bihbahani's (1706-1792) contribution to *wilayat al-faqih* in section *2.1.2 Historical survey of the doctrine*.

26. Haykal, op. cit., 129ff.

27. Depending on the specialty and the level of expertise of the *mujtahid*, the Shi'ites employed the doctrine of summing from here and there (*taba'ud*) in order to follow the most knowledgeable *mujtahid* in the field that they seek counsel in.

28. Abdallah Al-Nufaysi, *Dawr Al-Shi'a fi Tatawwur Al-Iraq Al-Siyasi Al-Hadith [The Role of the Shi'a in the Development of the Modern Political Iraq]*. Beirut: Al-Nahar, 1986, 30-86; Joyce N. Wiley, *The Islamic Movement of Iraqi Shi'as*. London: Lynne Rienner Publishers, 1992, 121-122; Juan Cole, *Sacred Space and Holy War: The Politics, Culture and History of Shi'ite Islam*. London: I. B. Tauris, 2002, 58-77; See also *Ara' fi Al-Marja'iyya Al-Shi'iyya [Views on the Shi'ite Religious Authority]*. Beirut: Dar Al-Rawda, 1994, especially, pp. 481-501.

29. Chibli Mallat, *The Renewal of Islamic Law: Muhammad Baqer as-Sadr, Najaf and the Shi'i International*. Cambridge: Cambridge University Press, 1993, 39-40.

30. Ali Ahmad Al-Bahadli, *Al-Hawza Al-'Ilmiyya fi Al-Najaf: Ma'alimuha wa Harakatuha Al-Islahiyya (1920-1980) [The Religious Seminary in Najaf: Features and Reformist Trends]*. Beirut: Dar Al-Zahra', 1993, 274. (It is worth mentioning that none of Hizbullah's leading cadres studied in *Qum*; rather all of them graduated from *Najaf*).

31. Ibid., 194-195; 270-275.

32. Ibid., 201-214.

33. Fu'ad Ibrahim, *Al-Faqih wa Al-Dawla: Al-Fikar Al-Siyasi Al-Shi'i [The Jurisprudent and the State: Shi'ite Political Thought]*. Beirut: Dar Al-Kunuz Al-Adabiyya, 1998. See also *Ara' fi Al-Marja'iyya Al-Shi'iyya*, op. cit.

34. 'Allamah Tabataba'i, "Taqiyyah" in: Seyyed Hossein Nasr, Hamid Dabashi, and Seyyed Vali Reza Nasr, (eds.), *Shi'ism: Doctrines, Thought, and Spirituality*. New York: State University of New York Press, 1988, 204-205.

35. Morris, "Taqiyah", op. cit., 317.

36. Enayat, op. cit., 176; Jafri, op. cit., 300.

37. R. Strothmann, "Takiya", in: M. TH Houtsma et al. (eds). *The Encyclopedia of Islam*. Vol. IV. (London: Luzac and Co., 1934), 628. It is worth mentioning that Enayat argues along similar lines. Enayat, op. cit., 179-80.

38. Tabataba'i, op. cit., 205.

39. Momen, op. cit., 183.

40. Enayat, op. cit., 176.

41. See also Qur'an 49:13. Morris, op. cit., 337.
42. Strothmann, op. cit., 628.
43. Jafri, op. cit., 299.
44. Enayat, op. cit., 176.
45. Jafri, op. cit., 298.
46. Enayat, op. cit, 175-77.
47. Strothmann, op. cit., 628.
48. Momen, op. cit, 183.
49. The "linkage between the divine investiture and the creation of an Islamic world order became a salient feature of Islamic ideological discourse almost from the beginning. Accordingly, the basic religious focus on the creation of just order and leadership, which can create and maintain it, orients the world view of Muslims in general and of the Shi'ite Muslims in particular". Abdulaziz Sachedina, "Activist Shi'ism in Iran, Iraq and Lebanon", in: Martin E. Marty and R. Scott Appleby, (eds). *Fundamentalisms Observed*. Vol. I. Chicago: The University of Chicago Press, 1991, 421.
50. *Muharram* is the first month of the year in the Muslim AH lunar calendar.
51. See "The Martyrdom of Husayn", in: Jafri, op. cit., 174-221.
52. For a substantial portion of Shi'ite history, these ritual celebrations were performed underground so as to avoid confrontation with the Sunni rulers. For instance, see the section entitled, "The Vitality of Religious Experience in Islam", in Sachedina, op. cit., 407-410.
53. Momen, op. cit., 220.
54. Strothmann contends that "It is also to be noticed that the *takiya* of the Shi'is is not a voluntary ideal…, but one should avoid a martyrdom that seems unnecessary and useless and preserve oneself for the faith and one's co-religionists". Strothmann, op. cit., 629.
55. Due to the strong impact of *taqiyya* and quietist waiting, most Shi'ite jurists forbid *jihad* during the occultation period. See Ahmad Al-Katib, *Tatawwur Al-Fikr Al-Siyasi Al-Shi'i: Min Al-Shura ila Wilayat Al-Faqih [The Development of the Shi'ite Political Thought: From Consultation to the Rule of the Jurisprudent]*. Beirut: Dar Al-Jadid, 1998, 292-299.
56. It is noteworthy that *ta'bi'a* has been practiced among most of the Muslim sects that were put in defensive situations, or felt that they had to fulfil the obligation of launching *jihad*.
57. See for instance, Abdulaziz Sachedina, "The Rule of the Religious Jurist in Iran" in: John L. Esposito and R.K. Ramazani (eds.), *Iran at the Crossroads*. (New York: Palgrave, 2001), 131-2, 145; Bernard Lewis, "The Shi'a in Islamic History", in: Martin Kramer (ed.), *Shi'ism, Resistance, and Revolution*. Boulder, CO.: Westview Press, 1987, 32.
58. Sachedina, "Activist Shi'ism in Iran, Iraq and Lebanon", 420.
59. Ibid., 408. (My emphasis).
60. Imam Khumayni refers to the renaissance of the Iranian people, which began since the June 1963 uprising, and is still being enlarged and deepened. See Imam Khumayni, *Sahifat Al-Thawra Al-Islamiyya: Nass Al-Wasiyya Al-Siyasiyya Al-Ilahiyya Lil-Imam Al-Khumayni, Qa'id Al-Thawra Al-Islamiyya [The (Religious) Book of the Islamic Revolution: The Text of the Political-Divine Will of Imam Khumayni, the Leader of the Islamic Revolution]*. Beirut: Iranian Cultural Centre, 1989, 19. Imam Khumayni wrote his will in 1404 AH/1983AD; he did minor editing to it after five years. It was revealed for the first time in the Islamic *Shura* Council, on June 4, 1989, one day after his death. Since its publication, Khumayni's will has been in the curriculum of every Iranian University.

61. Momen, op. cit., 105-123. Cf. Said Amir Arjomand, The Shadow of God and the Hidden Imam. Chicago: The University of Chicago Press, 1984, 109-209.

62. Momen, op. cit, 246-249. In more recent years, the Shi'ite resistance in Iraq and finally the resistance of Hizbullah in south Lebanon can be seen and comprehended in this context.

63. Ibid., 157.

64. Abdulaziz Sachedina, Islamic Messianism: The Idea of Mahdi in Twelver Shiism. Alabany, NY.: State University of New York Press, 1980, 6.

65. See for instance, Khaykh Muhsin Kadivar, Nazariyyat Al-Dawla fi Al-Fiqh Al-Shi'i: Buhuth fi Wilawat Al-Faqih [The Theory of the State in the Shi'ite Jurisprudence: Research in the Rule of the Religious Jurist]. Beirut: Dar al-Jadid, 2000. Kadivar argues that Shi'ite jurisprudence has laid the foundations of nine theories of wilaya.

66. Also known as al-Muhaqqiq al-Thani, a Lebanese activist from Jabal 'Amil, was one of those 'ulama who were instrumental in the dissemination of Shi'ism in Iran during the Safavid Dynasty. As mentioned earlier, under the Safavids, Shi'i Islam became Iran's official religion.

67. Momen, op. cit., 190.

68. Haykal, op. cit., 127-131.

69. Al-Shaykh Ahmad Al-Naraqi, Wilayat Al-Faqih. Introduction and Commentary by Sayyid Yasin Al-Musawi. Beirut: Dar Al-Ta'aruf lil Matbu'at, 1995, 107ff.

70. Tanbih Al-Umma wa Tanzih Al-Milla fi Wujub Al-Mashruta (Warning/Awakening of the Umma and the Purification of Religion in the Conditional/Required Duties) is considered the enlightened ideology of the Constitutional Revolution of 1906. This book is regarded as a rare document in the theory of political Shi'ism, in particular, and Islamic reformist discourse, in general.

71. Hisba is a religious principle sanctioned in the Qur'an: "Those who, if We establish them firmly in the land, will perform the prayer, give the alms, command the good and prohibit the evil. To Allah belongs the outcome of all affairs" (22:41). The Qur'an stipulates hisba as a necessity for the good of the community. Since it was incumbent upon the ruler to enjoin the good and forbid the evil, he executed the hisba by obeying the religious and moral injunctions of Islam, and he made his subjects comply with these injunctions. Hisba also covered a wide range of financial, administrative, political, and social matters. As such, hisba became a political interpretation of this religious principle. From here originates the usage of al-wilaya al-hisbiyya. See for instance "Jurisdictions based on the hisbi domain", in: Al-Shaykh Malik Mustapha Wehbe Al-'Amili, Al-Faqih wa Al-Sulta wa Al-Umma: Buhuth fi Walayat Al-Faqih [The Jurisprudent, The Authority, and the Umma: Studies in Wilayat Al-Faqih and the Umma]. Beirut: Al-Dar Al-Islamiyya, 2000, 252-256.

72. Al-taklif al-shar'i al-Ilahi refers to the delegated responsibility/obligation of the muqalidin – followers of the muqallad (emulated) in law and ritual – towards the muqallad. Al-taklif al-shar'i al-Ilahi will be referred to as taklif, which is loosely translated (by Hizbullah) as "legitimate and religious responsibility". It is worth mentioning that the concept of taklif is a term used for legal obligation in usul al-fiqh (the methodology of Islamic jurisprudence).

73. See also a review of Na'ini's book Tanbih Al-Umma in Al-Ghadir 2 (March 1991), 12-13, 69; and Nasr et al, (eds.), Expectation of the Millennium..., 314-318.

74. See Al-Shaykh Muhammad Bin Al-Hasan Al-Hurr Al-'Amili, Wasa'il Al-Shi'a [Shi'ite Rituals]. Volume 11 "Jihad". Beirut: Mu'assat Al-Hulul, Bayt Ihya' Al-Turath, 1993. All Shi'ite books ultimately refer to it being the most authoritative classical compilation of the Shi'ite

concordance of hadith and Shi'ite doctrines by the Lebanese Al-Hurr Al-'Amili who died in 1104 AH/1692 AD.

75. See Al-Shaykh Al-Rikabi, *Al-Jihad fi Al-Islam: Dirasa Mawdu'iyya Tahliliyya Tabhath bi Al-Dalil Al-'Ilmi al-Fiqhi 'an Al-Jihad wa 'Anasiruhu bi Al-Tanzil wa Al-Sunna [Al-Jihad in Islam: An Objective-Analytical Study that Researches the Jurisprudential-Scientific Evidence/Proof on Jihad and its Components in Revelation and Traditions]*. Beirut: Dar Al-Fikr Al-Mu'asir, 1997, 15-20 (Shi'ite author); and Bashir al-Bahrani, *Al-'Unf wa Al-Irhab wa Al-Jihad: Qura'a fi Al-Mustalahat wa Al-Mafahim [Violence, Terrorism, and Jihad: A Reading in Terminology and Concepts]*. Beirut: Dar Al-Hadi, 2003, 39-41 (Shi'ite author).

76. Al-Kulyami, Muhammad Ibn Ya'qub, *Al-Kafi*. Edited by 'Ali Akbar Ghaffari. Volume 5. Tehran: Maktabat Al-Saqquq, 1961, 2.

77. Al-Kulyami, op. cit., 4. Cf. *Al-Jihad wa Khisal Al-Mujahidin [Jihad and the Martyrs' Traits]*. Beirut: Markaz Baqiyyat Allah, 1999, 135-166.

78. At that time, the horses were the sign of conquest and the symbol of the military forces. It is worth mentioning that during battles and conquests, the horse riders (knights, cavaliers) were given more spoils than other fighters (infantry, for instance); the horse being the modern equivalent of a tank.

79. Ibn Babawayh, *Al-Amali*. Qum: Al-Bi'tha, 1997, 673.

80. This is in conformity with the specific meaning of *jihad* as the total devotion in performing one's religious duty, be it in action or in intention (desire).

81. *Al-Jihad wa Khisal Al-Mujahidin*, 135. The trait of "Dignity is the opposite of humiliation, and death to humiliation" is attributed to Imam Husayn and Imam Ali. Ibid., 54. See also *Nahj Al-Balagha*. Volume 6. Beirut: Dar Al-Adwa', 1986, 90.

82. *Al-Amali*, 553.

83. See the "Secrets of Jihad" in Al-'Arif Al-Qadi Sa'id Al-Qummi, *Asrar Al-'Ibadat [The Secrets of Worship]*. Beirut: Markaz Baqiyyat Allah, 1999, 137-150.

84. *Al-Jihad wa Khisal Al-Mujahidin*, 31-46. This book bases itself on a host of authoritative Shi'ite sources including: Al-Hurr Al-'Amili's *Wasa'il Al-Shi'a*; Khumayni's *Tahrir Al-Wasila* among other books; Imam 'Ali's *Nahj Al-Balagha* among other books; the four prominent Shi'ite collection of *hadith* books (Al-Kulyami's *Al-Kafi*; Al-Tusi's *Al-Tahdhib* and *Al-Istibsar*; Ibn Babawayh Al-Qummi's *Man La Yahduruhu Al-Faqih*), etc.

85. *Al-Jihad wa Khisal Al-Mujahidin*, 31-32.

86. Ibid., 32ff: Al-Kulyami, op. cit., Volume 5, 2.

87. For the sake of clarity I have numbered the eight mundane (worldly/material) relations. As would be demonstrated later on, Qasim refers to the same Qur'anic verse in order to substantiate his argument.

88. *Al-Jihad wa Khisal Al-Mujahidin*, 32-34.

89. Ibid., 43-46.

90. For instance, see Majid Fakhry, *The Qur'an: A Modern English Version*. Reading: Garnet Publishing Ltd., 1997, 118 (Lebanese Shi'ite author; I am almost always quoting the Qur'anic verses from his translation); A. Yusuf Ali, *The Holy Qur'an: Translation and Commentary*. Fourth printing. Lahore: Islamic Propagation Center, 1993, 456 (Pakistani Sunni author); Muhammad Taqi-ud-Din Al-Hilali and Muhammad Muhsin Khan, *Translation of the meanings of The Noble Qur'an in the English Language*. Madinah: King Fahd Complex for the Printing of The Holy Qur'an, 1420 A. H., 1999 A.D, 252 (Saudi Sunni author).

91. *Al-Jihad wa Khisal Al-Mujahidin*, 88; Al-Rikabi, op. cit., 265; and Al-Hurr Al-'Amili, op. cit., Volume 11 "Jihad", 48.

92. The Shah's regime was classified under this category.

93. Imam Khumayni, *Kashf Al-Asrar [The Revelation of Secrets]*. Beirut: Dar wa Maktabat Al-Rasul Al-Akram, 1992, 132-134; 192-194; and *Al-Hukumat al-Islamiyya [Islamic Government]*. Tehran: The Institute of Coordinating and Publishing Imam Khumayni's Heritage, 1996, 60-65; 138-144;191-199.

94. Imam Khumayni, as cited in: Hamid Algar, *Roots of the Islamic Revolution in Iran*. Revised and expanded edition. New York: Islamic Publications International, 2001, 130.

95. A literal traslation states, "was not present".

96. Imam Khumayni, *Kashf Al-Asrar*…, 169-170.

97. Imam Khumayni, *Al-Istiqama wa Al-Thabat [Straightforwardness and Steadfastness]*. Translated by Qazim Yasim. Beirut, 1992, 156-169.

98. Khumayni, *Al-Istiqama wa Al-Thabat*…, 303ff.

99. From now on, *al-waliyy al-faqih* will be referred to as *faqih*, who is the official Iranian *marja' al-taqlid* (authority of emulation).

100. Khumayni, *Al-Hukuma Al-Islamiyya*, 45ff.

101. Faleh Abdul-Jabar, "The Genesis and Development of Marja'ism versus the State", in: Faleh Abdul-Jabar (ed.), *Ayatollahs, Sufis And Ideologues: State, religion and Social Movements in Iraq*. (London: Saqi Books, 2002), 61-89.

102. Khumayni, *Al-Hukuma Al-Islamiyya*, 80ff.

103. Momen, op. cit., 196-97; 296.

104. For instance, (14:52); (15:2); (22:49); (33:40); (36:70).

105. Khumayni, *Al-Hukuma Al-Islamiyya*, 47.

106. Islamic law and jurisprudence regards this as a crime in its own right that has its stipulated legal penalties and punishments (*hudud*).

107. Khumayni, *Al-Hukuma Al-Islamiyya*, 86-88; 135-138.

108. It is worth noting that Imam Khumayni's infallibility is of a different nature than that of Prophet Muhammad, the Twelve Imams, and Fatima Al-Zahra'. However, there seems to be a consensus among Shi'ite jurists that Imam Khumayni has not committed any mistake. (See for instance, *Thawrat Al-Faqih wa Dawlatuhu: Qira'at fi 'Alamiyyat Madrasat Al-Imam Al-Khumayni [The Revolution of the Jurisprudent and his Government: Readings in the Global Nature of Imam Khumayni's School]*. Second edition. Compiled by Muhammad Mahdi Ruhani. Beirut: Mu'assat Al-Balagh, 2002). This claim is also substantiated by popular religion, where it is widely believed that Imam Khumayni conducted regular meetings with Imam al-Mahdi and did not take a decision except by consulting with him. However, according to official religion, Imam Khumayni is considered the deputy of Imam al-Mahdi in religious, social, and *political* domains.

109. Hamid Algar, "Development of the Concept of *velayat-i faqih* since the Islamic Revolution in Iran". Paper presented at London Conference on Wilayat al-faqih (June 1988), as quoted by Sachedina, "The Rule of the Religious Jurist…", 134, 136. (Italics in original). Also published in Farsi in *Kayhan* 13223 (16 *Jamadi Al-Awwal* 1409/ 6 January 1989).

110. See for instance, Hamid Mavini, "Analysis of Khomeini's Proofs for *al-Wilaya al-Mutlaqa* (Comprehensive Authority) of the Jurist", in: Linda S. Walbridge (ed.), *The Most Learned of the Shi'a: The Institution of Marja' Taqlid*. (Oxford: Oxford University Press, 2001), 183-201.

111. Imam Khumayni, *Tahrir Al-Wasila* as cited in *Al-Jihad wa Khisal Al-Mujahidin*, 35-37.

112. Cf. Prophet Muhammad's hadith: "The martyrs have certain dignities *[karamat]* that are not ascribed to the Prophets including me".

113. Imam Khumayni, "A Speech Given to a Delegation of Customs Officials", 27 March 1979, as cited in: Algar, *Roots of the Islamic Revolution in Iran*, 161ff.

114. Imam Khumayni, *Tahrir Al-Wasila*. Volume 1. Beirut: Dar Al-Ta'aruf, 1981, 485. *Tahrir Al-Wasila* is Imam Khumayni's *risala 'amaliyya*. See *1.1.3.2 Stages of ijtihad (independent reasoning) leading to marja'iyya.*

115. The most salient verses are the following: (61:11-12): "Believe in Allah and His Apostle and struggle [practice jihad] in the cause of Allah with your possessions and yourselves. This is far better for you, if only you knew. He will then forgive you your sins and admit you into gardens, beneath which rivers flow, and into the dwellings in the Garden of Eden. This is the great triumph". (49: 15): "Indeed, the believers are those who have believed in Allah and His Apostle, then were not in doubt, but struggled with their possessions and themselves in the cause of Allah. Those are the truthful ones". (9:41): "Charge forth, on foot or mounted, and struggle with your possessions and yourselves in the way of Allah. That is far better for you, if only you knew". (4:95): "Those of the believers who stay at home while suffering from no injury are not equal to those who fight for the cause of Allah with their possessions and persons. Allah has raised those who fight with their possessions and persons one degree over those who stay at home; and to each Allah has promised the fairest good. Yet Allah has granted a great reward to those who fight and not to those who stay behind". (3:169): "And do not think that those who have been killed ['martyred'] in the way of Allah as dead; they are rather living with their Lord, well-provided for".

116. Imam Khumayni as cited by The Lebanese Council of Muslim Ulama, *Masa'il Jihadiyya wa Hukm Al-'Amaliyat Al-Istishhadiyyah [Jihadi Issues and the Judgement of Martyrdom Operations]*. Beirut: Dar Al-Wihda Al-Islamiyya, 2002, 27-28.

117. Imam Khumayni, 1 November 1979, as cited in Richard T. Antoun, *Understanding Fundamentalism: Christian, Islamic, and Jewish Movements*. Oxford: Altamira Press, 2001, 43. Imam Khumayni offered Qur'anic substantiation on the notion of self-sacrifice.

118. Imam Khumayni as quoted by Joyce M. Davis, "The Child as Soldier Martyr: Iran's Mohammad Hosein Fahmideh", *Martyrs: Innocence, Vengeance and Despair in the Middle East*. New York: Palgrave Macmillan , 2003, 45.

119. The *Bassidji* comprised around half a million volunteer young Iranian boys, around the age of twelve, who fought in the front lines. These people were well known for their self-sacrifice. They were integrated in the *Pasdaran*, but they preserved their identity. See Farhad Khosrokhavar, *L'Islamisme et la Mort: Le Martyre Revolutionnare en Iran [Islamism and Death: The Revolutionary Martyrs in Iran]*. Paris: L'Harmattan, 1995, 415.

120. Imam Khumayni, *Al-Jihad Al-Akbar [Greater Jihad]*. Translated by Husayn Kurani. Tehran: Islamian Grand Library, 1980, 31-36.

121. Ibid., 22-23.

122. Ibid., 57-59; 67-82.

123. Ibid., 29.

124. Ibid., 24-25.

125. It is very difficult for an English translation to capture the meticulous difference or the nuance between the two.

126. Bilal N'im, "The Reality and the Concealed in Imam Khumayni's 'Irfan", *al-Intiqad* 1120 (29 July 2005).

127. For instance, see "Characteristics of *Marja' Al-Taqlid* and *Al-Waliyya Al-Faqih*", in *Fiqh Al-Shari'a [The Jurisprudence of the Shari'a]*. Volume I, fifth edition. Beirut: Dar Al-Malak, 2001, 17-19. See also *al-Shira'* 26 May and 4 August 1986.

128. Some of the authors who subscribe to this view are the following: Talib Aziz, "Fadlallah and the Remaking of the Marja'iyya", in: *The Most Learned of the Shi'a…*, 207; Ajami, op. cit., 213-

218; Fuller, op. cit., 28; and Martin Kramer, "The Oracle of Hizbullah", in: *Spokesmen for the Despised*. Edited by R. Scott Appleby. Chicago: The University of Chicago Press, 1997, 84.

129. This and the foregoing analysis crystallised as a result of the author's personal discussions with Hani 'Ali Abdallah, Fadlallah's political and press advisor, on at least two occasions: 27 December 2001 and 14 December 2005.

130. Muhammad Husayn Fadlallah, *Al-Haraka Al-Islamiyya: Humum wa Qadaya [The Islamic Movement: Worries and Causes]*. Fourth edition. Beirut: Dar Al-Malak, 2001, 65-108; 308-316.

131. Hani 'Ali Abdallah as well as Faruq Rizq and Ja'far 'Aqil, Fadlallah's Al-Mabarrat Association directors, warranted this and the foregoing analysis through personal discussions with the author on 14 December 2005. Even recently, it seems that Fadlallah's thought continues to influence Hizbullah. Since Fadlallah calls for active resistance to the Israeli occupation of Arab land, his book *Iradat Al-Quwwa* finds a special resonance to Hizbullah, especially after the nearly complete Israeli withdrawal from Lebanon in May 2000. In this connection Sayyid Hasan Nasrallah, Hizbullah's Secretary General, argues, "Because the power of right is not enough in a unipolar world controlled by the US, then it is imperative on us to possess the right of power along with the power of right". See his speech in the third anniversary of the liberation on May 25, 2003 at: http://www.nasrollah.org/arabic/hassan/khitabat/2003/khitabat93.htm (Last accessed April 2005).

132. Cf. "Fadlallah, who is considered close to Hizbollah but who rejects being called the organization's spiritual leader...". Daniel Sobelman, *Rules of the Game: Israel and Hizbullah After the Withdrawal from Lebanon*. Memorandum No. 69. Tel Aviv university: Jaffee Center for strategic Studies, January 2004, 117, at: http://www.tau.ac.il/jcss/memoranda/memo69.pdf.

133. Kramer, "The Oracle of Hizbullah", 84.

134. *Al-Harakat al-Islamiyya fi Lubnan*, op. cit., 175-176.

135. Al-Madini, *Amal wa Hizbullah...*, 203. For an insider's view on the relationship between Ayatullah Fadlallah and Hizbullah refer to: Hasan Fadlallah, *Al-Khiyar al-Akhar*, 83-89. Nabih Berri stressed that *AMAL* follows Fadlallah's *marja'iyya*. Adnan El-Ghoul, "At Shiite conclave, Berri backs Iran's nuclear quest: Observers see 'deal' to Boost Amal prestige", *Daily Star* 20 August 2004.

136. The living Imam is Imam al-Mahdi, whose occultation makes him away from people's sight. (See Qasim, *Hizbullah: Al-Manhaj...*, 388).

137. Salim Al-Hasani, *Al-Ma'alim Al-Jadida Lil-Marja'iyya Al-Shi'iyya [The New Features of the Shi'ite Marja'iyya]*. Third edition. Beirut: Dar Al-Malak, 1994, especially 48-58; see also Al-Madini, *Amal wa Hizbullah...*, 201.

138. This continued till Imam Khumayni's death in June 1989.

139. Talal Salman, *Sira Dhatiyya li Haraka Muqawina 'Arabiyya Muntasira: Hizbullah [An Autobiography of a Victorious Arab Resistance Movement: Hizbullah]*. Beirut: Al-Safir, June 2000, 4. See the following web page: http://www.nasrollah.org/arabic/hassan/sera/about002.htm. That is why it is not surprising that Hizbullah allocated, in its "Open Letter" or political constitution, a special section dealing with the dangers of *fitna*. See "Appendix A", section 22: "God is With the Unity of the Muslims".

140. Hasan Fadlallah, op. cit., 35; 163-183. As of 1998 the signature and motto changed to "Hizbullah – The Islamic *Resistance* in Lebanon". (Italics added for emphasis).

141. Ali Al-Kurani, a Hizbullah middle rank cadre, was the first to expose the social movement's mobilization strategies in his book entitled, *Tariqat Hizbullah fi Al-'Amal Al-Islami [Hizbullah's Method of Islamic Mobilization]*. Tehran, Maktab Al-I'lam Al-Islami: Al-Mu'assa Al-'Alamiyya, 1985, 9-20; 165-181.

142. Prospective recruits have to undergo stringent mobilizational training that might last for more than one year. During that period they undergo intensive Islamic cultural indoctrination, on the basis of which they are evaluated in terms of behaviour and action that should reflect the Shi'ite religious ideological norms that Hizbullah built its method of Islamic mobilization upon. After passing this stage the recruits have to be strictly disciplined (*intizam*) in two important categories: (1) following the orders in the chain of command or pyramidical structure, come what may; and (2) undergo intensive military training, which is a must incumbent upon all of Hizbullah's rank and file even though some of them might not be engaged at all in smaller military jihad while fulfilling their membership. See Sharif al-Husayni's article "*Hizbullah: Haraka 'Askariyya am Siyasiyya am Diniyya?* (Hizbullah: A Military or Political or religious Movement?)", under the section: "*Hala Mutafari'a 'an Al-Thawra Al-Islamiyya fi Iran* (An Upshot of the Islamic Republic of Iran). Beirut: *Al-Shira'* (17 March 1986), 14-21, especially 20-21.

143. Hasan Fadlallah, op. cit., 39-43; Qasim, op. cit., 23.

144. Cf. Saad-Ghorayed even goes as far as asserting that Hizbullah's "individual members are free to emulate another *marja'* as some of its adherents do". See *Hizbullah: Politics and Religion*, 65.

145. Qasim, op. cit., 75.

146. Al-Madini also confirms Qasim's stance and explanation. See *Amal wa Hizbullah*..., 176

147. Qasim, op. cit., 75-76.

148. There seems to be a consensus among the following that this is the case: Prof. Masud Islami (Former Rector of School of International Relations (SIR); Prof Hemmati (Expert on religion and philosophy, specialized in development and modernity; advisor to Khamina'i); Prof. Mohammad Reza Dehshiri (Head of Regional Studies Dept. at SIR and an expert on Iranian foreign policy); and Prof. Mohammad Reza Maleki (Director of Diplomacy and International Relations at SIR the Deputy Dean of School of Law and Political Science, Azad University, Karaj. He is an expert on the Middle East and the Arab-Israeli conflict). I conducted these interviews between August 30 and September 6, 2002. I also learned that Khamina'i is fully conversant with the ebb and flow of the Lebanese political system and public sphere even more than a local. This seems to explain why Hizbullah follows Khamina'i's injunctions.

149. Hizbullah's primary sources: Sheikh Hasan Trad; Sayyid Ibrahim Amin al-Sayyid; Ali Akbar Muhtashami; Shaykh Hasan Srur (*al-'Ahd*, no. 146).

150. *Al-Harakat al-Islamiyya fi Lubnan*, op. cit., 323-336. Cf Khumayni, *Al-Hukuma Al-Islamiyya*, 60ff.

151. He was *AMAL*'s deputy president. In 1982 he defected and founded Islamic *AMAL*, which later became part of Hizbullah.

152. Interview conducted by *al-Shira'* on October 26, 1983 as cited in *Al-Harakat al-Islamiyya fi Lubnan*, op. cit. 219-233.

153. As argued by Qasim in: *Al-Harb Al-Sadisa: Al-Ijtiyah Al-Sahyuni Li-Lubnan 1982 [The Sixth War: The Zionist Invasion of Lebanon 1982]*. Vol. II, Episode 3. Beirut: Dar Al-Manar Li-Intaj Al-Mar'i wa Al-Tawzi', 2002.

154. Qasim, op. cit., 44-45. The explanation of the Qur'anic verse (22:78) is borne out by Tabataba'i. Cf. *Al-Jihad wa Khisal Al-Mujahidin*, 31-37.

155. Qasim, op. cit., 53-54.

156. Ibid., 44.

157. Ibid., 55.

158. Ibid., 53.

159. See section 1 of the Open Letter: "The main sources of our culture are the venerable Qur'an, the infallible Sunna, and the rules and religious edicts made by the jurist (*faqih*), the authority of emulation. These sources are clear, uncomplicated, and accessible to all *without* exception and they need no theorisation or philosophy. All they need is abidance and application".

160. Qasim, op. cit., 51.

161. Ibid., 44.

162. Ibid., 55.

163. Ibid., 59-61.

164. "Ahzab Lubnan...", Part I (1979-1989). *NBN*, 21 July 2002.

165. 'Ali Al-Kurani, op. cit., 104-113.

166. Ibid., 143.

167. Ibid., 171-173.

168. Ibid., 175-177.

169. Qasim, op. cit, 58.

170. Ibid., 55.

171. Ibid., 61-62.

172. Qasim insinuates that Islamic movements and Hizbullah employ upbringing on the concept of martyrdom; that is why they were and still are victorious. While nationalistic movements use upbringing on the concept of victory, reaping nothing but defeat and treason. Ibid., 58-59.

173. Ibid., 58.

174. See Sami Moubayed, "Lebanon guided by the Nasrullah factor", *The Asia Times*, 26 February 2005. Via the internet at: http://atimes01.atimes.com/atimes/Middle_East/GB26Ak03.html.

175. Qasim, *Hizbullah: Al-Manhaj...*, 58.

176. See *Al-Harb Al-Sadisa...*, Vol. II, Episode 6. (Italics added for emphasis).

177. Al-Sayyid Muhammad Husayn Fadlallah, "*Al-Thawra Al-Islasmiyya fi Iran: Ta'amulat min Al-Dakhil* [The Islamic Revolution in Iran: Reflections from the Inside]", *Al-Muntalaq*, 8 (January 1980), 11-12, as cited by Kramer, "The Oracle of Hizbullah", 109.

178. Martin Kramer, *The Moral Logic of Hizbullah*. The Dayan Center for Middle Eastern and African Studies. Occasional Papers. 101. Tel Aviv University: The Shiloah Institute, August 1987,16.

179. *Al-Liwa'* 9 July 1984.

180. Although Imam Husayn did not blow himself (simply because there were no explosives at the time), Imam Husayn is considered *sayyid al-shuhada*, the "Lord of the Martyrs" and "The Immortal Maryr" according to Shi'ite religious doctrine since he faced a superior army in the battlefield knowing for sure that he was going to die. See Enayat, *Modern Islamic Political Thought...*, 181-194. Enayat includes martyrdom as one of the three "aspects of Shi'i modernism", the other two being constitutionalism and *taqiyya* (expedient dissimulation).

181. Imam Khumayni, *Kashf Al-Asrar...*, 169-170. Imam Khumayni, *Al-Istiqama wa Al-Thabat*, 156-169.

182. For a detailed discussion of Hizbullah's analysis of Imam Husayn's martyrdom see Na'im Qasim, *'Ashura: Madad wa Hayat ['Ashura: Replenishment and Life]*. Second expanded edition. Beirut: Dar Al-Hadi, 2003, especially pages 85-217.

183. Qasim, *Hizbullah: Al-Manhaj...*, 60.

184. Kramer, *The Moral Logic of Hizbullah*, 9.

185. Council of Muslim Ulama, op. cit., 25-42.

186. Fadlallah is referring to those, who during the annual commemoration of '*Ashura*, practice self-flagellation and self-immolation by beating their chests, slashing their scalps with swords, and whipping themselves with chains.

187. Speech by Fadlallah, *Al-Nahar* 27 September 1985, as cited by Martin Kramer in "Sacrifice and 'Self-Martyrdom' in Shi'ite Lebanon". *Terrorism and Political Violence* 3, (Autumn 1991) 3, 30-47 at: http://www.geocities.com/martinkramerorg/Sacrifice.htm, 9-10.

188. I compiled this material by heavy reliance on an extended dialogue with Hizbullah's deputy secretary general, Shaykh Na'im Qasim, on the subject of "*Al-Shahada wa al-'Ithar*" [Martyrdom and "Preference"] in the program entitled "*Al-Din wa Al-Hayat [Religion and life]*", *Al-Manar*, 10 October 2002.

189. Prophet Muhammad said: "The martyrs have certain dignities [*karamat*] that are not ascribed to the Prophets including me. If I die, I am washed and wrapped in a burial shroud; however, the martyr is neither washed nor wrapped in a burial shroud... The Angels wash him". See Al-Hurr Al-'Amili, *Wasa'il Al-Shi'a...*, 506-511, *hadiths* 1 to 12, *abwab ghusl al-mayyit* (sections of the washing of the dead), specifically *ghusl al-shahid* (the washing of the martyr), in *bab* 14 (section 14), *hadith* 7.

190. Sayyid Muhammad Husayn Fadlallah states this unequivocally as a fact. See *Fiqh Al-Shari'a [The Jurisprudence of the Shari'a]*. Volume I, first edition. Beirut: Dar Al-Malak, 1983, 192.

191. Hizbullah offered 1281 martyrs from the second Israeli invasion in June 1982 till the nearly complete Israeli withdrawal in May 2000.

192. Al-Khamina'i, '*Itr Al-Shahada...*, 17.

193. Interview with Sayyid Husayn al-Musawi conducted by *al-Shira'* on 26 October 1983.

194. Again Qasim affirmed that this is an immutable principle.

195. Qasim, *Hizbullah: Al-Manhaj...*, 62ff; Qasim, "*Al-Shahada wa al-'Ithar*".

196. *Masa'il Jihadiyya...*, 25-42.

197. "Ahzab Lubnan...", Part I (1979-1989); *Al-Harb Al-Sadisa...* From the perspective of theoretical and practical ethics, the foundation rests on the distinction between what psychological egoism calls suicide: "All voluntary human actions are selfishly motivated", and what normative ethical theories label as altruism. Suicide is the opposite of altruistic or self-sacrificial behaviour. Altruism is a supererogatory act, i.e. an act done beyond the call of moral duty or obligation. See Tom L. Beauchamp, *Philosophical Ethics: An Introduction to Moral Philosophy*. Second edition. New York: McGraw-Hill, Inc., 1991, 68-79, 241-244, 246-248; and Peter Singer, *Practical Ethics*. Second edition. Cambridge: Cambridge University Press, 1999, 243, 321, 334.

198. Qasim, *Hizbullah: Al-Manhaj...*, 62.

199. Ibid., 58-59.

200. Interview with Fadlallah, *Politique internationale* 29 (Autumn 1985), 268, as cited by Kramer in "Sacrifice and 'Self-Martyrdom' in Shi'ite Lebanon", 10.

201. Interview with Fadlallah, *Middle East Insight* 4 (June-July 1985), 2, 10-11, as cited by Kramer in "Sacrifice and 'Self-Martyrdom' in Shi'ite Lebanon", 10.

202. Sayyid Muhammad Husayn Fadlallah, *Al-Muqawama al-Islamiyya [The Islamic Resistance]*. Beirut: Imam al-Rida Publications, 1984, 18, as cited by Kramer in "Sacrifice and 'Self-Martyrdom' in Shi'ite Lebanon", 10.

203. See Amin Mustapha, *Al-Muqawama fi Lubnan: 1948-2000 [The Resistance in Lebanon: 1948-2000]*. Beirut: Dar Al-Hadi, 2003, 461. Although only Ahmad Qasir, the first Hizbullah martyr, could accomplish this goal, Hizbullah did not heed this safeguard and conducted eleven martyrdom operations after Qasir.

204. Qasim, *Hizbullah: Al-Manhaj...*, 62.

205. Interview with Fadlallah, *Monday Morning* 16 December 1985, as cited by Kramer in "Sacrifice and 'Self-Martyrdom' in Shi'ite Lebanon", 10.
206. Speech by Fadlallah, *Al-Nahar* 14 May 1985, as cited by Kramer in "Sacrifice and 'Self-Martyrdom' in Shi'ite Lebanon", 10-11.
207. Cf. "Islam's ability to dominate a state's identity is highly contested. While powerful Islamic movements exist within several states in the region [Middle East], these groups are encountering alternative definitions of community, based on divisions within Islam (Shia versus Sunni), race and language (Arab versus non-Arab), or clan and tribe… While some of these movements and some states are trying to increase Islamic influence and identity in other countries, the success of these efforts is not assured". Stephen Saideman, "Thinking Theoretically about Identity and Foreign Policy", in: *Identity and Foreign Policy in the Middle East*. Shibley Telhami and Michael Barnett (eds.). (London: Cornell University Press, 2002), 191.

Notes Chapter 3

1. The translation of the Open Letter is based on Hizbullah's original text. It is extracted from "Appendix A", with an indication of the corresponding page numbers as published in *al-'Ahd*. The Open Letter only outlined Hizbullah's political ideology; other documents elaborated the content of the political ideology.
2. Hizbullah's most notable political declarations referred to in this chapter are the following: "Jerusalem is the Holiest of our Causes" (29 June 1984); "Our Struggle with Israel is Doctrinal" (July 1984); "Resistance and Continued Struggle" (October 1984); "The American Threats and Confrontation" (28 October 1984); "Negotiations with Israel are Religiously Prohibited" (November 1984); "The Negotiations with Israel and the Treachery of the Lebanese Political System" (November 1985); Hizbullah's political declaration on the martyrdom of Ahmad Qasir (19 May 1985); Hizbullah's political declaration in the anniversary of the annulment of May 17 Agreement (23 May 1986); and Hizbullah's political declaration on the relations with Christians (31 May 1986). Also references are made to *al-'Ahd* and other sources like daily newspapers such as *al-Nahar*, *al-Safir*, *al-Liwa'*, *al-Anwar*, and *Kayhan;* and weeklies such as *al-Shira'* and *al-Masira*.
3. Member of the *Shura* Council and the first Secretary General of Hizbullah in 1989.
4. Member of the *Shura* Council and the leader of the Islamic Resistance.
5. Sayyid Abbas' brother. The only civilian in the leadership. Member of the *Shura* Council, AMAL's deputy president; he founded Islamic AMAL, which later became part of Hizbullah.
6. He was Hizbullah's first spokesman and he read the Open Letter; member of the Shura Council.
7. Fadlallah is a local Lebanese Ayatollah who is respected by Hizbullah.
8. Member of the *Shura* Council and the head of Hizbullah's Executive Council in 1987.
9. Member of the *Shura* Council.
10. Z'aytir was a leading Hizbullah cadre at the time. *Nazra 'ala Tarh Al-Jumhuriyya Al-Islamiyya fi Lubnan [An Outlook at the Proposal of the Islamic Republic in Lebanon]*. Beirut: Al-Wikala Al-Sharqiyya lil-Tawzi', 1988.
11. Kurani, a Hizbullah middle rank cadre, was the first to expose the social movement's mobilization strategies in his book entitled, *Tariqat Hizbullah fi Al-'Amal Al-Islami [Hizbullah's Method of Islamic Mobilization]*. Tehran, Maktab Al-I'lam Al-Islami: Al-Mu'assa Al-'Alamiyya, 1985.

12. In order to denote the Islamic order, Hizbullah uses "Islamic state", "Islamic government", and "Islamic Republic" interchangeably, maybe because Imam Khumayni called his book *Islamic Government* and labelled Iran as the "Islamic Republic", not "Islamic State". Till 2000, Hizbullah's flag contained the expression "The Islamic Revolution in Lebanon". Still other Hizbullah cadres referred to the Islamic Republic in Lebanon (*Al-Jumhuriyya Al-Islamiyya fi Lubnan*).

13. Sayyid Ibrahim Amin Al-Sayyid, *Al-'Ahd* (21 *Dhul-Qadah* 1404/ 17 August 1984).

14. See Section 13: "Words to the Christians in Lebanon".

15. These are called the "purposes of the shari'a" (*maqasid al-shari'a*), which are discussed in chapter 4.

16. The term was coined in 1973 by Gustavo Rutierrez, a Peruvian Catholic priest. In brief, liberation theology is a Biblically inspired doctrine that exhorts the Church to employ its resources in order to liberate the world populace from poverty, oppression, injustice, and inequality in order to secure social and economic justice.

17. See Section 8: "Our Friends". This explanation on this specific section of the Open Letter was accorded to me through two separate interviews with Hajj Imad Faqih and Sayyid Ibrahim Al-Musawi on November 2, 2004 and October 29, 2004 respectively. Faqih is a Hizbullah social welfare and public relations officer; al-Musawi is a Hizbullah media cadre who is an *al-Manar* TV editor and *al-Intiqad* weekly newspaper columnist.

18. See Section 2: "The Oppressors are in concordance in fighting us", Section 8: "Our Friends", Section 21: "International front for the oppressed", and Section 14: "Our story with the world oppressors".

19. According to Yusuf 'Ali, the context of the "passage was the question of migration from places where Islam was being persecuted and suppressed. Obviously the duty of the Muslims was to leave such places, even if it involved forsaking their homes, and join and strengthen the Muslim community among whom they could live in peace and with whom they could help in fighting the evils around them. But the meaning is wider. Islam does not say: 'Resist not evil'. On the contrary it requires a constant, unceasing struggle against evil. For such struggle it may be necessary to forsake home and unite and organise and join our brethren in assaulting and overthrowing the fortress of evil. For the Muslim's duty is not only to enjoin the good but to prohibit evil. To make our assault we must be prepared to put ourselves in a position in which such assault would be possible, and God's earth is spacious enough for the purpose. 'Position' includes not only local position, but moral and material position. For example, we must shun evil company where we cannot put it down, but organise a position from which we can put it down". However, he adds, "If through physical [smaller military jihad], mental, or moral incapacity [persuasive jihad], we are unable to fight the good fight, we must rest content with putting up with evil and just guarding ourselves from it. God's gracious Mercy will recognise and forgive our weakness if it is real weakness, and not merely an excuse". (*The Holy Qur'an...*, 211-212).

20. Fadlallah, *Ma' Al-Hikma...*, 46-54. This bears some similarity to the Prophetic tradition where the Prophet spent 13 years in Mecca practicing his call and succeeded in converting only 83 people to Islam. When his life was in danger, according to Islamic belief, God ordered him to emigrate to Medina. He heeded and consolidated his call, and made of Medina the base for spreading the mission of Islam.

21. By political Maronism Hizbullah means the leading Maronite notables and their retinue, which constitute the symbols of the Lebanese political system. Their retinue included the Sunni prime minister and the Shi'a speaker who were completely under their command blindly exercising their political whim and will. The late PM Sami al-Solh said

that the PM is only "ketchup" in the hands of the president. Thus, from 1943 till 1990 the Muslims, in general, and the Shi'as, in particular, had been politically marginalized since the Maronites wielded economic and political power and had absolute control of the country's resources and riches.

22. See Section 2: "The Oppressors are in concordance in fighting us", Section 8: "Our Friends", Section 21: "International front for the oppressed", and Section 14: "Our story with the world oppressors".

23. Z'aytir, op. cit., 63.

24. Ibid., 75-80.

25. Sayyid Muhammad Husayn Fadlallah, *Ma' Al-Hikma fi Khat Al-Islam [Wisdom in the Way of Islam]*. Beirut: Dar Al-Wafa', 1985, 47.

26. Z'aytir, op. cit., 200.

27. At least the six verses mentioned below.

28. *Al-'Ahd* no. 9 (*Dhul-Qadah* 1404/ August 1984), 9. See also Qasim, *Hizbullah: Al-Manhaj...*, 388. Hizbullah's English home page quotes (28:4) in the following manner: "And we desire to bestow a favour upon those who were deemed weak in the land and make them the Imams and make them heirs" See http://www.hizbollah.org/english/frames/index_eg.htm. According to Yusuf 'Ali, "God's plan was to protect them as they were weak, and indeed to make them custodians and leaders in His Faith, and to give them in inheritance a land 'flowing with milk and honey'. Here they were established in authority for such time as they followed God's Law". See *The Holy Qur'an...*, 1002.

29. Yusef 'Ali commented on this verse, "Muslims were reminded that they were a small band in Mecca; despised and rejected; living in a state of insecurity for their persons, their lives, their property, and those of their dependents; persecuted and exiled and how by the Grace of God they found a safe asylum in Medina, how they found friends and helpers, how their many needs were cared for, and how at length they generated strength and numbers enough to defeat the forces of godlessness, injustice, and oppression". *The Holy Qur'an...*, 421.

30. Hizbullah remained working underground and released its first political declarations in 1984.

31. Amin Al-Sayyid, *Al-'Ahd* (21 *Dhul-Qadah* 1404/ 17 August 1984). See also *Al-Hukumat al-Islamiyya [Islamic Government]*. Tehran: The Institute of Coordinating and Publishing Imam Khumayni's Heritage, 1996, 60-62; 64-65.

32. Sayyid Muhammad Husayn Fadlallah, *Al-Islam wa Mantiq Al-Quwwa [Islam and the Logic of Power]*. Beirut: Dar Al-Huruf, 1987, 171ff.

33. Sayyid Muhammad Husayn Fadlallah, *Al-Muqawama al-Islamiyya [The Islamic Resistance]*. Beirut: Al-Dar Al-Islamiyya, 1986, 47.

34. *Al-'Ahd* (21 *Dhul-Qadah* 1404/ 17 August 1984).

35. See sections 2, 8, 14, and 21 of the Open Letter.

36. Cf. *Al-Hukumat al-Islamiyya*, 60-62; 64-65.

37. Cf. *The Constitution of the Islamic Republic of Iran*. Chapter Ten entitled "Foreign Policy", article 154. Tehran, Department of Translation and Publication, Islamic Culture and Relations Organization: Alhoda Publishers and Distributors, 1997, 118.

38. See Section 7: "Our objectives in Lebanon".

39. Khumayni, *Al-Hukuma Al-Islamiyya*, 60ff.

40. Sharif al-Husayni, "*Hizbullah: Haraka 'Askariyya am Siyasiyya am Diniyya?* (Hizbullah: A Military or Political or religious Movement?)". Beirut: *Al-Shira'* (17 March 1986), 20.

41. See Section 7: "Our objectives in Lebanon".

42. See Hizbullah's political declaration in the third anniversary of the annulment of May 17, 1983 agreement with Israel. *Al-'Ahd* 100 (15 Ramadan 1406/ 23 May 1986), 11.·

43. Ibid. See also Section 9: "We are committed to Islam, but we do not impose it by force".

44. Qasim, *Hizbullah: Al-Manhaj…*, 39.

45. A canton refers to a religious mini-state inside the Lebanese sate, or a state within state. In Hizbullah's case founding a Shi'ite canton in the areas under its control, would have implied establishing a mini-Islamic state or a replica of an Islamic state in miniature. Unlike others, Hizbullah neither established a mini-state – having its own ports, airports, and civil administration – within the Lebanese state, nor did Hizbullah call for federalism. During the mid 1980s the issue of establishing cantons along sectarian lines in Lebanon was high on the agenda among most religious denominations, including the Christians. For instance, Habib Matar, the deputy president of the National Liberal Party (*Hizb al-Wataniyyin al-Ahrar*) has stated in 1986 that his call to the Vatican of establishing a Christian state in Lebanon should not be viewed as a call for the disintegration of Lebanon; rather the Christian state would be erected on all the Lebanese soil. Matar questioned, "Why don't the Christians in the East have a save haven or a small state?" When he was asked what should the Muslims do, he replied: "Its their own problem. There are a lot of empty areas in the Arab world [where they can go], or let them be governed by the Christian state and this is better for them". (*Al-Masira* last week of March 1986). A similar view was earlier announced by Bashir Jumayyel who said in 1982 that the Maronites are aiming at converting Lebanon into a Christian state in which all the Christian Arabs can live in. As to the borders of the alleged Maronite state, Z'aytir claims they are constantly expanding. (Muhammad Z'aytir, *Al-Mashru' Al-Maruni fi Lubnan: Juzuruhu wa Tatawwuratuhu [The Maronite Project in Lebanon: Roots and Development]*. Beirut: Al-Wikala Al-'Alamiyya lil-Tawzi', 1986, 14. Since this book contains 1136 pages of severe political-ideological bashing against the Maronites, it is officially banned in Lebanon. (The book's cover portrays a blue map of Lebanon with a black cross in its midst).

46. Sayyid Hasan Nasrallah, *Al-'Ahd* 95 (9 Sha'ban 1406/ 18 April 1986), 11.

47. This mirrors Khumayni who argued that Islam is a state, *shari'a*, and a just government that upholds the rule of law and accords people serenity. *Al-Hukuma Al-Islamiyya*, 86-88.

48. See Section 9.

49. Z'aytir, *Nazra 'ala Tarh Al-Jumhuriyya Al-Islamiyya fi Lubnan*, 57-60.

50. Ibid., 52-57.

51. Non-Muslim people of the Book living under Islamic protection. Non-Muslim monotheists (Jews and Christians) enjoying a protected status under Muslim rule for exchange of a poll tax (*jizya*), of which only those who fought alongside the Muslims were exempted from.

52. See Hizbullah's Political Declaration of 31 May 1986.

53. For the connection between the good political order (Islamic state) and the application of justice to all groups, including minorities, see the following Qur'anic verses: (4:28); (42:15); (5:8); (5:42); (6:152); and (16:90).

54. Fadlallah was referring to one of the maxims of Islamic jurisprudence (*qawa'id al-fiqh*), which states that the warding off vices is preferable to obtaining interests.

55. See the section entitled, "Power and its Relationship to the Sovereignty and Islam", in: Fadlallah, *Al-Islam wa Mantiq Al-Quwwa*, 245-259.

56. 'Ali Al-Kurani, op. cit., 181.

57. Kurani added that neither Israel nor the US care about the Lebanese Christians, since they have cost them too much and given too little benefit in return. Ibid., 191.

58. Z'aytir, *Nazra 'ala Tarh Al-Jumhuriyya Al-Islamiyya fi Lubnan*, 106.

59. *Al-Safir* 7 September 1985.

60. Z'aytir contended that the Maronites engaged for the past 700 years in a systematic campaign of deporting Muslims until they had virtual control over Mount Lebanon. He also claimed that there was an international decision behind this move so that the West would benefit from Maronite following and collaboration.

61. Z'aytir, *Al-Mashru' Al-Maruni fi Lubnan*, op. cit., 11-12.

62. See Section 11:"Why do we confront the existing regime?"

63. See Section 12: "Our stance towards the opposition". The Open letter referred to the Lebanese president, Bashir Jumayyel as a "butcher" and chastised his brother Amin Jumayyel – who were both members of the Maronite right-wing Palangist party – for attempting to crush Hizbullah's endeavour of establishing an Islamic state. Hizbullah criticised Amin Jumayyel for destroying the homes of the displaced persons, attacking mosques, and ordering the Lebanese army to bombard the quarters of the downtrodden and oppressed people in the southern suburbs of Beirut. Also, Hizbullah vehemently blasted Amin Jumayyel for (1) inviting NATO troops to strengthen his regime and to fight the oppressed; and (2) signing the May 17, 1983 accord with Israel, which made Lebanon a sphere of influence of Israel and the US. (See Section 5: "Zionist-Phalagist coordination").

64. See Section 6:"Our basic enemies", and Section 7:"Our objectives in Lebanon".

65. According to Z'aytir these are the "Crusader capitals in Europe and America" headed by "the Pope of the Crusaders in Rome". Z'aytir, *Nazra 'ala Tarh Al-Jumhuriyya Al-Islamiyya fi Lubnan*, 77.

66. Ibid., 75-80. Islamists are committed, serious, honest, faithful, politically engaged Muslims who uphold religion as a guiding principle in all aspects of life. Thus, Islamists employ religious discourse as their distinguishing identity.

67. *Jahiliyya* began about 500 AD and lasted until the rise of Islam in 610 AD.

68. Z'aytir, *Nazra 'ala Tarh Al-Jumhuriyya Al-Islamiyya fi Lubnan*, 86-88.

69. Al-Kurani, op. cit., 179-181.

70. Z'aytir, *Nazra 'ala Tarh Al-Jumhuriyya Al-Islamiyya fi Lubnan*, 169-174.

71. Ibid., 209-213.

72. Ibid.,106-107.

73. Ibid., 76.

74. Ibid., 75-80.

75. Ibid., 80-81.

76. Ibid., 103-104.

77. Ibid., 86-88.

78. See Lebanese daily newspapers of 8 February 1988. As such, Hizbullah resorted to a confrontational rhetoric with the Phalangists and the Lebanese state, but confined its military confrontation to the Lebanese Communist Party (from 1984-85) and *AMAL* (1988-1990).

79. Z'aytir, *Nazra 'ala Tarh Al-Jumhuriyya Al-Islamiyya fi Lubnan*, 243-245.

80. From a historical perspective, Mackey argues, "Lebanon's Christians... are not a monolithic but a collection of distinctive groups possessing marked diversities. They broadly divide into three major denominational groups – the Maronites and the Melkites, both Roman Catholic, and Greek Orthodox, who are part of the Eastern Orthodox church... The Maronites reject inclusion in the Arab world outright; the Greek Orthodox accept their status as part of that world; and the Melkites vacillate between the two attitudes. However, all Lebanese Christians perceive as imperiled their survival as a religious minority trapped

in a sea of Islam". Sandra Mackey, *Lebanon: Death of a Nation*. New York: Congdon and Weed Inc., 1989, 30. As cited in Joyce M. Davis, *Martyrs: Innocence, Vengeance and Despair in the Middle East*. New York: Palgrave Macmillan, 2003, 80.

81. It seems that from the early 1980s till 1990 no political dialogue or high level contact had been established between Hizbullah and the Christians. What took place were sideline meetings conducted in the *Biqa'* and the *Dahiya*. Besides that, the general framework that Hizbullah operated in was that there was a general prohibition in dealing with the Christians, especially the Maronites. (Hasan Fadlallah, *Al-Khiyar al-Akhar...*, 137).

82. See Section 13: "Words to the Christians in Lebanon".

83. Ibid.

84. I prefer to translate *da'wa* as Islamic propagation or call, rather than "Islamic indoctrination" as some authors do.

85. Z'aytir, *Nazra 'ala Tarh Al-Jumhuriyya Al-Islamiyya fi Lubnan*, 60-61.

86. See Section 13: "Words to the Christians in Lebanon". Kurani interprets this is a clear reference to the Jews who did not honour their covenant with the Prophet as stipulated by the Constitution of Medina. Al-Kurani, *Tariqat Hizbullah...*, 160.

87. See Section 9: "We are committed to Islam, but we do not impose it by force".

88. Z'aytir, *Nazra 'ala Tarh Al-Jumhuriyya Al-Islamiyya fi Lubnan*, 103-104.

89. See Hizbullah's political declaration in the anniversary of the annulment of May 17, 1983 agreement with Israel. *Al-'Ahd* 100 (15 Ramadan 1406/ 23 May 1986), 11.

90. Hizbullah's political declaration of November 1984, entitled "Negotiations with Israel are Religiously Prohibited".

91. Kurani referred to the Hizbullah's " distinguished cultural (educational) project of the Liberation of Jerusalem" and enmity to the Zionist entity as one of the principal pillars of its political ideology. He explained that before Hizbullah's distinguished mobilizational culture came to the fore, the Lebanese Muslims, and especially the Shi'ites of the South, considered resisting Israeli occupation as an idiocy. He added that Hizbullah's mobilizational political ideology altered this capitulating mentality and galvanised the masses to join the Islamic Resistance to fight the occupation and liberate Lebanon as a first step in the road to liberate Jerusalem. Kurani argues that Hizbullah has a holistic liberation project of individual and social reform, among it the liberation of Jerusalem, which is different than the political fight of other groups against Israel. (See "The Seventh Trait in Hizbullah's Culture: The Culture of Liberation of Jerusalem", in: Al-Kurani, *Tariqat Hizbullah...*, 177-178).

92. Hizbullah's political declaration of 29 June 1984, entitled "Jerusalem is the Holiest of our Causes".

93. See the program entitled "*Ahzab Lubnan: Hizbullah: Al-Jiz' Al-Awwal* [Lebanese Parties: Hizbullah, Part I]" (1979-1989), *NBN*, 21 July 2002. Also, Hizbullah's political declaration of 29 June 1984, entitled "Jerusalem is the Holiest of our Causes", unequivocally equates Khumayni's statement with Musa al-Sadr's statements.

94. See Section 15: "Israel must be completely obliterated".

95. See Hizbullah's political declarations of July 1984, entitled "Our Struggle with Israel is Doctrinal", and of September and October 1984: the first on the occasion of the second anniversary of the massacres in the Palestinian camps; the second on the anniversary of *'Ashura*.

96. See Section 24: "A final word regarding international organizations". Hizbullah seems to be lobbying for something stronger than the now defunct UN Resolution 3379, which stipulates that Zionism is a form of racism.

97. Z'aytir, *Nazra 'ala Tarh Al-Jumhuriyya Al-Islamiyya fi Lubnan*, 198.

98. See Section 3: "America is behind all our catastrophes".

99. See Hizbullah's political declaration of 19 May 1985.

100. "That is, by punishing them severely".

101. As a symbolic gesture of support to the Islamic *umma*, in general, and the Palestinians, in particular, Hizbullah's annual celebration of the "Day of Jerusalem" is always inaugurated by a military parade emanating from the "constructed" *Khaybar* gate.

102. Sayyid Abbas Al-Musawi, *al-Safir* 7 September 1985. See also Na'im Qasim, *Al-Harb al-Sadisa...*, 1982.

103. See also Imam Khumayni, *Sahifat Al-Nour [A Compilation of Khumayni's Works]*, Volume 10. Beirut: n.d., 164-171.

104. See *Al-'Ahd* 18 *Jamad Al-Awwal* 1410/ 15 December 1989.

105. See Hizbullah's political declaration of November 1984, entitled "Negotiations with Israel are Religiously Prohibited". See also *Al-'Ahd* no. 20. Hizbullah's political declaration entitled, "Negotiations and the Treachery of the (Lebanese Political) System", issued in November 1985 reiterated the same themes. In almost all their speeches, Hizbullah's leaders confirm that they are willing to fight for liberating southern Lebanon and Palestine, rather than submitting to either Israel or the US. They continuously reiterate the centrality of their struggle against Israel. Tufayli declared that if the whole world makes peace with Israel, Hizbullah would continue to fight the Zionists even if Israel withdraws from South Lebanon. He added that the peace documents would be torn, and that there would be no normalization with the enemy and the resistance would continue. *Al-Shira'* 31 August 1986.

106. See Section 15: "Israel must be completely obliterated". In conformity with the Open Letter and its political declarations, Hizbullah voiced its rejection to the peace settlement (peace process) and the Madrid Peace Conference, arguing that it serves the interests of the Great Satan (the US) and the Little Satan (Israel), at the expense of the interests of the Arabs and Muslims. The Madrid Peace Conference was supposed to be the conference of destiny for Lebanon, the Middle East, the Palestinian cause, and the struggle on an existential level between the Zionists and the Arabs and the Muslims. (The Madrid accord resulted from the Madrid Peace Conference, which was held in October-November 1991). See Sayyid Abbas' speech on the thirteenth anniversary of the commemoration of the disappearance of Imam Musa Al-Sadr, 31 August 1991.

107. *Al-'Ahd* 20 *Safar* 1406/ 25 October 1985; *Al-'Ahd* 12 *Sha'ban* 1407/ 10 April 1987; *Al-'Ahd* 24 *Safar* 1408 / 16 October 1987.

108. It is alleged that he was killed because of his multi-volume book entitled, *The Causes Responsible for Materialist Tendencies in the West*. See http://www.al-islam.org/al-tawhid/1-west.htm

109. Saddam executed him on April 9, 1980. It is no wonder that Hizbullah considers Imam Musa al-Sadr and Sayyid Muhammad Baqir al-Sadr among its ideologues and leaders.

110. See Section 22: "God is with the unity of Muslims".

111. Z'aytir, *Nazra 'ala Tarh Al-Jumhuriyya Al-Islamiyya fi Lubnan*, 123-127.

112. Ibid., 107.

113. Al-Kurani, op. cit., 199ff.

114. Fadlallah, *Min Ajl Al-Islam [For The Sake of Islam]*. Beirut: Dar Al-Ta'arruf, 1989, 129.

115. Z'aytir, *Nazra 'ala Tarh Al-Jumhuriyya Al-Islamiyya fi Lubnan*, 127.

116. Al-Kurani, op. cit., 178.

117. Norton, *Amal and the Shi'a...*,121ff; Hasan Fadlallah, op. cit., 133ff; Sharara, *Dawlat Hizbullah...*, 346-350. Talal Salman, *Sira Dhatiyya li Haraka Muqawina 'Arabiyya Muntasira: Hizbullah [An Autobiography of a Victorious Arab Resistance Movement: Hizbullah]*. Beirut:

Al-Safir, June 2000, 11. See the following web page: http://www.nasrollah.org/arabic/hassan/sera/about002.htm (Last accessed April 2005).

118. See Hasan Fadlallah, op. cit., 145-147. Sharara, op. cit., 346-350.

119. For details on Hizbullah's military confrontation with the Lebanese Communist Party (from 1984-85), see See Augustus R. Norton, "Hizballah of Lebanon: Extremist Ideas vs. Mundane Politics", *Council on Foreign Relations*, (February 2000), 14-15; Norton, "Lebanon", *Yearbook on International Communist Affairs: Parties and Revolutionary Movements*. Stanford: Hoover Institutionalization Press, 1987, 449-53; Sharara, op. cit., 349-350; and al-Husayni, "Hizbullah: Haraka…", 15.

120. The Islamic Republic embedded in its hierarchal organizational structures "The World Forum for Proximity of Islamic Schools of Thought" (*Al-Majma' Al-'Alami lil-Taqrib byna Al-Madhahib Al-Islamiyya*), which, since 1988, has been annually organizing a conference in Tehran on the unity of the Muslims in order to consolidate inter-Islamic ecumenical activities. Hizbullah's leading cadres receive the spotlight in such gatherings. (See respectively the Farsi and Arabic websites of *Majma'-e Jahani-ye Baraye Taqrib-e baine Mazaheb-e Eslami*. at: http://www.taghrib.ir/site/aboutus.htm and http://www.taghrib.org/arabic/index.htm. See also Wilfried Buchta, *Who Rules Iran? The Structure of Power in the Islamic Republic*. Washington, DC: The Washington Institute for Near East Policy and the Konrad Adenaueur Stiftung, 2000, 49ff).

121. The Constitution of the Islamic Republic of Iran. Chapter Ten entitled "Foreign Policy", article 152. Tehran, Department of Translation and Publication, Islamic Culture and Relations Organization: Alhoda Publishers and Distributors, 1997, 117. Imam Khumayni argued that defending Islam and Hizbullah is a fundamental constant in the policy of the Islamic Republic. (See *Al-Kalimat Al-Qisar: Al-Islam wa A'malina [Short Words: Islam and our Works]*. Beirut: n.d., 187). Hizbullah annually commemorates Imam Khumayni's call to the unity of the Muslims through meetings and dialogue among Muslim scholars and religious leaders of all confessions.

122. See Section 21: "International Front for the Oppressed"; and Z'aytir, *Nazra 'ala Tarh Al-Jumhuriyya Al-Islamiyya fi Lubnan*, 127.

123. See Section 22: "God is with the unity of Muslims".

124. "*Fitna* is worse than slaughter" (2:191); "Fight them until there is no *fitna*" (2:193); "And know that your wealth and your children are a *fitna*, and with Allah is a great reward" (8:28); "As to the unbelievers, they are friends of one another. If you do not support the Muslims and subdue the unbelievers, there will be great *fitna* and corruption in the land" (8:73).

125. Fadlallah, *Al-Islam wa Mantiq…*, 171-172.

126. "And obey Allah and His Apostle and do not quarrel among yourselves lest you lose heart and your strength dissipates. And stand fast, for Allah is on the side of those who stand fast" (8:46).

127. "And fear a discord which will not only inflict the wrongdoers among you…" (8:25).

128. Z'aytir, *Nazra 'ala Tarh Al-Jumhuriyya Al-Islamiyya fi Lubnan*, 123-127.

129. See Section 22: "God is with the unity of Muslims". Z'aytir reiterates the same discourse. See *Nazra 'ala Tarh Al-Jumhuriyya Al-Islamiyya fi Lubnan*, 123-127.

130. Ibid., 123.

131. See Section 22: "God is with the unity of Muslims".

132. 'Ali al-Kurani, op. cit., 147-163.

133. *Al-'Ahd* 7 February 1986; *Kayhan* 27 July 1986; *Al-'Ahd* 11 Sh'ban 1407AH/ 10 April 1987.

134. *Al-'Ahd* no. 146, (12 Shaban 1407 AH/ 10 April 1987), 7.

135. Z'aytir, *Nazra 'ala Tarh Al-Jumhuriyya Al-Islamiyya fi Lubnan*, 54.

136. See Section 3 of the Open Letter: "America is behind our catastrophes".

137. See Hizbullah's political declaration entitled, "The American Threats and Confrontation", 28 October 1984.

138. See Sections 3, 6, 7, and 20: "America is behind our catastrophes"; "Our main enemies"; "Our objectives in Lebanon"; and "Defeatist Arab regimes".

139. *Al-Liwa'* 1 July 1986. In its major constituencies, Hizbullah's banner "America is behind all our catastrophes" appeared and below it a US flag was depicted with bombs instead of stars.

140. Fadlallah, *Min Ajl Al-Islam*, 62.

141. Ibid., 129.

142. Fadlallah, *Al-Islam wa Mantiq Al-Quwwa*, 293ff.

143. See the Open Letter: sections, 1, 2, 6, 13, and 20.

144. Hizbullah's reference to the Qur'anic verse on East and West gets another touch since its original use, as a mystical interpretation, is different from the East and West of the cold war. See Yusuf 'Ali, op. cit., 907-908; 920-924.

145. See Section 10: "The bare minimum of our aspirations", Section 11: "Why do we confront the existing regime", and Section 21: "International front for the oppressed".

146. "The Spiritual-Dynamic Force of the Islamic Revolution: Second Episode", *Al-'Ahd* (10 *Shawwal* 1405AH/ 28 June 1985), 9.

147. "The Spiritual-Dynamic Force of the Islamic Revolution..."; See also Ayatullah Murtada Mutahhari book entitled, *The Causes Responsible for Materialist Tendencies in the West* at http://www.al-islam.org/al-tawhid/1-west.htm (Last accessed August 2005).

148. "The Spiritual-Dynamic Force of the Islamic Revolution..."

149. *Al-'Ahd* (21 *Dhul-Qadah* 1404/ 17 August 1984).

150. Z'aytir, *Nazra 'ala Tarh Al-Jumhuriyya Al-Islamiyya fi Lubnan*, 161-165; 244-249.

151. See Section 23: "An appeal to the 'ulama of Islam".

152. Khumayni said in more than one occasion that if people knew that a shop owner is dishonest and immoral, then they would say that Mr. X is dishonest and immoral; if they found out that a trader is cheating then, then they would say that Mr. X is a cheater; however, if they knew that a Muslim religious scholar (*'alim*), God forbid, is not upright, then they would generalize and say that all religious scholars are not upright (perverted) and the religion (Islam) as a whole is not upright. Hizbullah appropriated this section of the Open Letter, almost word by word, from the section entitled, "The Grave Responsibilities of the Muslim *'Ulama*", in: Imam Khumayni's *Al-Jihad Al-Akbar [Greater Jihad]*. Translated by Husayn Kurani. Tehran: Islamian Grand Library, 1980, 9-10. Cf. Norton's failure to translate and contextualise this concept of greater jihad. Augustus Richard Norton, *Amal and the Shi'a Struggle for the Soul of Lebanon*. Austin: University Press of Texas, 1987, 185.

153. "The Spiritual-Dynamic Force of the Islamic Revolution: The Ideological and Social Change... A New Conception of Jihad", 10 *Shawwal* 1405AH/ 28 June 1985, 9.

154. This is reminiscent of Khumayni's argument in *Al-Jihad Al-Akbar*, 8.

155. This mirrors, more or less, Khumayni's list of the traits of the practitioner of greater jihad. (*Al-Jihad Al-Akbar*, 10-11).

156. *Al-'Ahd* (10 *Shawwal* 1405AH/ 28 June 1985), 9.

157. Sayyid Muhammad Husayn Fadlallah, *Khutuwat 'ala Tariq Al-Islam [Steps on the Way to Islam]*. Beirut: Dar Al-Huruf, 1986, 47.

158. Nasrallah was referring to the October 23, 1983 suicidal operation that claimed the lives of 241 Marines near the Beirut airport.

159. See Nasrallah's lecture entitled, "Revolutionary Mobilization in the Process of Change" delivered at the headquarters of "The Lebanese Union of Muslim Students" on January 27, 1986.

160. Fadlallah, *Al-Islam wa Mantiq al-Quwwa*, 193ff.

161. *Al-Safir* 28 July 1986.

162. See the program entitled "Ahzab Lubnan: Hizbullah: Al-Jiz' Al-Awwal (1979-1989) [Lebanese Parties: Hizbullah, Part I]", *NBN*, 21 July 2002.

163. See Martin Kramer, *The Moral Logic of Hizbullah*. The Dayan Center for Middle Eastern and African Studies. Tel Aviv University: The Shiloah Institute. Occasional Papers. 101 (August 1987), 7, 9.

164. *Al-Safir* 19 August 1986.

165. Due to security reasons, in 1982 Hizbullah neither disclosed its first martyr's name, Ahmad Qasir, nor claimed responsibility for its first martyrdom operation. On May 19, 1985, Hizbullah issued a political declaration in which it offered a political-ideological legitimisation of its first martyrdom operation to the Arab and Islamic *umma*: "In the name of God the Mortal Blower of the oppressors, In recognition of the Islamic Resistance to the glorified blood of its martyrs; in emphasizing the leading and great sacrifices in the name of Islam that is the vanguard of an underground war of liberation [against the Israeli soldiers] so that the martyrs will remain an eternal light in the faithful generations' march towards *al-Aqsa* [Mosque in Palestine], the Islamic Resistance announces on the occasion of the honourable celebration of the martyrs (of *Dayr Qanun al-Nahr*) the name of its dignified martyr, the hero of the triumphant first martyrdom operation against the Israeli headquarters in *Jal al-Bahr* [Tyre], the operation of *Khaybar*, the operation that spread terror in the heart of the Zionist enemy [Israeli], convulsed its foundations and military balance, and signified a great historical conquest against the Jews, he is the martyr Ahmad Qasir (Haydar). We [Hizbullah] promise the illuminated blood of the martyrs, in the dark nights of *Jabal 'Amil*, the continuation of the march until the victory of the oppressed [is consummated]". (See Hizbullah's political declaration, 19 May 1985. Also published in *Al-'Ahd* 4 Ramadan 1405AH /24 May 1985).

166. Sayyid Ibrahim Amin al-Sayyid, *Al-'Ahd* 22 Jamad al-'Awwal 1407/ 23 January 1987, as cited by Martin Kramer in: "Sacrifice and 'Self-Martyrdom' in Shi'ite Lebanon". *Terrorism and Political Violence* 3, (Autumn 1991) 3, 30-47 at: http://www.geocities.com/ martinkramerorg/Sacrifice.htm.

167. Iranian Revolutionary Guards.

168. Interview with Sayyid Abbas al-Musawi, *Al-'Ahd* 22 *Safar* 1408/ 16 October 1987, as cited by Martin Kramer in: "Hizbullah: The Calculus of Jihad". In *Fundamentalisms and the State: Remarking Polities, Economics, and Militance*. Vol. III. Chicago: The University of Chicago Press, 1993, 539-56, via the Internet at: http://www.martinkramer.org/pages/899528/ index.htm, 9.

169. This is corroborated by Wensinck: "suicide, under whatever circumstances, is forbidden in Islam". A. J. Wensinck, "The Oriental Doctrine of the Martyrs", in: *Mededeelingen der Koninklijk Akademie van Wetenschappen, Afdeeling Letterkunde; dl. 53, nr. 6*. Amsterdam: Koninklijk Akademie van Wetenschappen (KNAW publications), 1922, 153.

170. See for instance, Farhad Khosrokhavar, *L'Islamisme et la Mort: Le Martyre Revolutionnare en Iran [Islamism and Death: The Revolutionary Martyrs in Iran]*. Paris: L'Harmattan, 1995, especially 258-267; Richard T. Antoun, *Understanding Fundamentalism: Christian, Islamic, and Jewish Movements*. Oxford: Altamira Press, 2001; and Farhad Khosrokhavar, *Les Nouveaux Martyrs D'Allah [God's New Martyrs]*. Paris: Flammarion, 2002.

171. Fadlallah, *Min Ajl Al-Islam*, 48-52.

172. Hizbullah is not monopolising the use of religion, as Roy seems to imply, rather the party employs the word Hizbullah in an extended, inclusive, and progressive sense, which includes all believers from all religious denominations. Hajj Muhammad Al-Jammal, Hizbullah's spokesman, argued along these lines on the occasion of receiving a Danish delegation – composed of students, researchers, faculty, mainly from Arhus University and the University of Southern Copenhagen, and some Danish journalists – at the CIO, 30 March 1999. Cf. Olivier Roy, *Globalised Islam: The Search for A New Umma*. Revised and updated edition. London: Hurst and Company, 2004, 249, 329.

173. Cf. As'ad Abu Khalil, "Ideology and Practice of Hizbollah in Lebanon: Islamization of Leninist Organizational Principles", *Middle Eastern Studies*, 27 (July 1991), 3, 395; and Roy, op. cit., 247-248.

174. "Now, whether or not an Islamist movement [Hizbullah] becomes truly radical hinges *on whether or not it rejects the very validity and legitimacy of the local state* and seeks universal revolution to undermine it in the name of the ideal *umma* (italics in original)… Yet other Muslim radicals, perhaps non-violent, possess utopian views that perceive the creation of an 'Islamic state' as the solution to all problems, or as a way to empower the Muslim world and restore the power of the Muslim civilization". Fuller, *The Future of Political Islam*, 17, 88.

175. Fadlallah, *Al-Islam wa Mantiq Al-Quwwa*, 258ff.

176. Imam Khumayni issued a *fatwa* stressing that the Lebanese system is illegitimate and criminal. In 1986 Khamina'i clarified Khumayni's *fatwa* arguing for the necessity of the Muslims to rule Lebanon since they comprise the majority of the population. (Al-Madini, *Amal wa Hizbullah…*, 162-163; Sharara, op. cit., 342). The chief of staff of the Iranian revolutionary guards in Lebanon stressed that Hizbullah and the Revolutionary Guards are going to bring down the Martonite regime just as the Iranians brought down the Shah. (*Al-Anwar* 9 February 1988).

177. Sayyid Muhammad Husayn Fadlallah, "Reflections on the Muslim-Christian Dialogue", A lecture delivered at the American University of Beirut, 22 December 1987.

178. Sharara, op. cit., 348.

179. "The Union of Muslim Ulama" was established in the wake of the Israeli invasion in June 1982.

180. See *Al-Harakat al-Islamiyya fi Lubnan* and Al-Kurani, *Tariqat Hizbullah…*, especially 147-163.

181. Imam Khumayni, *Al-Kalimat Al-Qisar: Al-Islam wa A'malina [Short Words: Islam and our Words]*, p. 193, as cited in: Rafiq Sulayman Fidda, *Athar Al-Imam Al-Khymayni ala Al-Qadiyya Al-Filastiniyya [Imam Khymayni's Impact on the Palestinian Cause]*. Beirut: n.d., 170.

182. Westoxification, a term coined in the 1960s by an Iranian intellectual called Jalal al-Ahmad, denotes the venomous Western civilizational influence and hegemony on other civilizations and cultures.

Notes Chapter 4

1. "Views and Concepts", "Statement of Purpose", and "Identity and Goals" are Hizbullah's self-descriptions, which include aspects of its political ideology and political program. The first was circulated via al-Manar TV, the second via Hizbullah's Press Office, and the third via Hizbullah's official website. See "Appendix A".

2. Hizbullah's second Secretary General, assassinated on February 16, 1992.

3. Deputy Secretary General of Hizbullah since 1991.

4. Hizbullah's third Secretary General since 1992.

5. In 1997 he was a member of Hizbullah's Political Council and the head of Hizbullah's Central Press Office.

6. A middle rank cadre who is columnist at *al-Intiqad*, Hizbullah weekly newspaper.

7. The director of Hizbullah's think tank, CCSD (Consultative Centre for Studies and Documentation), and a member of Hizbullah's Political Council.

8. The current head of Hizbullah's 12-member parliamentary Bloc entitled, "Loyalty to the Resistance"; previously the head of Hizbullah's Political Council.

9. The ex-head of Hizbullah's social institutions and the current head of Hizbullah's "Islamic Resistance Support Association".

10. Political Council member and foreign relations officer.

11. Hizbullah's current head of the Executive Council.

12. Farid El-Khazen, "Political Parties in Postwar Lebanon: Parties in Search of Partisans", *Middle East Journal*, 57 (Autumn 2003), 4, 612.

13. Hizbullah's Central Press Office, 3 January 1991. As will be shown later, Hizbullah included these principles in its parliamentary elections programs.

14. Sayyid Abbas' political program is compiled from: *Kawkab Al-Shahada…*; Hiyan Rizq, *Sayyid Al-Qada…*; Al-Shaykh Muhammad Ali Khatun, *Amir Al-Qafila…*; *Qudwat Al-Tha'rin…*; and *Sayyid Shuhada Al-Muqawama…*

15. As will be conveyed later, these points figured our prominently in Hizbullah's parliamentary elections programs.

16. As Sayyid Abbas put it, "If the populace of the Muslims and the oppressed give paramount importance to the resistance, then it would be fruitful". He added, "the *umma* is living the eventuality of *jihad* and the heroics of the freedom fighters (*mujahidin*)". Sayyid Abbas argued that this model of resistance should be emulated in all parts of the world that are suffering from occupation.

17. The author considers this as an indirect reference to the two and a half year *AMAL*-Hizbullah war that ended in November 1990, the ending of the 16-year old civil war, and Tufayli's schism (See chapter one and the "Chronology" in "Appendix D").

18. The *AMAL*-Hizbullah war was fought in the South and *Dahiya*; the Lebanese civil war moved from one place to another, thus engulfing almost all of Lebanon.

19. Sayyid Abbas added this is of vital importance since fortifying the domestic front leads the populace to engulf and embrace the Islamic Resistance, thus leading to its continuation and viability.

20. Lebanonisation signifies Hizbullah's enrolment in Lebanese domestic political life. It is worth mentioning that in political science, "Lebanonisation of nation-states" refers to fragmentation or tribalism, a usage completely different than the one employed here. See for instance Benjamin. J. Barker, *Jihad vs. McWorld*. New York: Times Books, 1995; and James N. Rosenau, *Along the Domestic-Foreign Frontier: Exploring Governance in a Turbulent World*. Cambridge: Cambridge University Press, 1997.

21. The Lebanese myriad or mosaic refers to the ethnic composition of the Lebanese communities that comprise Lebanon, including the officially recognised 18 sects.

22. This stance goes in line with Sayyid Abbas' famous slogans: "We will serve you with our eyebrows"; "We [Hizbullah] will fight deprivation, as we fight the [Israeli] occupation".

23. Personal interview, 31 December 2001.

24. Qasim, *Hizbullah: Al-Manhaj…*, 267-273.

25. Cf. Saad-Ghorayeb, *Hizbullah: Politics and Religion*, 2002, 67-68.

26. Qasim, op. cit. 267-268.

27. Islamists are committed, serious, honest, faithful, politically engaged Muslims. Islamism is holistic in its approach since it is "*a religious-cultural-political framework for engagement on issues that most concern politically engaged Muslims*". (Italics in the original; my underlining). Fuller, *The Future of Political Islam*, 193. The three elements of Hizbullah's identity are embedded in this definition.

28. Qasim, op. cit., 268-269.

29. Since 1992, all Hizbullah's deputies in the parliament have been males.

30. Qasim, op. cit., 269-270.

31. Cf. Open Letter and Ch 4 on Hizbullah's views on the acceptance of the other.

32. Qasim, op. cit., 270-271.

33. Ibid., 271.

34. It is usually composed of the *Shura* Council members in addition to the Political Council members.

35. Hizbullah voiced this worry in its election program. In fact, the Resistance was the first entry (article, point) in Hizbullah's 1992 election program, and the most elaborated entry by far, making it the main priority.

36. Qasim, op. cit., 271-272.

37. Saad-Ghorayeb argues that Khamina'i's 'blessing' of Hizbullah's decision implies that he did not issue a *fatwa*. She relies on a secondary source (*al-Diyar*) to make this claim. (See Saad-Ghorayeb, op. cit., 68).

38. Qasim, op. cit., 272-273.

39. The most salient verse repeatedly referred to by Hizbullah is the following: "We wish to favour the downtrodden [oppressed] in the land and make them leaders [Imams] and make them the inheritors; And establish (*numakin*) them firmly in the land..." (28:5-6). As mentioned in chapter three, the oppressed were established in authority or were empowered because they followed God's Law. Other Qur'anic verses quoted by Hizbullah are: (12:21); (12:56); (12:54); (18:84); (7:10); (46:26); (6:6); (22:41); (18:95); and (28:57).

40. Yusuf 'Ali comments on the following verse by arguing: "The justification of the righteous in resisting oppression when not only they but their Faith is persecuted and when they are led by a righteous Imam, is that it is a form of self-sacrifice. They are not fighting for themselves, for land, power, or prestige. They are fighting for the right". (See *The Holy Qur'an...*, 862). As will be argued in the conclusion (3.4), this verse stresses the Qur'anic concept of human empowerment (*tamkin*).

41. See the cover page of *Mu'tamar Al-Baladiyyat Al-Awwal [The First Municipal Conference/Convention]*. Beirut: Hizbullah's Central Press Office, 16 July 2002.

42. See the introduction to Hizbullah's 1992 election program.

43. See the introduction to Hizbullah's 1996 election program.

44. See the seventh article: "Foreign policy". The same stance was reiterated in Hizbullah's 1997 "Views and Concepts" in the sections entitled, "*Hizbullah- Lebanon*" and "*Hizbullah between Peace and violence*".

45. See Appendixes A, B, and C.

46. Nasrallah, *Al-'Ahd* 26 August 1994.

47. Qasim, op. cit., 38.

48. Since in Lebanese politics the issue of majority-minority is a very sensitive issue, Nasrallah stressed the unity and solidarity among the Lebanese by clarifying that when he or Hizbullah speaks about the majority and minority, he does not speak about the Muslim majority and the Christian minority (God forbid); rather he speaks about a Muslim-Christian majority and a Muslim-Christian minority. See Nasrallah's speech in the

commemoration of "Jerusalem Day" on 12 November 2004. http://www.nasrollah.org/audio/hassan/2004/quds12112004.html (Last accessed April 2005).

49. Identity and Goals. Nasrallah expressed the same views in al-'Ahd 16 February 1998.

50. Nasrallah, Lebanese Broadcasting Corporation (LBC) 24 September 1995.

51. Al-'Ahd no. 441.

52. Nasrallah, Al-'Ahd 6 April 1994.

53. Nasrallah's speech on July 10, 2001. Al-Manar and al-Nour 10 July 2001; al-Safir 11 July 2001. See also Nasrallah's speech "On the Occasion of the End of the Summer Activities for 'Sayf Association' ", 4 September 2004, http://www.nasrollah.org/audio/hassan/2004/anshita04092004.html.

54. Nayef Krayyem, Hawla Al-Dawla Al-Mansuba li Hizbullah [On Hizbullah's Alleged State]. Beirut: Hizbullah's Educational Mobilization Unit, 1997, 41.

55. The ex-Hizbullah MP, George Najm, used to read, while wearing a cross, Hizbullah's political declarations, that are inaugurated with, "In the name of Allah, the Merciful and Compassionate".

56. See various Lebanese daily newspapers of the month of April 2002, especially al-Safir of 18, 20, and 23 April 2002.

57. Hizbullah's Central Press Office.

58. Hizbullah's Central Information Unit, "A Reading in Papal Guidance", 9-15.

59. That conference saw an unprecedented concordance of ideas, especially those pertaining to religious and moral issues, between the Vatican and the Islamic Republic of Iran.

60. Hizbullah's Central Information Unit, "A Reading in Papal Guidance", 16-25.

61. At that time, he was the head of Hizbullah's Political Council (politburo).

62. Hizbullah's Central Information Unit, "A Reading in Papal Guidance", 26-37.

63. "Identity and Goals".

64. Al-Nour, 6:00 GMT News, 17 January 2004.

65. It is worth mentioning that the abolition of political sectarianism is stipulated in article 95 of the Ta'if Agreement. All that has been achieved till now on the way to the abolishment of political sectarianism is that, in 2004, the Lebanese parliament formed a committee, which is supposed to pave the way for the establishment of the "National Body for the Abolishment of Political Sectarianism".

66. Hizbullah's 1992 election program, second article: " The abolishment of political sectarianism".

67. See the second article: " Achieving equality and establishing the just state".

68. Hizbullah's Central Information Unit, "A Reading in Papal Guidance", 14.

69. See article 4: "The building of the state of law and institutions, and the promotion of political participation".

70. See Nasrallah's 10 July 2001 Speech, al-Safir 11 July 2001.

71. Daily Star 5 February 2004.

72. See the second article: " Achieving equality and establishing the just state".

73. In addition to the Maronites, Hizbullah embarked on a political dialogue with the Christian notables and clergy from all religious denominations such as Greek Orthodox, Greek Catholic, Protestants, Armenians, Syriacs, Assyrians, etc.

74. See the "Introduction" and "Hizbullah and Dialogue", in "Views and Concepts".

75. As mentioned in chapter two, the concept of taklif is a term used for legal obligation in the methodology of Islamic jurisprudence (usul al-fiqh).

76. Hizbullah's nominees to positions in the governmental apparatus portrayed ambitious expectations in serving the public interest. (See the introduction to Hizbullah's 1992 election program). Hizbullah employs a periodic rotation policy among its cadres, a

great majority of whom are the product of the European system of education, rather than Islamic schools and universities.

77. By Qur'anic concepts I mean either explicitly stated in the Qur'an, or derived from a Qur'anic doctrine by way of correlation with religion, interpretation in a religious mode, and authentication in the Qur'an, Sunna, and *shari'a*.

78. See for instance: (42:38) "Their affair being a counsel *[shura]* among themselves", (3:159), and (2:233). It seems that Hizbullah interprets *shura* as some form of *ijma'* based on the Shi'ite variant of the hadith: "The Imams will not confer upon an error", instead of "The *umma* will not confer upon an error"

79. See for instance: (3:23) and (4:105).

80. See for instance: (2:213); (10:19); (5:48); (32:25)

81. See for instance: (8:41); (73:20); (2:277); (4:172); (5:12); and (22:41).

82. See *Mu'tamar Al-Baladiyyat Al-Awwal*, 16ff. Also Hajj Muhammad Ra'd and Dr. Ali Fayyad explained the abovementioned concepts to me in personal interviews conducted in December 2001. See Muhammad Jawad Maghniyyé, *'Ilm Usual Al-Fiqh fi Thawbihi Al-Jadid [The Science of the Principles of Jurisprudence in its New Garment]*. Beirut: Dar Al-Tayyar Al-Jadid, 1988, especially 225-232; 363-365. Cf Ahmad S. Moussalli, *The Islamic Quest for Democracy, Pluralism, and Human Rights*. Gainesville, FL: University Press of Florida, 2001.

83. Interview conducted by Fadeel M. Abun-Nasr on 24 April 2002, as cited in his book entitled *Hizbullah: Haqa'iq…*, 132-133.

84. Bilal N'im, "*Al-Islam fi Shumuliyatihi Al-Tashri'iyya* [Islam as a Comprehensive (System of) Legislation]". *Al-Intiqad* 1065 (9 July 2004).

85. Hizbullah argues that every human being has a natural disposition to worship the divine or God. Hizbullah's Islamic propagation or call (*da'wa*) aims to wake up this element of human nature.

86. Bilal N'im, op. cit. (Italics added for emphasis).

87. *Al-Safir* 7 June 2005.

88. *Lebanese National News Agency* 10 August 2005.

89. See for instance Martyr Murtada Mutahhari's two books: *The Role of Reason in Ijtihad* at http://www.al-islam.org/al-tawhid/reason-ijtihad.htm and *The Role of Ijtihad in Legislation* at http://www.al-islam.org/al-tawhid/ijtihad-legislation.htm. See also Maghniyyé, op. cit.

90. Cf. Saad-Ghorayeb who contends that Hizbullah's political program and ideology do not contain or leave room for a socio-economic program. op. cit., 196, note 2.

91. See Appendix B.

92. *Al-Manar* and *al-Nour* 10 July 2001; *al-Safir* 11 July 2001.

93. It annually holds regular conclaves in order to study and evaluate the socio-economic situation, and it issues its recommendations in a publicised document.

94. This "Working Document" was divided into two main sections. The first section prescribed a ten-point working plan whose objective was to constructively alleviate the socio-economic situation, while the second section stipulated a ten-point strategy directed at finding constructive solutions to the workers' and syndicates' demands. See *al-Intiqad* 1074 (10 September 2004).

95. See, for instance, Nasrallah's speech in commemoration of the municipal councils and majors of the South, 30 June 2004, http://www.nasrollah.org/audio/hassan/2004/baladiat30062004.html

96. http://www.naimkassem.org/materials/activity/2004/aml_hizb.htm. See also *Al-Nour*, 5:00 GMT News, 5 April 2004.

97. *Al-Nour* 5 GMT News 22 May 2004. Hizbullah has been able to build an efficient and responsive organization that meets many of the needs of its constituents while avoiding the tag of corruption that taints the Lebanese political system and its institutions as a whole. Knowing that the national public debt reached $35 billion by June 2004 and is expected – according to the late Lebanese Prime Minister, Rafiq Hariri – to reach $45 billion in 2007, the socio-economic agenda seems to be Hizbullah's most salient feature of its political program after the May 2000 Israeli withdrawal. It is worth mentioning that the economic situation is so severe that a lot of the youth, predominantly males, are either emigrating or working abroad.

98. Conspicuous consumption refers to "Thorstein Veblen's term for a change from the Protestant ethic to an eagerness to show off wealth by the elaborate consumption of goods." James M. Henslin, *Sociology: A Down-To-Earth Approach*. New York: Allyn and Bacon, 2003, 411. See Thorstein Veblen, *The Theory of the Leisure Class*. New York: Macmillian, 1912.

99. See the section entitled, "*Hizbullah and Human Rights*", in "Views and Concepts".

100. Cf. Peter Burke, *History and Social Theory*. New York: Cornell University Press, 1992; Richard Bulliet, *Islam: The View from the Edge*. New York: Colombia University Press, 1994.

101. Hajj Husayn Shami was the ex-head of Hizbullah's social institutions and is the current head of Hizbullah's "Islamic Resistance Support Association". See "*Hizbullah In Haka* [Hizbullah Speaks Out]", *Hurriyat* 9 (Fall 1997), 34-41. Beirut: CRED.

102. See the section entitled, "*Hizbullah and Human Rights*", in "Views and Concepts".

103. Hizbullah has efficiently contributed in providing humanitarian services to the citizens in various Lebanese areas without discrimination between one citizen and another, or one sect and another.

104. Shami, *Hizbullah In Haka*.

105. Personal interview, 2 November 2004. Faqih, an engineer by profession and Nasrallah's second cousin, is Hizbullah's social welfare and public relations officer of the "Organization of the Seal of the Prophets" (*Mujama' Khatim Al-A fnbiya'*) in *Nwayri-Bashura*, a heavily populated Sunni area of Beirut.

106. See the section entitled, "*Hizbullah and Human Rights*", in "Views and Concepts".

107. Some of Hizbullah's civil institutions and NGOs are the following: The Institution of The Good Loan (*Jam'iyyat Mu'ssat al-Qard al-Hasan*), established in 1982; The Martyrs' Foundation (*Mu'assat Al-Shahid*), founded in 1982; The Association of Islamic Health (*Jam'iyyat Hayy'at al-Sihiyyat al-Islamiyyat*), founded in 1984; Institution of Construction and Development (*Jam'iyyat Mu'ssat Jihad al-Bina' al-Inma'iyyat*), founded in 1984; *Al-'Ahd* (Hizbullah's weekly mouthpiece), established in 1984, renamed *Al-Intiqad* in 2001; The Association of the Relief Committee of Imam Khumayni (*Jam'iyyat lajnat al-Imdad al-Khayriyyat al-Islamiyyat*), established in 1987; CCSD (Hizbullah's think tank), founded in 1988; *Al-Nour* radio station, established in 1988. (In November 2004 al-Nour satellite transmission covered the globe); The Wounded Foundation (*Mu'assat Al-Jarha*), established in 1990; The Educational Foundation (*Al-Mu'asasa al-Tarbawiyya*), established in 1991; *Al-Manar* TV station, founded in 1991. (In September 2000, in the wake of the second Palestinian *Intifada*, *al-Manar* started its satellite transmission); etc.

108. Talal Salman, *Sira Dhatiyya li Haraka Muqawina 'Arabiyya Muntasira: Hizbullah [An Autobiography of a Victorious Arab Resistance: Hizbullah]*. Beirut: Al-Safir, 2000, 12.

109. "Hizbullah's Statement of Purpose", Central Press Office, 20 March 1998. Hizbullah's 2004 "Identity and Goals" reiterated the same issues.

110. Hala Jaber calls these "religious taxes" Jaber, *Hezbollah: Born with a Vengeance*, 151; the author prefers to call them 'religious donations'.

111. Interview with Faqih, 2 November 2004.
112. Shami, *Hizbullah In Haka*; Interview with Faqih, 2 November 2004.
113. See "Appendix C", Sections 5 and 7.
114. Yusuf 'Ali comments on the verse by arguing, "That is, spend your wealth in charity and good works. It is God who has given it to you, and you should spend it in God's cause. Nor should you forget the legitimate needs of this life, as misers do, and most people become misers who think too exclusively of their wealth. If wealth is not used properly, three evils will follow: (1) its possessor may be a miser and forget all claims due to himself and those about him; (2) he may forget the higher needs of the poor and needy, or the good causes which require support; and (3) he may even misspend on occasions and cause a great deal of harm and mischief". *The Holy Qur'an…*, 1023.
115. See the section entitled, "*Hizbullah and Human Rights*", in "Views and Concepts".
116. This resonates Sayyid Abbas' important statement: "We will fight deprivation, as we fight the occupation". Sayyid Ibrahim Amin Al-Sayyid, Hizbullah's Political Council head, while calling for occasional economic conferences, repeatedly stated the need to alleviate "political desertification" as well as the problem of political and party life in Lebanon. See http://www.dirasat.net/indexarab.htm for Hizbullah's workshops and conferences on domestic and socio-economic issues.
117. He means Hizbullah did not solely exist to rid Lebanon of the Israeli occupation.
118. Faqih emphasised that Hizbullah's will, determination, and reliance on God accomplished this "divine victory" over the Israeli forces occupying Lebanon. Thus, using the banner of Islam, Hizbullah dealt with the populace and the world for the benefit of the people and the "message".
119. Personal interview, 2 November 2004.
120. Cf.: "It is important to remember, however, that Hezbollah was never involved in meting out 'just punishment' to the Christian militias and had never kidnapped, car bombed or sniped at Lebanese civilians as most other militias had at one time or another". Harik, *Hezbollah: The Changing Face of Terrorism*, 67.
121. Nasrallah and Muhammad Ra'd, as cited in the program entitled "*Ahzab Lubnan: Hizbullah: Al-Jiz' Al-Awwal* [Lebanese Parties: Hizbullah, Part I]", *NBN*, 21 July 2002.
122. Nasrallah's speech on July 10, 2001. *Al-Manar* and *al-Nour* 10 July 2001; *al-Safir* 11 July 2001. See also Nasrallah's 4 September 2004 speech, op. cit. Hajj Imad Faqih explains that Hizbullah refuses to engage in such acts and operate on the ground, simply because these acts will eventually dirty its hands, an eventuality Hizbullah can not afford to happen. (Personal interview, 2 November 2004).
123. For instance, see "Identity and Goals"; its 1996 election program, article one: "Resistance and occupation"; and its 2000 election program, article one: "Resistance and liberation".
124. "Views and Concepts".
125. Nasrallah bases his argument on the Lebanese government's official position/stance as conveyed by the Lebanese permanent delegate to the UN, on September 2, 2004, in the wake of the adoption of US-French backed UN Security Council Revolution 1559, which indirectly referred to Hizbullah as a militia calling on the Lebanese government to disband it and disarm it. The Lebanese delegate argued that in Lebanon there are no militias, rather a Resistance (Hizbullah's Islamic resistance) that is officially recognized and embraced by the Lebanese government. See Nasrallah's 4 September 2004 speech, op. cit. This reasoning has been reiterated by the Lebanese cabinet's policy statement of July 2005.

126. The socio-political indicators of the LMCB testify to its secularist-nationalist nature. See the section entitled, "The formation of the Multi-confessional Lebanese Brigades" in Chapter 1.

127. Mirrored from *Yadi'ot Ahronot*, as cited in *al-safir* 12 December 2005.

128. Hizbullah's "Educational Mobilization" photocopied *al-Safir* issue and wrote the above quotation at the bottom of the page, distributing it at Lebanese colleges and universities.

129. Ayatullah Fadlallah, Personal interview, October 1999.

130. Qasim, op. cit., 294, 320, 327.

132. Ibid., 286.

133. Ibid., 77.

133. Hajj Muhammad Ra'd, Personal interview, 31 December 2001. See also the interview conducted by Fadeel M. Abun-Nasr on 24 April 2002, as cited in his book entitled *Hizbullah: Haqa'iq…*, 132. Also Dr. Ali Fayyed employed the same reasoning when I interviewed him in December 2001.

134. Hajj Muhammad R'ad, Hizbullah's Central Information Unit, "A Reading in Papal Guidance", 33-36. These dimensions of civil society are also clearly salient in all of Hizbullah's parliamentary elections programs.

135. As stipulated in the "Constitution of Medina".

136. See Nasrallah's interview with *al-Safir* 28 June 2000.

137. I think Qasim is using the world ideology to connote a system or order or basis for political and social action.

138. Qasim, op. cit., 39-40.

139. See http://www.naimkassem.org; *Al-Nour*, 6:00 GMT News, 10 February 2004; *Al-Safir* 10 February 2004.

140. Personal interview, 2 November 2004.

141. The last issue of *al-'Ahd* was number 896, dated 6 April 2001/ 12 *Muharram* 1422 AH; the first issue of *al-Intiqad* was number 897, dated 20 April 2001/ 26 *Muharram* 1422 AH.

142. Hizbullah reiterated that Lebanon is characterized by an Arab identity and belonging. Hizbullah's Central Information Unit, "A Reading in Papal Guidance", 23.

143. See article 7: "Foreign policy".

144. See article 2: "Lebanese foreign policy".

145. See article 2: "Lebanese foreign policy".

146. See Nasrallah's interview with *al-Jazeera* 25 May 2000. When Nasrallah started his visit to Iran on July 4, 2001 he was received as a head of state.

147. See Nasrallah's interview with *al-Safir* 28 June 2000.

148. Qasim, op. cit., 77.

149. Interview with Na'im Qasim, "*Salun al-Sabt* [Saturday's Saloon]", *Sawt Lubnan* 25 January 2003. See also Nasrallah's fiery speech on the occasion of a funeral procession for three Hizbullah "martyrs" who died fighting the Israeli forces in the Lebanese border village of *Ghajar* on November 25, 2005: "We are allied with Syria and Iran from the stance of Lebanon's *maslaha* to liberate its occupied land. However, the Islamic Resistance's orders come from Beirut". See *al-Intiqad* 1138 (2 December 2005), 7-8.

150. Hizbullah's Central Information Unit, "A Reading in Papal Guidance", 13; 36.

151. See "Politburo member lauds Hizbullah's role", *Daily Star* 1 September 2003.

152. Al-Musawi is referring to the UN Resolution 1559.

153. *Daily Star* 18 June 2005.

154. Interview with Reuters as reported by *al-Safir* 17 August 2005.

155. See Lebanese daily newspapers of 8 August 2005 and *al-Intiqad* 1122 (12 August 2005).

156. See Nasrallah's speech to Hizbullah's Women's Organization during an *iftar* organized by the "Islamic Resistance Support Association", 13 October 2005.

157. See the program entitled "Ahzab Lubnan...", *NBN*, Part III.

158. After the creation of the post of Secretary General in 1989, the Secretary General headed the *Shura* Council.

159. Qasim, op. cit., 76.

160. Ibid., 76.

161. Idem.

162. "Ahzab Lubnan...", *NBN*, 21 July 2002.

163. Khatami's visit to Lebanon in May 2003 falls in this regard. In his speeches Khatami praised Hizbullah's successful resistance against the Israeli occupation and praised Hizbullah's May 2000 feat, namely, the liberation of southern Lebanon from the 22-year old Israeli occupation, thus setting a precedent in the Arab-Israeli conflict. However, Khatami did not only concentrate on Hizbullah's military capabilities, rather he called on it, as he has done in his 1997 visit, to continue pursuing a policy of *infitah* towards the other sectarian-confessional communities in Lebanon and to graduate intellectuals line in line with freedom fighters. Khatami called Lebanon the land of freedom and dialogue. Khatami's positive attitude towards Lebanon prompted Elias Aoudé, the Greek Orthodox Bishop of Beirut, to say that if all the Lebanese loved Lebanon as Khatami did, then none of the calamities that rocked Lebanon will ever have happened. *Al-Nour* 5:00 GMT News 15 May 2003.

164. Interview with Qasim, op. cit., *Sawt Lubnan* 25 January 2003.

165. Qasim, op. cit., 77-78.

166. Ibid., 76-77.

167. See the first article of its 1992 election program: "The Resistance".

168. See the video clip entitled "Death to Israel" on *Al-Manar* TV.

169. "Identity and Goals".

170. See the introduction and first article in its 1992, 1996, and 2000 election programs.

171. See "Views and Concepts", section entitled "*Hizbullah-Lebanon*".

172. Hizbullah's Central Information Unit, "A Reading in Papal Guidance", 20.

173. See http://www.knesset.gov.il/main/eng/home.asp; *AFP* 31 July 2003; and " 'Communal Punishment and Racial Discrimination': Knesset Approves Barring the Palestinians from Obtaining the [Israeli] Nationality"; *Al-Safir* 1 August 2003.

174. Qasim, op. cit., 250.

175. Keeping in mind the Qur'anic prohibition of killing women, children, and elderly, Nasrallah conceded that this talk has its heavy price from the perspective of the overall *shar'i*, moral, and *jihadi* responsibilities.

176. Nasrallah rationalizes this stance by arguing that the Palestinians do not need anyone to fight on their behalf. They are capable of fighting on their own using their rifles, bombs, and the bodies of their martyrs in order to rapture the Zionist disgrace and humiliation and defeat the Zionist entity. See http://media.manartv.com/clips/clip25.ram (Last accessed August 2004).

177. Nasrallah's speech in the commemoration of "The Jerusalem (Quds) Day", Beirut, 14 December 2001. I would like stress that – contrary to the Palestinians who have blown themselves into Israeli civilians – Hizbullah has never done so. Hizbullah did not engage in any suicide operation against Israeli civilians in its 18-year struggle with the Israeli forces occupying south Lebanon. Rather, all its field and martyrdom operations targeted Israeli military and intelligence personnel. Further, Hizbullah has never conducted any suicide operation in Israel; rather, it left it to the discretion of the Palestinians to do so.

178. Muhammad Ra'd, Personal interview, 31 December 2001. Nasrallah also emphasized this stance in his September 28, 2001 speech in commemoration of the first anniversary of the *Intifada*.
179. See the video clip entitled "Death to Israel" on *Al-Manar* TV.
180. Hizbullah refers to the Middle East peace process as the "peace settlement".
181. See the first article in its 1992, 1996, and 2000 election programs.
182. *Al-'Ahd* 887 (2 February 2001); *al-Safir* 31 January and 1 February 2001; *al-Afkar* 965 (12 February 2001).
183. This is a standard Hizbullah policy iterated by Qasim's and Nasrallah on several occasions, some of which are the following: Qasim's speech of 28 May 2002 at AUB entitled, "The Experience of the Resistance and the Future of the *Intifada*", and Nasrallah's speech of 18 June 2002 in the occasion of the "First Convention of the Parliamentarians who are Defending the Palestinian Cause". See respectively www.nasrallah.net; *al-Intiqad* 955 (31 May 2002), 16; *al-Intiqad* 958 (21 June 2002), 6-7.
184. The attacks claimed the lives of 191 innocent civilians and wounded around 1,400 others.
185. See Nasrallah's speech in the weekly commemoration of the martyrdom of Youssef Mir'i, 14 March 2004, at: http://www.nasrollah.org/audio/hassan/2004/youssef14032004.html (Last accessed April 2005).
186. See Nasrallah's speech on the first day of *Muharram* 1425 AH, 20 February 2004, at: http://www.nasrollah.org/arabic/hassan/khitabat/2004/khitabat005.htm. (Last accessed April 2005).
187. See "Views and Concepts", the section entitled, *"Hizbullah and the Resistance"*. See also Hizbullah's 1998 "Statement of Purpose".
188. "Identity and Goals".
189. See the first article in Hizbullah's 1992, 1996, 2000, and 2005 parliamentary elections programs. Section 6 of Hizbullah's 2004 municipal elections program, which is dedicated to socio-economic issues, stressed the consolidation of the resistance society, in order to substantiate the already existing resistance identity.
190. See Hizbullah's 1998 "Statement of Purpose", and the first article of its 2000 election program: "Resistance and Liberation". Hizbullah credits itself for inspiring the flare up of the Palestinian Intifada on September 28, 2000.
191. Nasrallah personally thanked the Lebanese authorities, which testifies to the importance Hizbullah accords to this decision and its positive impact on Hizbullah's domestic role. (See "Hizbullah's celebration of the two governorates equals a distinguished *jihadi* operation". *Al-Mustaqbal* 8 July 2003).
192. Hizbullah is the only Lebanese political party or group that is not known to have misappropriated or stolen public funds.
193. See Nasrallah's speech in commemoration of the municipal councils and majors of the South, 30 June 2004, http://www.nasrollah.org/arabic/hassan/khitabat/2004/khitabat014.htm (Last accessed April 2005).
194. See Nasrallah's speech in commemoration of the municipal councils and majors of the *Biqa'*, 4 July 2004, http://www.nasrollah.org/arabic/hassan/khitabat/2004/khitabat015.htm (Last accessed April 2005).
195. See the introduction to Hizbullah's 1992 election program.
196. "Identity and Goals".
197. See the introduction to Hizbullah's 2000 election program: "Our loyal Lebanese populace".
198. See "Views and Concepts", the section entitled *"Hizbullah and Human Rights"*.

199. See Nasrallah's speech on the first day of *Muharram* 1425 AH, 20 February 2004, at: http://www.nasrollah.org/arabic/hassan/khitabat/2004/khitabat005.htm. (Last accessed April 2005).

200. Condoleeza Rice, the US National Security Advisor, tried to explain suicide operations arguing, "[A] sense of *hopelessness* provides a fertile ground for ideologies of hatred that persuade people to forsake university educations, careers and families and aspire instead to blow themselves up – taking as many innocent lives with them as possible". (Italics added for emphasis). (See "Bush adviser Condoleeza Rice peddles democratic blueprint for Middle East", *AFP* 7 August 2003). Barbara Victor subscribes to a similar view. In her study on "Palestinian women suicide bombers", she contends that the main motive for this "fatal cocktail" is that a "culture of death" entered into the psyche of the Palestinian people as a result of hopelessness, social stress, and depression, which these relatively destitute women suffered from. See her book entitled: *Army of Roses: Inside the World of Palestinian Women Suicide Bombers*. PA: Rodale Press, 2003.

201. Qasim, op. cit., 61-64. (Italics added for emphasis).

202. See the program entitled "*Al-Din wa Al-Hayat [Religion and Life]*", *Al-Manar*, 10 October 2002.

203. See Sayyid Hasan Nasrallah's speech delivered in *Nabi Shit* on 16 February 2003 in the commemoration of the martyrdom of Sayyid Abbas al-Musawi and Shaykh Raghib Harb, as well as the 18th anniversary of the inauguration of the party. (http://www.nasrollah.org)

204. Sayyid Hasan Nasrallah, http://media.manartv.com/clips/clip11.ram

205. Sayyid Hasan Nasrallah, Lebanese Broadcasting Corporation (March 1997), as cited by Saad-Ghorayeb, *Hizbullah: Politics and Religion,* 133.

206. A few days after Sept. 11, Ayatullah Khamina'i condemned the attacks, "Our stance is that of Islam: we denounce the massive killing of people... these calamities are condemned in whichever place they occur". See http://www.nasrollah.org/arabic/khaminai/khitabat/2001/khitabat007.htm In commenting on the London July 7, 2005 attacks Iran said that the recourse to violence in order to achieve particular goals is totally condemned. *Al-Intiqad* 1117 (8 July 2005)

207. 56 people died, including the 4 suicide bombers, and around 700 hundred were insured. *Al-Intiqad* 1117 (8 July 2005); *al-Safir* 8 July 2005.

208. For an elaboration of Hizbullah's views see: Joseph Alagha, "Hizbullah, Terrorism, and Sept. 11" *ORIENT: German Journal for Politics and Economics of the Middle East*, 44 (September 2003), 3, 385-412; and "Hizbullah and Martyrdom", *ORIENT*, 45 (March 2004), 1, 47-74.

209. Fadlallah, a Press Release, 12 September 2001, (www.bayynat.org.lb); *al-Safir*, 14 September 2001; Interview by Sarkis Na'um in *al-Nahar*, published in instalments in issues from 19-26 September 2001; Interview with *al-Zaman Magazine* 27 November 2001.

210. See the political declaration entitled, "Hizbullah regrets lives lost and warns the US not to resort to unjust policies", issued by the "Central Press Office", 16 September 2001, www.hizbollah.org. (English mistakes are not corrected). (Last accessed August 2004).

211. www.bayynat.org.lb; al-Intiqad 1117 (8 July 2005); *al-Safir* 8 July 2005.

212. See Hizbullah's 1996 and 2000 parliamentary elections programs, articles 3 to 6, and 3 to 7 respectively. See also Hizbullah's 2004 municipal elections program, especially the opening paragraph.

213. In that case, members of the Resistance who are unwilling to participate in civil life will be accommodated in the Lebanese Army and all the party's weapons will be handed in to the Lebanese Army, as other militias had done in conformity to the Ta'if Agreement.

214. Contestation refers to "Opportunities to oppose the government, form political organizations, express oneself on political matters without fear of government reprisals, read and hear alternative points of view, vote by secret ballot in elections in which candidates of different parties compete for votes and after which the losing candidates peacefully yield their claim to office to the winners, etc". Robert A. Dahl, *Polyarchy: Participation and Opposition*. New Haven: Yale University Press, 1971, 20.

215. I take cooptation to refer to the "disarming" of opposition by the invitation of opposition leaders to become part of a ruling elite or structure.

216. I use empowerment to describe a process by which a marginalized group experiences an accretion to its power without continuously setting out to do so at the expense of others. However, the key term here is "power" which is a much-debated term.

217. Cf. Saad-Ghorayeb, op. cit., 171 ff. It is worth mentioning that the abolished UN Resolution 3379, which stipulated Zionism as a form of racism, can be interpreted as anti-Semitic.

218. Even before the creation of Israel, Antun S'adé, the Syrian Social Nationalist Party (SSNP) Christian founder, as early as the 1920s, employed an uncompromising discourse, namely, "Our contact with the Jews is a contact of a foe to a foe". S'adé's statement could be considered anti-Semitic because he discriminated against the Jews as a race.

219. Cf. Hamzeh who relegates Hizbullah's political and economic *jihad*, most notably parliamentary representation and involvement in elected professional bodies, to the status of persuasive *jihad* or smaller non-military *jihad*. A. Nizar Hamzeh, *In the Path of Hizbullah*. Syracuse: Syracuse University Press, 2004, 39.

220. See the introduction to Hizbullah's 1996 election program in "Appendix B".

Notes Chapter 5

1. Nasrallah, "Ahzab Lubnan...", Part I *NBN*, 21 July 2002.

2. Nasrallah, see the program entitled "Ahzab Lubnan...", *NBN*, Part III.

3. Wilfried Buchta, *Who Rules Iran? The Structure of Power in the Islamic Republic*. Washington, DC: The Washington Institute for Near East Policy and the Konrad Adenaueur Stiftung, 2000.

4. Which is also a precedent since 1981.

5. After the liberation, or the nearly complete Israeli withdrawal from south Lebanon in May 2000, Hizbullah erected two small stone pillars, one representing the Great Satan (US), and the other the Little Satan (Israel), so that people could throw stones at them, thus emulating the symbolic act of stoning the Devil at *Mina*, in Saudi Arabia during the *Hajj*. By this Hizbullah solved the problem of cross-border fire by the Israeli soldiers against the Lebanese stone throwers who used to target them across the fenced border.

6. According to Maloney the functions of political Islam in foreign policy, which characterize Iran's identity, are the following: Persian nationalism, pan-Islamism, and revolutionary anti-imperialism. (Suzanne Maloney, "Identity and Change in Iran's Foreign Policy", in: Raymond Hinnebusch and Anoushiravan Ehteshami (eds.), *The Foreign Policy of Middle East States*. Boulder, Co.: Lynne Rienner Publishers, 2002, 88-116).

7. Cf. Joseph Alagha, "Hizbullah, Terrorism and Sept. 11", *ORIENT: German Journal for Politics and Economics of the Middle East*, 44 (September 2003), 3, 396-397; 405-410.

8. *Bidnayyil*'s Speech, 20 May 2001; Interview with al-*Jazeera*, 25 May 2001.

9. "We note that these [international] organizations do not constitute a podium for the oppressed nations, and in general, they remain ineffective and inefficient due to the

procedural hegemony and domination of the world oppressors on its decisions…" See section 24: "A final word regarding international organizations".

10. On a theoretical level, this is most likely warranted by the following logic: "Transnational identities, while quite important, may be very limited in their long-term impact because politicians [Nasrallah] respond more strongly to domestic audiences than to opinions held by citizens of other countries". Saideman, "Thinking Theoretically…", 194.

11. Judith Palmer Harik, *Hezbollah: The Changing Face of Terrorism*. London: I.B. Tauris, 2004, 2; 168.

12. This logic is also based on Hizbullah's distinction among the four senses of martyrdom. For an elaboration of this argument see: Joseph Alagha, "Hizbullah and Martyrdom", *ORIENT*, 45 (March 2004), 1, 47-74.

13. As cited by Hasan 'Izzeddine, "How is Hizbullah looked upon and how does it introduce itself?" Paper delivered as a contribution to an LAU (Lebanese American University) conference on "Arab Stereotyping", 6-9 November 2001, p. 6. The same article was published in *Al-Safir* 12 November 2001.

14. See Nasrallah's interview on September 24, 1998 in "Hot Spot" (*Nuqta Sakhina*) on al-Jazeera TV. Nasrallah stresses that in Iran, the Islamic Revolution was not a military coup d'état; rather it was accompanied by people's choice. Ayatullah Khumayni himself made a referendum about this issue and made the people participate in drafting the constitution. Basing himself of the Iranian precedent, Nasrallah states that an Islamic state can neither be established by a strong-armed political party by restoring to force nor by a coup d'état.

15. Interview with Ali Fayyad, conducted by Abun-Nasr on 17 April 2002, op. cit., 127.

16. Qasim, op. cit., 38.

17. Al-Madini, op. cit., 162-163; Sharara, op. cit., 342.

Notes Chapter 6

1. Saad-Ghorayeb, "Factors Conducive…", 295.

2. Fuller and Francke, *The Arab Shi'a…*, 231.

3. Wright, "Lebanon", 62.

4. See Al-Husayni, "*Hizbullah: Haraka 'Askariyya…*", 18-19. Imam Khumayni held "the idea that the divisiveness of political parties has no place among Muslims who all belong to the Party of God". Momen, *An Introduction to Shi'i Islam…*, 297. In other words, this is in line with Khumayni's conception that in Islam there are no political parties, the concept being a Western invention. Even up till now there are no political parties in Iran as such, which are allowed to participate in the political life of the Islamic Republic. Raymond Hinnebusch and Anoushiravan Ehteshami (eds.), *The Foreign Policy of Middle East States*. Boulder, Co.: Lynne Rienner Publishers, 2002, 295-296ff.

5. Hizbullah's election lists and parliamentary representation included Sunnis and Christians.

6. For instance, in the 2004 municipal elections, Beirut and Tripoli voter turnout was around 20% and 30% respectively, while in the *Biqa'* it was 70%. In the 2005 parliamentary elections voter turnout in Beirut was around 28%, while in the South and *Biqa'* it was respectively 45% and 52%.

7. Hizbullah indicated points of convergence with the Papal guidance on the issue of secularism. Ra'd emphasized that national coexistence under the umbrella of the human values, which are affirmed both by Christianity and Islam, is much better for society than

the adoption of secularism. (See Hizbullah's Central Information Unit, "A Reading in Papal Guidance", 30-31).

8. See chapter one, the section entitled: *"The employment of al-taklif al-shar'i in the elections".*

9. Olivier Roy, *Globalised Islam: The Search for A New Umma.* Revised and updated edition. London: Hurst and Company, 2004, 61.

10. Na'im Qasim, *Al-Safir* 20 May 2002.

11. See http://www.naimkassem.org; *Al-Nour*, 6:00 GMT News, 9 February 2004; *Al-Safir* 9 February 2004.

12. This is in line with Nasrallah's call of greater *jihad* against the self and corruption in Lebanon. (See chapter four).

13. Hajj Imad Faqih, Personal interview, 2 November 2004. (See chapter four).

14. See Nasrallah's speech to Hizbullah's Women's Organization during an *iftar* organized by the "Islamic Resistance Support Association", 13 October 2005.

15. *Al-Safir* 3 September 2005; *Al-Safir* and *Daily Star* 6 September 2005. Nasrallah is reported to have said: "Resistance is a reaction against aggression; when the aggression ends, resistance ends". See his interview with *Al-'Arabiyya* 2 September 2005.

16. I mention two prominent occasions of Hizbullah's employment of the "if theory". The first during Sharon's incursion into the West Bank in April 2002; the second during the prisoner's negotiation phase with Israel that resulted in the watershed January 2004 exchange.

17. Shaykh Na'im Qasim is reported to have said that, when he annually performs the *hajj*, every year, he is astonished by the growing number of people from various places and countries in the Muslim world who congratulate him on Hizbullah's model of resistance. This illustrates, to a degree, the far-reaching nature of *al-Manar* TV: "In 2004, it was estimated that about 10 million people watched *al-Manar*". See Sami Moubayed, "Lebanon guided by the Nasrullah factor", *The Asia Times*, 26 February 2005. Via the internet at: http://atimes01.atimes.com/atimes/Middle_East/GB26Ak03.html

18. It started broadcasting to the five continents in November 2004, in addition to its previous satellite broadcasting to Middle East, North Africa, and Europe.

19. See Section 2.6 in chapter 4.

20. See Appendixes A, B, and C.

21. Between 17-19 February 2004, the CCSD organized – at the prestigious Crown Plaza Hotel located in Hamra Ras-Beirut – a conference entitled "The Islamic World and Europe: From Dialogue towards Understanding". The conference was co-organized by: The Centre for the Study of Islam and Christian-Muslim Relations (CSIC) at the University of Birmingham, the German Orient Institut (Beirut), and the Friedrich Ebert Stiftung Foundation (Beirut); in cooperation with: *la Revue Confluences-Méditerranée* (Paris), les éditions l'Harmattan (Paris), the Austrian Embassy (Beirut), and the *Ijtihad* Journal (Beirut). The conference pamphlet stated, "The conference deals with the clarification of terminology… [it] discuss[es] international issues… [and] attempts at bridging the gap between diverging perceptions to reach a common language to start from. So, finding a common expression of equally shared concerns prevents building up an 'axis of evil' of whatever kind". The conference aims "to set the preconditions for the establishment of a 'permanent committee for dialogue' open for everyone, thus enabling continuing exchanges on the same level in the future… The main aim of such a dialogue is to identify basic values and concepts to fill them with commonly shared contents in order to develop an approach to a mutual understanding. From this basis, a further discussion of politically problematic

issues concerning the relationship between Arab-Islamic and European societies should be fruitful". See the CCSD website: http://www.dirasat.net/indexarab.htm

22. Mainly, low-key and closed nature meetings.

23. The meeting took place at Hizbullah's secretariat-general headquarters and lasted for 75 minutes. Dr. Ali Fayyad, the head of the CCSD, attended the meeting. "The assembly discussed the issue of the European-Mediterranean partnership, particularly the relations between Lebanon and the EU". The meeting resulted in broadening the cooperation between the EU Commission and Hizbullah, thus establishing common working committees in order to study mutually important dossiers. (See http://www.nasrollah. org/english/index.htm and the Lebanese daily newspapers of 11 September 2004). In a similar vein, Bernhard Bot – the Dutch Foreign Minister, whose country headed the EU presidency from July till December 2004, in a meeting with the Israeli foreign minister, Sylvan Shalom, during the UN General Assembly's meeting in New York – labelled Hizbullah as a resistance or "struggle" movement (verzettsbeweging / strijdbeweging) stressing the need of conducting dialogue with it. (See Lebanese daily newspapers of 24 September 2004). It is worth mentioning that Hizbullah praised the Spanish Prime Minister's call to a coalition between the Western civilization and the Arab-Islamic one. See Mahmud Rayya, "Bila Muwaraba", al-Intiqad 1076 (24 September 2004).

24. Khamini's endorsement of the Iraqi constitution is from the stance of maslaha. (IRNA 21 October 2005 Friday prayer's speech). Likewise, Iran's allowing the US to use its airspace and to roll its tanks across the Khurasan region in its war on Afghanistan, falls within the domain of maslaha.

Notes Chapter 7

1. Unless otherwise specified, translations are mine. My translation is not always literal; rather it is intended to capture the over all meaning and the message behind the text.

2. The Open Letter was published as "Al-Nass Al-Harfi Al-Kamil li-Risalat Hizbullah ila al-Mustad'afinin [The Original Text in Full of Hizbullah's Open Letter to the Oppressed]", al-'Ahd (Friday 3 Jamadi al-Thani 1405 AH, 22 February 1985), 5-8. The Open Letter was read one week earlier, on Saturday, February 16, 1985, by Hizbullah's spokesman at the time Sayyid Ibrahim Amin al-Sayyid.

3. Cf. al-husnayayn in Chapter 2. The word husnayayn in (9:52) is taken to refer to martyrdom (of the self) and victory (for the umma): "Say: 'Do you expect for us anything other than one of the two fairest outcomes (martyrdom and victory); while we await for you that Allah will smite you with a punishment, either from Him, or at our hands?' So wait and watch, we are waiting and watching you".

4. A reference to Imam Husayn and his "martyrdom" at Karbala'.

5. Al-'Ahd (Friday 3 Jamadi al-Thani 1405 AH), 5.

6. Idem. It is most likely that this verse offers/shelters Hizbullah with a religious legitimacy for its political ideology. The verse refers to the idea of free choice and free will, whereby in the end the people (believers) find out that religion is the Truth. Thus, religion is found through freedom of choice, and not by imposition of the truth. The application of this is that Hizbullah will not impose its faith or ideology on anyone. The choice is ultimately left to the individual, but S/he must be aware of the Qur'anic injunction. My interpretation is borne out by the following explanation: "Our choice in our limited Free-will involves a corresponding personal responsibility. We are offered the Truth: again and again is

it pressed on our attention. If we reject it, we must take all the terrible consequences which are prefigured in the Fire of Hell. Its flames and roof will completely enclose us like a tent. Ordinarily there is water to quench the heat of thirst: here the only drink will be like molten brass, thick, heavy, burning, sizzling. Before it reaches the mouth of the unfortunates, drops of it will scald their faces as it is poured out". A. Yusuf Ali, *The Holy Qur'an: Translation and Commentary*. Fourth printing. Lahore: Islamic Propagation Center, 1993, 738.

7. Idem. The 3 words in bold – Islam, *wilayat al-faqih (al-waliyy al-faqih)*, *jihad* – are supposed to refer to Hizbullah's religious ideology. Translation taken from http://www.ict.org.il/Articles/Hiz_letter.htm with few modifications in order to capture the meaning conveyed in the original Arabic text.

8. Idem. http://www.ict.org.il/Articles/Hiz_letter.htm

9. *Al-'Ahd*, op. cit., 5.

10. Translation taken from http://www.ict.org.il/Articles/Hiz_letter.htm. Philip Habib was a Lebanese-American envoy and negotiator sent by the US Administration to diffuse and solve the crisis that resulted from the June 1982 Israeli invasion of Lebanon.

11. *Al-'Ahd*, op. cit., 5.

12. A reference to the "ethnic cleansing" that was practiced by the Christian Militias against the Shi'as in East Beirut and the Christian areas between 1975-1976 (See chapter 1).

13. Lebanese Forces are the military wing of the Phalangists.

14. Bashir Jumayyel, the head of the Phalangist Christian militia, was elected president on August 23, 1982. On September 14, 1982, he was assassinated by a car bomb.

15. Lebanese president from 1976-1982.

16. Amin Jumayyel, Bashir's brother, was elected as president of the Lebanese Republic on September 23, 1982. He remained in office for the next six years.

17. *Al-'Ahd*, op. cit., 5-6. http://www.ict.org.il/Articles/Hiz_letter.htm

18. Ibid., 6. http://www.ict.org.il/Articles/Hiz_letter.htm

19. Idem. http://www.ict.org.il/Articles/Hiz_letter.htm

20. Idem.

21. Idem. http://www.ict.org.il/Articles/Hiz_letter.htm

22. Idem.

23. Idem.

24. http://www.ict.org.il/Articles/Hiz_letter.htm

25. *Al-'Ahd*, op. cit., 6.

26. By Lebanese political system is meant "political Maronism" and the sectarian division of governmental and vocational posts.

27. *Al-'Ahd*, op. cit., 6. http://www.ict.org.il/Articles/Hiz_letter.htm

28. A politico-military consortium of the Christian right militias. Now it is defunct.

29. *Al-'Ahd*, op. cit., 6-7. http://www.ict.org.il/Articles/Hiz_letter.htm

30. On March 19, 1982 the UN Security Council issued resolution 425 calling for the unconditional withdrawal of the Israeli forces from Lebanon. In order to help restore the Lebanese state's sovereignty to the border, the UN established the United Nations Interim Force in Lebanon (UNIFIL), a 5000 interim peacekeeping force, which was sent to Lebanon as of March 23, 1982. According to the UN website, the "UNIFIL was created in 1978 to confirm Israeli withdrawal from Lebanon, restore the international peace and security, and help the Lebanese Government restore its effective authority in the area". http://www.un.org/Depts/dpko/missions/unifil/index.html

31. *Al-'Ahd*, op. cit., 7. http://www.ict.org.il/Articles/Hiz_letter.htm

32. Idem. http://www.ict.org.il/Articles/Hiz_letter.htm

33. Idem.
34. Idem.
35. This is a contextual reference to the 1985 Israeli withdrawal from *Nabatiyyé* and *Tyre* and the formation of its self-declared "Security Zone". (See Chronology and Chapter 1).
36. Cf. SSNP nationalist discourse of "In you is a power, which if actualised will change the course of history". See Alagha (2004).
37. *Al-'Ahd*, op. cit., 7.
38. Idem.
39. Idem. http://www.ict.org.il/Articles/Hiz_letter.htm
40. Ibid., 7-8.
41. *Al-'Ahd*, op. cit., 8.
42. Idem.
43. Hizbullah appropriated this section of the Open Letter, almost word by word, from the section entitled, "The Grave Responsibilities of the Muslim *'ulama*", in: Imam Khumayni's *Al-Jihad Al-Akbar [Greater Jihad]*. Translated by Husayn Kurani. Tehran: Islamian Grand Library, 1980, 9-10. The same statement of refining the self before refining others is repeated and born out in the article entitled, "The Spiritual-Dynamic Force of the Islamic Revolution – Second Episode: The Ideological and Social Change... A New Conception of Jihad", in: *al-'Ahd* (10 Shawwal 1405/28 June 1985), 9. Cf. Norton's failure to translate and contextualise this concept of greater jihad. Augustus Richard Norton, *Amal and the Shi'a Struggle for the Soul of Lebanon*. Austin: University Press of Texas, 1987, 185.
44. Saddam executed him on April 9, 1980. Hizbullah leaders (*al-qada*) or ideologues are listed, from ascending to descending order, as follows: Imam Khumayni (Iranian), Imam Khamina'i (Iranian), the martyr al-Sayyid Muhammad Baqir al-Sadr (Iraqi), Sayyid Musa al-Sadr (Iranian-Lebanese), the martyr al-Sayyid Abbas al-Musawi (Lebanese), Sayyid Hasan Nasrallah (Lebanese), and the martyr Shaykh Raghib Harb (Lebanese). (See http://www.nasrollah.org/english/index.htm; last accessed August 2004). Thus, not all of Hizbullah's leaders are *fuqaha'* (plural of *faqih*), even though they are all clergymen. Also, it appears that Hizbullah's most prominent ideologues are transnational, rather than Lebanese. The word "*Rahbar*" in Persian, which means leader of the Islamic Revolution, is the title assumed by Khumayni, and after his death, it was accorded to Khamina'i when he succeeded him in 1995.
45. *Al-'Ahd*, op. cit., 8.
46. Idem, 8. Thus, the Open Letter ended as it started: with a Qur'anic substantiation. Hizbullah is not claiming the absolute Truth, since Truth is from God. God is the only Truth, we (Hizbullah) do not know if our discourse reveals the Truth. If there is anybody who refuses our ideas and discourse, then God will be the ultimate judge. However, Hizbullah claims the truth, but not the ultimate Truth, which is only known by God. This seems in line with classical Islamic discourse where the wrong is perceived from the self, and not from God. Therefore, Hizbullah is trying to employ a pluralist discourse, which is very different from post-modernist discourse and philosophy because it is based on the metaphysical underpinning of relations underscoring the difference between the relative truth and the absolute transcendent Truth. While the post-modernists seem to be agnostic, the Islamists, including Hizbullah, seem to be theists. After all, God is transcendent: "None knows God but God" (*la y'rif Allah illa Allah*). This seems in line with what Imam 'Ali has said: "incapability of cognisance is cognisance" (*al'ajzu 'an al-idrak al-idrak*). The solution might be the *hadith qudsi*: "I [God] was a hidden treasure and I wanted to be known, so I created and through me, they knew me" (*kuntu kanzan makhfiyyan fa aradtu an u'raf fa khalaqtu al-khalq fa bi 'arafuni*). [I think this *hadith* is related to the Islamic explanation

of cosmology. Although there is a controversial discussion among Islamic scholars about the validity of this *hadith* making it highly vulnerable to criticism, there seems to be a clue in the Qur'an to justify this *hadith* since it is written that human beings are created in the image of God. Thus, the existential aspect of human life is related to or goes back to or is ultimately referred back to God. It is worth mentioning that Ibn 'Arabi had argued that this *hadith* is correct through God's revelation to him (*sahih bi-al-mukashafa*), which is a speculative way of defending his argument]. The weakness is that human beings never fully understand God; this is the true understanding. Thus, one does not know God, but only the signs of God i.e. *'alam* (creature) and verses of the scripture, both are referred to as *aya* and both are signs; this is the way God reveals Himself to us. That is why we say *Rab al-'alamin* (God of the creatures). Thus, human beings understand the signs, not the absolute, and Hizbullah seems to imply and abide by this interpretation. In short, when Hizbullah opposes itself and its discourse to the oppressors (*al-qawn al-zalimin*), it is indirectly claiming truth on its side. Therefore, there is an aspect of relativism in Hizbullah's discourse. Remark: it is worth mentioning that from a theological perspective, *aya* has different meanings; however, it is very important to look at the generic meaning. The generic meaning of *aya* is signs, but the specific meaning is a sentence in the scripture (verse). Both uses are warranted in the Qur'an. Generic sense: "There are in the creation of Heavens and the earth and the alteration of night and day real signs *[ayat]* for people and understanding" (3:190); verse in the scripture: "Yet they are not all alike; some of the people of the Book are a nation upstanding, that recite God's signs *[ayat]* in the watches of the night, bowing themselves" (3:113).

47. http://almashriq.hiof.no/lebanon/300/320/324/324.2/hizballah/hizballah-background. html (Last accessed August 2005).

48. http://almashriq.hiof.no/lebanon/300/320/324/324.2/hizballah/statement01.html (Last accessed August 2005).

49. http://www.hizbollah.org/english/frames/index_eg.htm (Last accessed August 2004).

50. Although Hizbullah translated *jumhuriyya Islamiyya* (Islamic Republic) as Islamic Government, I prefer to stick to the exact translation as mentioned in the original Arabic text.

51. The 1996 April Understanding.

52. My translation is based upon Hizbullah's original document released by Hizbullah's Central Press Office in July 1992.

53. This is reminiscent of socialist-Marxist discourse.

54. A reference to the 1985 Israeli withdrawal and its formation of its self-declared "Security Zone". (See Chronology and Ch 1).

55. This is a clear stress on Hizbullah's resistance identity.

56. Lebanon lost the Seven Villages to Israel during the 1948 war. (See for instance, Al-Jam'iyya Al-Ijtima'iyya Al-Thaqafiyya Li-Abna' Al-Qura Al-Sabi', *Al-Qura Al-Sabi'Al-Lubnaniyya Al-Muhtalla: Dirasa Qanuniyya-Ijtima'iyya [The Seven Lebanese Occupied Villages: A Legal-Social Study]*. First edition. Beirut: Al-Markaz Al-Istishari Lil-Dirasat, November 2003). The Arabs of Wadi Khaled have been granted the Lebanese nationality in 1994.

57. It is ironic to note that up till now, this has not been accomplished.

58. This has been accomplished in 2003 by the government sponsored Centre of Research and Development (*Markaz Al-Buhuth wa Al-Inma'*).

59. http://almashriq.hiof.no/lebanon/300/320/324/324.2/hizballah/hizballah-platform. html (Last accessed August 2005). As translated from a four-page document entitled "*Al-Barnamaj Al-Intikhabi Li-Hizbullah*", issued by Hizbullah's Central Press Office in the

summer of 1996. In the translation, I denote where every page in the original Arabic text ends.

60. Yusuf 'Ali argues, "The Way of God (*sirat-ul-Mustaqim*) is a Straight Way. But men have strayed from it in all directions. And there are numerous Paths by which they can get back to the Right Way, the Way in which the purity of their own nature, and Will and mercy of God, require them to walk. All these numerous Paths become open to them if once they give their hearts in keeping to God and work in the right Endeavour (*jihad*) with all their mind and soul and resources. Thus will they get out of the Spider's web of this frail world and attain to eternal Bliss in the fulfilment of their true destiny". *The Holy Qur'an...*, 1048.

61. Ibid., p. 1.

62. Ibid., p. 2.

63. Ibid., p. 3.

64. Ibid., p. 4.

65. My translation is based upon "The Electoral Program of Hizbullah: Priorities and Continuations", *Al-'Ahd* 863 (18 August 2000), 4.

66. In addition to being plagued by sectarianism and confessionalism, the Lebanese system is characterised by nepotism and favouritism. It is based on the slogans of "I'll scratch your back, if you scratch mine" and "What will I get out of it?", etc.

67. This seems to refer to the demarcation of the Blue line, in which Lebanon gained back 17,756,600 square meters of its southern land along the Israeli border, and the seven villages that were stripped out from Lebanon during the 1948 war with Israel.

68. This clause is mentioned in Preamble of Lebanon's 1990 constitution that was the fruit of the Ta'if Agreement.

69. On August 5, 2004, a new pension-retirement plan, which would create the much-anticipated public retirement system, was approved by the Lebanese Cabinet; however, its implementation still awaits the parliament's approval. It is ironic to note that such a plan was proposed in 1965 by the Social Affairs Minister, but it never came into effect.

70. Although Hizbullah did not publish a full pledged political program, its 2005 election program could be outlined from the speeches and stances of its leaders, most notably Shaykh Na'im Qasim. See Qasim's interview with *al-Intiqad* 26 April 2005: "Our Alliances are Political *par excellence* and are Based on a Political Program"; Qasim's speech on 29 April 2005 commemorating the death of Prophet Muhammad; and *al-Nour* 5:00 GMT News 30 April 2005.

71. I was told by Hizbullah cadres that this is an edited and appended version of the 1998 municipal election program after the recommendations of Hizbullah's "First Municipal Conference" held on 16 July 2002. It is worth mentioning that these points have been outlined, before, during, and after the elections, but not in considerable detail, in the following *al-Intiqad* issues: 1054 (23 April 2004); 1055 (30 April 2004); 1056 (7 May 2004); 1057 (14 May 2004); 1058 (21 May 2004); 1059 (28 May 2004); 1060 (4 June 2004).

72. See the cover page of *Mu'tamar Al-Baladiyyat Al-Awwal [The First Municipal Conference/ Convention]*. Beirut: Hizbullah's Central Press Office, 16 July 2002.

73. Ibid., 3.

74. Ibid., 4.

75. Ibid., 5-6.

76. Ibid., 7.

77. This is a pressing problem in Lebanon that caused most of the male population to emigrate.

78. *Mu'tamar Al-Baladiyyat...*, 7-8.

79. Ibid., 9.
80. Ibid., 10.
81. Ibid., 10-11.
82. In the Pre-Ta'if Lebanese constitution, there was an article placing women, children, and handicapped in the same clause (*al-mar'a wa al-tifl wa al-mu'aq*). Hizbullah added old age to this category/classification.
83. *Mu'tamar Al-Baladiyyat...*, 11.
84. Ibid., 12.
85. Ibid., 13.
86. It is estimated the there are 20 million Lebanese expatriates; 5 times more than the total population of Lebanon, which is estimated to be 4 million. See "The diaspora: Lebanon's secret weapon against economic collapse ", *AFP* (*Agence France-Presse*), 20 July 2004.
87. *Mu'tamar Al-Baladiyyat...*, 14.
88. Ibid., 15.
89. Ibid., 16.
90. See http://www.nasrollah.org/english/hassan/sera/sira.htm
91. See Nasrallah's speech in the 5th day of Muharram, 1425 A.H., 24 March 2004.
92. *Al-Safir* 18 May 1995.
93. Sobelman, *Rules of the Game...*, 47-48.
94. See Chapter 4.
95. See Nasrallah's speech in the commemoration of "Jerusalem Day" on 12 November 2004. http://www.nasrollah.org/audio/hassan/2004/quds12112004.html
96. A book or an article, unless otherwise specified.
97. The Social Science Research Council of American.

English Summary

The Shifts in Hizbullah's Ideology

Religious Ideology, Political Ideology, and Political Program

The Lebanese Shiʻite resistance movement, Hizbullah, is going through a remarkable political and ideological transformation. Hizbullah was founded in 1978 by various sectors of Lebanese Shiʻite clergy and cadres, and with Iranian backing as an Islamic movement protesting against social and political conditions. Over the years 1984/5 to 1991, Hizbullah became a full-fledged social movement in the sense of having a broad overall organization, structure, and ideology aiming at social change and social justice, as it claimed. Starting in 1992, it became a mainstream political party working within the narrow confines of its pragmatic political program. The line of argument in this dissertation is that Hizbullah has been adjusting its identity in the three previously mentioned stages by shifting emphasis among its three components: (1) from propagating an exclusivist religious ideology; (2) to a more encompassing political ideology; and (3) to a down-to-earth political program.

In these three stages, however, Hizbullah's identity as an Islamic *jihadi* (struggle) movement remained as one of its *thawabit* (immutable set of values), but the justifications of Islamic principles, in particular, *jihad* altered. The important shifts in Hizbullah's ideology in the three stages tackle the following topics: *wilayat al-faqih* (guardianship of the jurisprudent or jurisconsult); oppressors and oppressed, with special focus on the US and Israel; *jihad* and martyrdom; Islamic state; Hizbullah's relations with the Lebanese Christians; and Lebanonisation (integration) or *infitah* ("opening up").

The dissertation's findings suggest that the causes behind the shifts in Hizbullah's ideology are due to the alterations in the local Lebanese domestic dimension, as well as the regional and international dimensions. Hizbullah's own internal dynamic changed, Iranian politics shifted, and the international situation has been transformed. However, the focus has been primarily set on the alterations in Hizbullah's internal dynamics.

Hizbullah relies on the balance between the actual and the possible, shifting its stance from rejectionism and opposition (religious and political ideology strategies) to accommodation and conformity (political program policies). Usually, this makes it modify its strategies from hawkish (religious and political ideology discourse) to dovish policies (political program discourse) according to changing political circumstances. Since the end of the Civil War in 1990, Hizbullah has been confronting major developments in Lebanon: prominently, the emergence of a pluralist public sphere and increasing openness toward other communities, political parties, and interest groups in the Lebanese myriad. This resulted in a change in Hizbullah's discourse and priorities. The mixed confessional space in Lebanon led Hizbullah to modify its position from marginalisation, and branding the Lebanese state with unrighteousness and infidelity, to *infitah*. Through this process, the party became a major player in the Lebanese milieu. It continued to alter its stance and change its political rules from Islamisation to Lebanonisation, which implies integration in the public sphere. This was accomplished through active participation in the political system that involved contestation, cooptation, and empowerment. Therefore, the logic of operating within the bounds of the Lebanese state has prevailed over the logic of revolution.

While keeping its doctrinal principles in sight, Hizbullah is persistent in honouring its overall political program. Consequently, from time to time and as opportunities arise, Hizbullah might put aside, temporarily, its ideological program by leading a dynamic program without specifying a rigid political program. Hizbullah favours the incremental model of decision-making and employs piecemeal social engineering that requires a thorough discussion by the Hizbullah leadership of each issue at a time. Although it seems that Hizbullah does not have a ready-made formula to deal with all problems and possibilities that might arise, Hizbullah's *Shura* (Consultative) Council makes readily available answers to all questions. However, since its enemies, especially Israel, might benefit from this information, Hizbullah reserves the right of not disclosing these alternatives and contingency measures to the public.

As a mainstream political party, Hizbullah operates according to *Realpolitik* calculations of political expediency, benefit, and *maslaha* (interest). The party's gradual involvement in "normal" Lebanese politics – by joining the parliament, municipal councils, and cabinet – with the limitations that implies, begs the question of how much it is willing to be co-opted into the Lebanese political system and state institutions. Hizbullah's political victories in 2005 illustrated the patriotic-nationalistic character of a party that is supported, not only by its major Shi'ite constituency, but also by many Sunnis, Druze and Christians. Depending on popular support, Hizbullah aims to portray itself as the biggest political force in Lebanon. Although Hizbullah denies it, its success at balancing its nationalist political commitments, on the one hand, and its Islamic background, on the other, came at the price of compromise (even on some doctrinal issues). Through arguing for civil peace, social freedoms, and a functioning civil society, Hizbullah attempted to preserve its Islamic identity while working within the domain of the Lebanese state's sovereignty and inside the confines of a non-Islamic state and a multi-confessional polity. On these grounds, Hizbullah conferred de facto recognition upon the Lebanese state, and its supporters know this. Thus, Hizbullah ended up as being unable to cross the boundaries of an "ordinary" political party.

One should be careful not to read too much into the 2005 parliamentary elections and Hizbullah's decision to join the cabinet. It is interesting to note, here, that since the cabinet reflects the power balances in the parliament, it is obvious that any popular dismay with the parliament will be extended to the cabinet, and vice versa. However, Hizbullah's electoral success suggests that the party has been able to win the "hearts and minds" of many Lebanese voters, especially in its major Shi'ite constituencies. This has confirmed the efficiency of its *infitah* policy of agreeing to participate in a pluralist political process, while maintaining respect its for integrity and probity in its socio-economic work. Through its NGOs, Hizbullah has triumphantly portrayed itself as a Lebanese nationalist political party working in favour of the "wretched of the earth," without confessional fear or favour. Rafiq al-Hariri's assassination, along with the Syrian withdrawal and its aftermath, accelerated the political changes within Hizbullah. It may be argued that disarming and becoming an "ordinary" political party, far from causing the party's demise, would boost its domestic political power even further. Nevertheless, Hizbullah could not have faired so well in Lebanese domestic affairs without its two regional backers, Syria and Iran. Even though there is an ideological-strategic alliance between Hizbullah and Iran, on the one hand, and a political-strategic partnership between Hizbullah and Syria, on the other, the dissertation endeavours to demonstrate that Hizbullah is not a tool of policy in Syrian and Iranian hands. Rather, Hizbullah has pursued an independent course of decision-making and action that suits the particularities and specificities of the Lebanese political equation by putting into practice its political program of Lebanonisation, *infitah*, and integration in the Lebanese public sphere.

Nederlandse samenvatting van het proefschrift

De verschuivingen in Hezbollah's ideologie

Religieuze ideologie, politieke ideologie en politiek programma

De Libanese sjiïtische verzetsbeweging Hezbollah ondergaat een opmerkelijke politieke en ideologische transformatie. Hezbollah werd in 1978 met Iraanse steun opgericht door verschillende sectoren van de sjiïtische geestelijkheid en zijn kaders, als een Islamitische beweging van protest tegen maatschappelijke en politieke omstandigheden. Gedurende de jaren 1984/85 tot 1991 groeide Hezbollah uit tot een volledig ontwikkelde sociale beweging, in die zin dat het ging beschikken over een alomvattende organisatie, structuur en ideologie, die aanspraak maakte op doeleinden op het gebied van maatschappelijke verandering en sociale rechtvaardigheid. Vanaf 1992 werd het een prominente politieke partij die werkzaam is binnen de nauw omschreven grenzen van haar eigen pragmatische politieke programma. De centrale argumentatie in deze dissertatie luidt dat Hezbollah haar identiteit gedurende de hierboven genoemde drie stadia heeft aangepast door het accent te verschuiven tussen haar drie componenten: 1) van het propageren van een exclusivistische religieuze ideologie; 2) naar een meer omvattende politieke ideologie; en 3) naar een realistisch politiek programma.

Gedurende deze drie stadia bleef Hezbollah's identiteit als een islamitische *jihadistische* (strijd-) beweging echter een van zijn *thawabit* (verzameling van vaste waarden), maar de rechtvaardigingen van Islamitische principes, en met name die van *jihad*, veranderden. De belangrijke verschuivingen in Hezbollah's ideologie gedurende de drie stadia hadden betrekking op de volgende onderwerpen: *wilayat al-faqih* (voogdij van de rechtsgeleerde of rechtsadviseur); onderdrukkers en onderdrukten, vooral van toepassing op de VS en Israël; *jihad* en martelaarschap; islamitische staat; Hezbollah's relaties met de Libanese christenen; en Libanisering (integratie) of *infitah* ("politiek van openheid").

De bevindingen van deze dissertatie geven aan dat de oorzaken van de verschuivingen in Hezbollah's ideologie toegeschreven moeten worden aan de veranderingen die plaatsvonden. Hezbollah's eigen interne dynamiek veranderde, de Iraanse politiek verschoof en ook de internationale situatie is veranderd. De dissertatie richt zich echter allereerst op de veranderingen binnen Hezbollah's interne dynamiek.

Hezbollah borduurt voort op het evenwicht tussen het feitelijke en het mogelijke en het schuift zijn standpunt van afwijzing en oppositie (strategieën van religieuze en politieke ideologie) op in de richting van aanpassing en conformiteit (politiek van het politieke programma). Doorgaans brengt dit de beweging ertoe om zijn haviken-beleid (discours van religieuze en politieke ideologie) bij te stellen in de richting van duiven-beleid (discours van het politieke programma) in overeenstemming met veranderende politieke omstandigheden. Sinds het einde van de burgeroorlog in 1990 ging Hezbollah de confrontatie aan met belangrijke ontwikkelingen in Libanon. De meest prominente daarvan zijn het tot stand komen van een pluralistische openbare sfeer en een toenemende openheid ten aanzien van andere (confessionele) gemeenschappen, politieke partijen en belangengroepen in de Libanese myriade. Dit bracht een verandering in Hezbollah's discours en prioriteiten met zich mee. De gemengde confessionele ruimte in Libanon leidde ertoe dat Hezbollah zijn standpunt, dat eerst gekenmerkt werd door zelf-isolatie en het brandmerken van de Libanese staat als zijnde onrechtvaardig en ongelovig, aanpaste in de richting van *infitah*. Door dit proces werd de partij een belangrijke speler in het Libanese milieu. Het bleef haar standpunt en haar politieke regels omtrent Islamisering wijzigen in de richting van Libanisering, hetgeen integratie in de openbare sfeer met zich meebrengt. Dit was het resultaat van actieve deelname aan het politieke systeem dat (legale politieke) strijd, inkapseling en *empowerment* met zich meebracht. Aldus heeft de logica van het opereren binnen de grenzen van de Libanese staat het gewonnen van de logica van de revolutie.

Terwijl Hezbollah haar doctrinaire principes in het oog blijft houden, volhardt de beweging in het honoreren van haar politieke programma als geheel. Bijgevolg kan Hezbollah op tijdelijke basis en al naar gelang de mogelijkheden die zich voordoen haar ideologische programma opzij schuiven door een dynamisch programma naar voren te halen, zonder een rigide politiek programma te specificeren. Hezbollah geeft de voorkeur aan een periodiek model van besluitvorming en past een stapsgewijze vorm van maatschappijhervorming toe die een grondige bespreking van elke kwestie door de leiding van Hezbollah vereist op het geëigende moment. Ook al schijnt Hezbollah geen pasklare formule te hebben om met alle problemen en mogelijkheden die zich kunnen voordoen om te gaan, Hezbollah's *Shura* (consultatieve) Raad stelt haar antwoorden op alle vraagstukken beschikbaar. Aangezien echter haar vijanden, en vooral Israël, hun voordeel kunnen doen met deze informatie, behoudt Hezbollah zich het recht voor om deze alternatieven en noodmaatregelen niet openbaar te maken.

Als prominente politieke partij opereert Hezbollah in overeenstemming met overwegingen van *Realpolitik*, politieke opportuniteit, politiek voordeel en *maslaha* (belang). De geleidelijk toenemende betrokkenheid van de partij bij het "normale" Libanese politieke leven – door in het parlement, de gemeenteraden en het kabinet zitting te nemen – met alle beperkingen die dat met zich meebrengt, roept de vraag op in hoeverre het bereid is om zich in te laten kapselen in het Libanese politieke systeem en de staatsinstellingen. Hezbollah's politieke overwinningen bij de verkiezingen in 2005 illustreren het patriotisch-nationalistische karakter van een partij die niet alleen door haar hoofdzakelijk sjiïtische achterban gesteund wordt, maar ook door vele Soennieten, Druzen en Christenen. Al naar gelang de steun die het geniet onder de bevolking probeert Hezbollah zich te presenteren als de grootste politieke kracht in Libanon. Ook al wordt het door Hezbollah ontkend, haar succes in het balanceren van haar nationalistische politieke engagement met haar Islamitische achtergrond bracht een prijs met zich mee in de vorm van compromissen (zelfs ten aanzien van enkele doctrinaire kwesties). Hezbollah probeerde in het kader van haar activiteiten binnen het domein van de Libanese staatssoevereiniteit en binnen de grenzen van een niet-Islamitische staat en een multi-confessioneel staatsbestel haar Islamitische identiteit te handhaven door zich ten gunste van civiele vrede, sociale vrijheden en een functionerende civiele maatschappij uit te spreken. Daarmee heeft Hezbollah de Libanese staat feitelijk erkend, en haar aanhangers weten dat. Aldus bleek Hezbollah er uiteindelijk niet toe in staat om de status van een "gewone" politieke partij te overstijgen.

Men moet ook weer niet te veel opmaken uit de deelname aan de verkiezingen in 2005 en aan Hezbollah's beslissing om tot het kabinet toe te treden. Het is in dit verband interessant om op te merken dat aangezien het kabinet een afspiegeling is van de machtsverhoudingen in het parlement, het duidelijk is dat elke onvrede onder de bevolking ten aanzien van het parlement ook het kabinet zal treffen, en omgekeerd. Hezbollah's electorale successen geven echter aan dat de partij erin geslaagd is om de "harten en de geesten" van vele Libanese kiezers te winnen, vooral onder haar belangrijkste sjiïtische achterbannen. Dit heeft de doeltreffendheid van haar *inti-*

fah-beleid van instemming met deelname aan een pluralistisch .politiek proces bevestigd, terwijl de beweging het respect voor de integriteit en de rechtschapenheid van haar eigen sociaal-economische activiteiten handhaafde. Door middel van haar NGO's heeft Hezbollah zichzelf op triomfalistische wijze afgeschilderd als een Libanese nationalistische politieke partij die ten gunste van de "verworpenen der aarde" werkzaam is, zonder confessionele angst of bevoordeling. De aanslag op Rafiq Hariri heeft samen met de Syrische terugtrekking en zijn nasleep de politieke veranderingen binnen Hezbollah versneld. Men zou kunnen stellen dat, verre van het teweegbrengen van het verdwijnen van de partij, Hezbollah's proces van ontwapening en ontwikkeling tot een "gewone" politieke partij haar politieke macht alleen maar heeft versterkt. Toch zou Hezbollah het niet zo goed hebben gedaan in Libanese binnenlandse aangelegenheden zonder de steun van twee mogendheden in de regio, Syrië en Iran. Ook al bestaat er – enerzijds – een ideologisch-strategisch bondgenootschap tussen Hezbollah en Iran en – anderzijds – een politiek-strategisch partnerschap tussen Hezbollah en Syrië, deze dissertatie probeert aan te tonen dat Hezbollah niet een politiek instrument in Syrische of in Iraanse handen is. Hezbollah heeft veeleer een onafhankelijke koers van besluitvorming en handelen gevolgd die in overeenstemming is met de eigenaardigheden en de specifieke kenmerken van het Libanese politieke leven door haar politiek programma van Libanisering, *intifah* en integratie in de Libanese openbare sfeer in de praktijk te brengen.